the **Witch** of **Artemis**

VOL. 1

CREATED BY
YUI HARA

TOKYOPOP®

HAMBURG // LONDON // LOS ANGELES // TOKYO

The Witch of Artemis Volume 1
Created by Yui Hara

Translation - Alexis Kirsch
English Adaptation - Karen S. Ahlstrom
Copy Editor - Sarah Kniss
Retouch and Lettering - Star Print Brokers
Production Artist - Michael Paolilli
Graphic Designer - Kenneth Chan

Editor - Cindy Suzuki
Print Production Manager - Lucas Rivera
Managing Editor - Vy Nguyen
Senior Designer - Louis Csontos
Art Director - Al-Insan Lashley
Director of Sales and Manufacturing - Allyson De Simone
Associate Publisher - Marco F. Pavia
President and C.O.O. - John Parker
C.E.O. and Chief Creative Officer - Stu Levy

A **TOKYOPOP** Manga

TOKYOPOP and are trademarks or registered trademarks of TOKYOPOP Inc.

TOKYOPOP Inc.
5900 Wilshire Blvd. Suite 2000
Los Angeles, CA 90036

E-mail: info@TOKYOPOP.com
Come visit us online at www.TOKYOPOP.com

ISBN: 978-1-4278-1554-5

First TOKYOPOP printing: September 2010
10 9 8 7 6 5 4 3 2 1
Printed in the USA

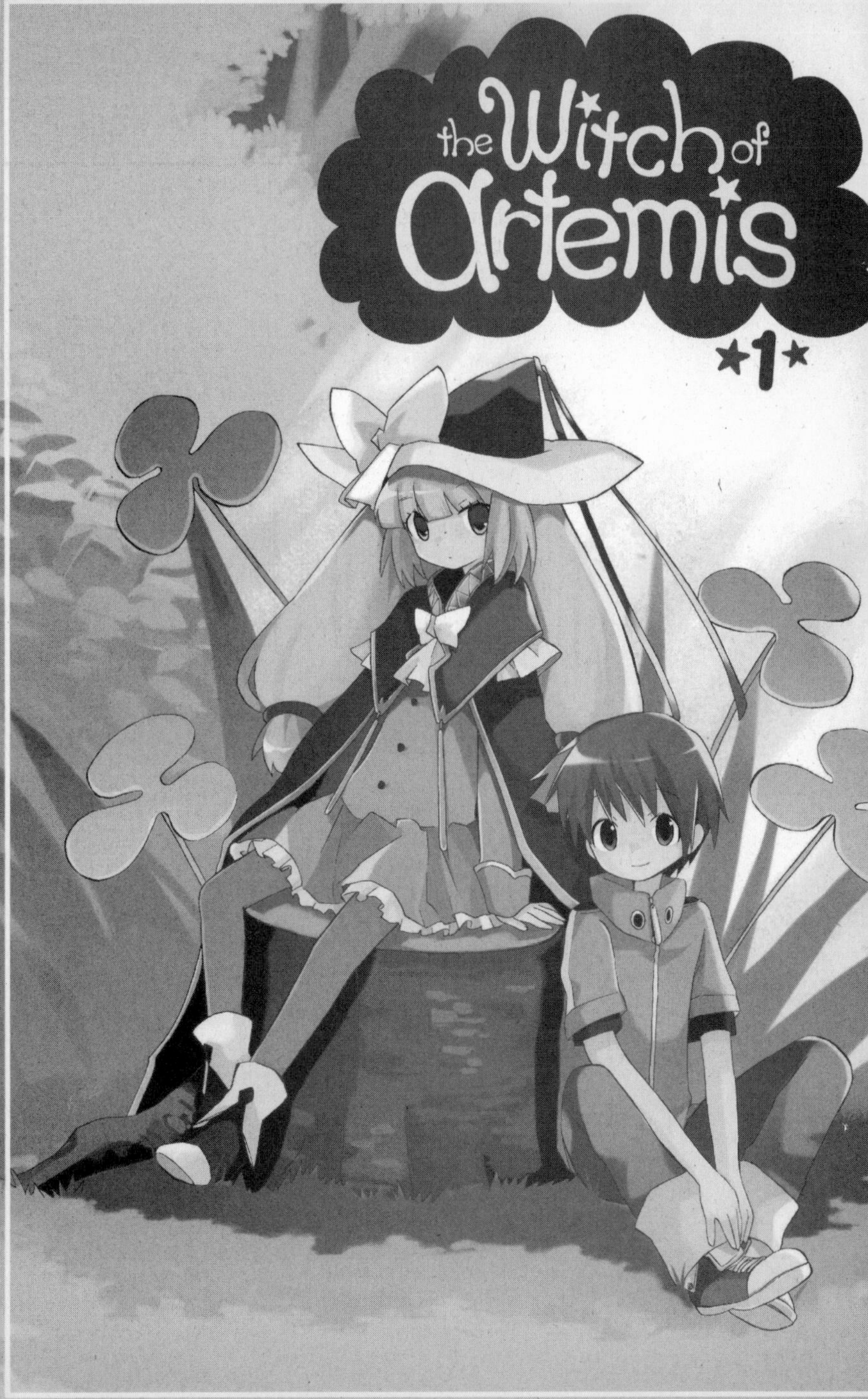
the Witch of Artemis
1

the Witch of Artemis

1

The witch in the ARTEMIS

CONTENTS

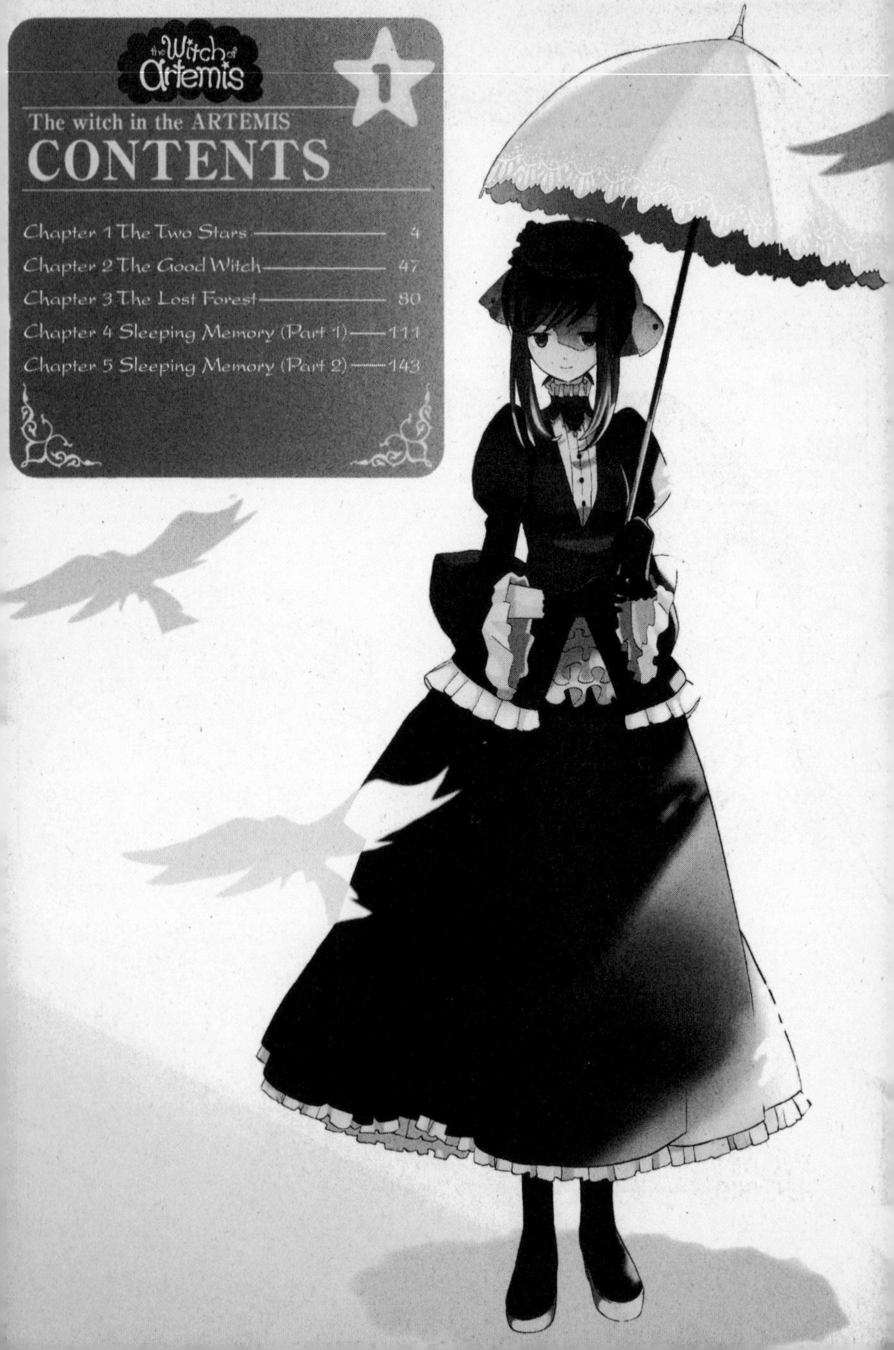

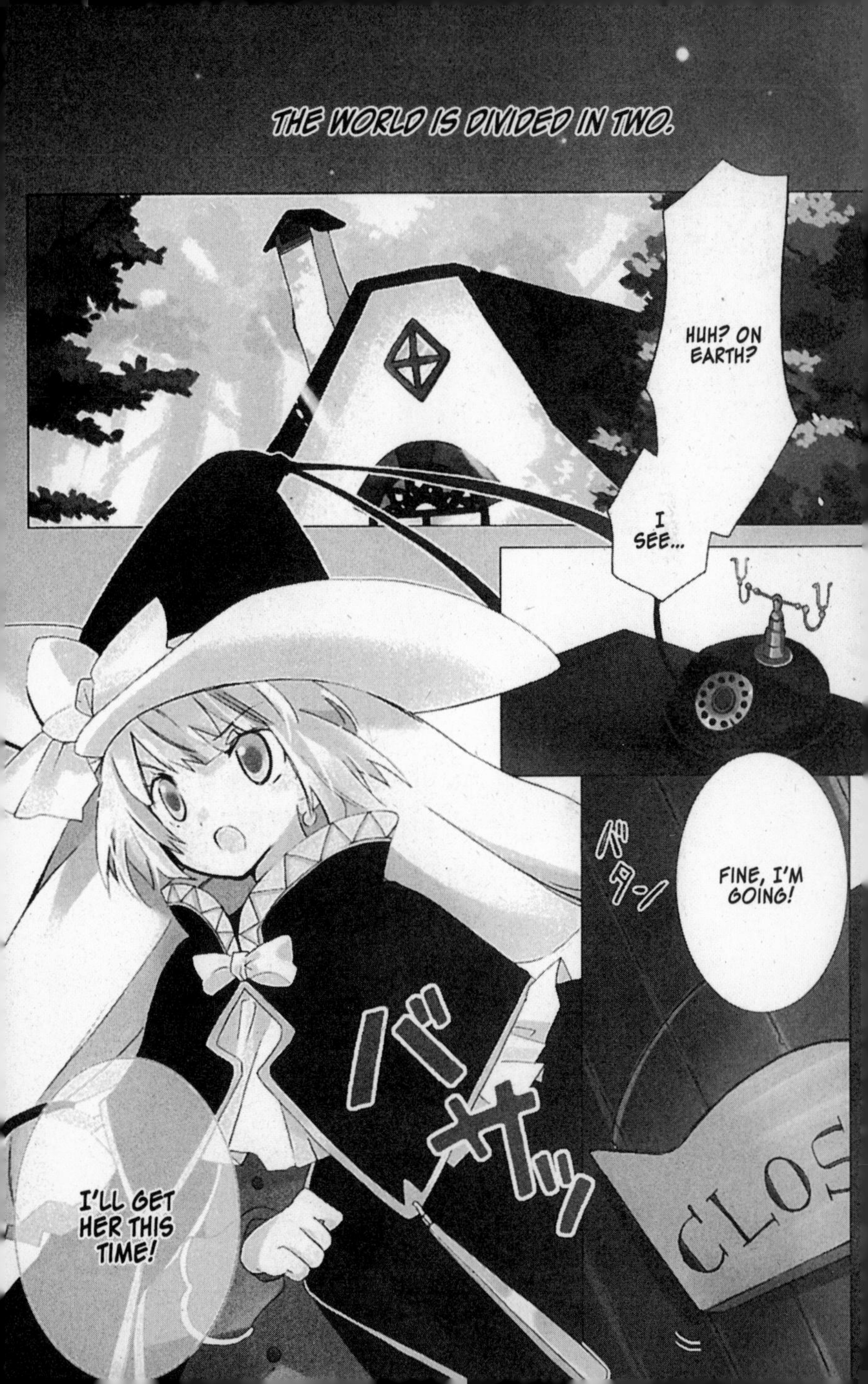
THE WORLD IS DIVIDED IN TWO.
HUH? ON EARTH?
I SEE...
バタン
FINE, I'M GOING!
バサッ
CLOS
I'LL GET HER THIS TIME!

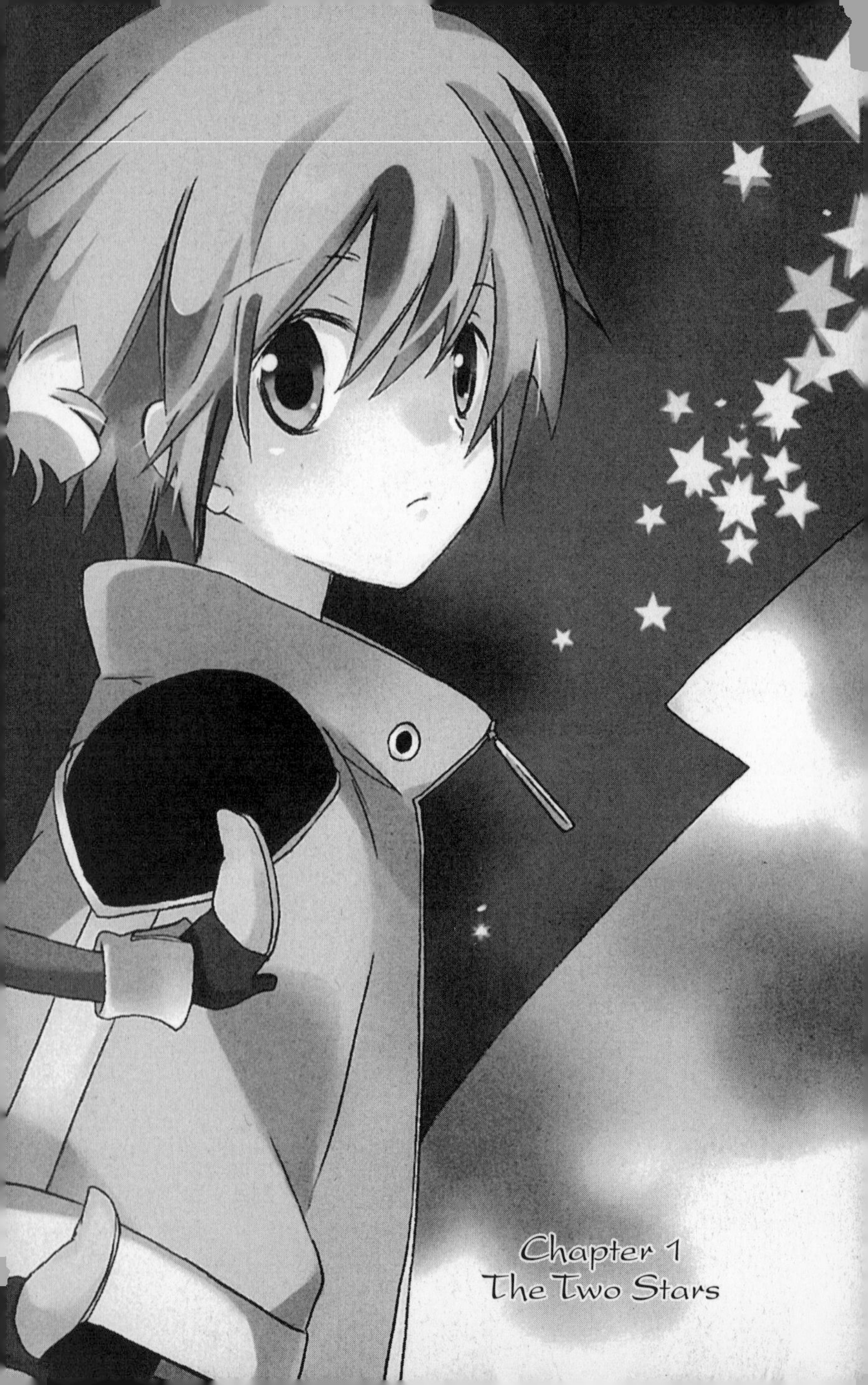
Chapter 1
The Two Stars

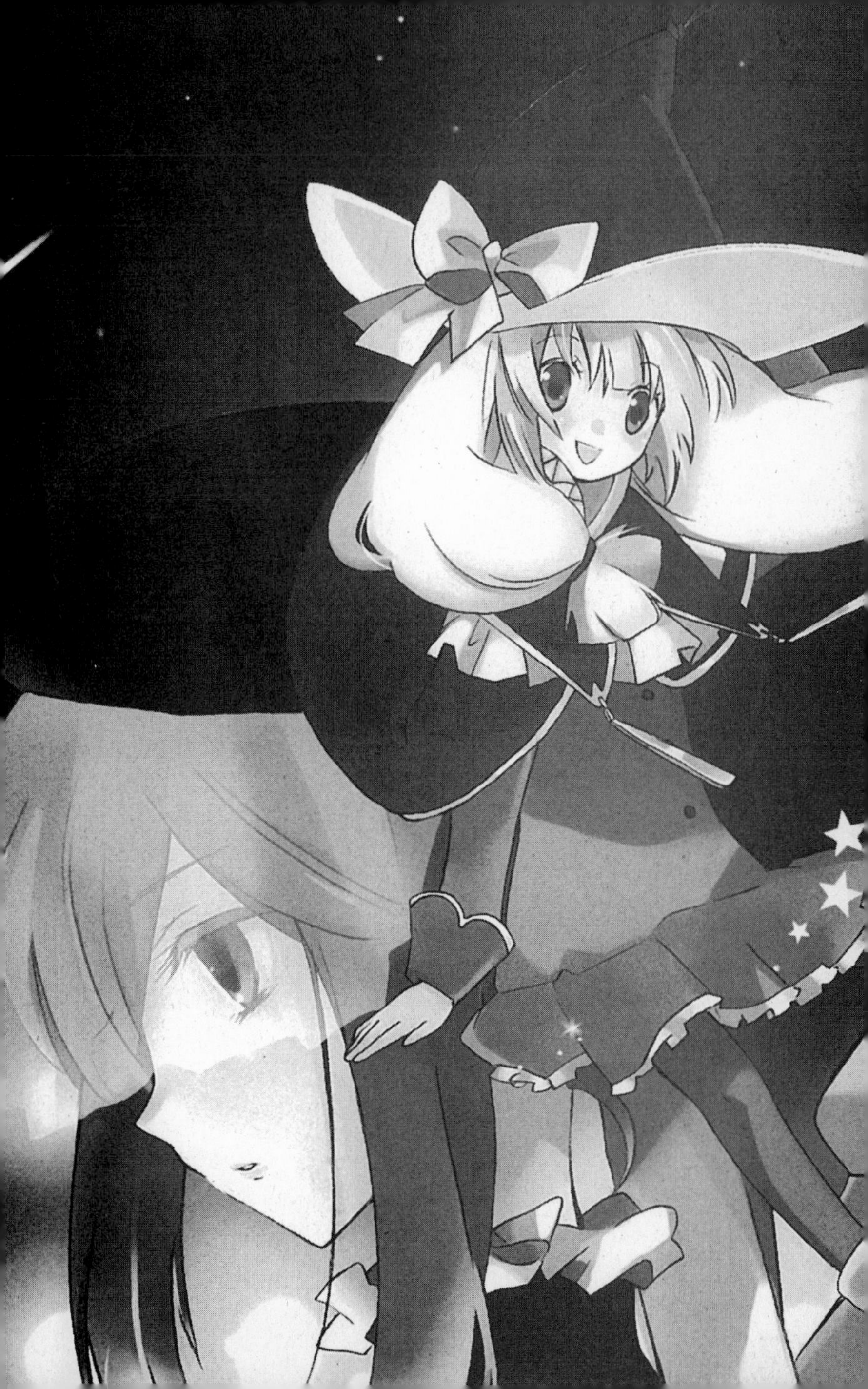

the Witch of Artemis

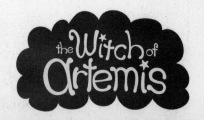

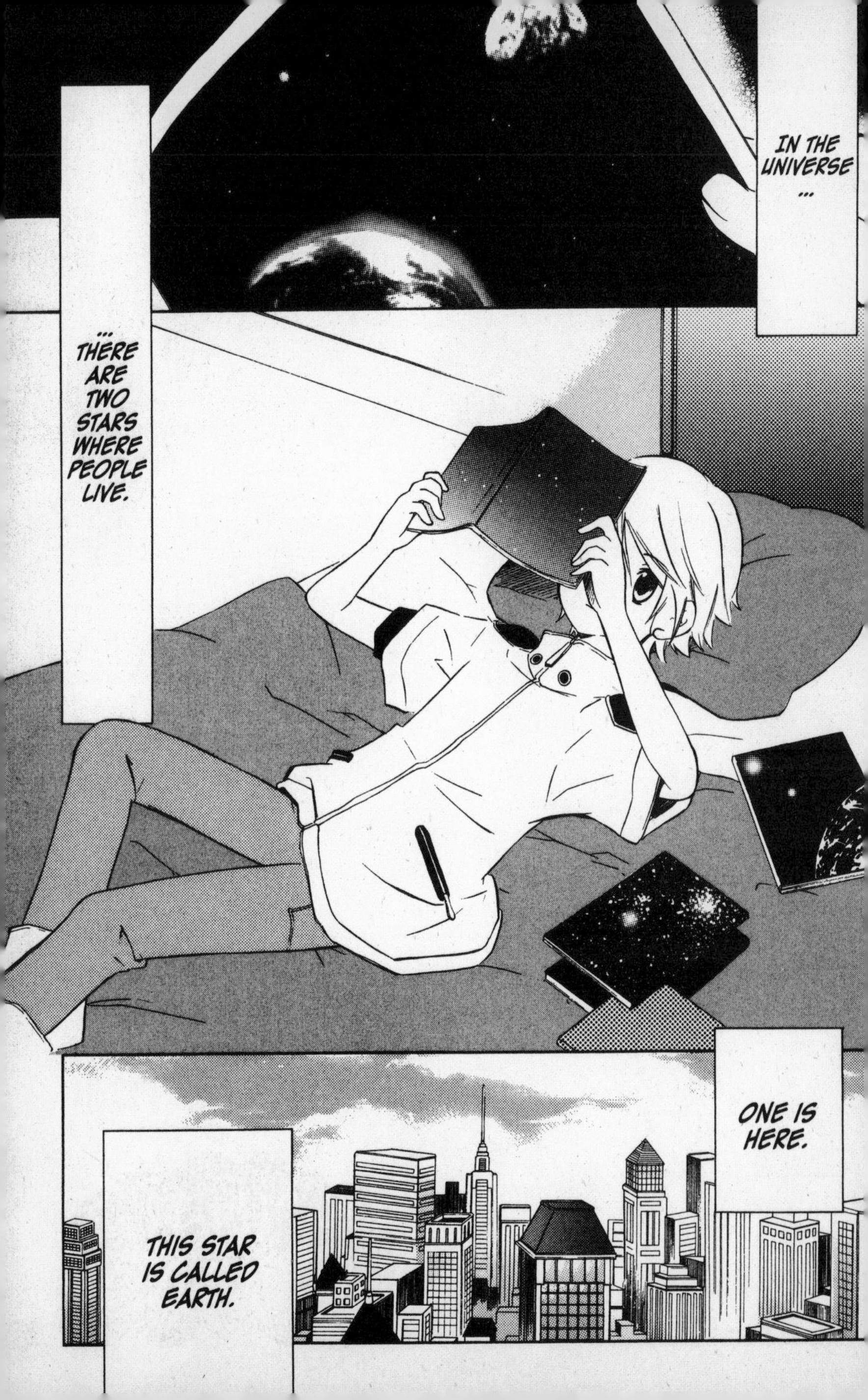
IN THE UNIVERSE ...
... THERE ARE TWO STARS WHERE PEOPLE LIVE.
ONE IS HERE.
THIS STAR IS CALLED EARTH.

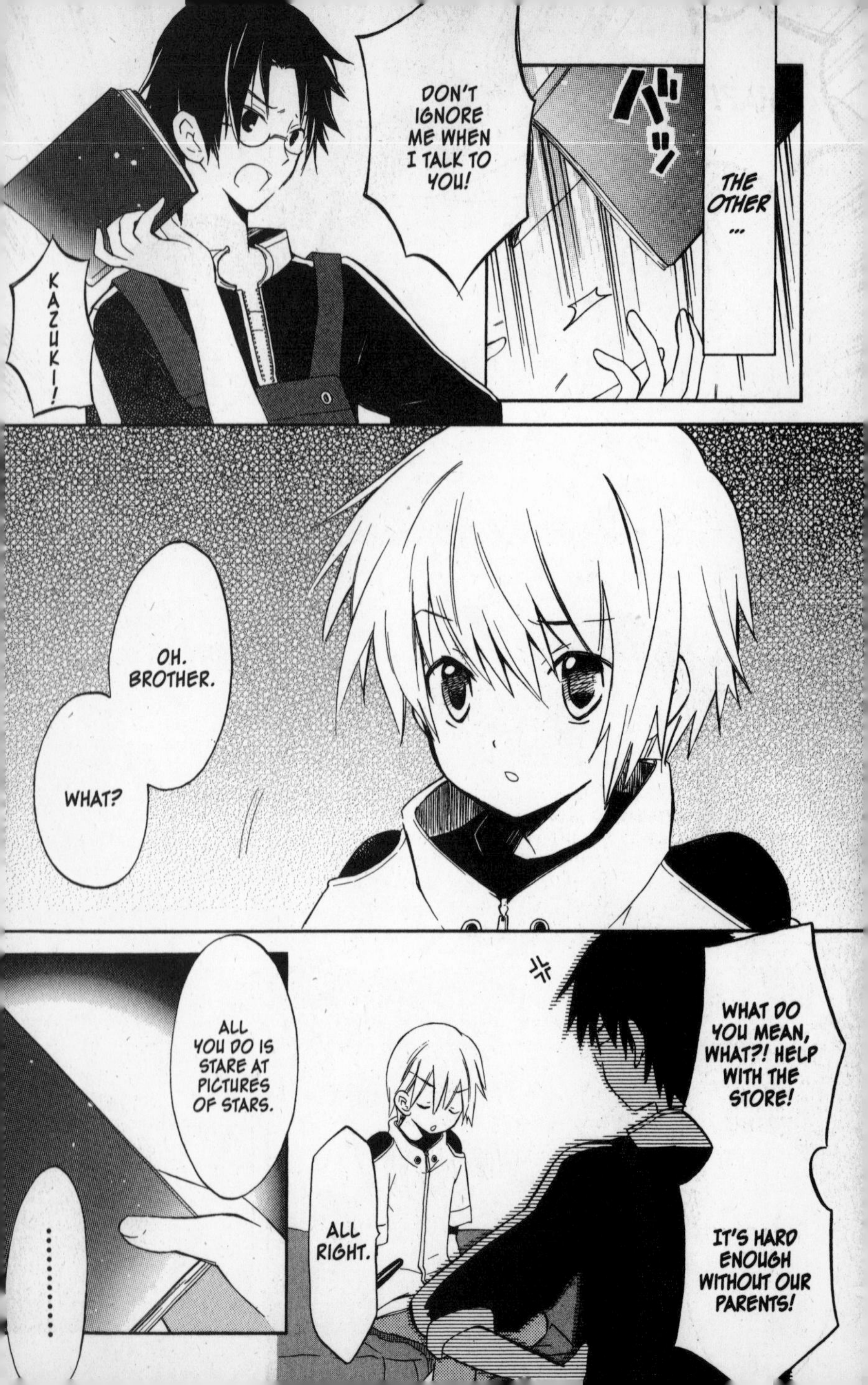
バッ
THE OTHER ...
DON'T IGNORE ME WHEN I TALK TO YOU!
KAZUKI!
OH. BROTHER.
WHAT?
WHAT DO YOU MEAN, WHAT?! HELP WITH THE STORE!
IT'S HARD ENOUGH WITHOUT OUR PARENTS!
ALL YOU DO IS STARE AT PICTURES OF STARS.
ALL RIGHT.
......

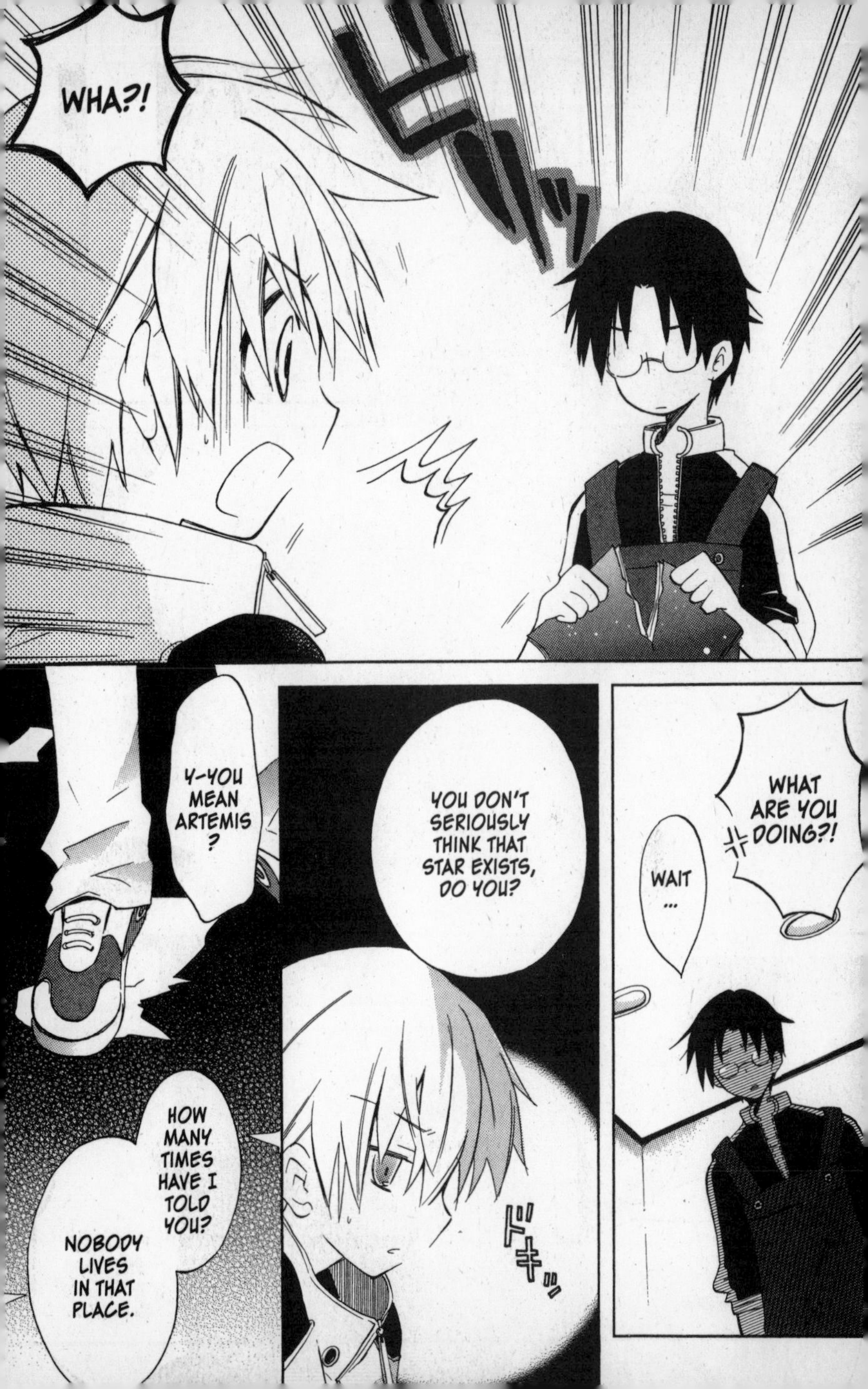
WHA?!
WHAT ARE YOU DOING?!
WAIT ...
YOU DON'T SERIOUSLY THINK THAT STAR EXISTS, DO YOU?
ドキッ
Y-YOU MEAN ARTEMIS ?
HOW MANY TIMES HAVE I TOLD YOU?
NOBODY LIVES IN THAT PLACE.

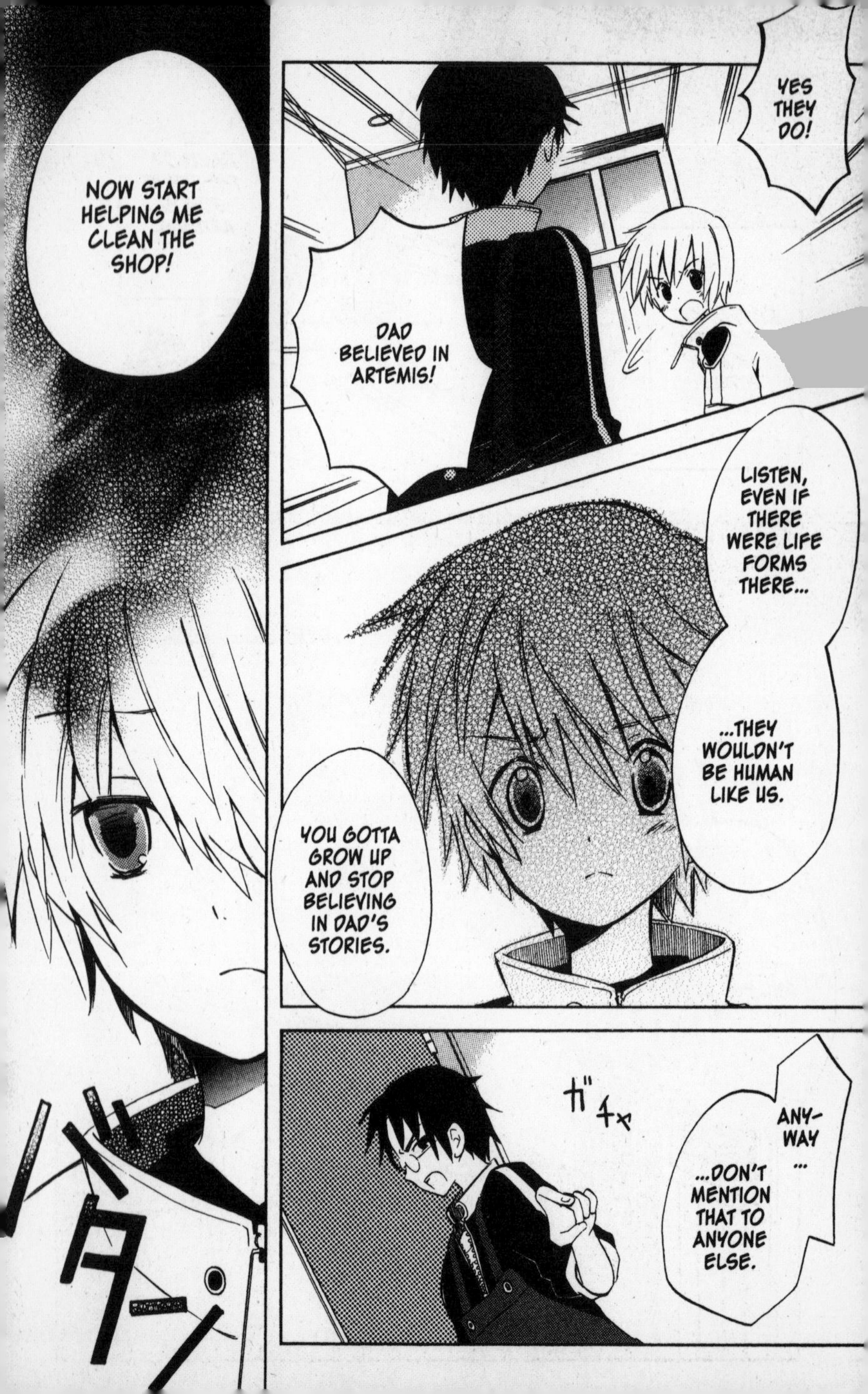
YES THEY DO!
DAD BELIEVED IN ARTEMIS!
LISTEN, EVEN IF THERE WERE LIFE FORMS THERE...
...THEY WOULDN'T BE HUMAN LIKE US.
YOU GOTTA GROW UP AND STOP BELIEVING IN DAD'S STORIES.
ガチャ
ANY-WAY...
...DON'T MENTION THAT TO ANYONE ELSE.
NOW START HELPING ME CLEAN THE SHOP!

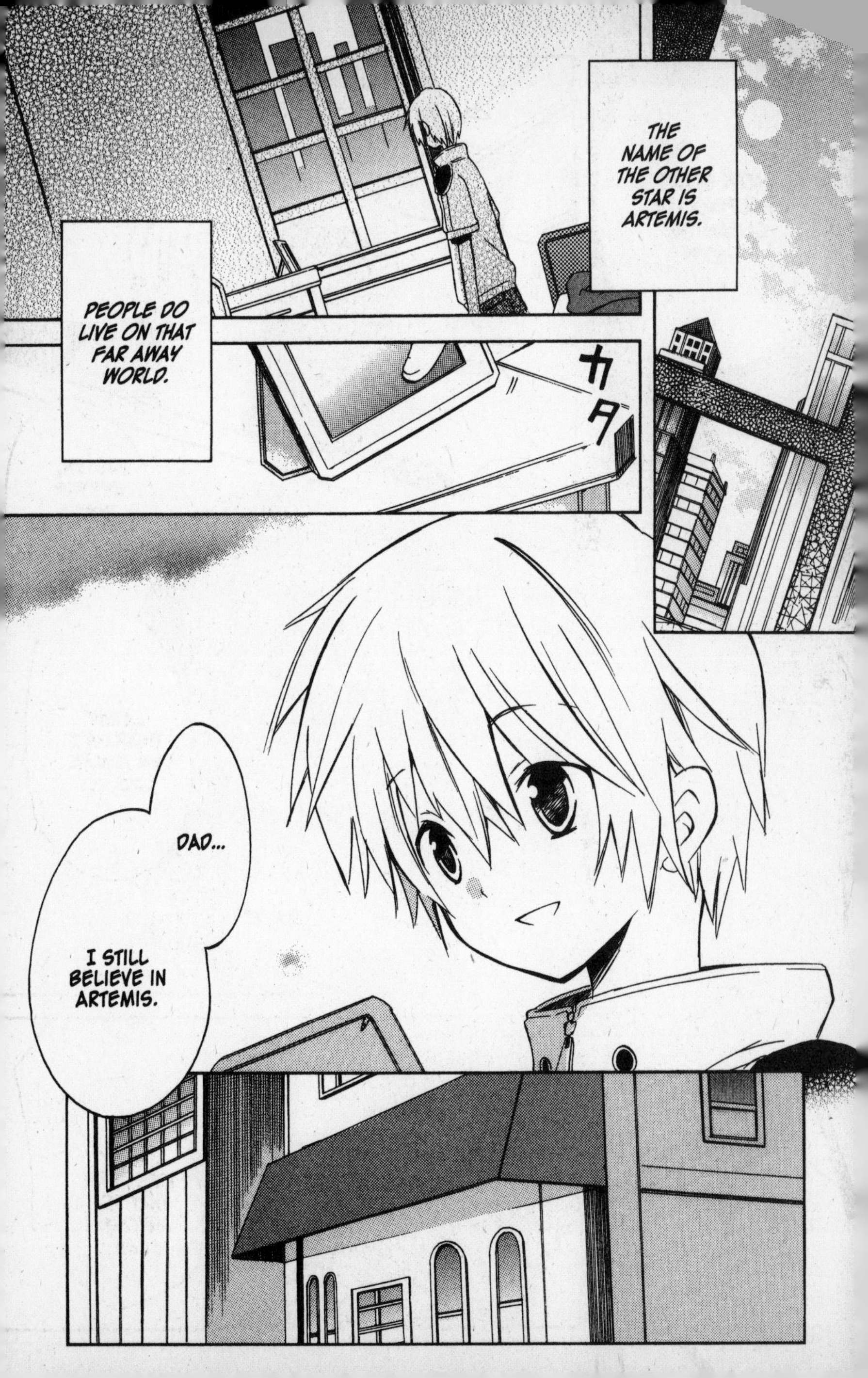
THE NAME OF THE OTHER STAR IS ARTEMIS.
PEOPLE DO LIVE ON THAT FAR AWAY WORLD.
カタ
DAD...
I STILL BELIEVE IN ARTEMIS.

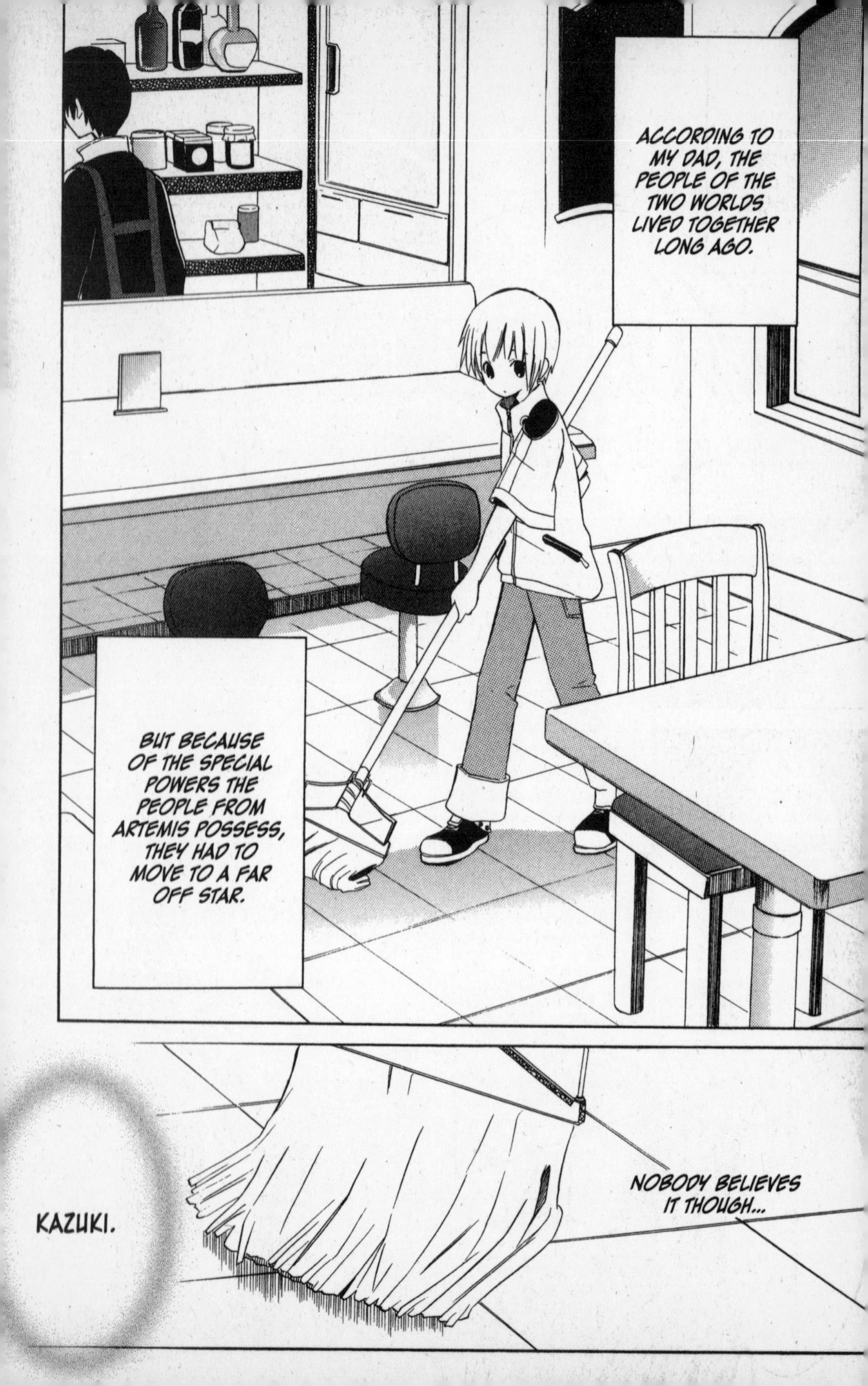
ACCORDING TO MY DAD, THE PEOPLE OF THE TWO WORLDS LIVED TOGETHER LONG AGO.
BUT BECAUSE OF THE SPECIAL POWERS THE PEOPLE FROM ARTEMIS POSSESS, THEY HAD TO MOVE TO A FAR OFF STAR.
NOBODY BELIEVES IT THOUGH...
KAZUKI.

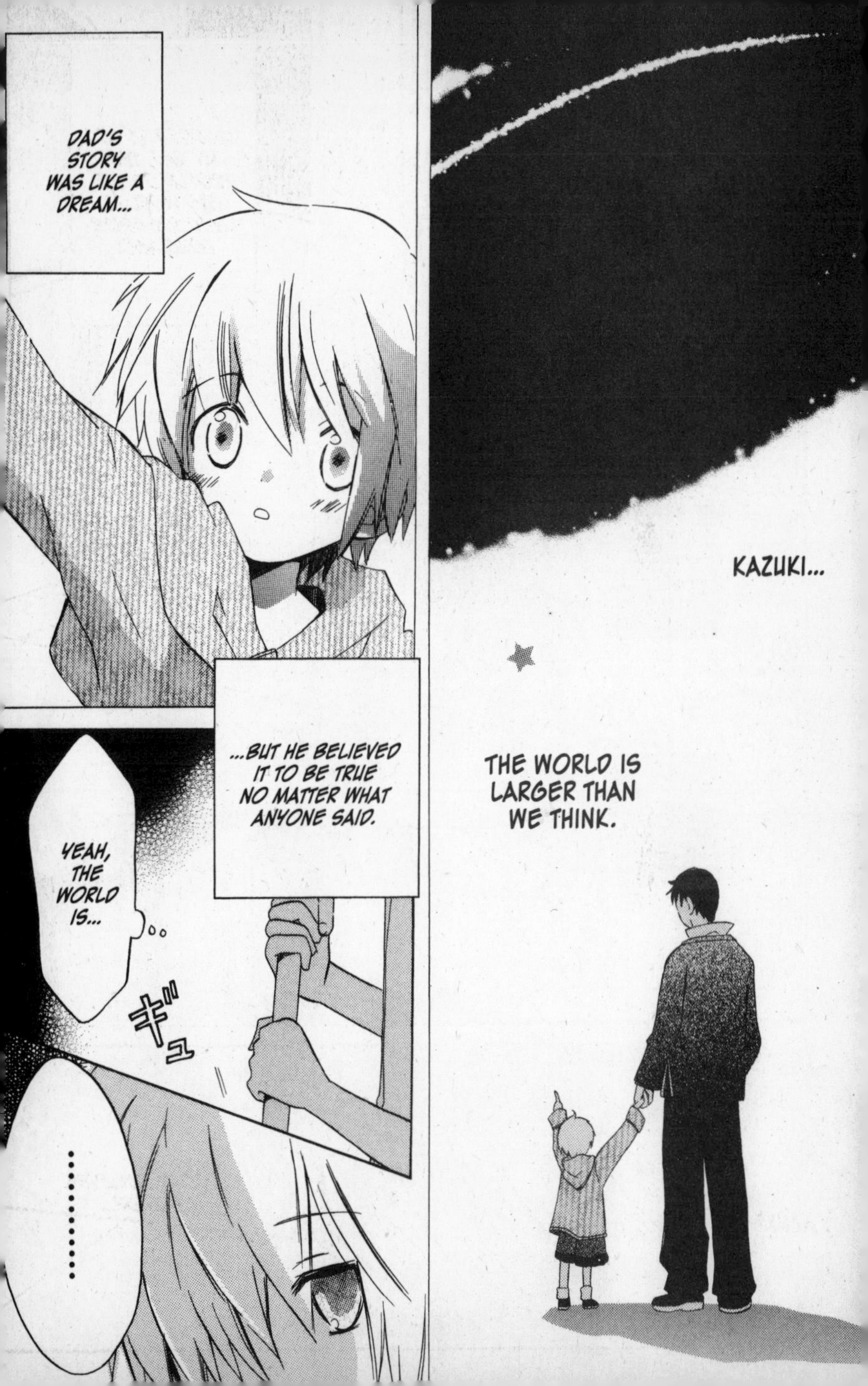
KAZUKI...
THE WORLD IS LARGER THAN WE THINK.
DAD'S STORY WAS LIKE A DREAM...
...BUT HE BELIEVED IT TO BE TRUE NO MATTER WHAT ANYONE SAID.
YEAH, THE WORLD IS...
ギュ
....

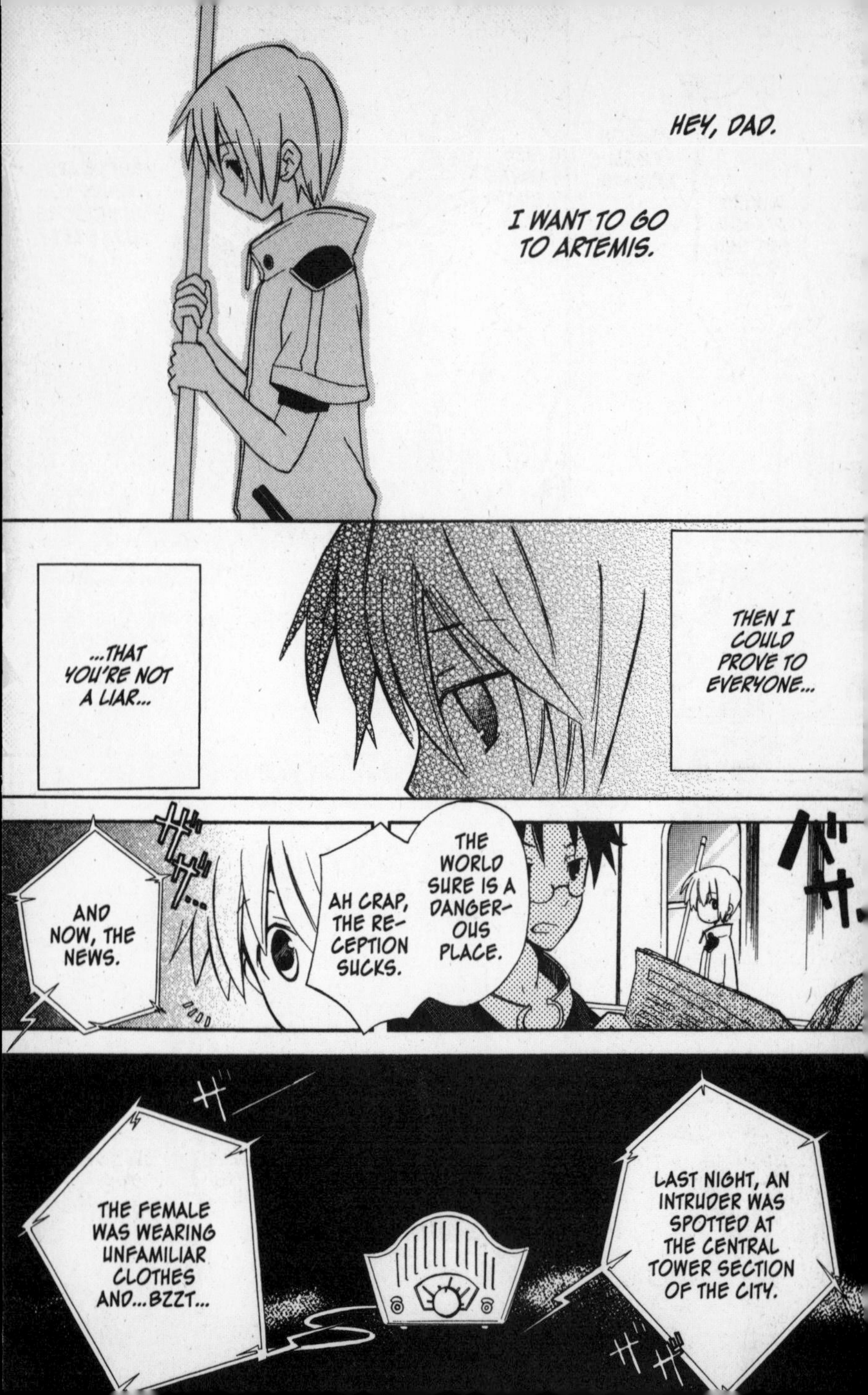
HEY, DAD.
I WANT TO GO TO ARTEMIS.
THEN I COULD PROVE TO EVERYONE...
...THAT YOU'RE NOT A LIAR...
THE WORLD SURE IS A DANGER-OUS PLACE.
AH CRAP, THE RE-CEPTION SUCKS.
AND NOW, THE NEWS.
LAST NIGHT, AN INTRUDER WAS SPOTTED AT THE CENTRAL TOWER SECTION OF THE CITY.
THE FEMALE WAS WEARING UNFAMILIAR CLOTHES AND...BZZT...

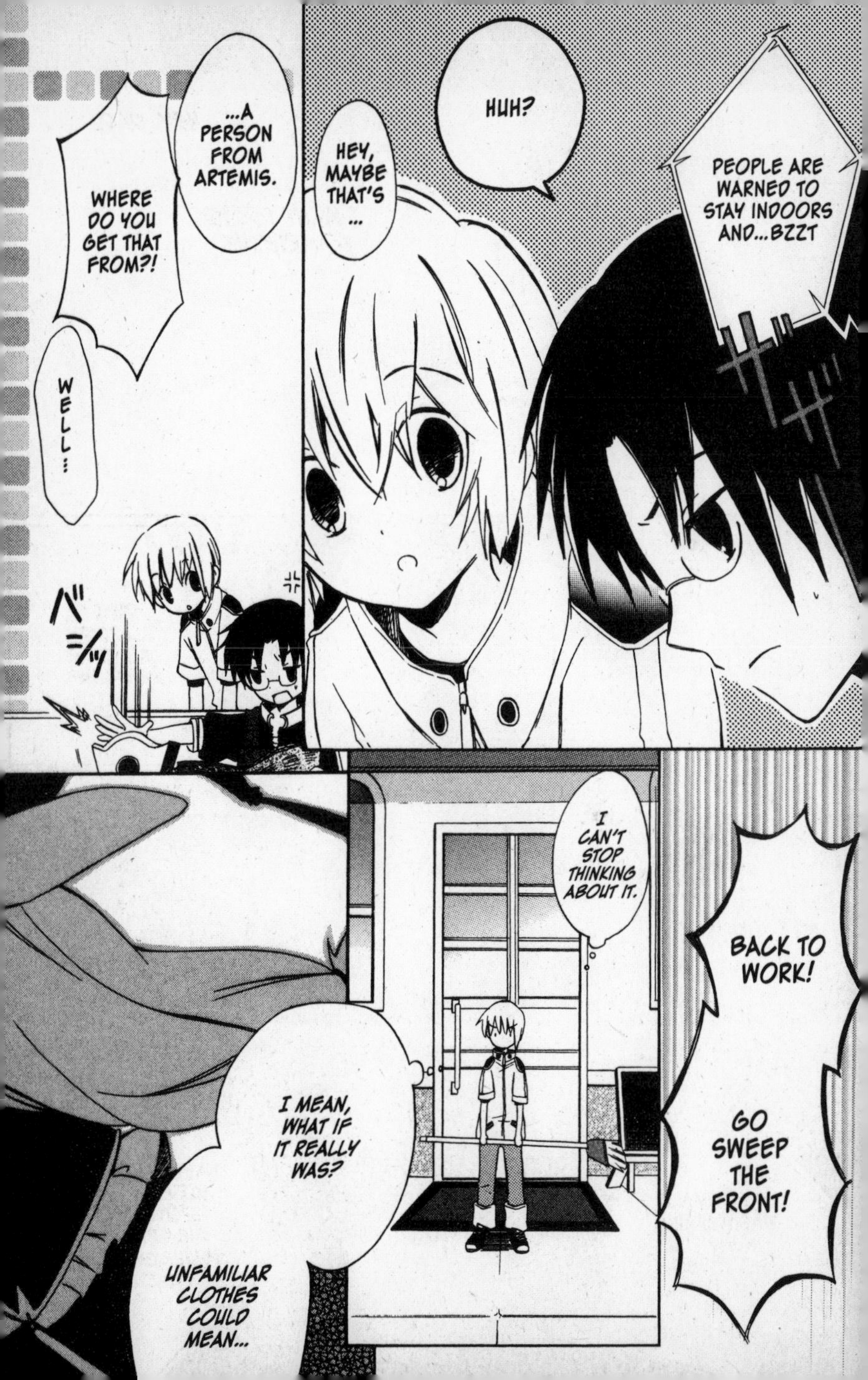
PEOPLE ARE WARNED TO STAY INDOORS AND...BZZT
HUH?
HEY, MAYBE THAT'S ...
...A PERSON FROM ARTEMIS.
WHERE DO YOU GET THAT FROM?!
WELL...
BACK TO WORK!
GO SWEEP THE FRONT!
I CAN'T STOP THINKING ABOUT IT.
I MEAN, WHAT IF IT REALLY WAS?
UNFAMILIAR CLOTHES COULD MEAN...

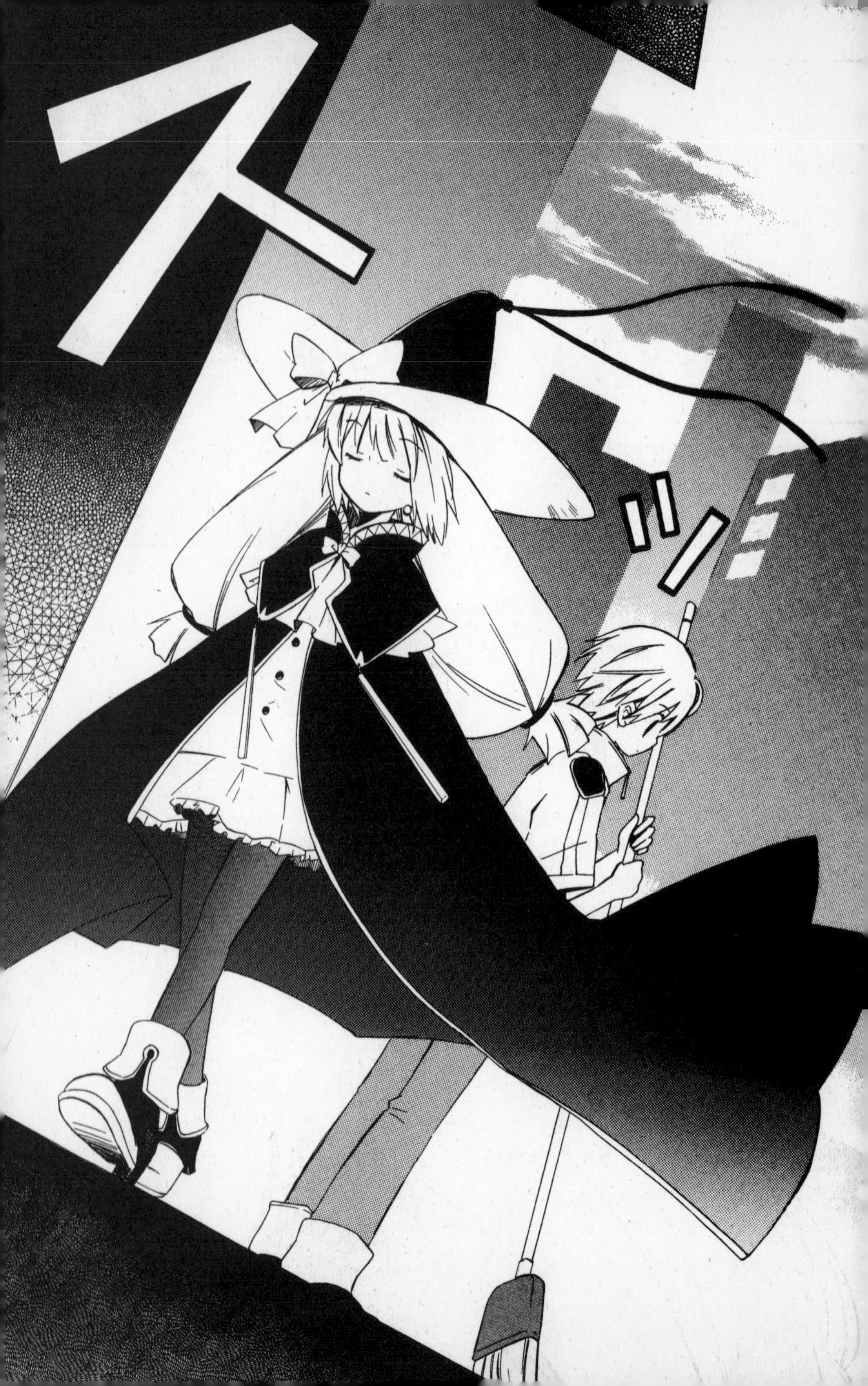

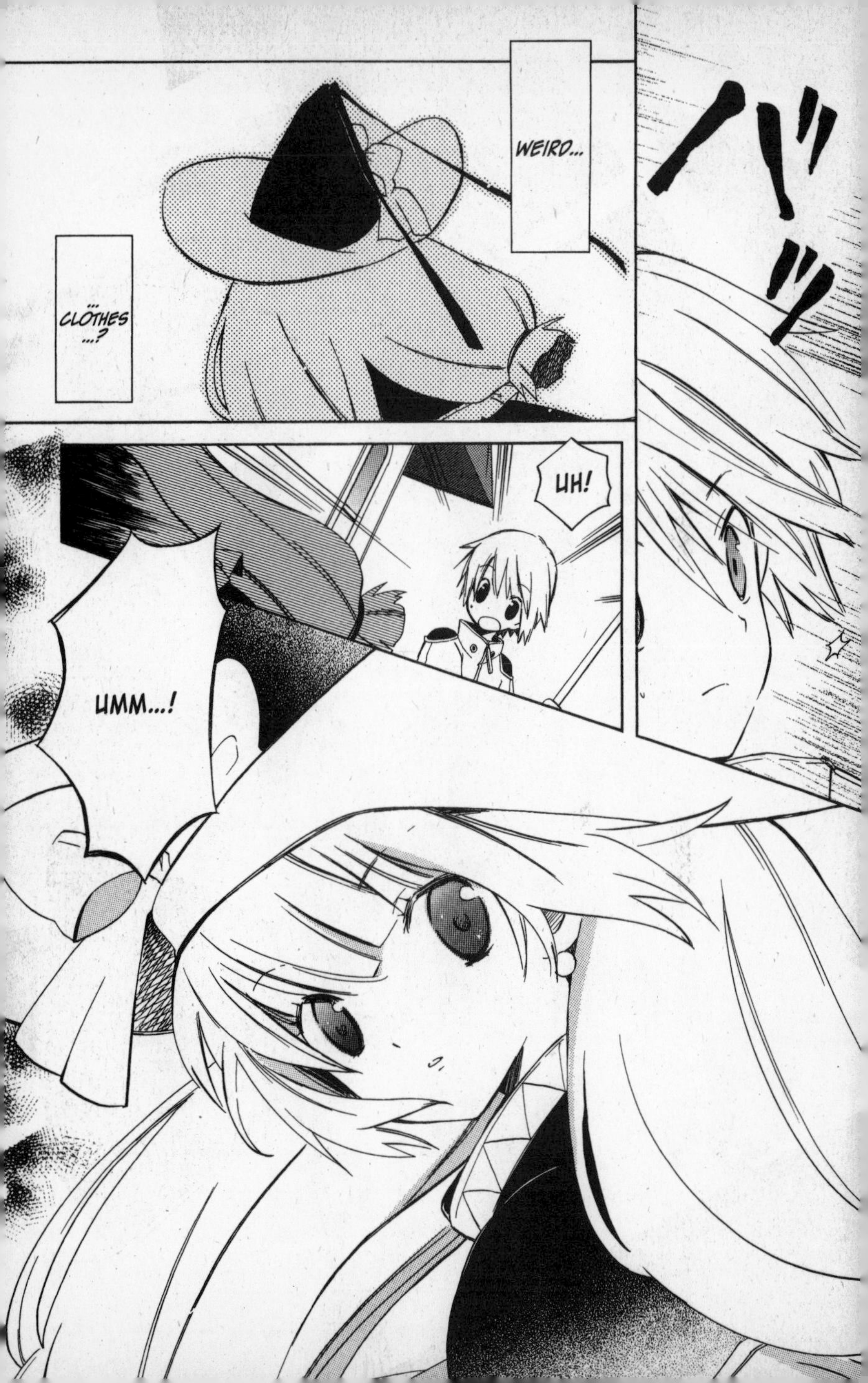
バッ
WEIRD...
...CLOTHES...?
UH!
UMM...!

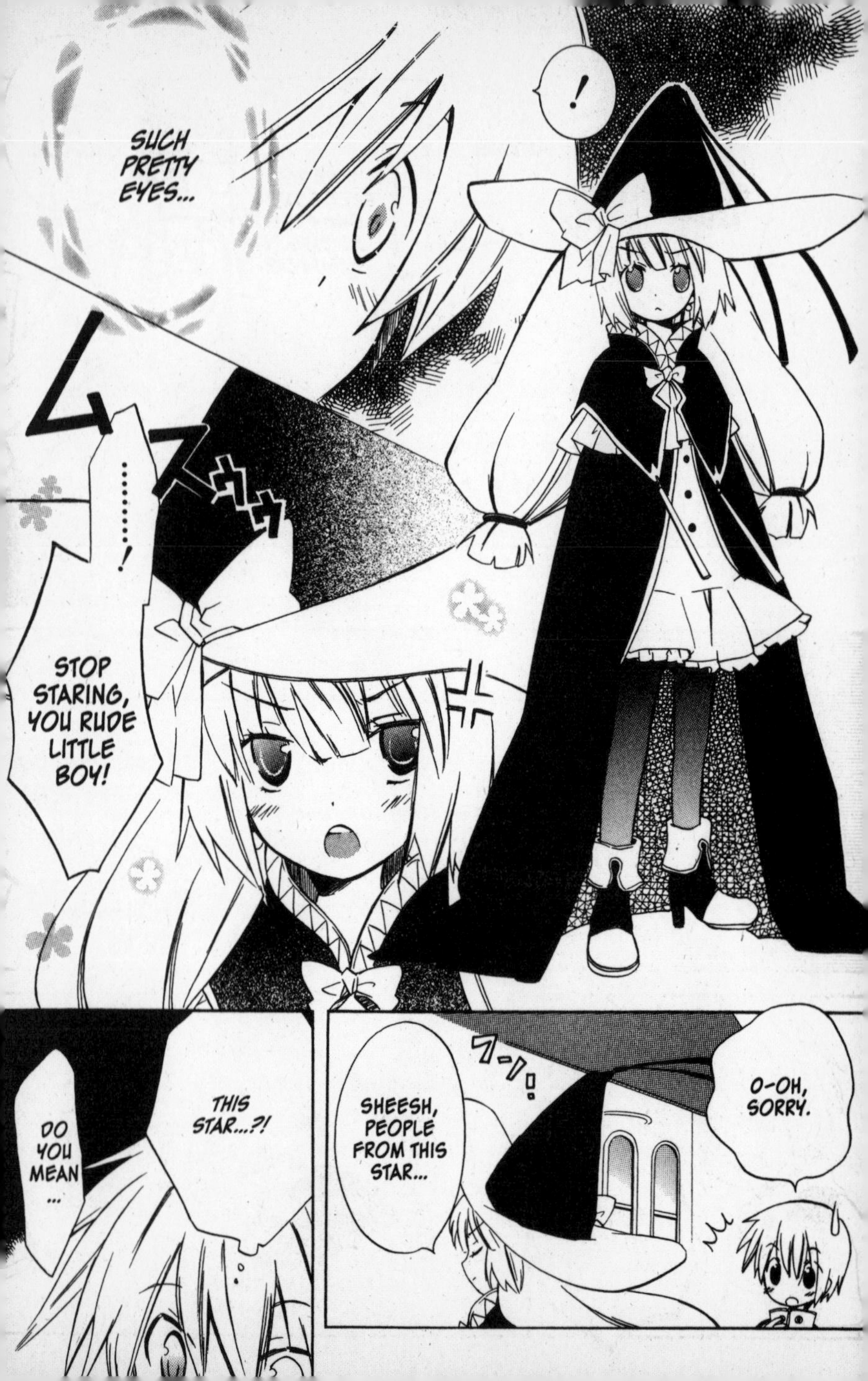
!
SUCH PRETTY EYES...
......!
STOP STARING, YOU RUDE LITTLE BOY!
O-OH, SORRY.
SHEESH, PEOPLE FROM THIS STAR...
THIS STAR...?!
DO YOU MEAN ...

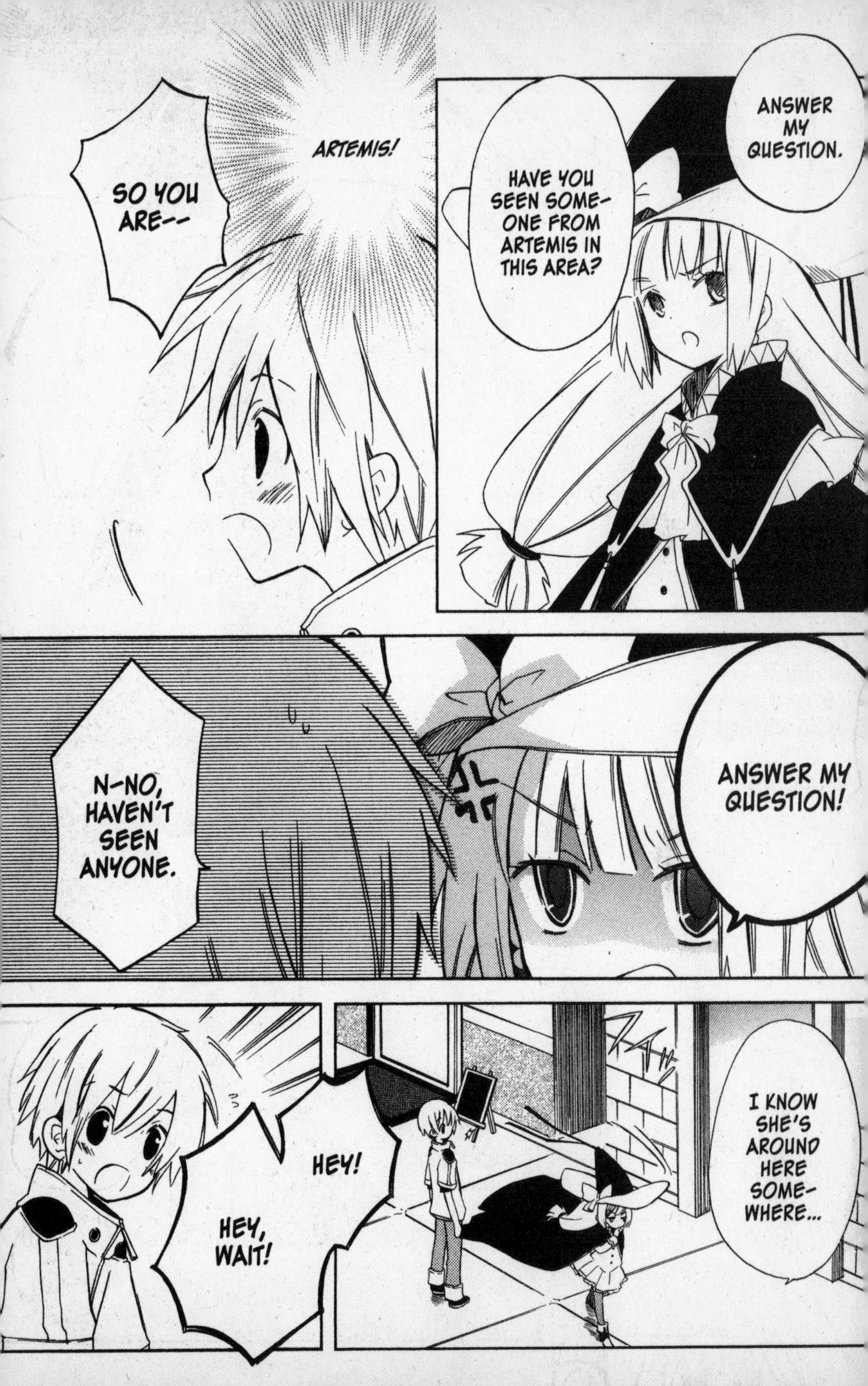
ANSWER MY QUESTION.
HAVE YOU SEEN SOME-ONE FROM ARTEMIS IN THIS AREA?
ARTEMIS!
SO YOU ARE--
ANSWER MY QUESTION!
N-NO, HAVEN'T SEEN ANYONE.
I KNOW SHE'S AROUND HERE SOME-WHERE...
HEY!
HEY, WAIT!

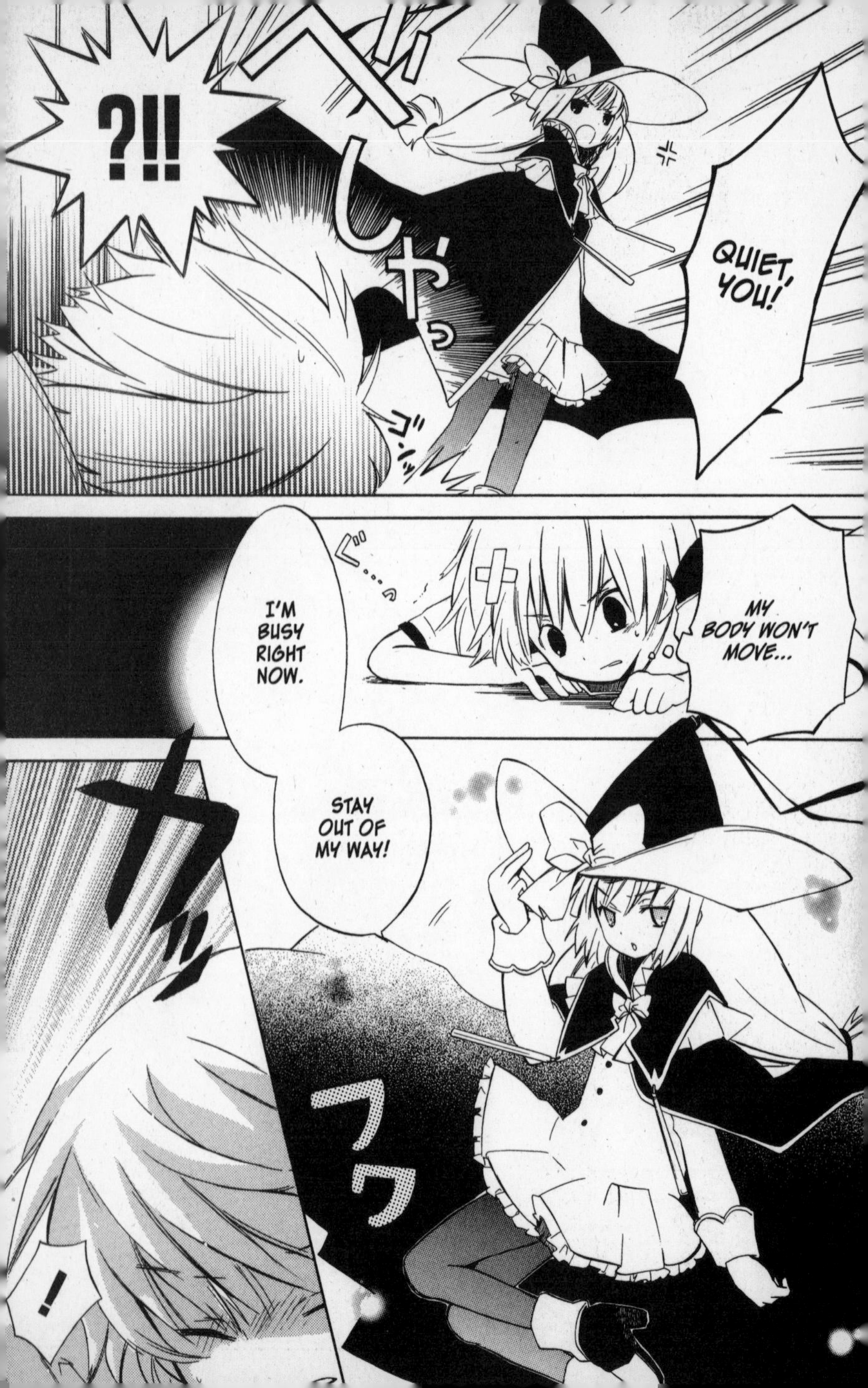
QUIET, YOU!
?!!
MY BODY WON'T MOVE...
I'M BUSY RIGHT NOW.
STAY OUT OF MY WAY!
!

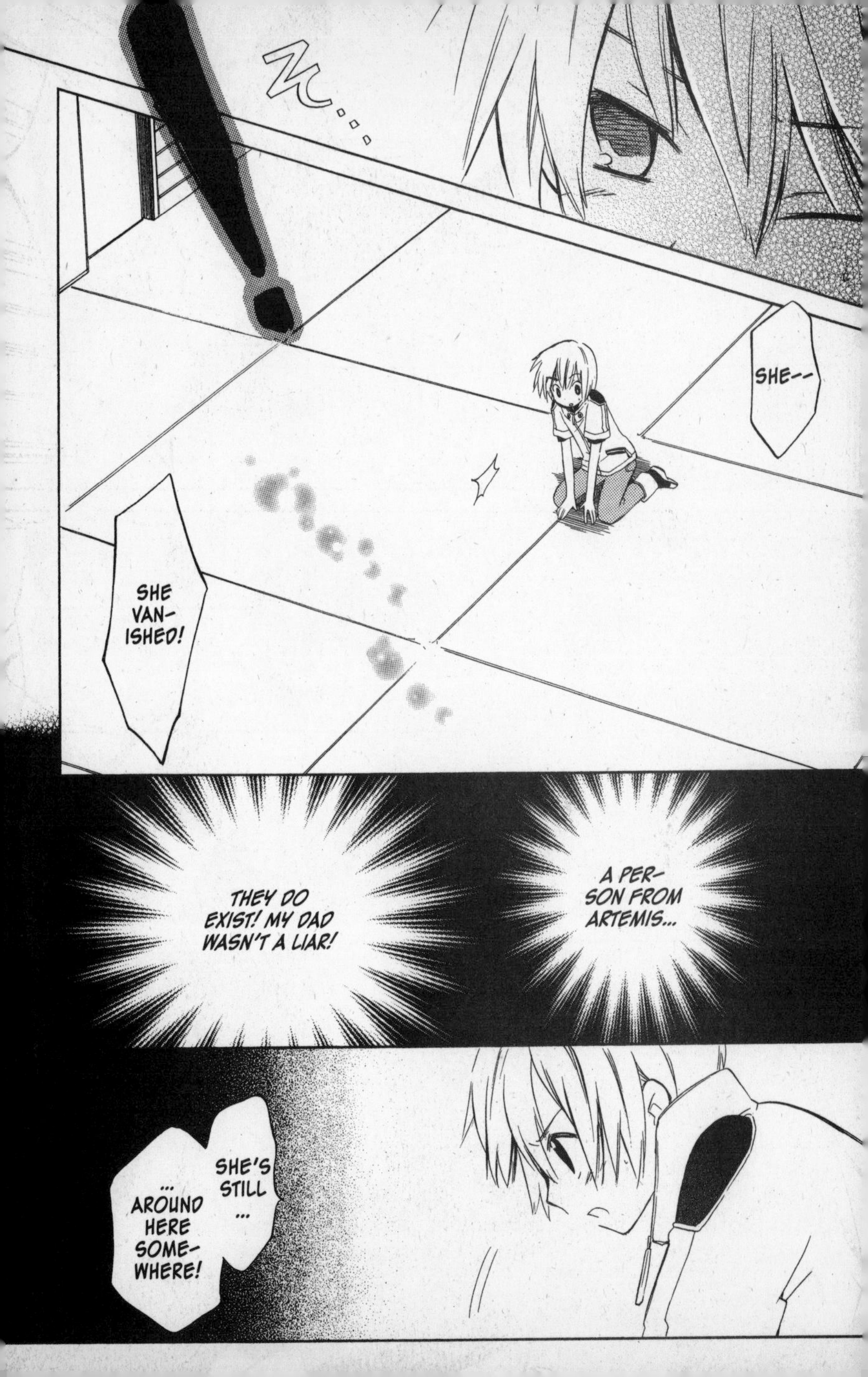
SHE--
SHE VAN-ISHED!
A PER-SON FROM ARTEMIS...
THEY DO EXIST! MY DAD WASN'T A LIAR!
SHE'S STILL ...
... AROUND HERE SOME-WHERE!

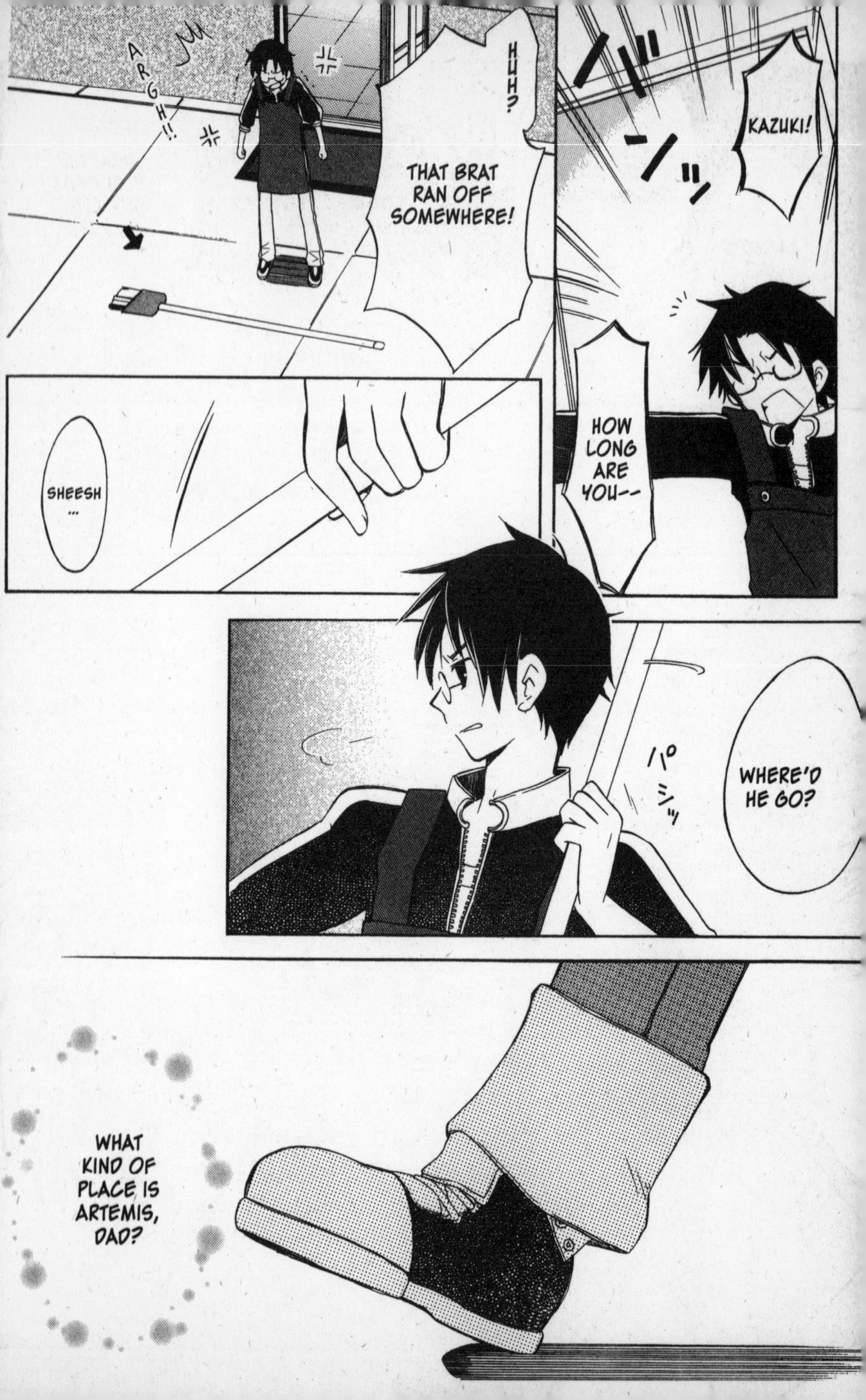
KAZUKI!
HOW LONG ARE YOU--
HUH?
THAT BRAT RAN OFF SOMEWHERE!
ARGH!!
SHEESH...
WHERE'D HE GO?
WHAT KIND OF PLACE IS ARTEMIS, DAD?

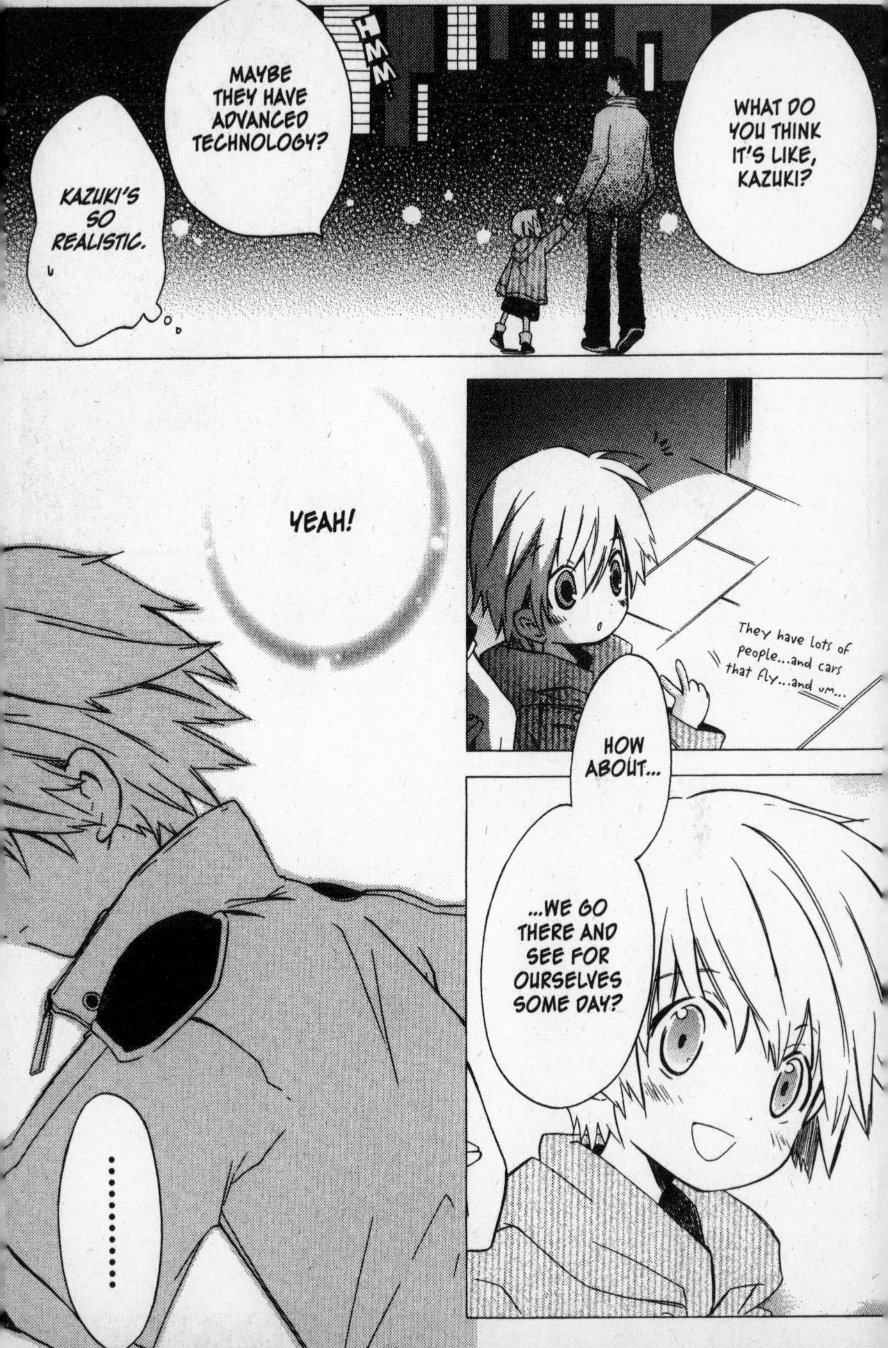
WHAT DO YOU THINK IT'S LIKE, KAZUKI?
HMM
MAYBE THEY HAVE ADVANCED TECHNOLOGY?
KAZUKI'S SO REALISTIC.
They have lots of people...and cars that fly...and um...
HOW ABOUT...
...WE GO THERE AND SEE FOR OURSELVES SOME DAY?
YEAH!
....

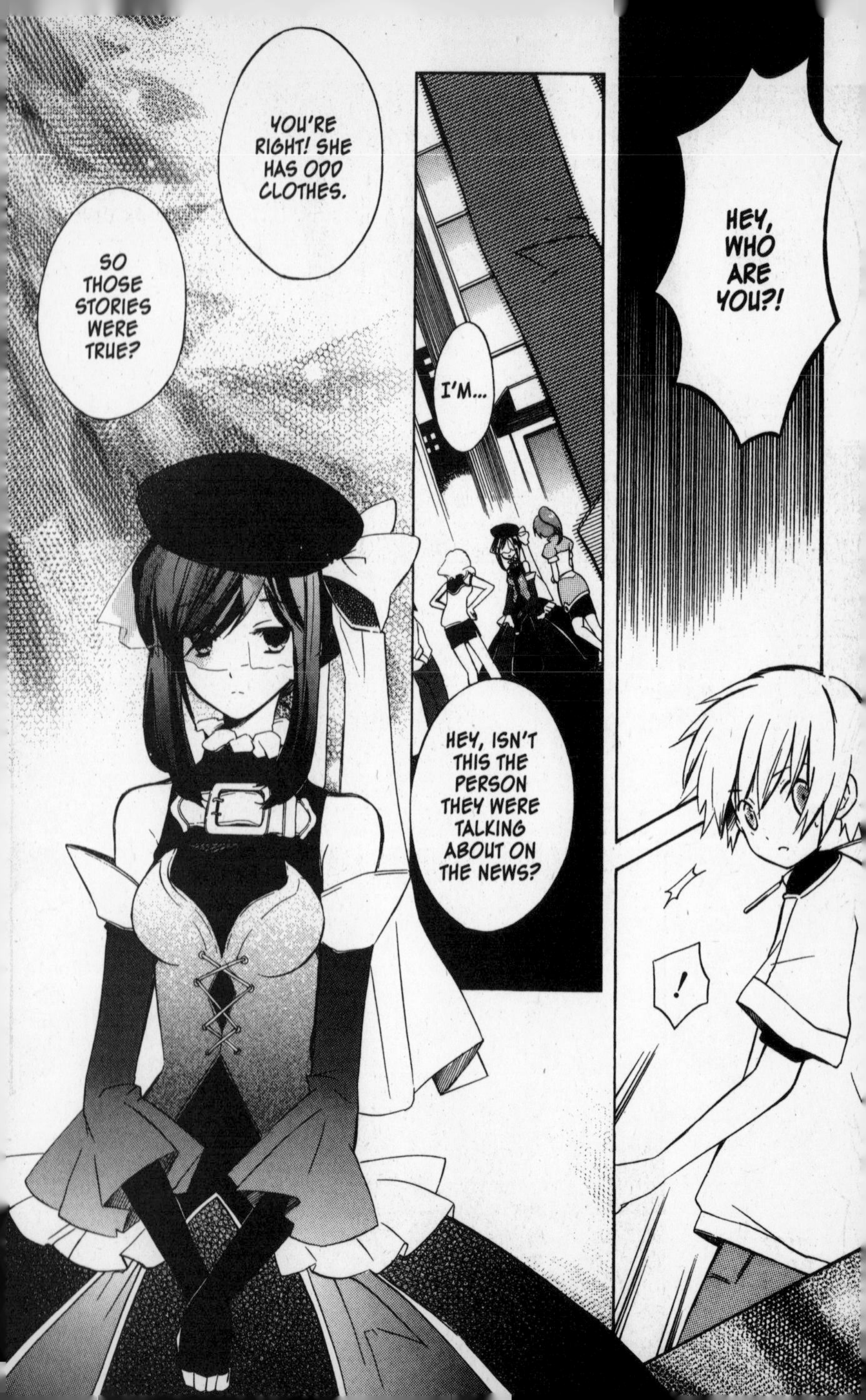
HEY, WHO ARE YOU?!
!
I'M...
HEY, ISN'T THIS THE PERSON THEY WERE TALKING ABOUT ON THE NEWS?
YOU'RE RIGHT! SHE HAS ODD CLOTHES.
SO THOSE STORIES WERE TRUE?

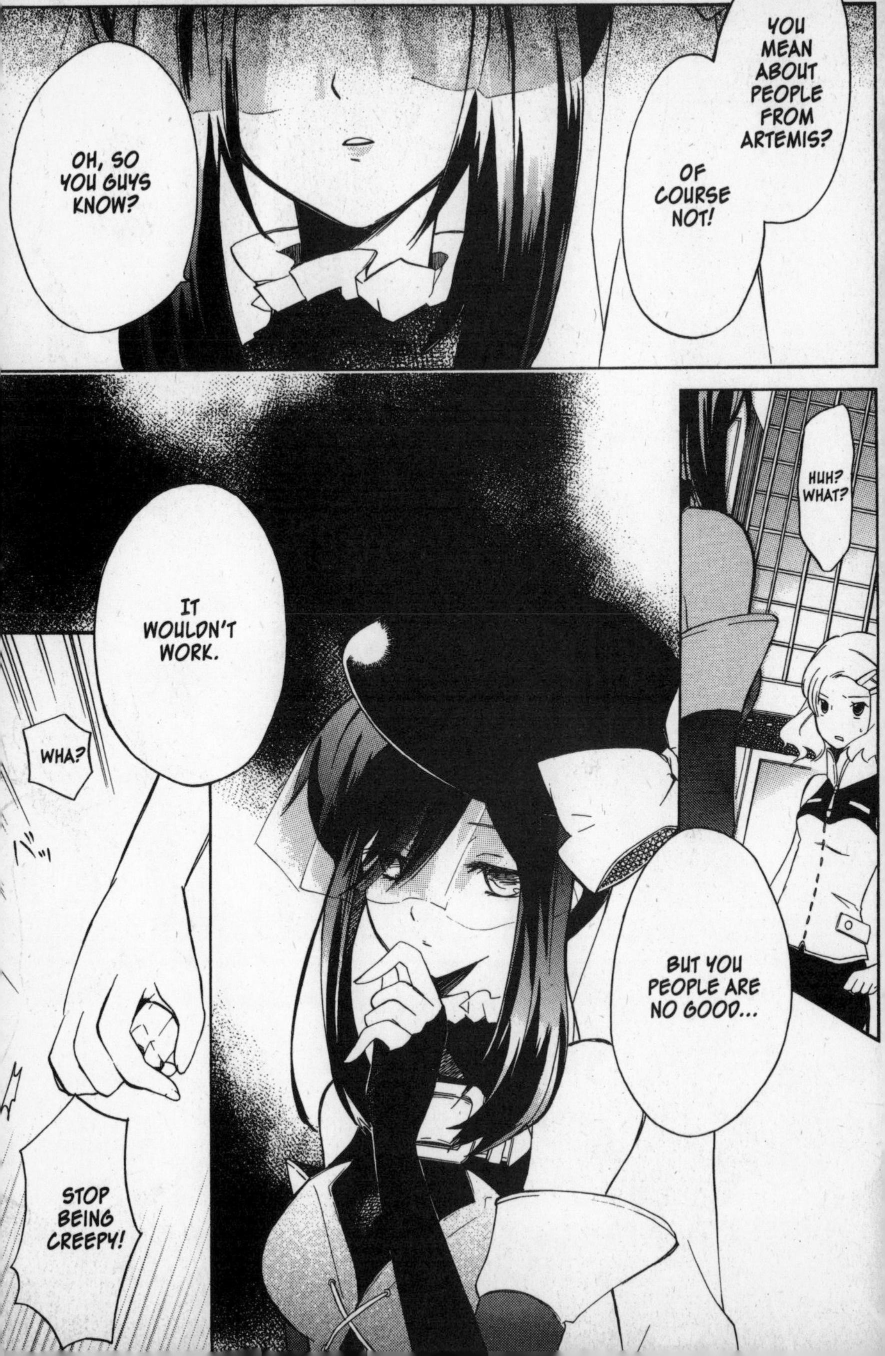
YOU MEAN ABOUT PEOPLE FROM ARTEMIS?
OF COURSE NOT!
OH, SO YOU GUYS KNOW?
HUH? WHAT?
BUT YOU PEOPLE ARE NO GOOD...
IT WOULDN'T WORK.
WHA?
バッ
STOP BEING CREEPY!

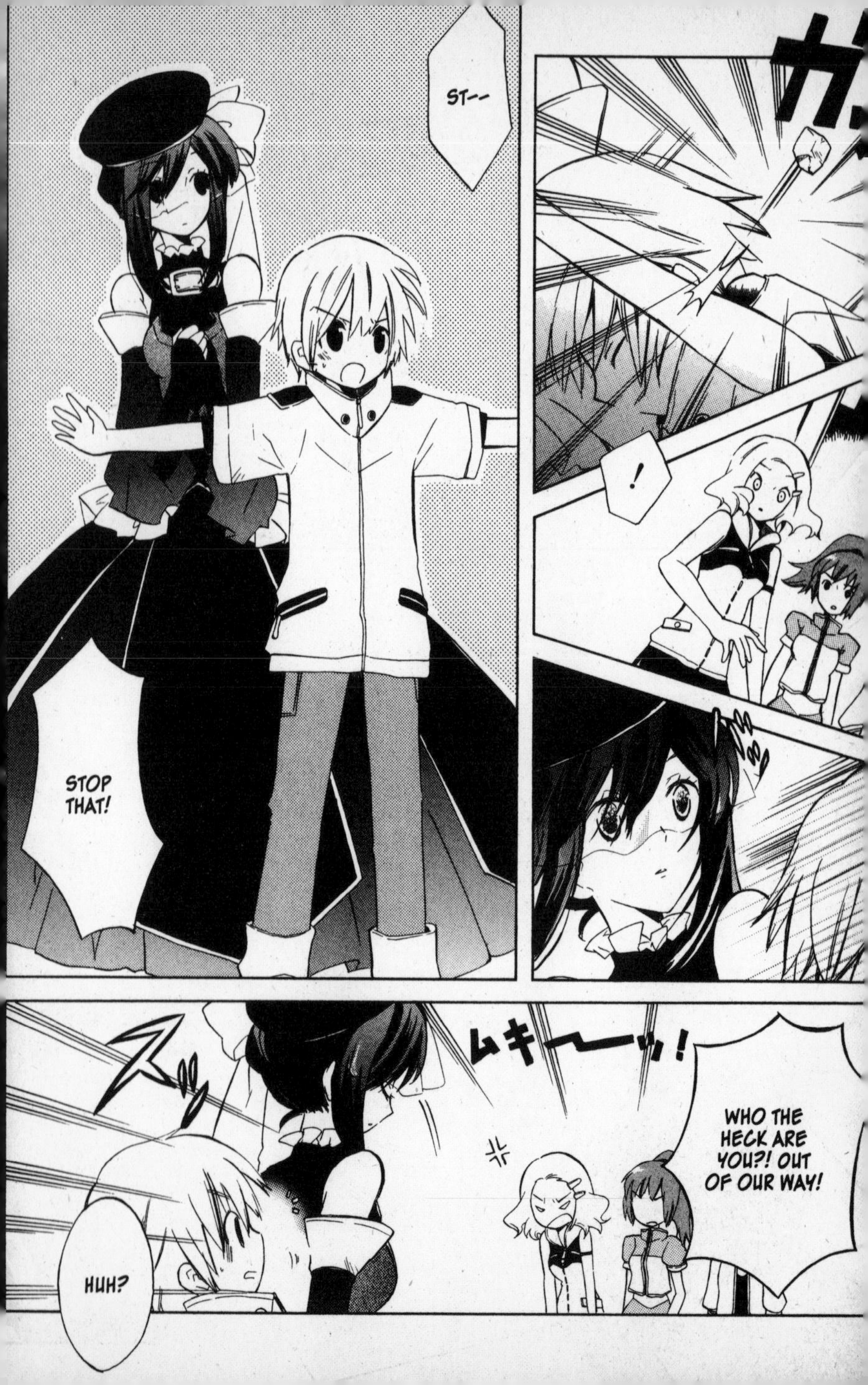
!
ST--
STOP THAT!
WHO THE HECK ARE YOU?! OUT OF OUR WAY!
ムキーーッ!
HUH?

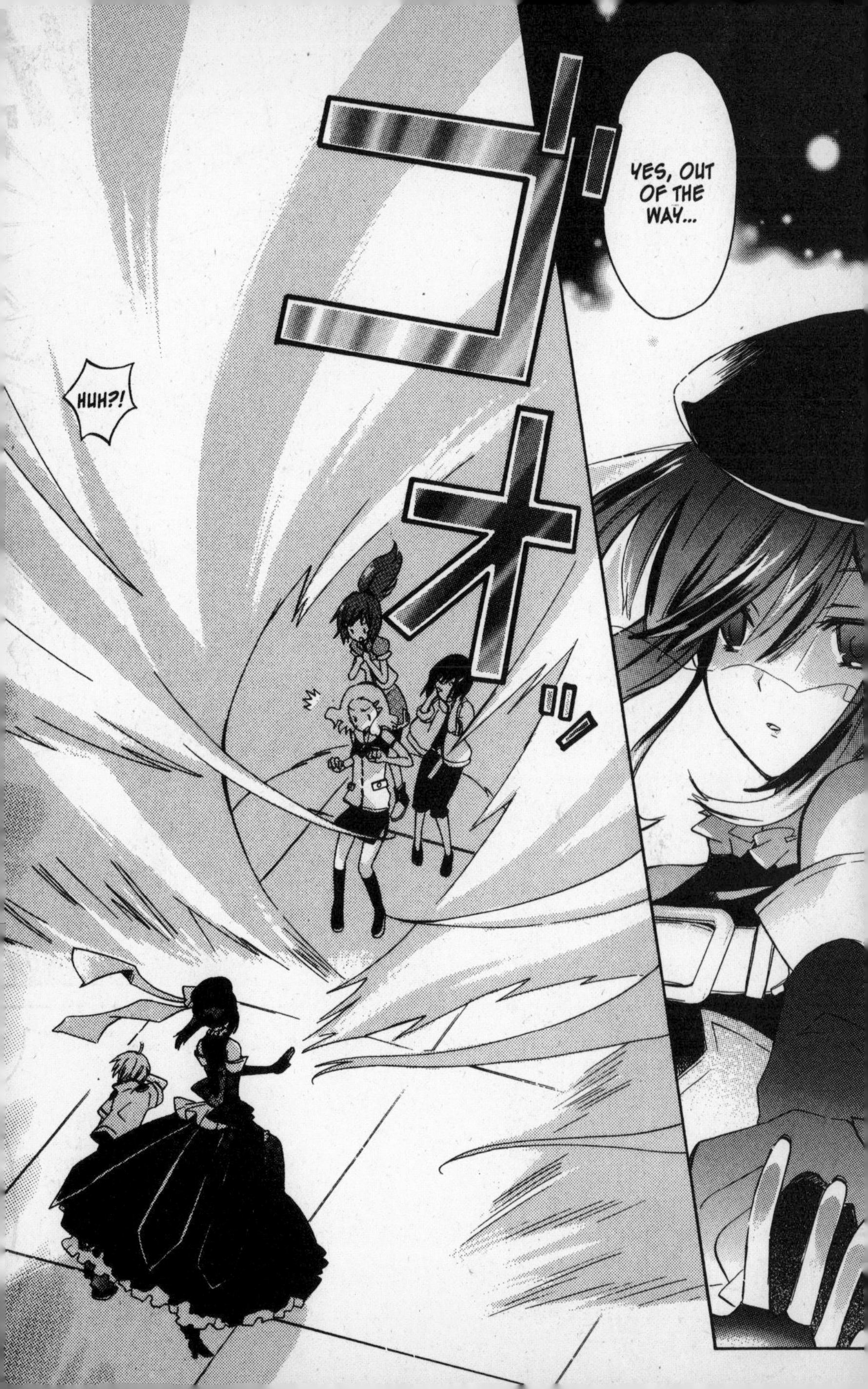
YES, OUT OF THE WAY...
ゴオッ
HUH?!

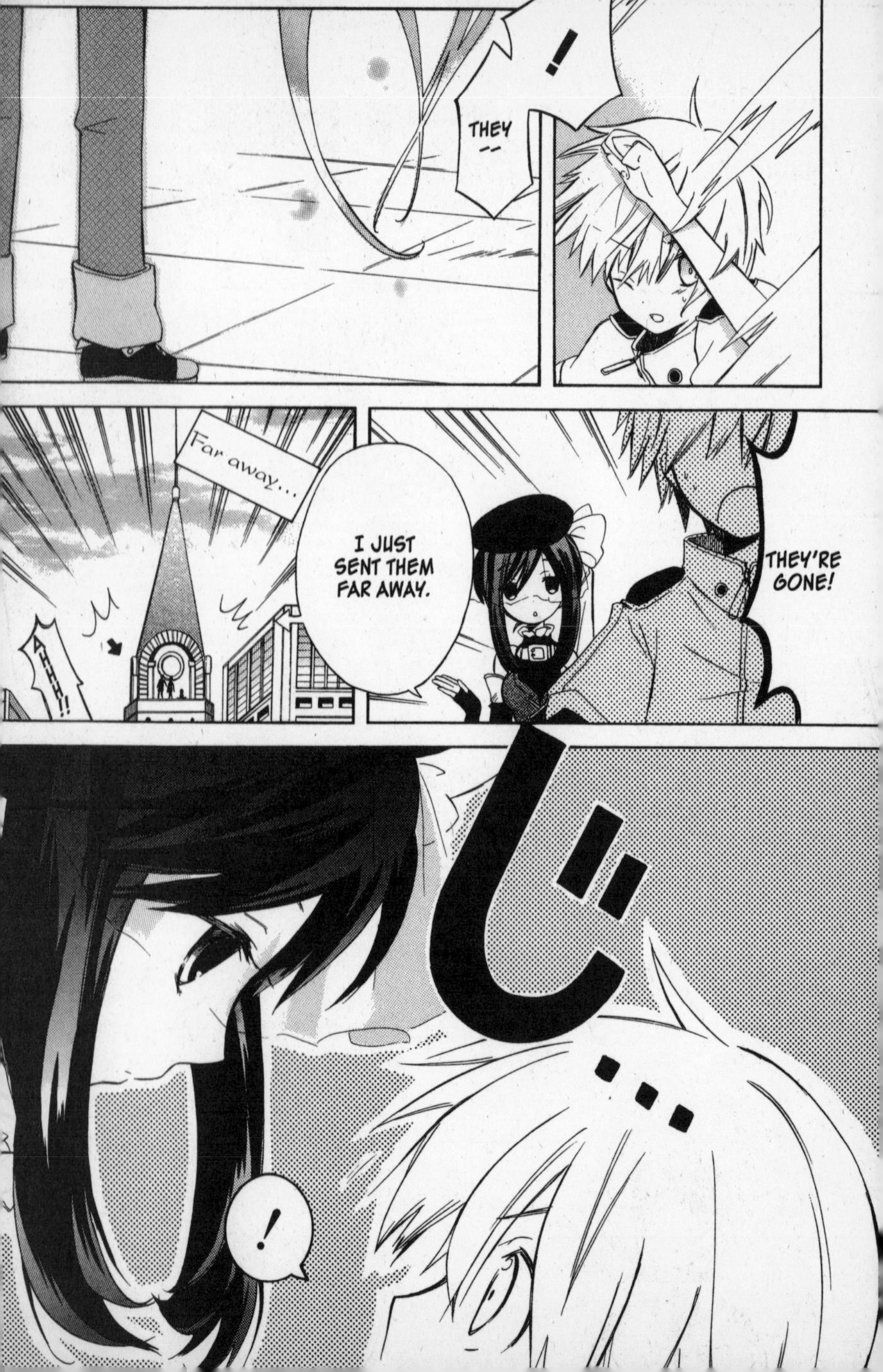
!
THEY --
THEY'RE GONE!
I JUST SENT THEM FAR AWAY.
Far away...
AHHH!!
じ
...
!

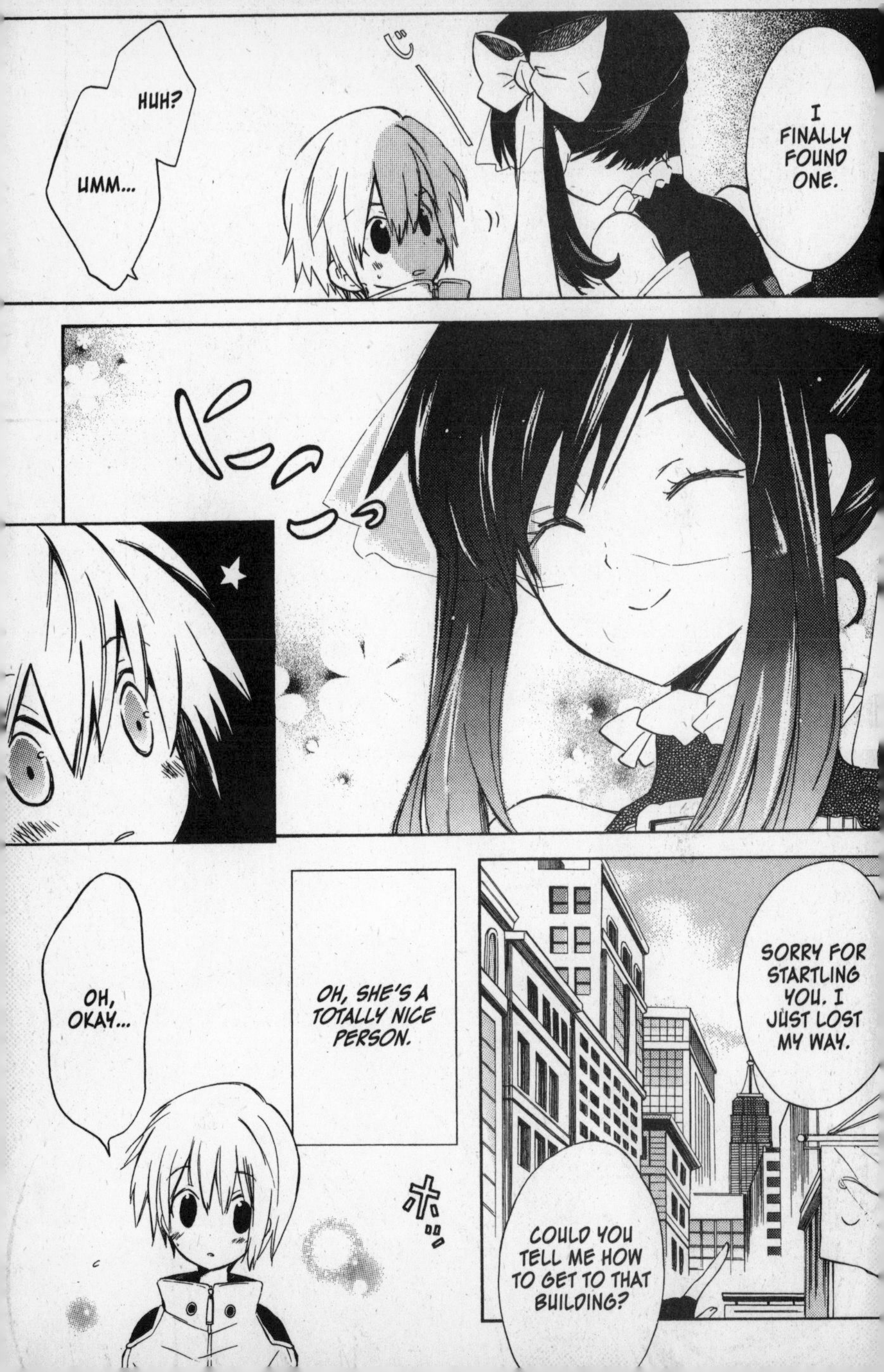
I FINALLY FOUND ONE.
HUH?
UMM...
SORRY FOR STARTLING YOU. I JUST LOST MY WAY.
COULD YOU TELL ME HOW TO GET TO THAT BUILDING?
OH, SHE'S A TOTALLY NICE PERSON.
OH, OKAY...

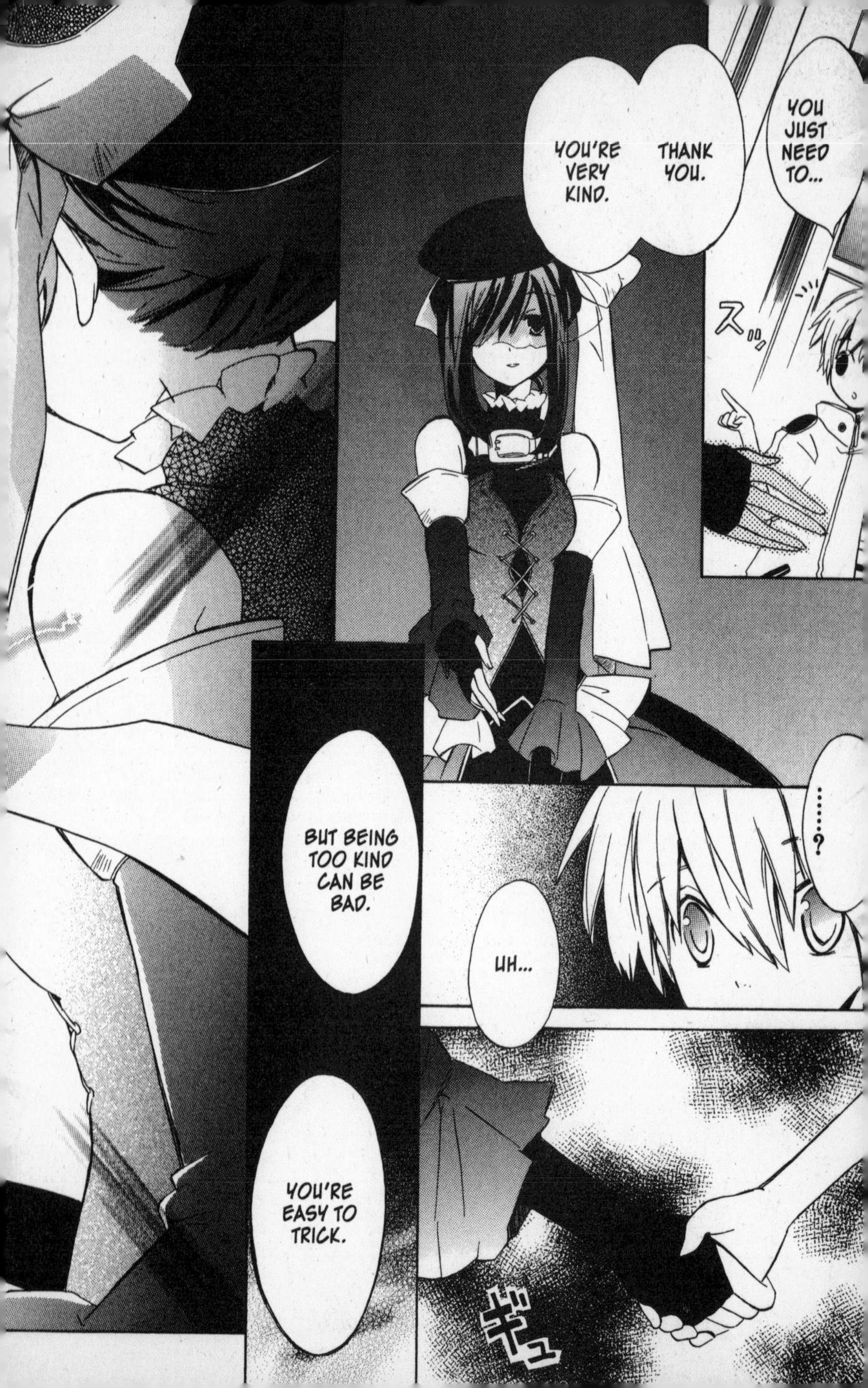
YOU JUST NEED TO...
スッ
THANK YOU.
YOU'RE VERY KIND.
BUT BEING TOO KIND CAN BE BAD.
......?
UH...
YOU'RE EASY TO TRICK.
ギュ

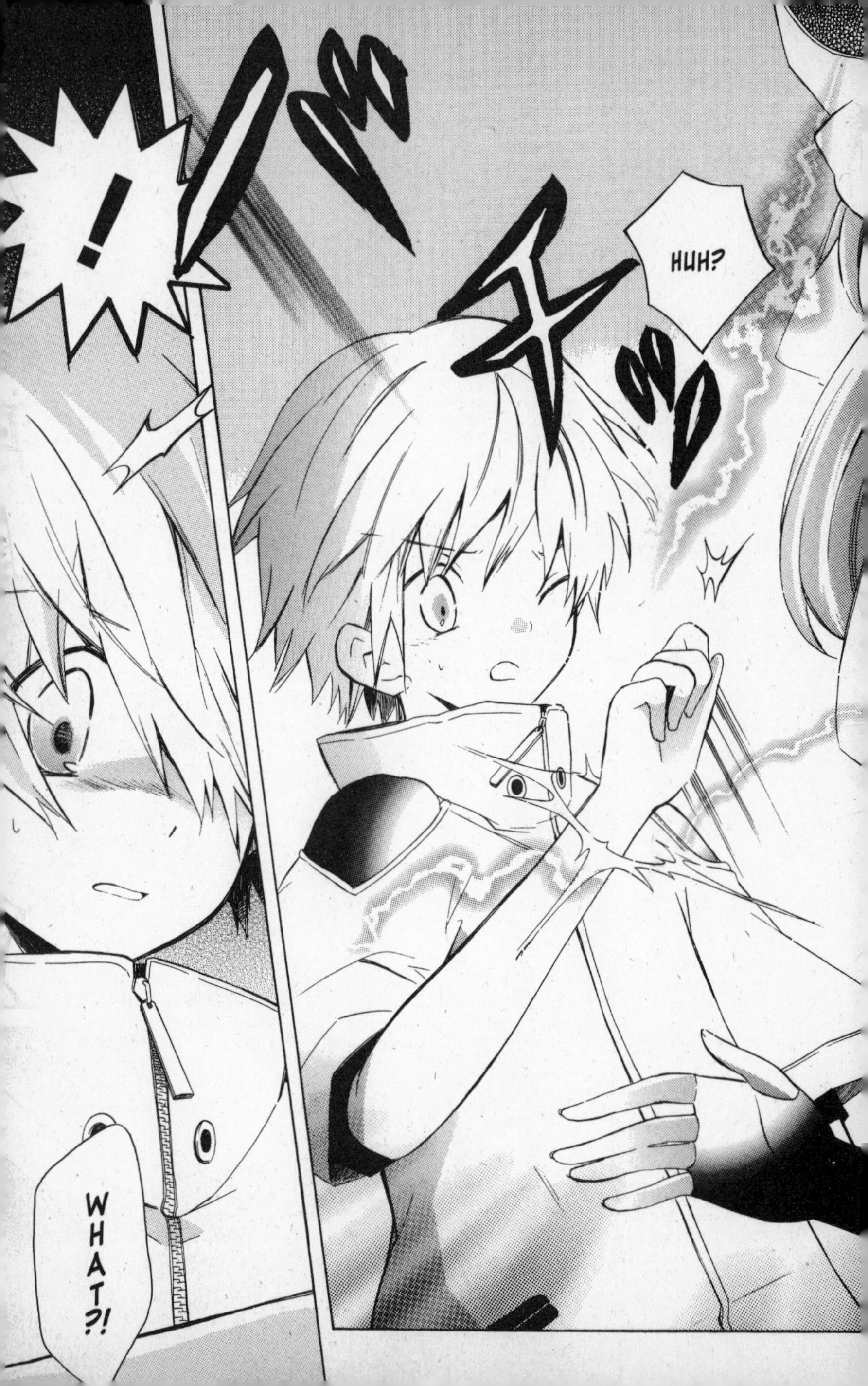
HUH?
!
WHAT?!

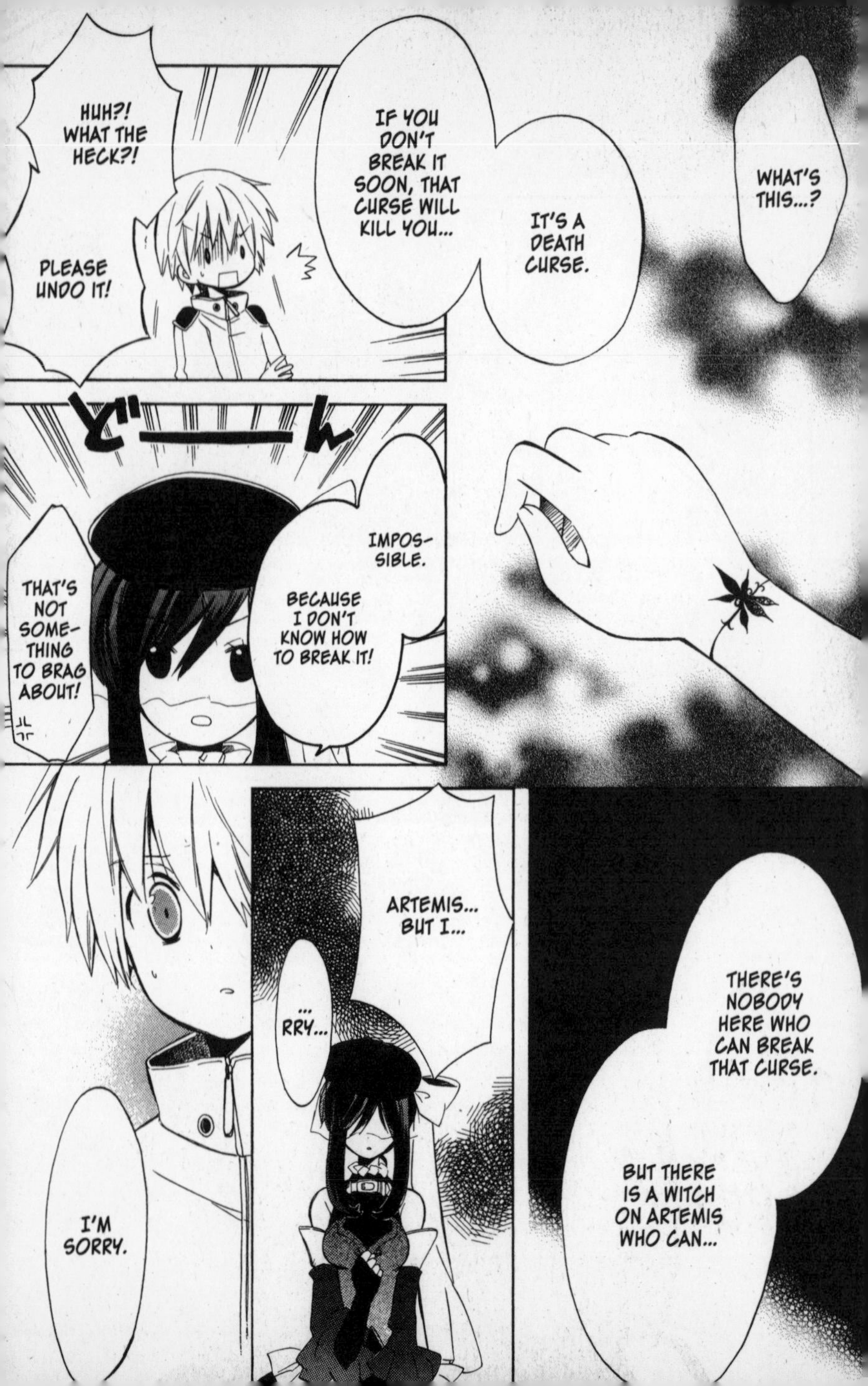
WHAT'S THIS...?
IT'S A DEATH CURSE.
IF YOU DON'T BREAK IT SOON, THAT CURSE WILL KILL YOU...
HUH?! WHAT THE HECK?!
PLEASE UNDO IT!
どーーーん
IMPOS-SIBLE.
BECAUSE I DON'T KNOW HOW TO BREAK IT!
THAT'S NOT SOME-THING TO BRAG ABOUT!
THERE'S NOBODY HERE WHO CAN BREAK THAT CURSE.
BUT THERE IS A WITCH ON ARTEMIS WHO CAN...
ARTEMIS... BUT I...
...RRY...
I'M SORRY.

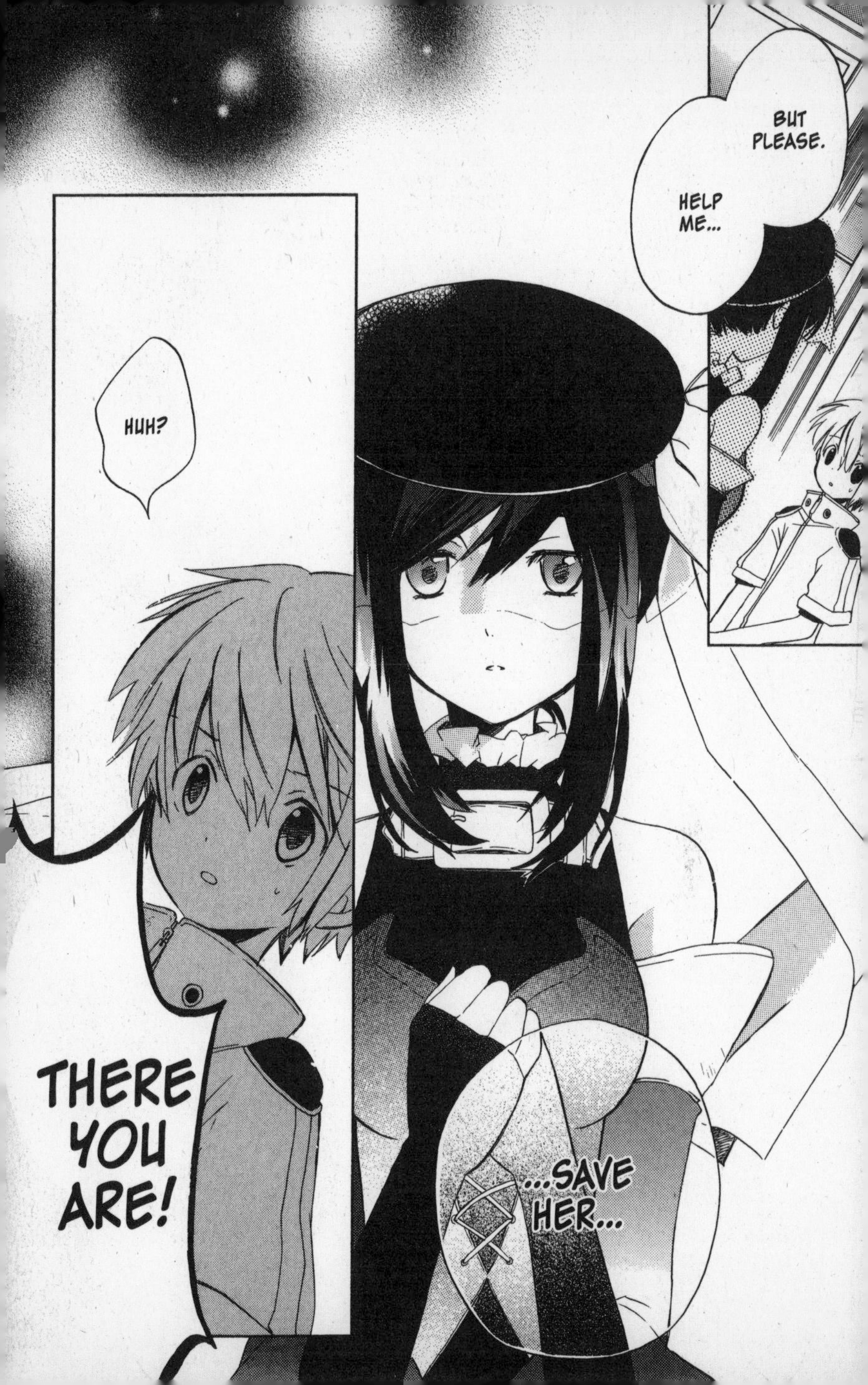
BUT PLEASE.
HELP ME...
...SAVE HER...
HUH?
THERE YOU ARE!

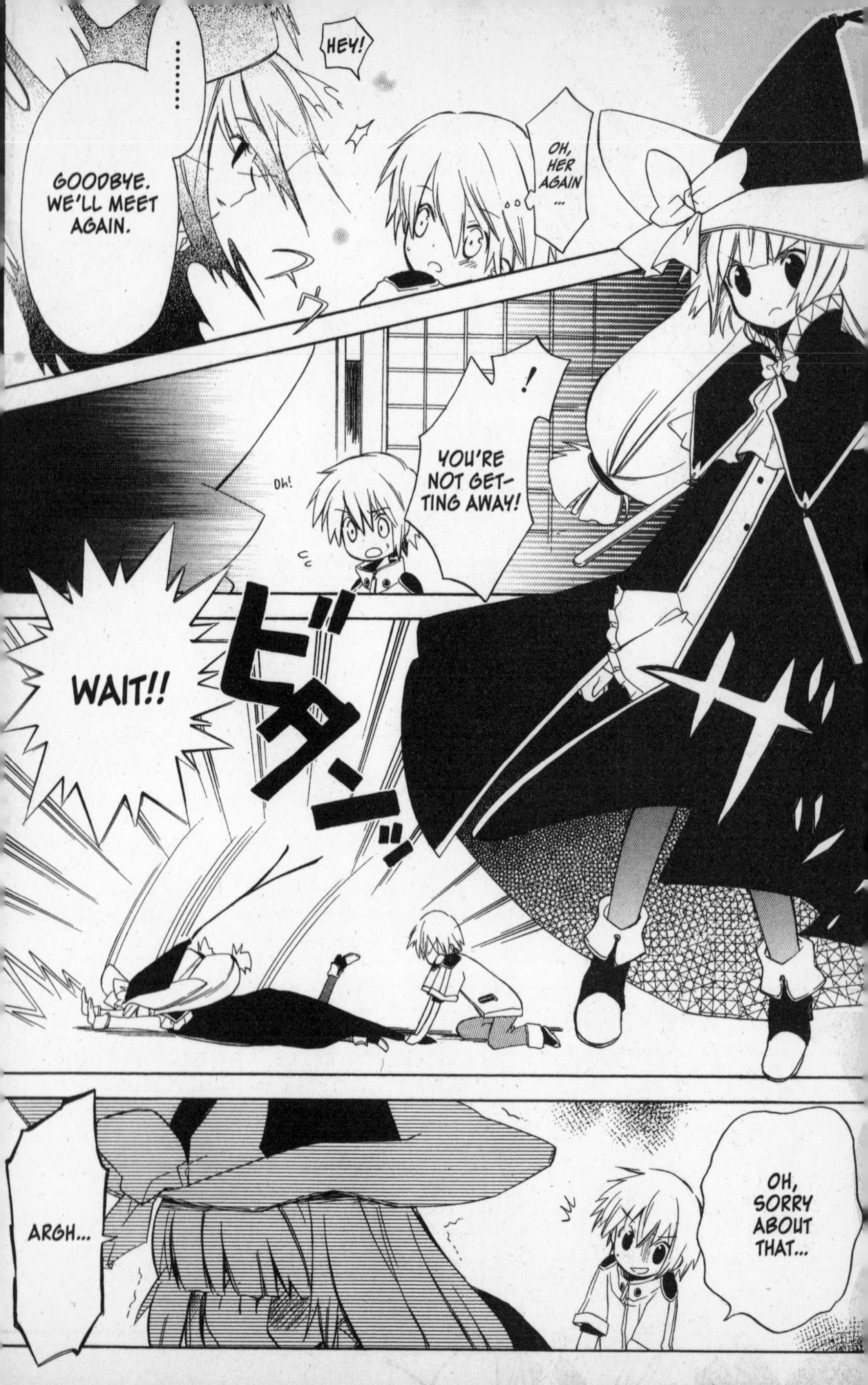

OH, HER AGAIN...
HEY!
......
GOODBYE. WE'LL MEET AGAIN.
!
YOU'RE NOT GET-TING AWAY!
Oh!
WAIT!!
ビダーンッ
OH, SORRY ABOUT THAT...
ARGH...

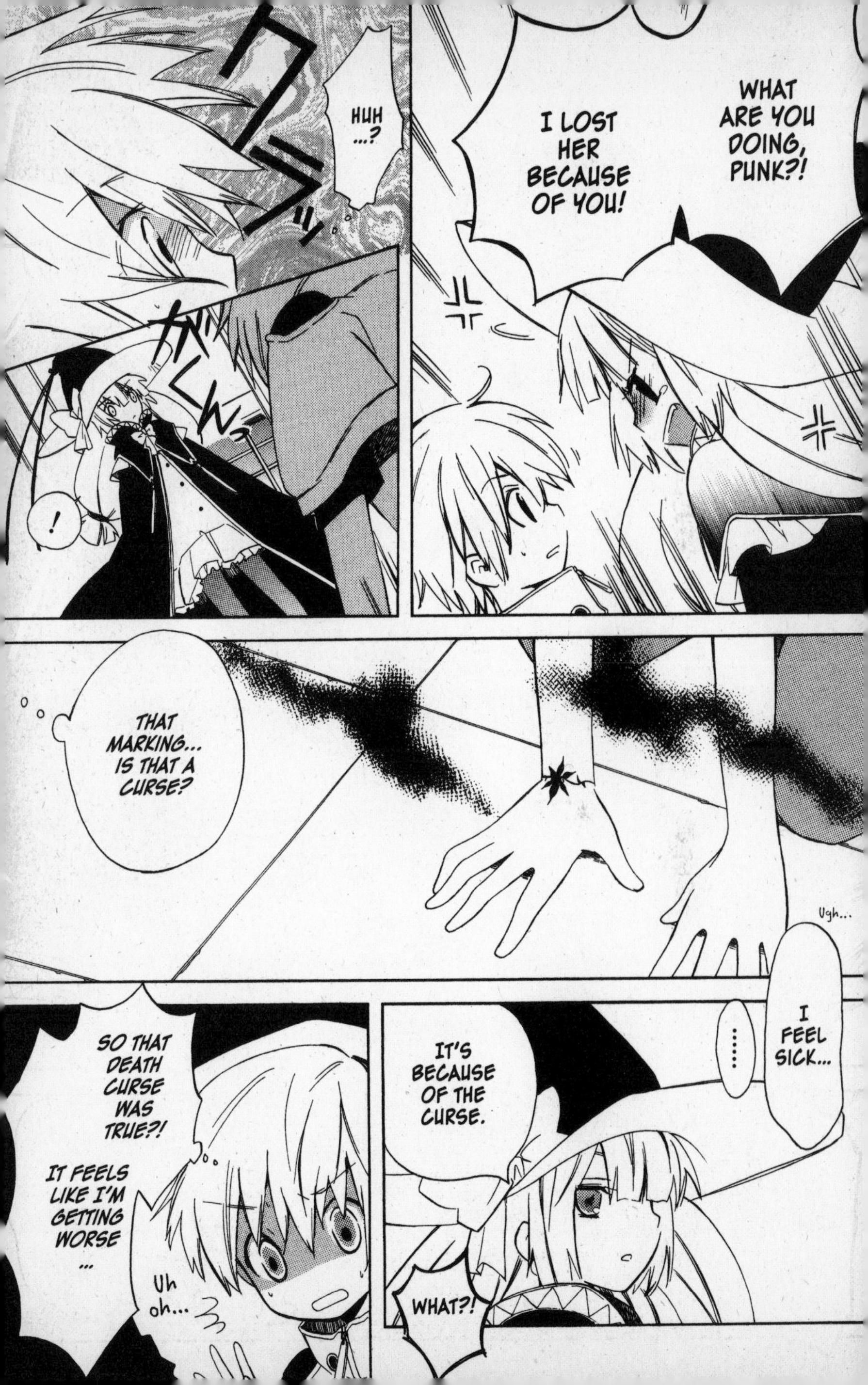
WHAT ARE YOU DOING, PUNK?!
I LOST HER BECAUSE OF YOU!
HUH ...?
!
THAT MARKING... IS THAT A CURSE?
Ugh...
I FEEL SICK...
......
IT'S BECAUSE OF THE CURSE.
WHAT?!
SO THAT DEATH CURSE WAS TRUE?!
IT FEELS LIKE I'M GETTING WORSE ...
Uh oh...

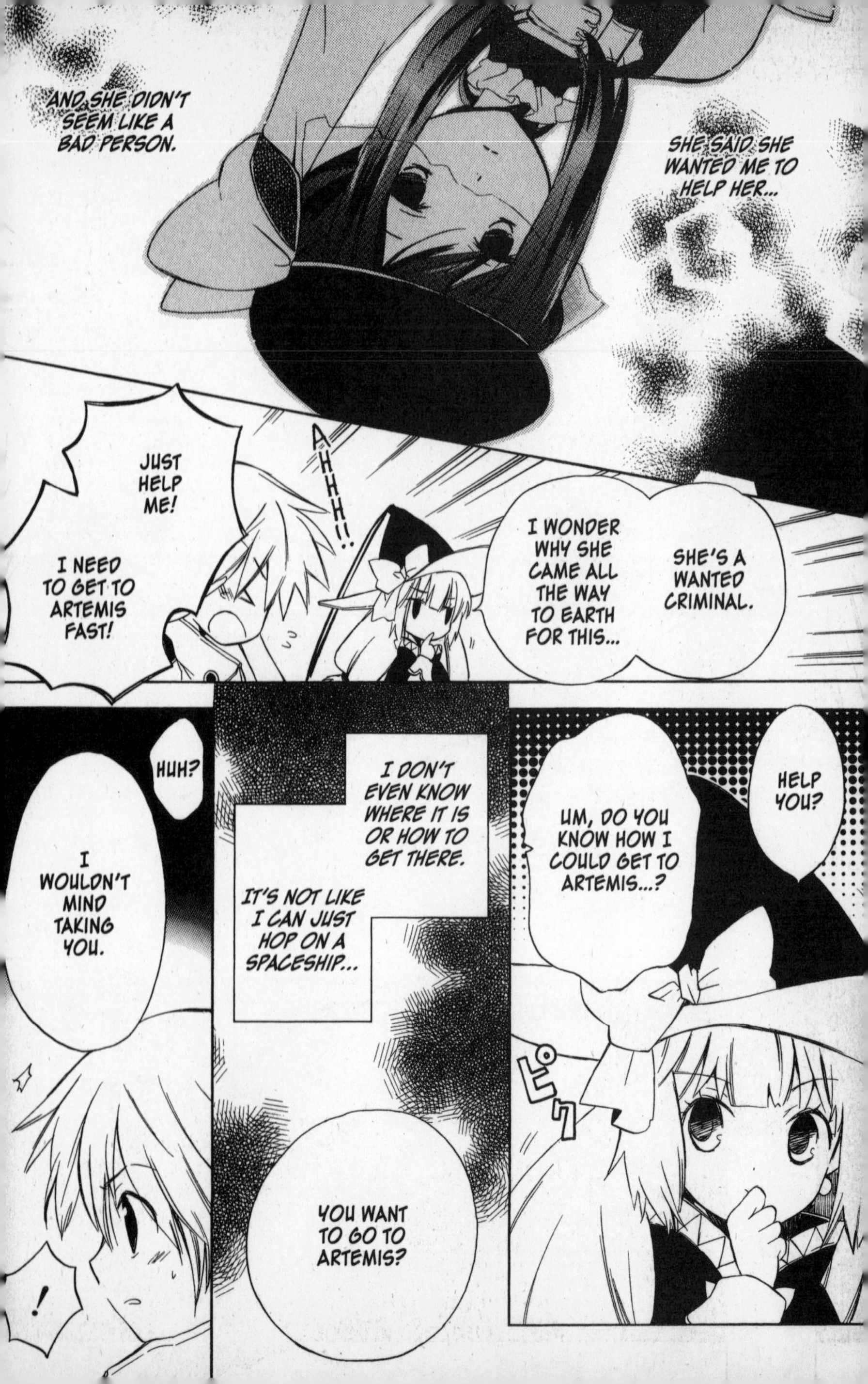
SHE SAID SHE WANTED ME TO HELP HER...
AND SHE DIDN'T SEEM LIKE A BAD PERSON.
SHE'S A WANTED CRIMINAL.
I WONDER WHY SHE CAME ALL THE WAY TO EARTH FOR THIS...
AHHHH!!
JUST HELP ME!
I NEED TO GET TO ARTEMIS FAST!
HELP YOU?
UM, DO YOU KNOW HOW I COULD GET TO ARTEMIS...?
ピク
I DON'T EVEN KNOW WHERE IT IS OR HOW TO GET THERE.
IT'S NOT LIKE I CAN JUST HOP ON A SPACESHIP...
YOU WANT TO GO TO ARTEMIS?
HUH?
I WOULDN'T MIND TAKING YOU.
!

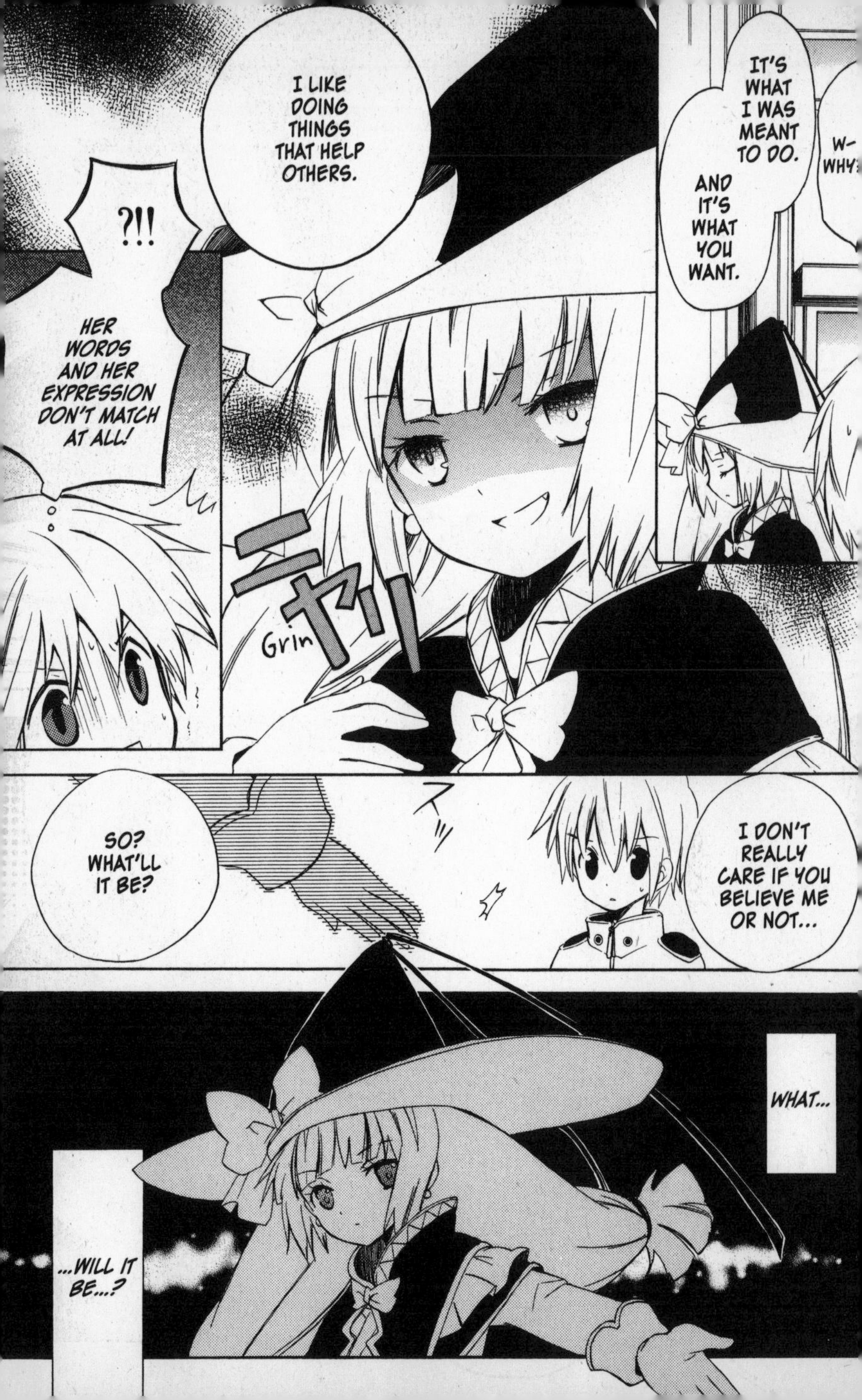
W- WHY
IT'S WHAT I WAS MEANT TO DO.
AND IT'S WHAT YOU WANT.
I LIKE DOING THINGS THAT HELP OTHERS.
Grin
?!!
HER WORDS AND HER EXPRESSION DON'T MATCH AT ALL!
I DON'T REALLY CARE IF YOU BELIEVE ME OR NOT...
SO? WHAT'LL IT BE?
WHAT...
...WILL IT BE...?

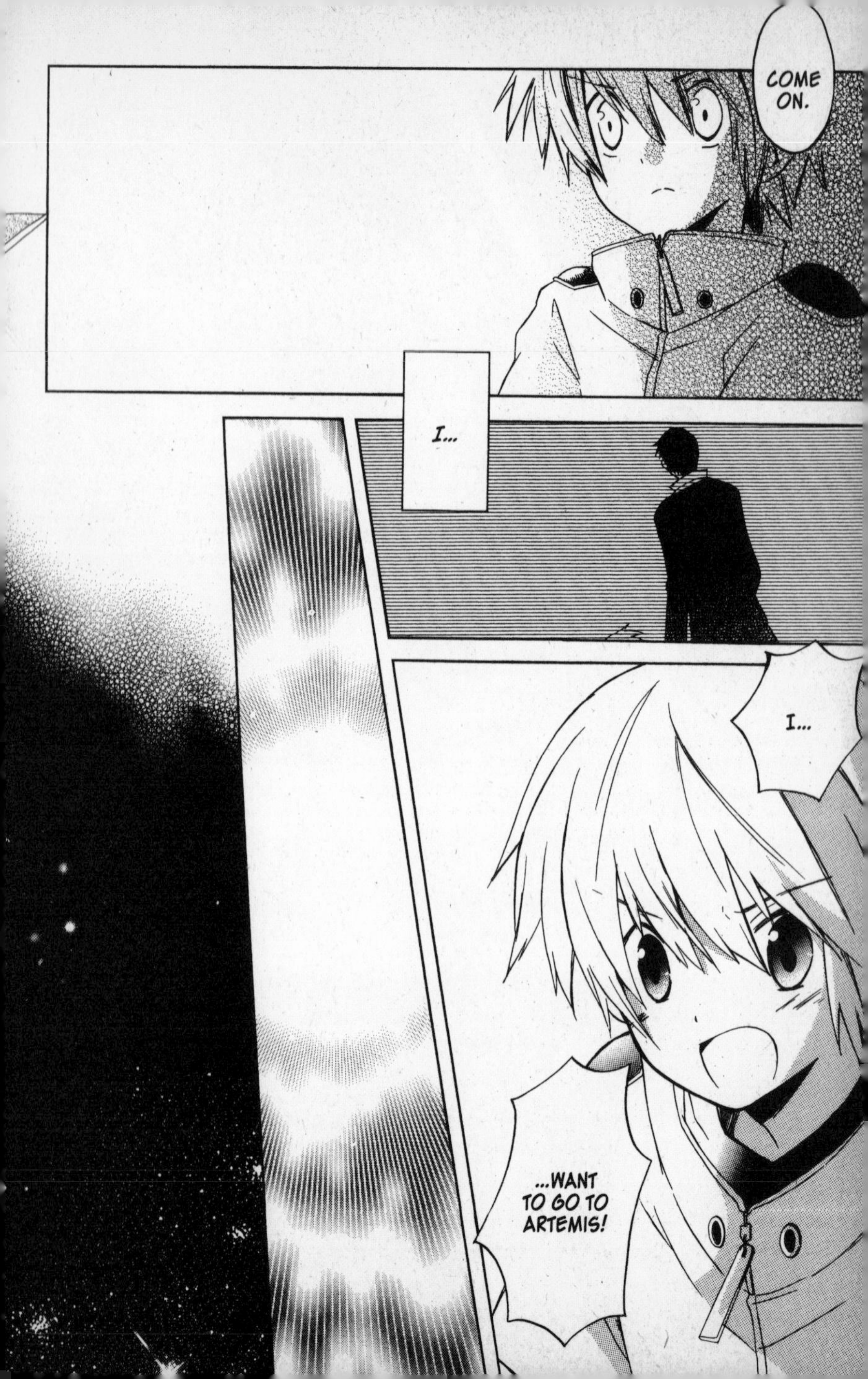
COME ON.
I...
I...
...WANT TO GO TO ARTEMIS!

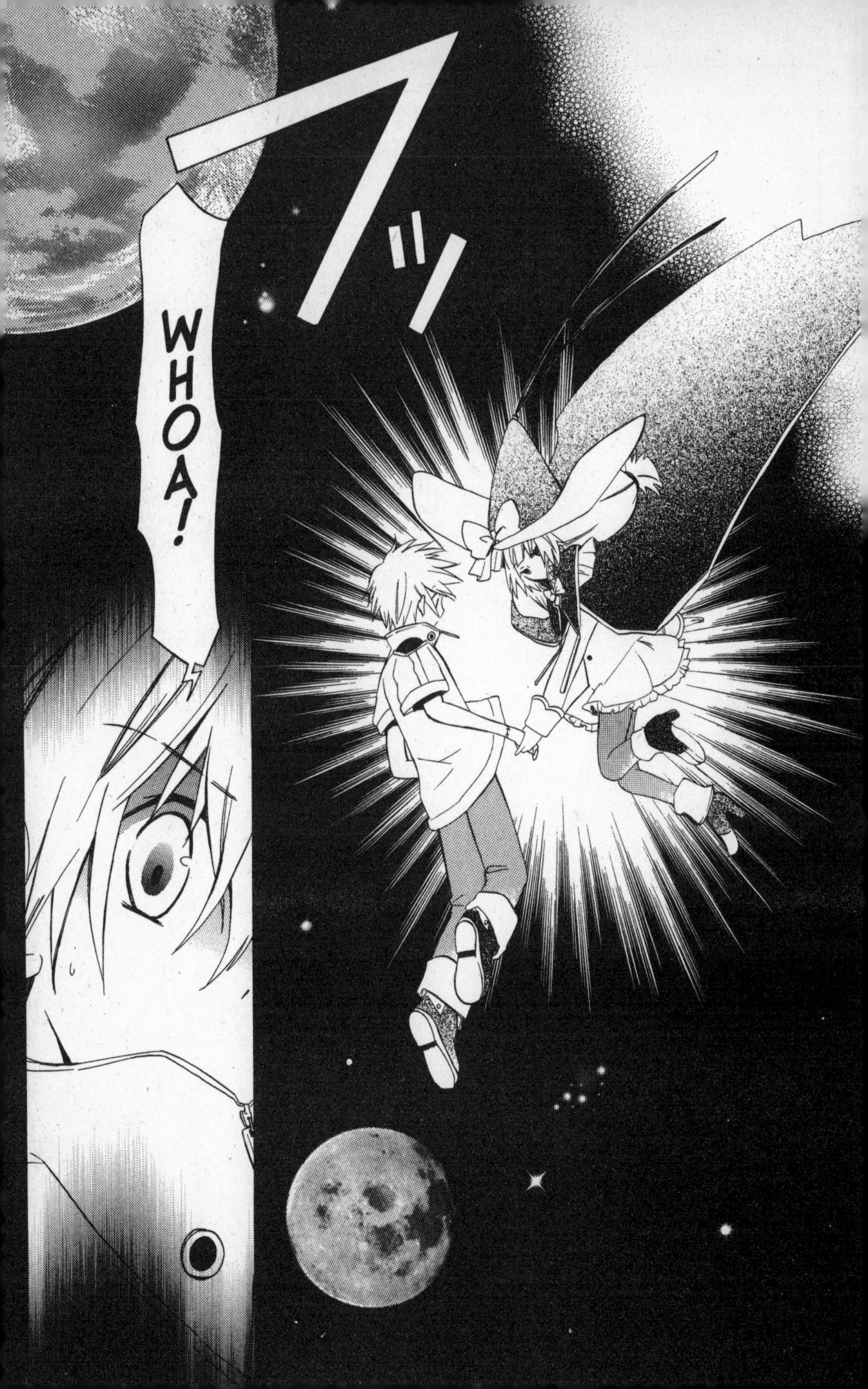
WHOA!

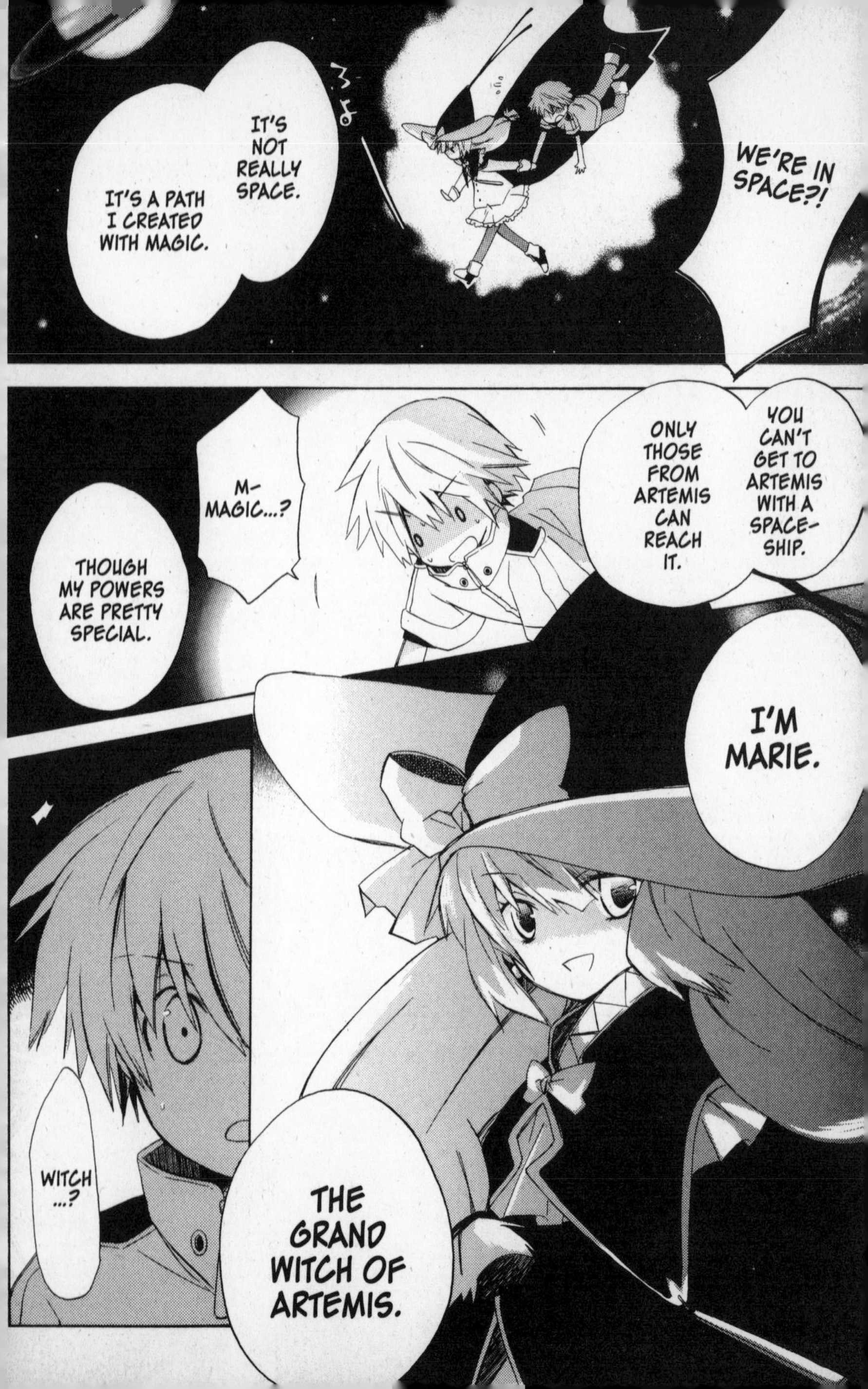
WE'RE IN SPACE?!
IT'S NOT REALLY SPACE.
IT'S A PATH I CREATED WITH MAGIC.
YOU CAN'T GET TO ARTEMIS WITH A SPACE-SHIP.
ONLY THOSE FROM ARTEMIS CAN REACH IT.
M-MAGIC...?
THOUGH MY POWERS ARE PRETTY SPECIAL.
I'M MARIE.
THE GRAND WITCH OF ARTEMIS.
WITCH ...?

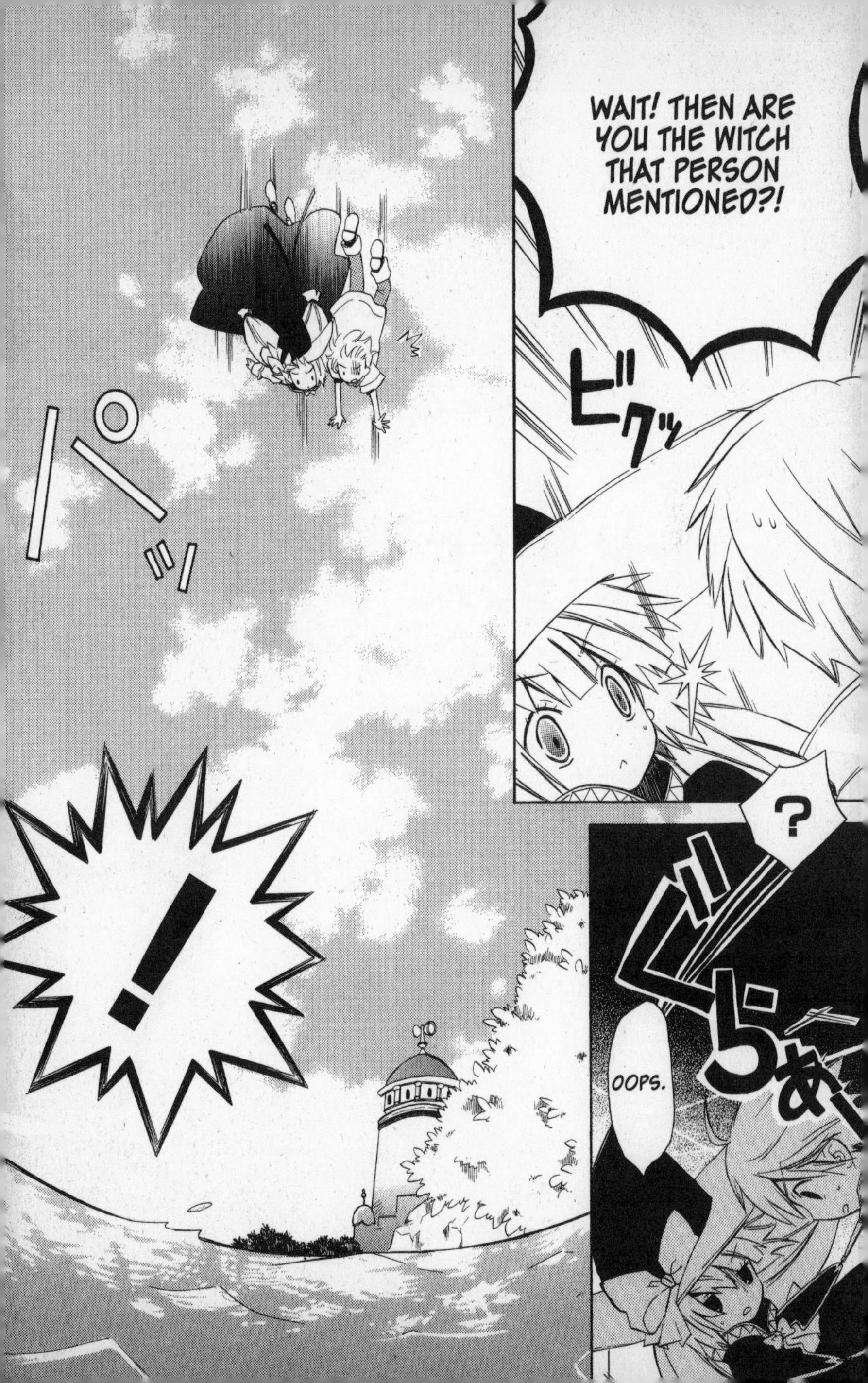
WAIT! THEN ARE YOU THE WITCH THAT PERSON MENTIONED?!
ビクッ
?
OOPS.
!

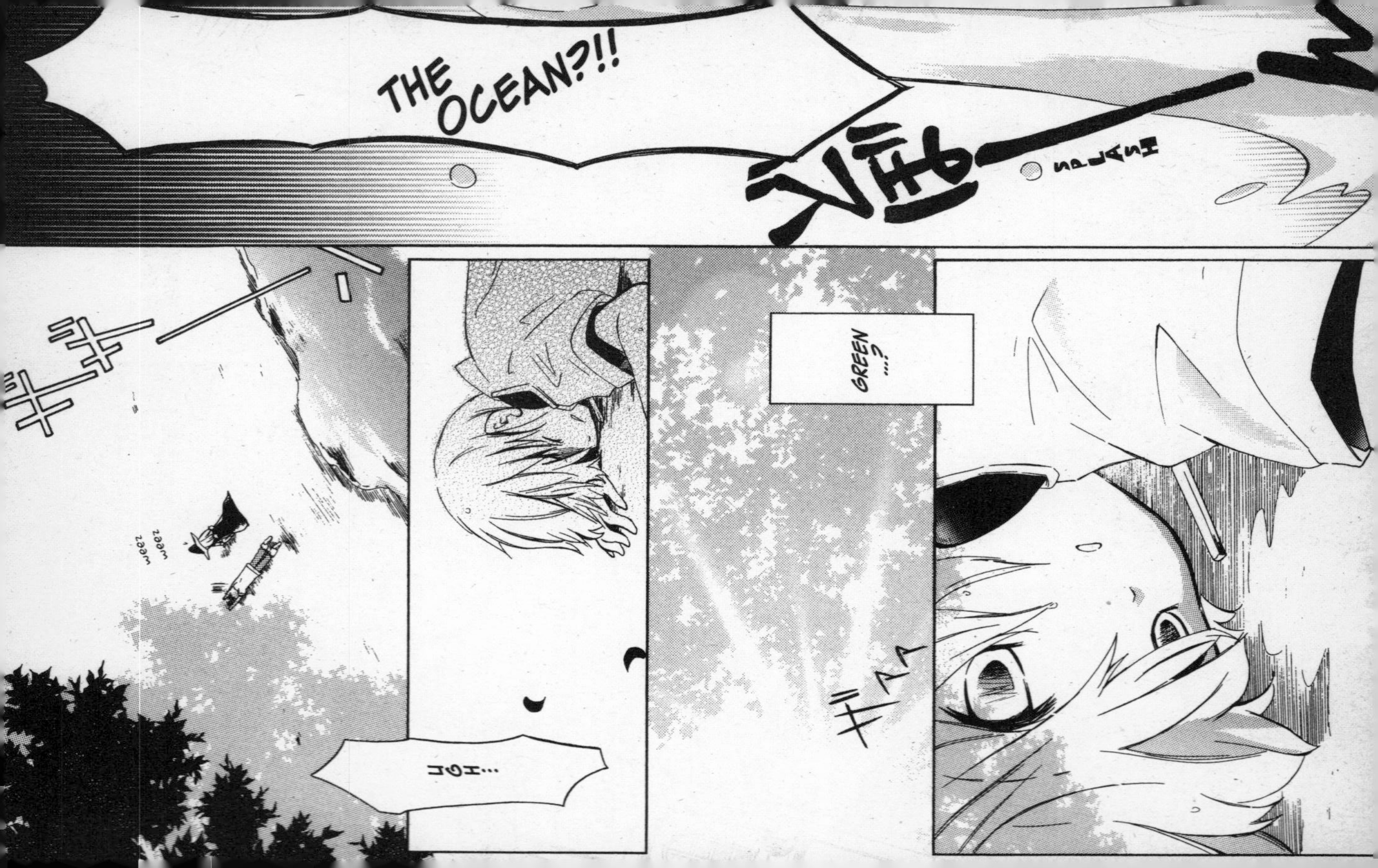
SPLASH
THE OCEAN?!!
GREEN ...?
UGH...
weez weez

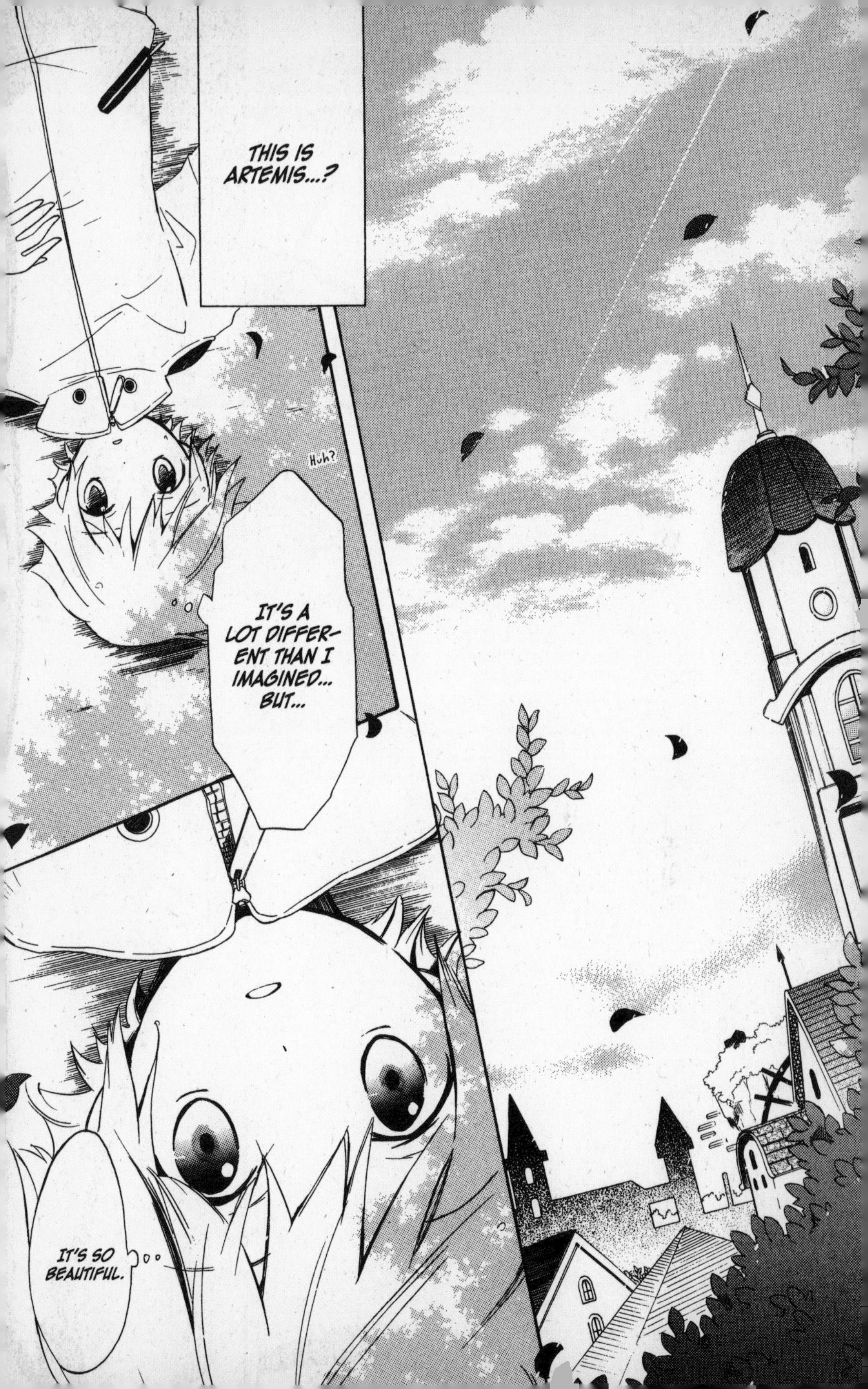
THIS IS ARTEMIS...?
Huh?
IT'S A LOT DIFFER-ENT THAN I IMAGINED... BUT...
IT'S SO BEAUTIFUL.

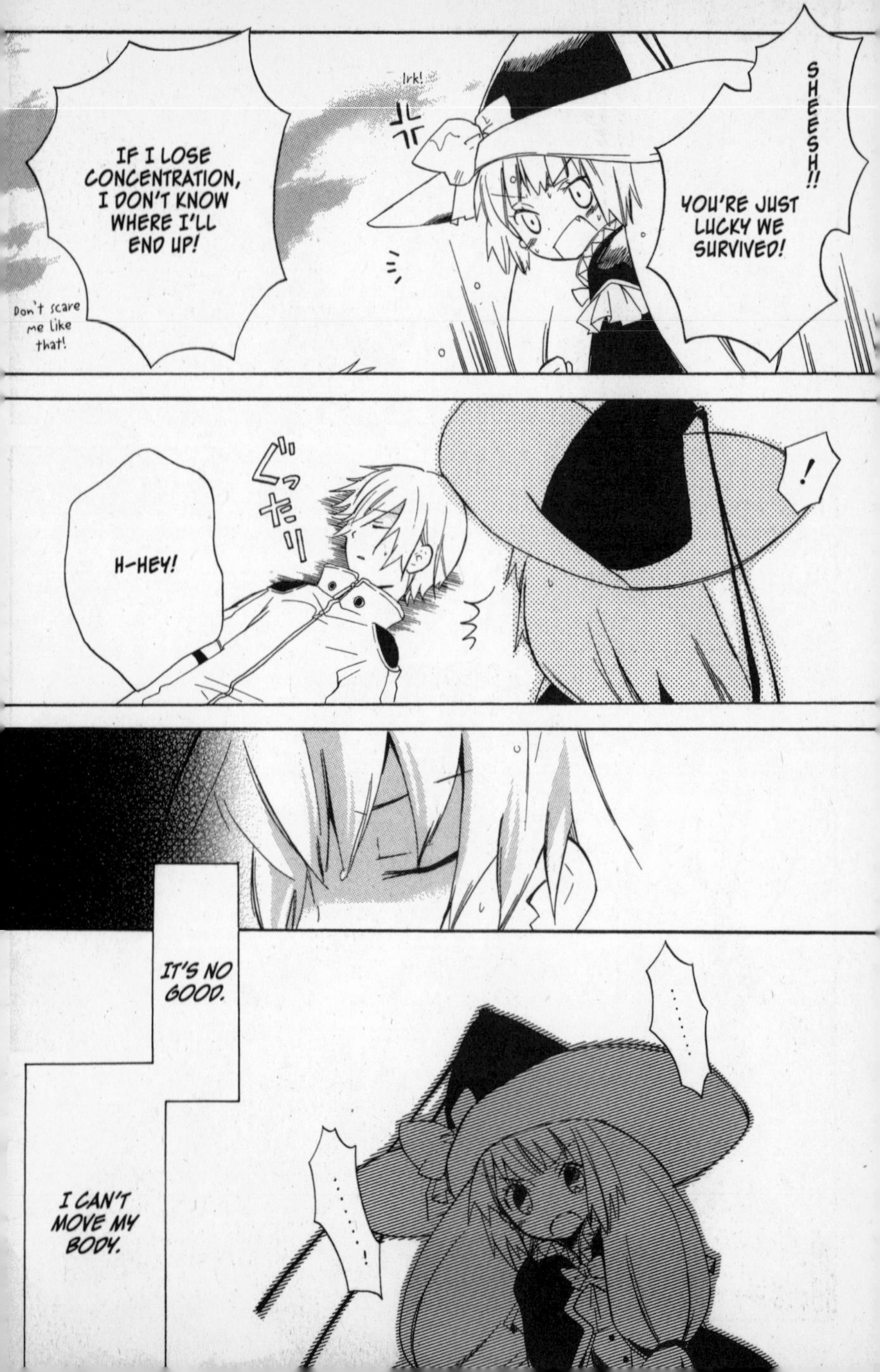
SHEESH!!
YOU'RE JUST LUCKY WE SURVIVED!
Irk!
IF I LOSE CONCENTRATION, I DON'T KNOW WHERE I'LL END UP!
Don't scare me like that!
!
ぐったり
H-HEY!
......
......!
IT'S NO GOOD.
I CAN'T MOVE MY BODY.

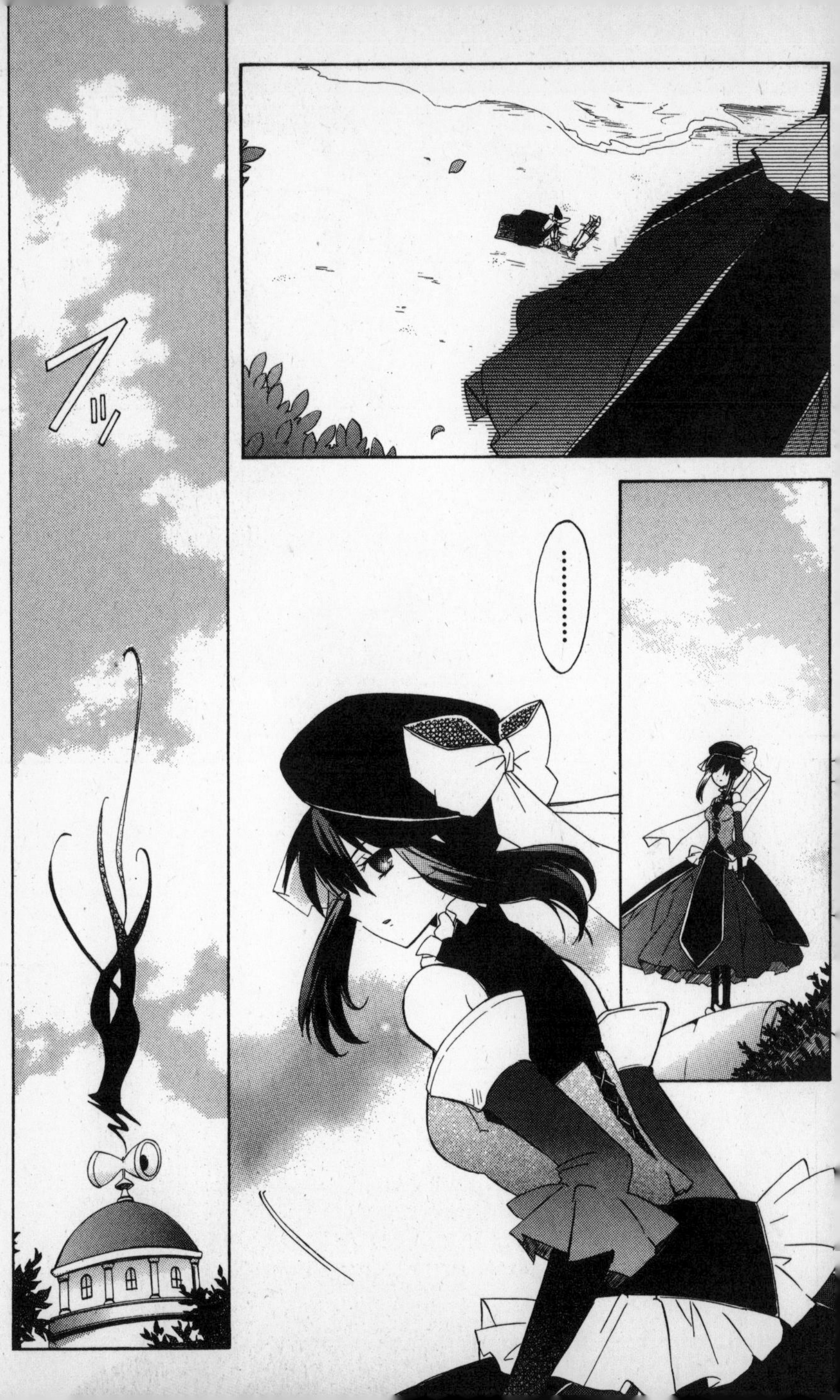
……
フッ

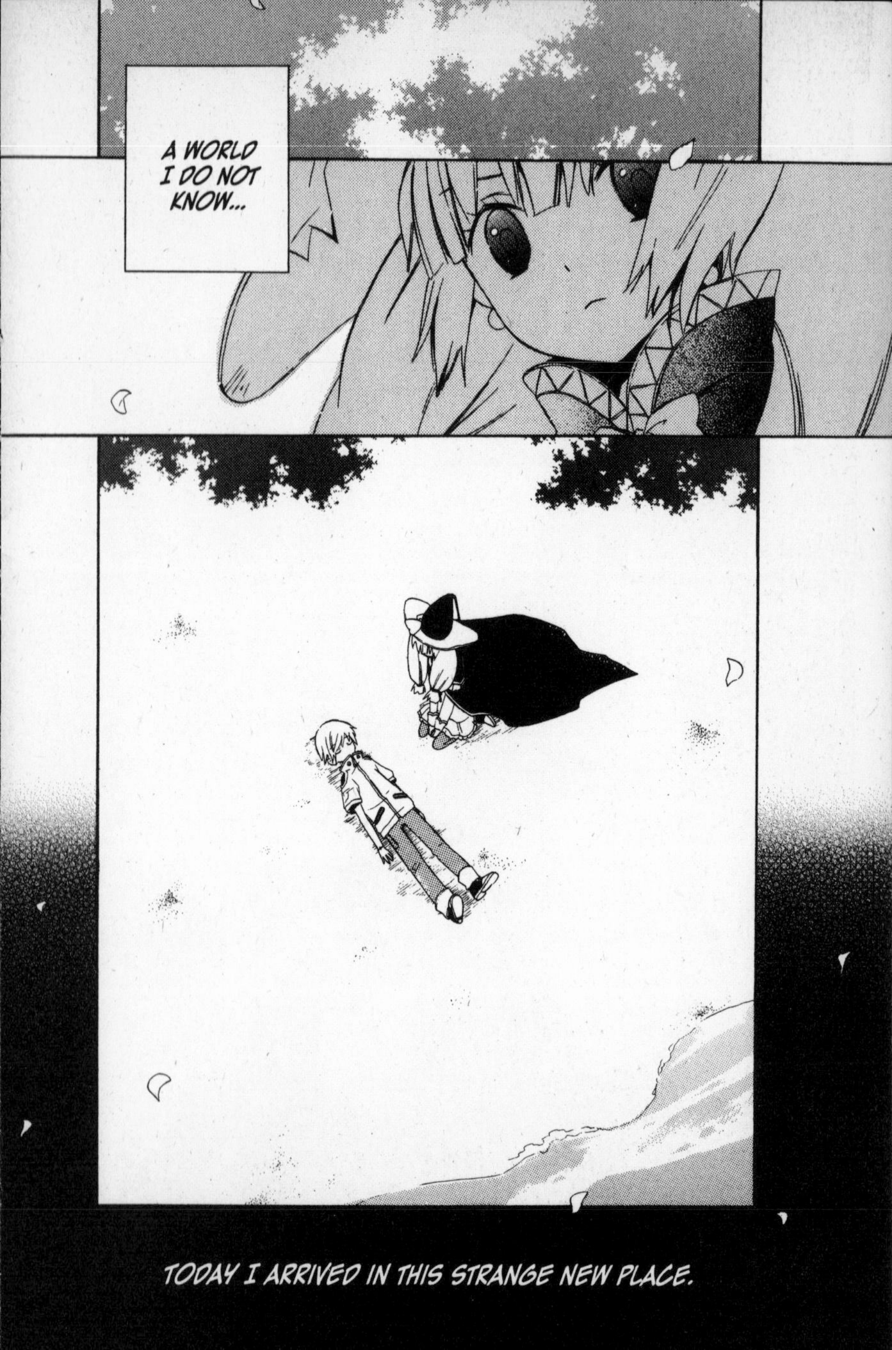
A WORLD I DO NOT KNOW...
TODAY I ARRIVED IN THIS STRANGE NEW PLACE.

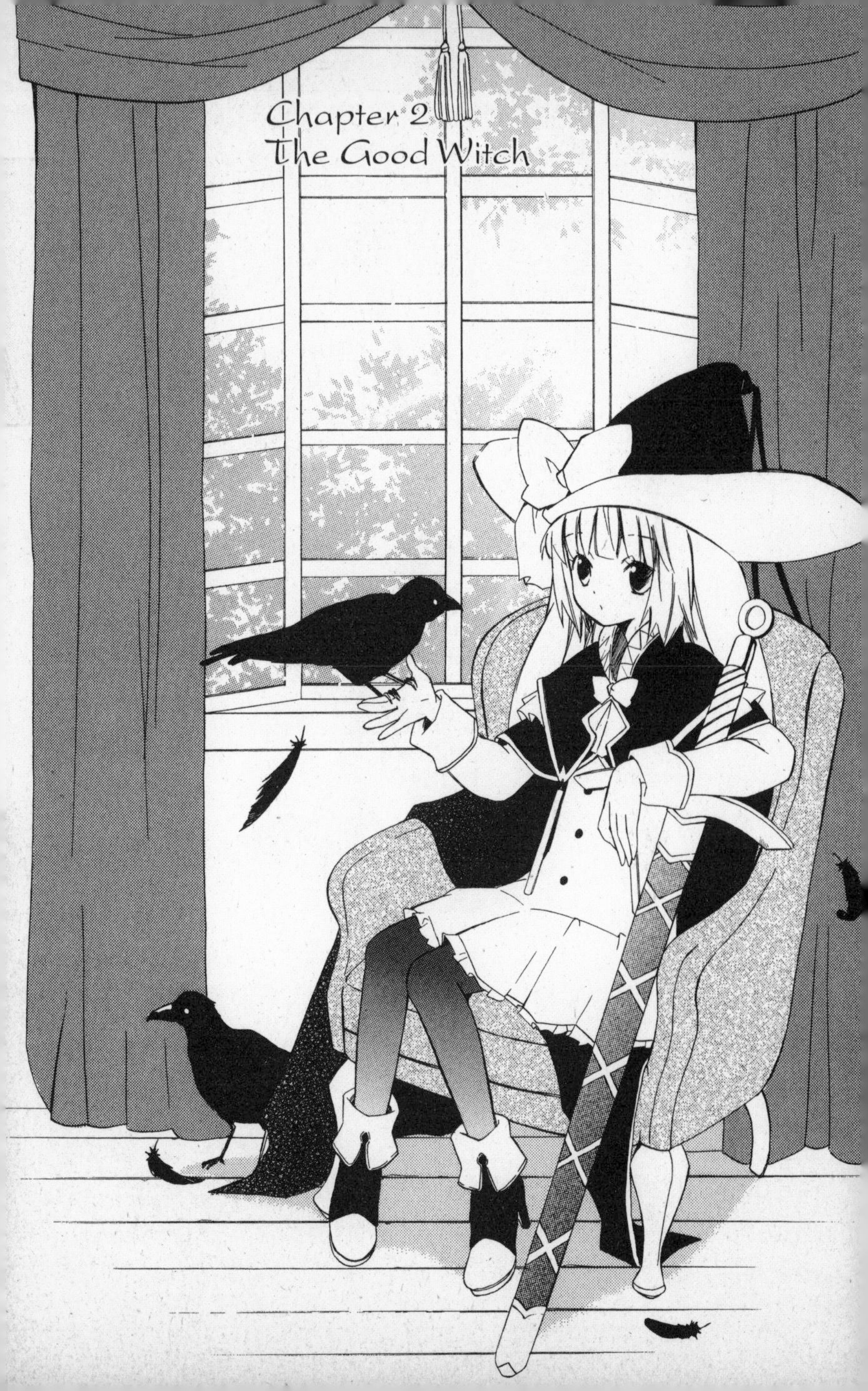
Chapter 2
The Good Witch

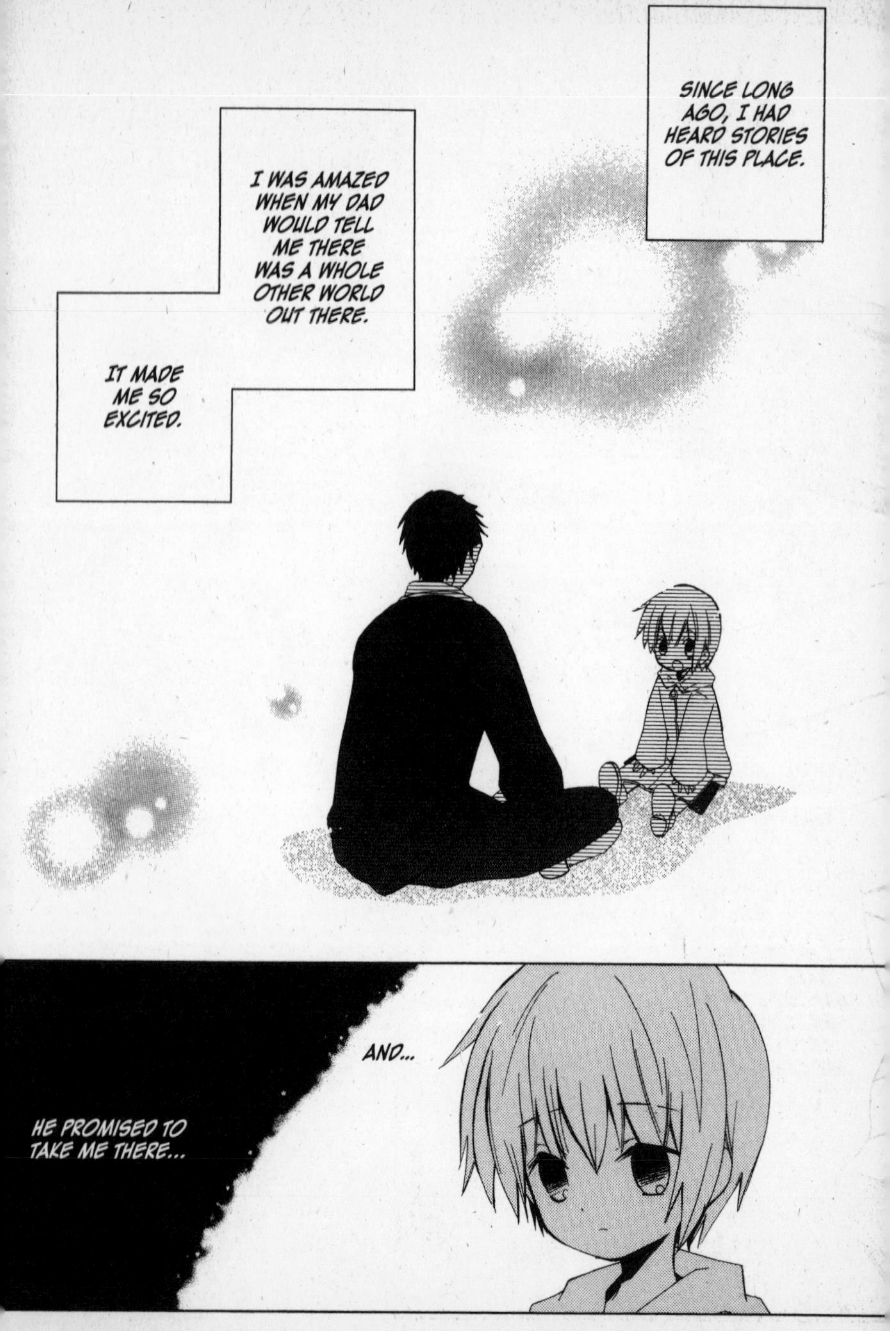
SINCE LONG AGO, I HAD HEARD STORIES OF THIS PLACE.
I WAS AMAZED WHEN MY DAD WOULD TELL ME THERE WAS A WHOLE OTHER WORLD OUT THERE.
IT MADE ME SO EXCITED.
AND...
HE PROMISED TO TAKE ME THERE...

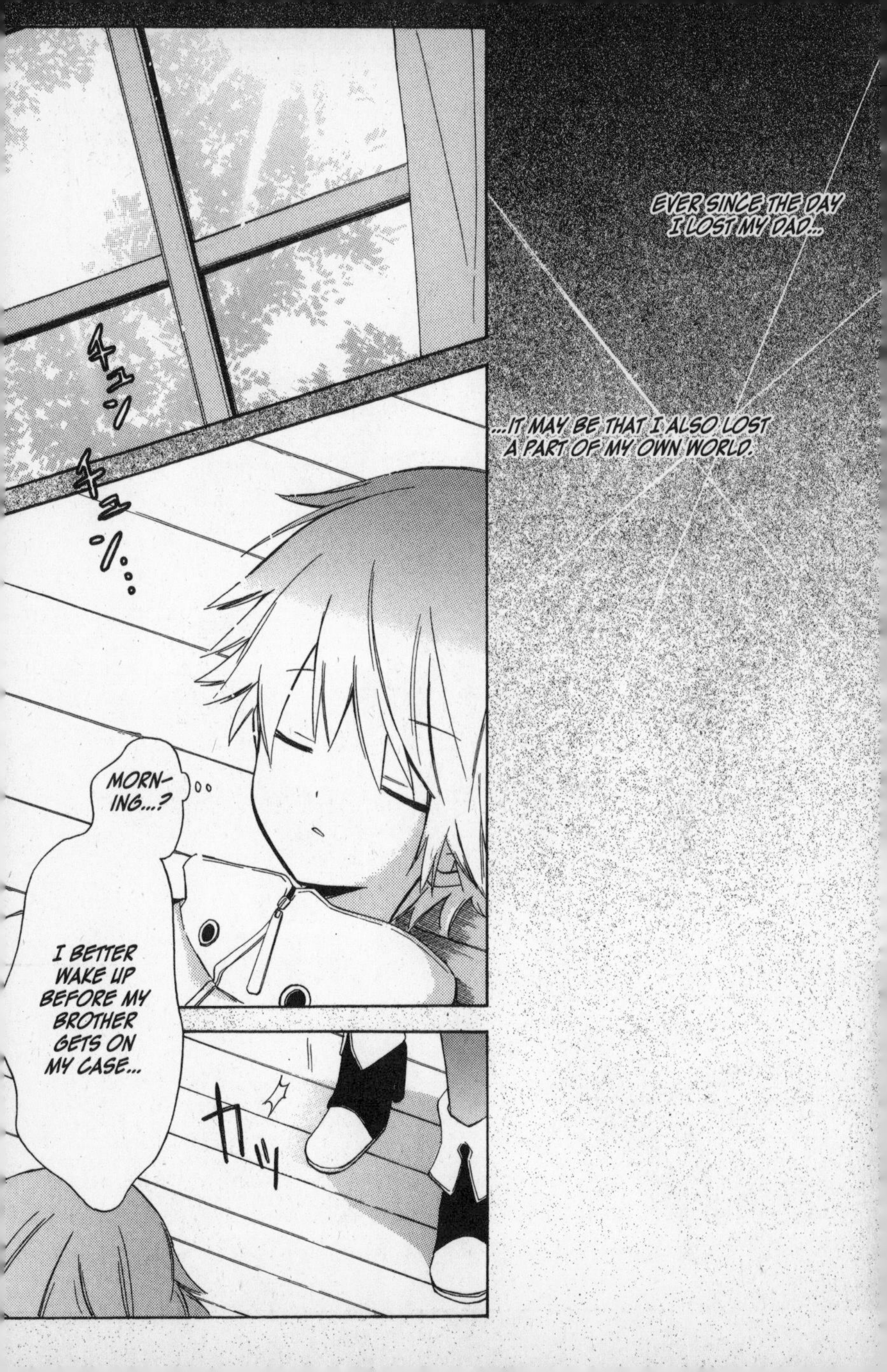
EVER SINCE THE DAY I LOST MY DAD...
...IT MAY BE THAT I ALSO LOST A PART OF MY OWN WORLD.
チュン チュン...
MORN-ING...?
I BETTER WAKE UP BEFORE MY BROTHER GETS ON MY CASE...
ガッ

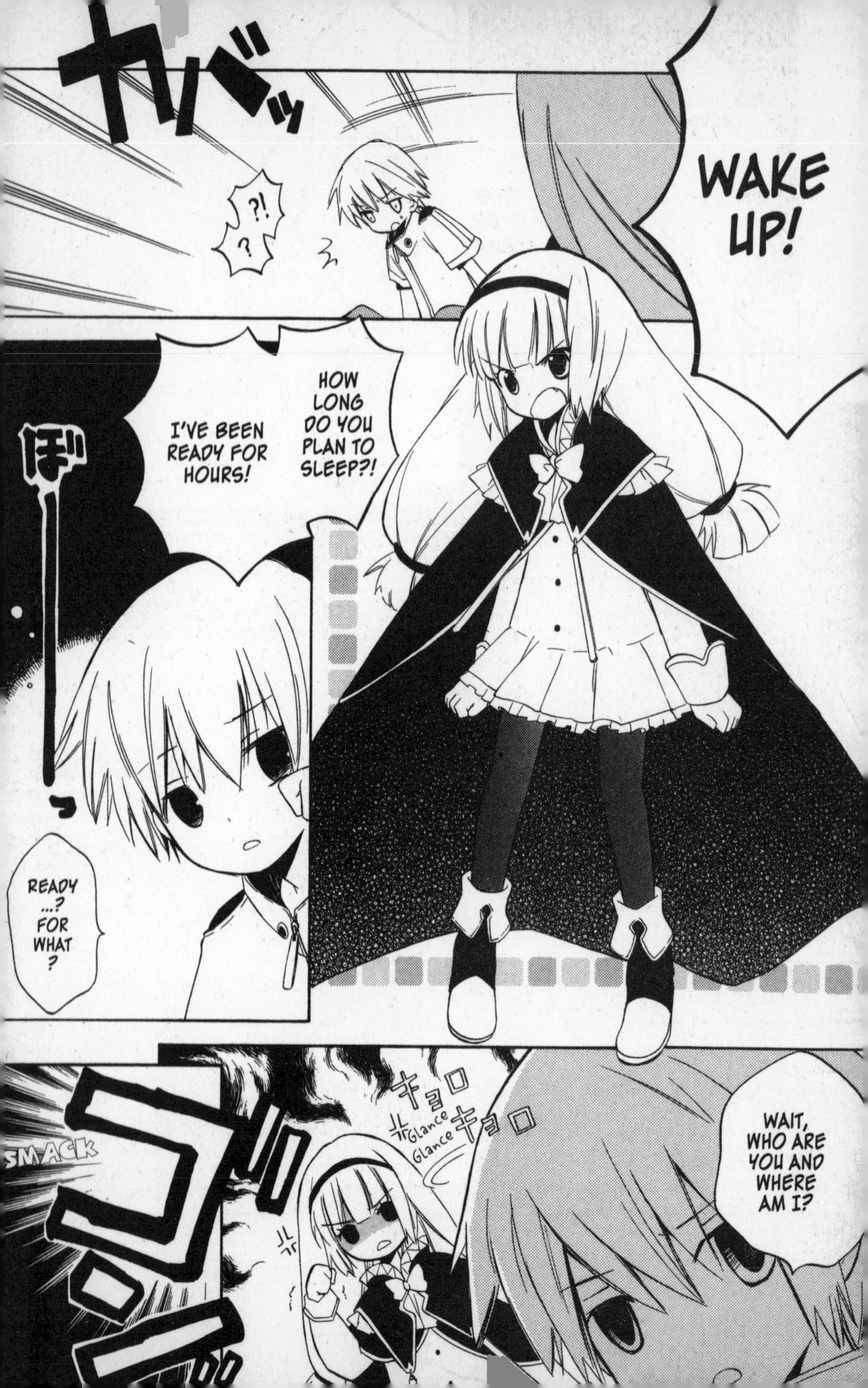
WAKE UP!
?!
?
ガバッ
HOW LONG DO YOU PLAN TO SLEEP?!
I'VE BEEN READY FOR HOURS!
ぼー…
READY ...? FOR WHAT ?
WAIT, WHO ARE YOU AND WHERE AM I?
キョロ Glance
キョロ Glance
ゴンッ
SMACK

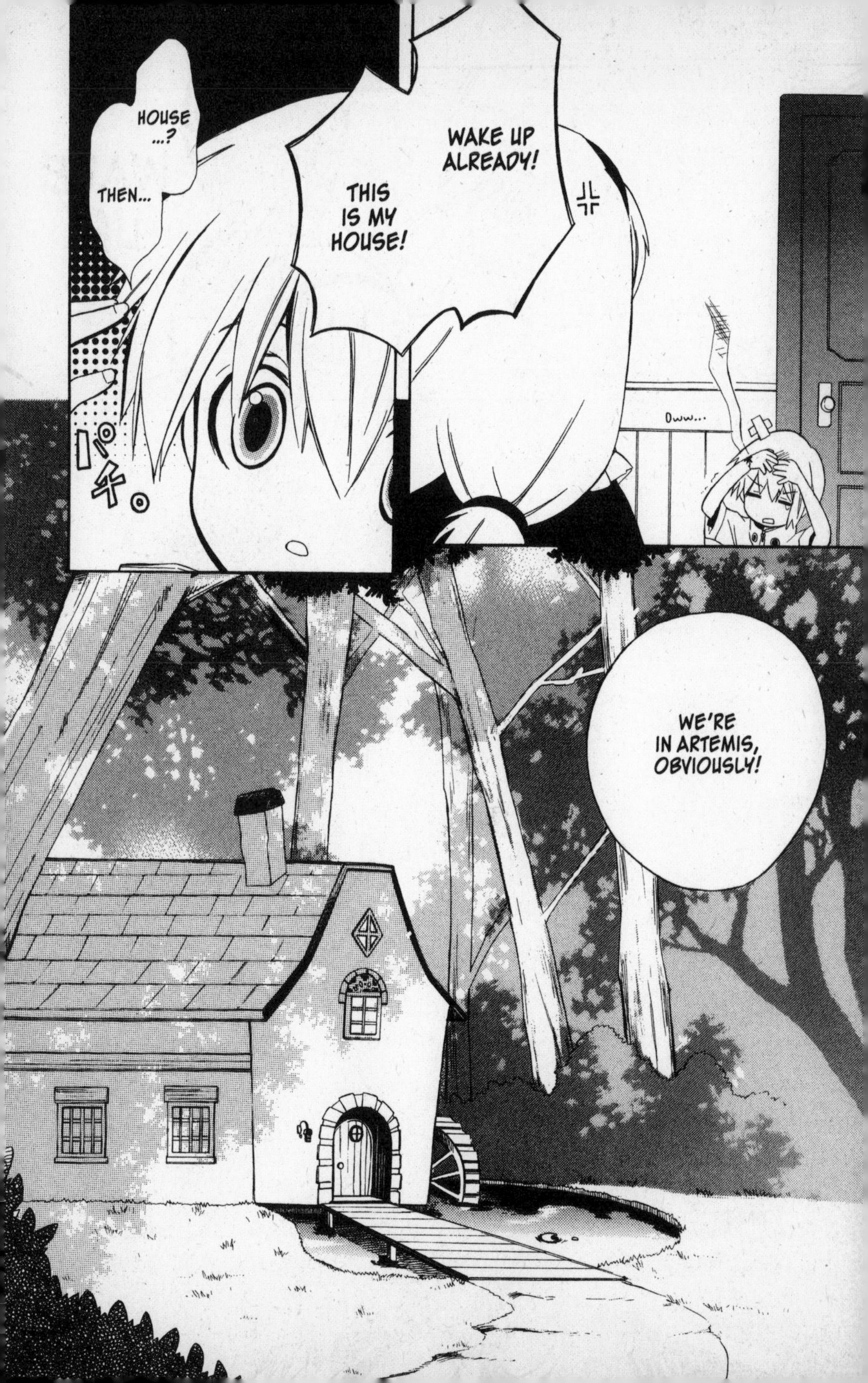
WAKE UP ALREADY!
THIS IS MY HOUSE!
Oww...
HOUSE ...?
THEN...
パチ。
WE'RE IN ARTEMIS, OBVIOUSLY!

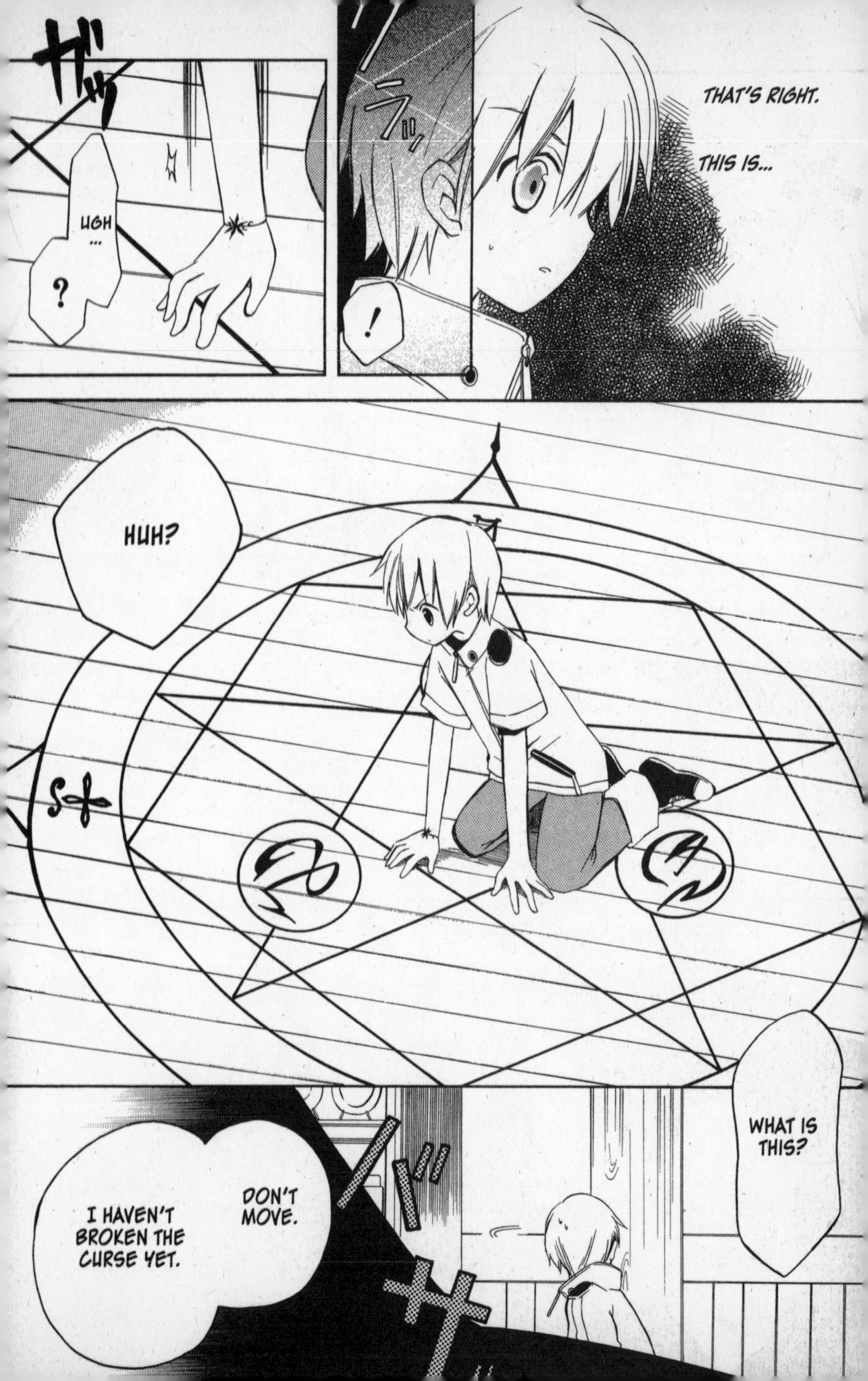
THAT'S RIGHT.
THIS IS...
!
UGH...
?
HUH?
WHAT IS THIS?
DON'T MOVE.
I HAVEN'T BROKEN THE CURSE YET.

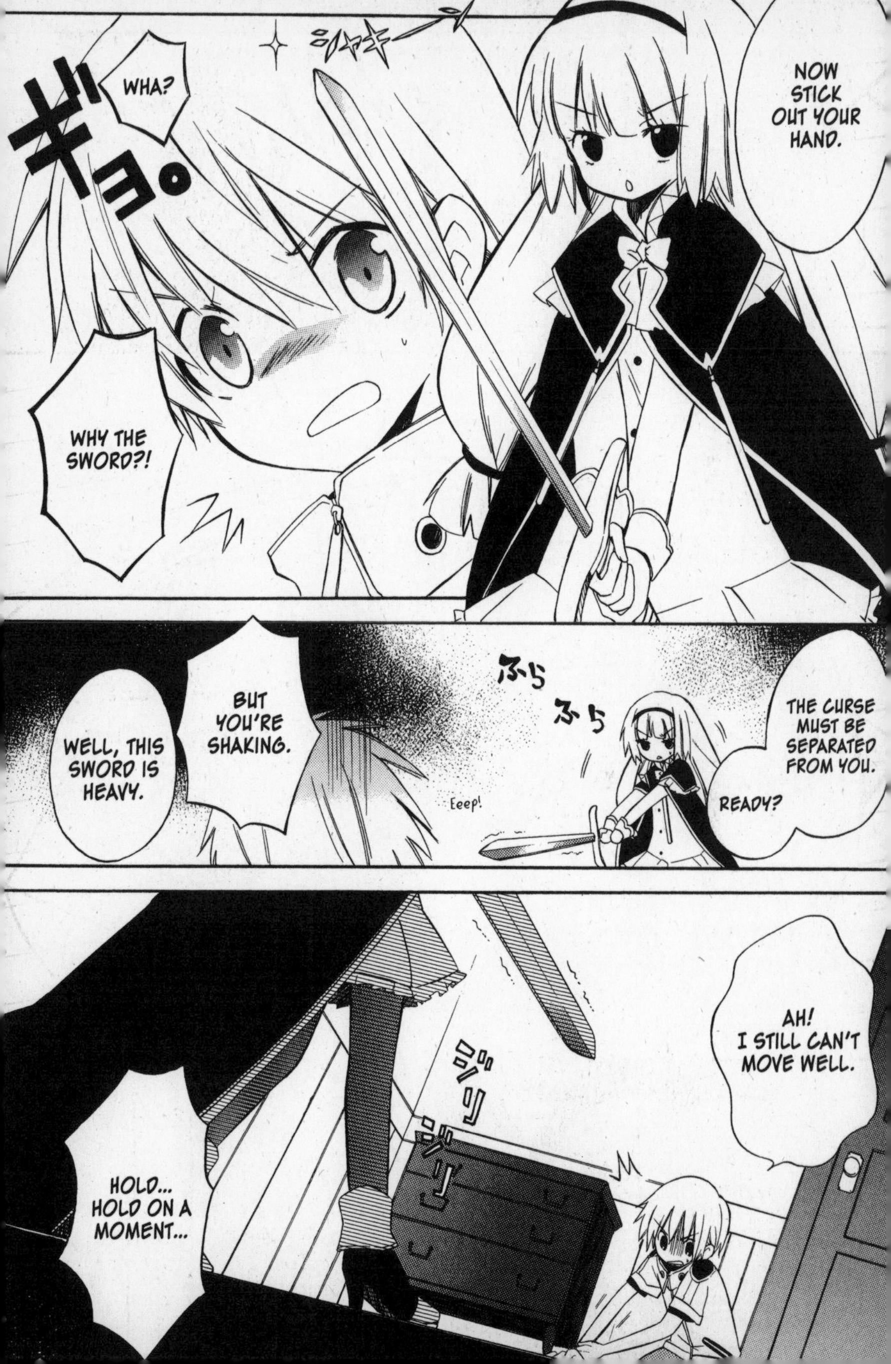
NOW STICK OUT YOUR HAND.
シャキ
WHA?
ギョ。
WHY THE SWORD?!
THE CURSE MUST BE SEPARATED FROM YOU.
READY?
ふら ふら
Eeep!
BUT YOU'RE SHAKING.
WELL, THIS SWORD IS HEAVY.
AH! I STILL CAN'T MOVE WELL.
ジリ ジリ
HOLD... HOLD ON A MOMENT...

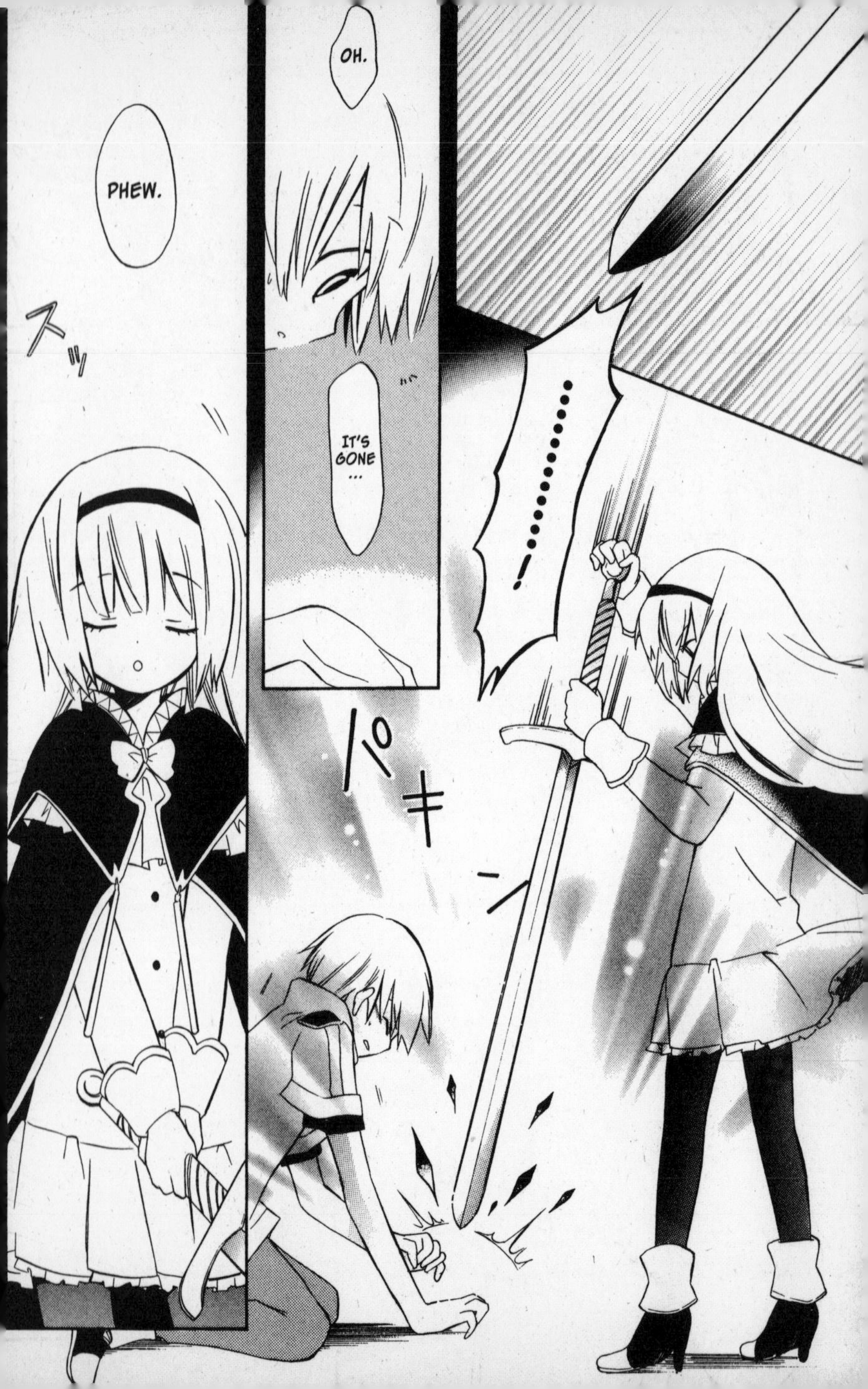

......!
パキーン
OH.
IT'S GONE ...
PHEW.
スッ

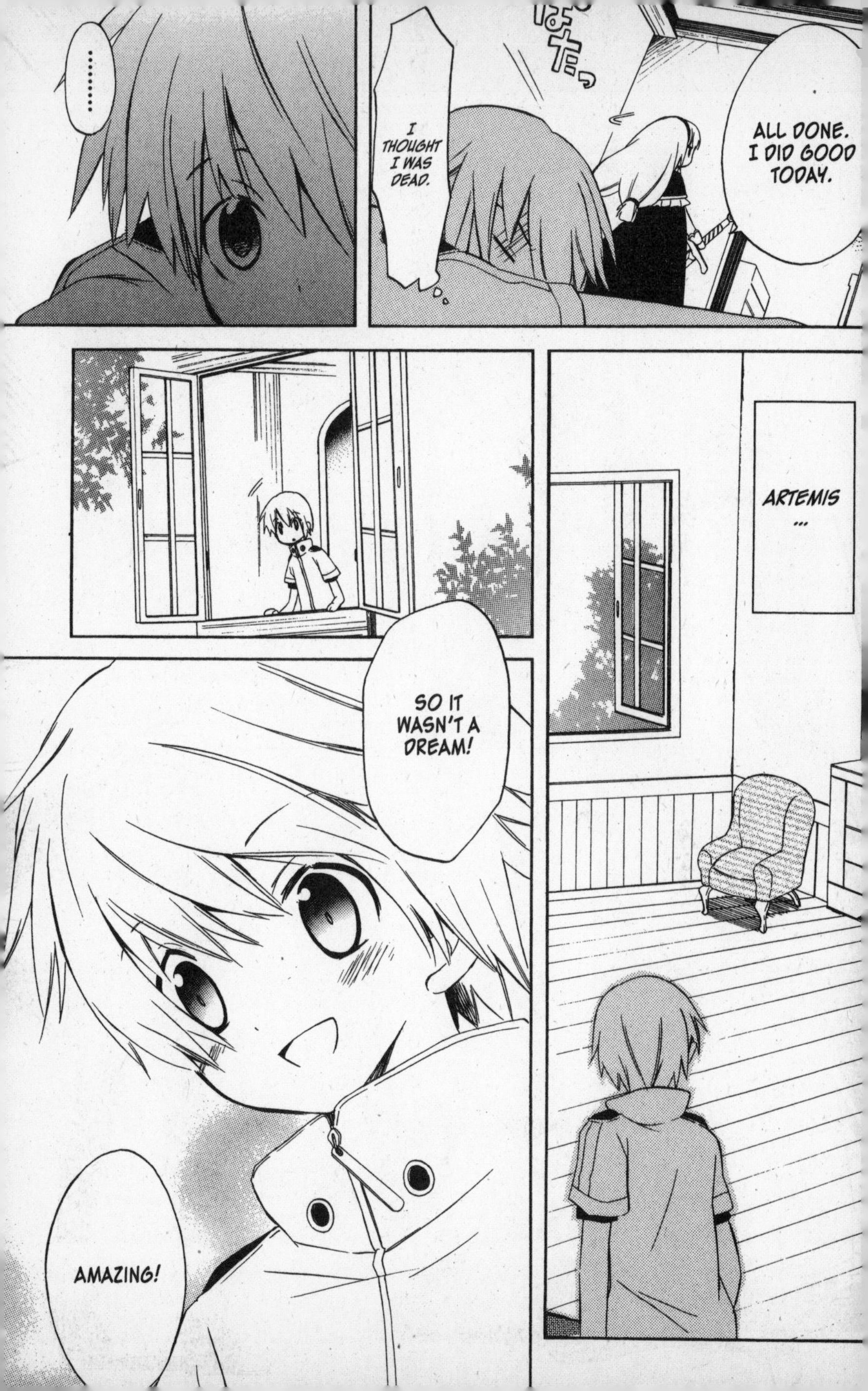

ぱたっ
ALL DONE. I DID GOOD TODAY.
I THOUGHT I WAS DEAD.
......
ARTEMIS ...
SO IT WASN'T A DREAM!
AMAZING!

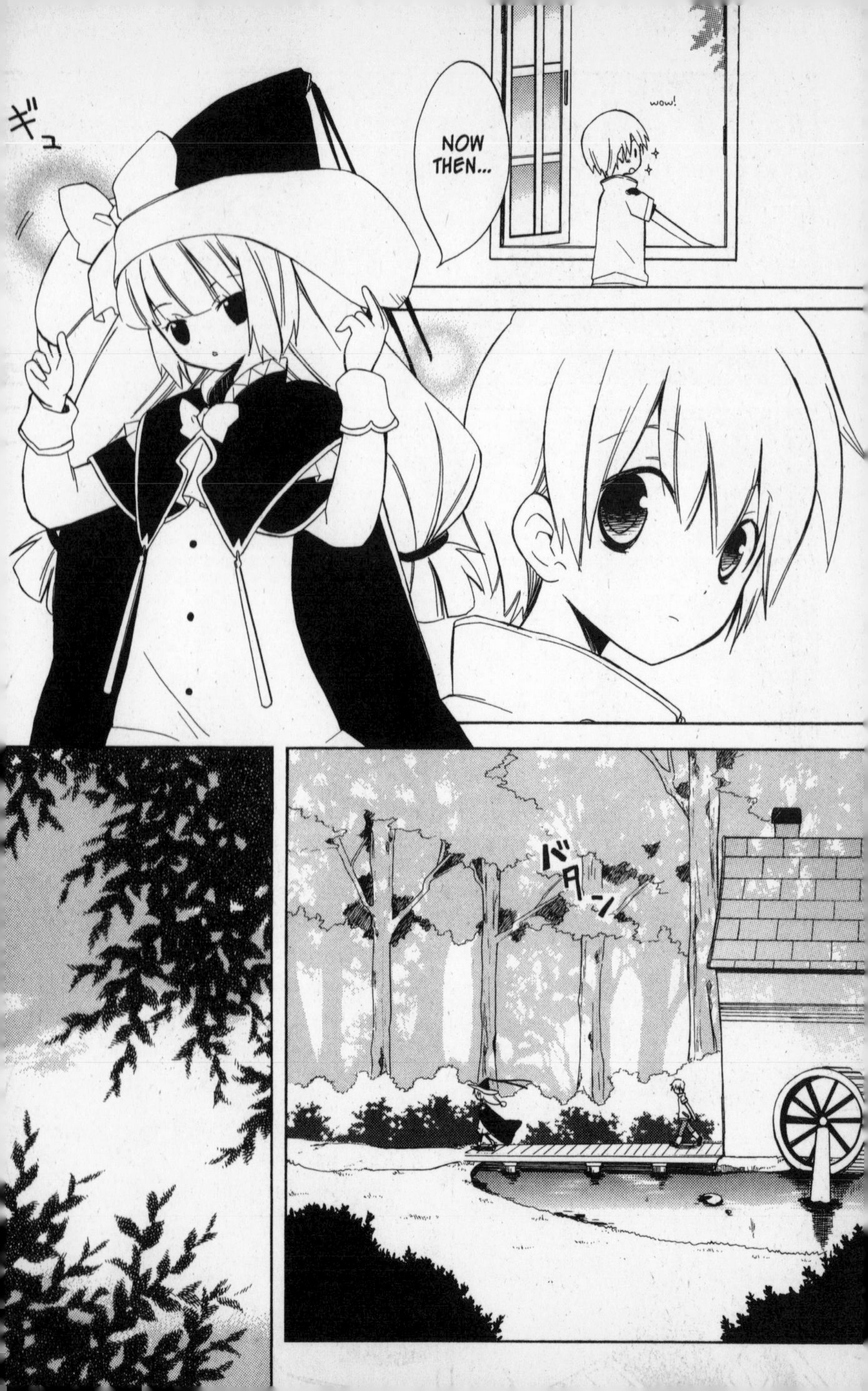
wow!
NOW THEN...
ギュ
バタン

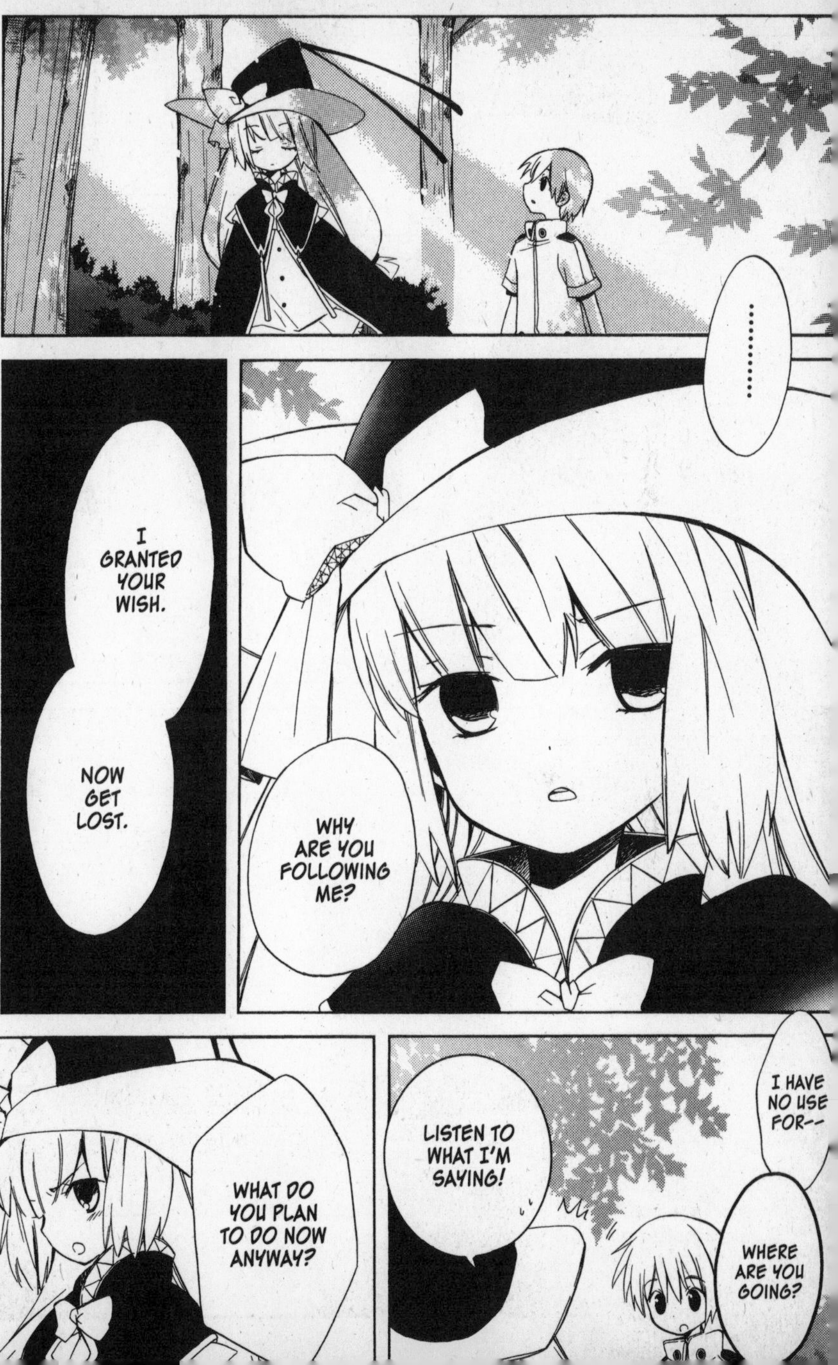
......
WHY ARE YOU FOLLOWING ME?
I GRANTED YOUR WISH.
NOW GET LOST.
I HAVE NO USE FOR--
WHERE ARE YOU GOING?
LISTEN TO WHAT I'M SAYING!
WHAT DO YOU PLAN TO DO NOW ANYWAY?

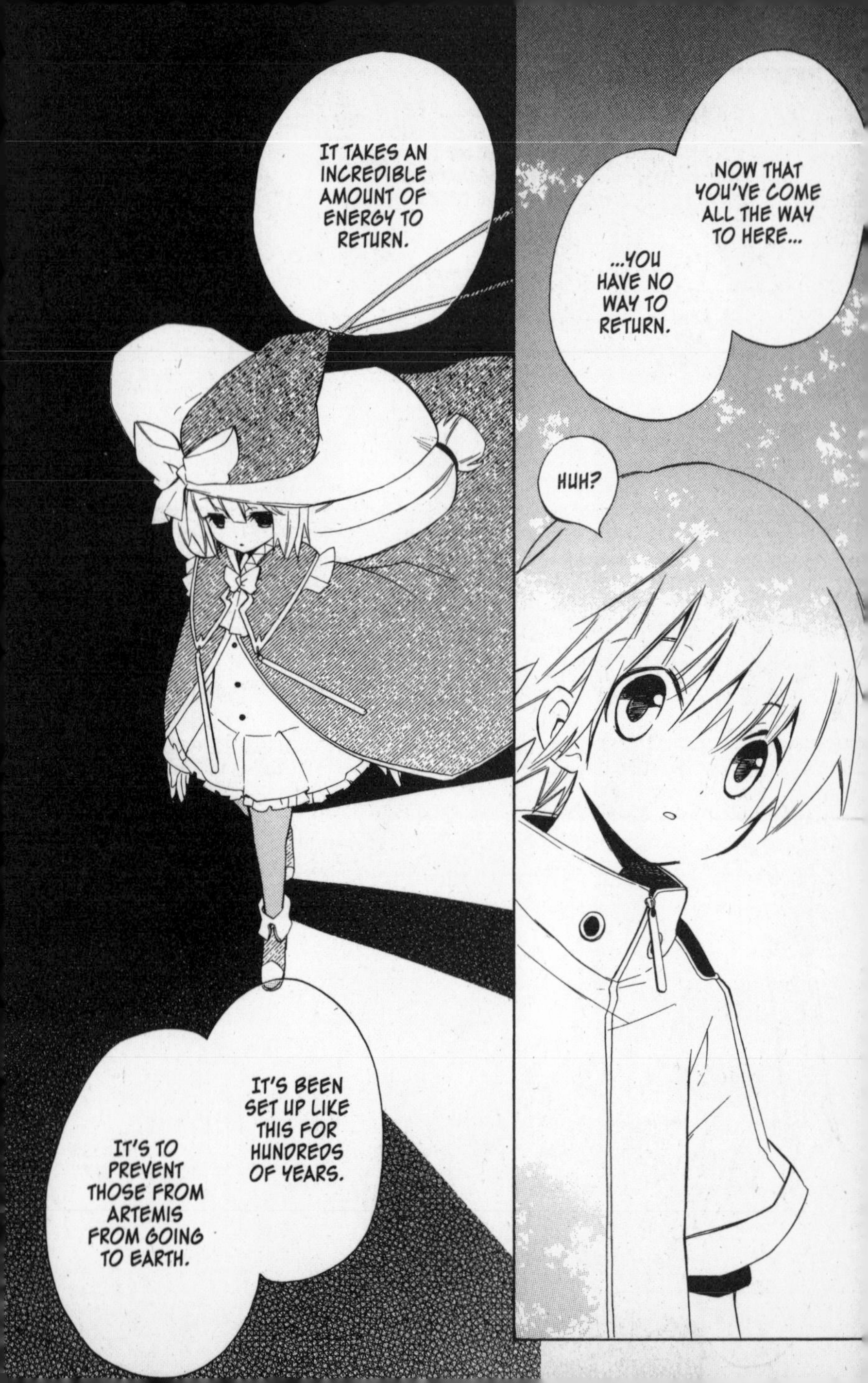
NOW THAT YOU'VE COME ALL THE WAY TO HERE...
...YOU HAVE NO WAY TO RETURN.
HUH?
IT TAKES AN INCREDIBLE AMOUNT OF ENERGY TO RETURN.
IT'S BEEN SET UP LIKE THIS FOR HUNDREDS OF YEARS.
IT'S TO PREVENT THOSE FROM ARTEMIS FROM GOING TO EARTH.

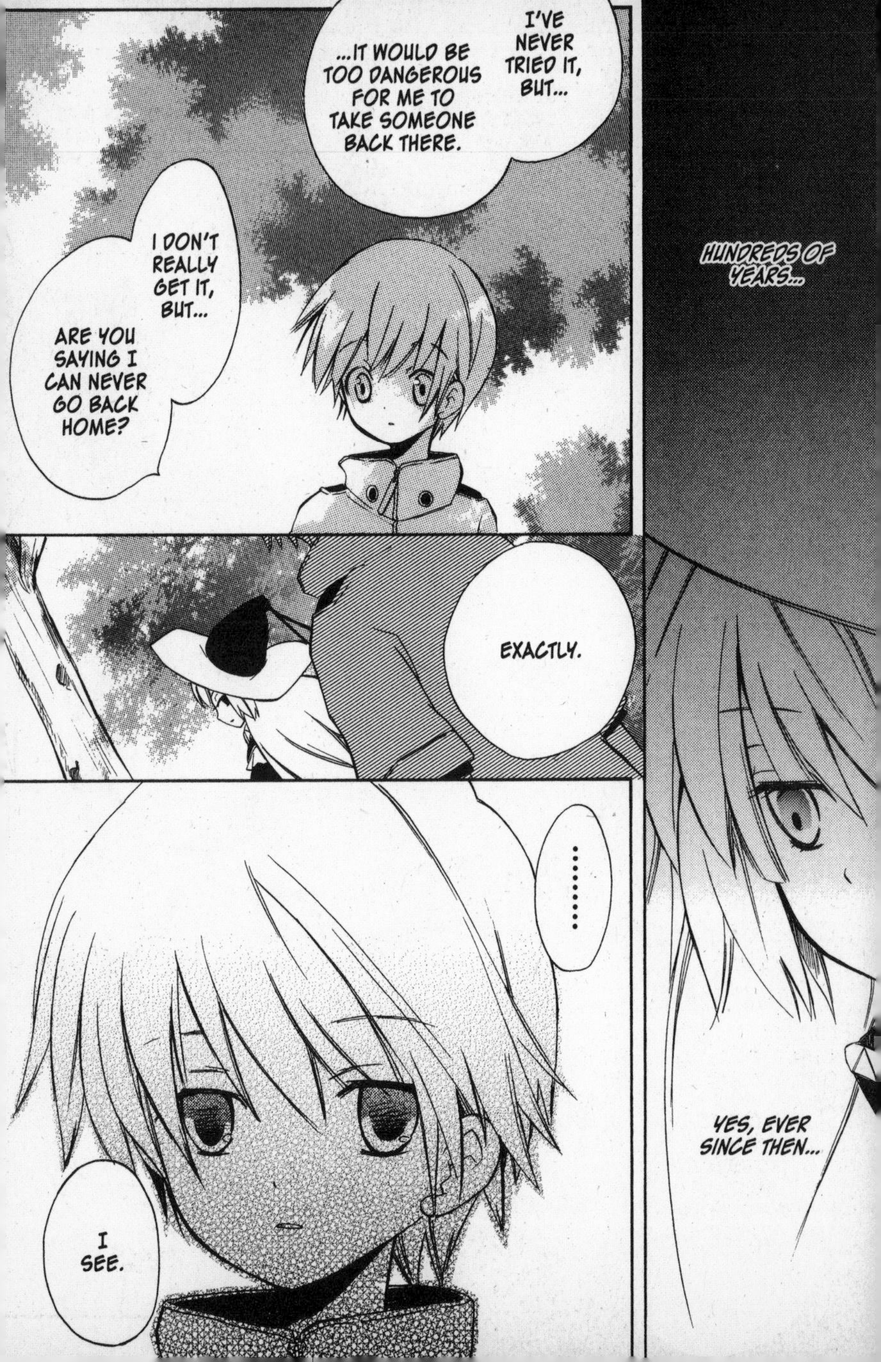
HUNDREDS OF YEARS...
YES, EVER SINCE THEN...
I'VE NEVER TRIED IT, BUT...
...IT WOULD BE TOO DANGEROUS FOR ME TO TAKE SOMEONE BACK THERE.
I DON'T REALLY GET IT, BUT...
ARE YOU SAYING I CAN NEVER GO BACK HOME?
EXACTLY.
....
I SEE.

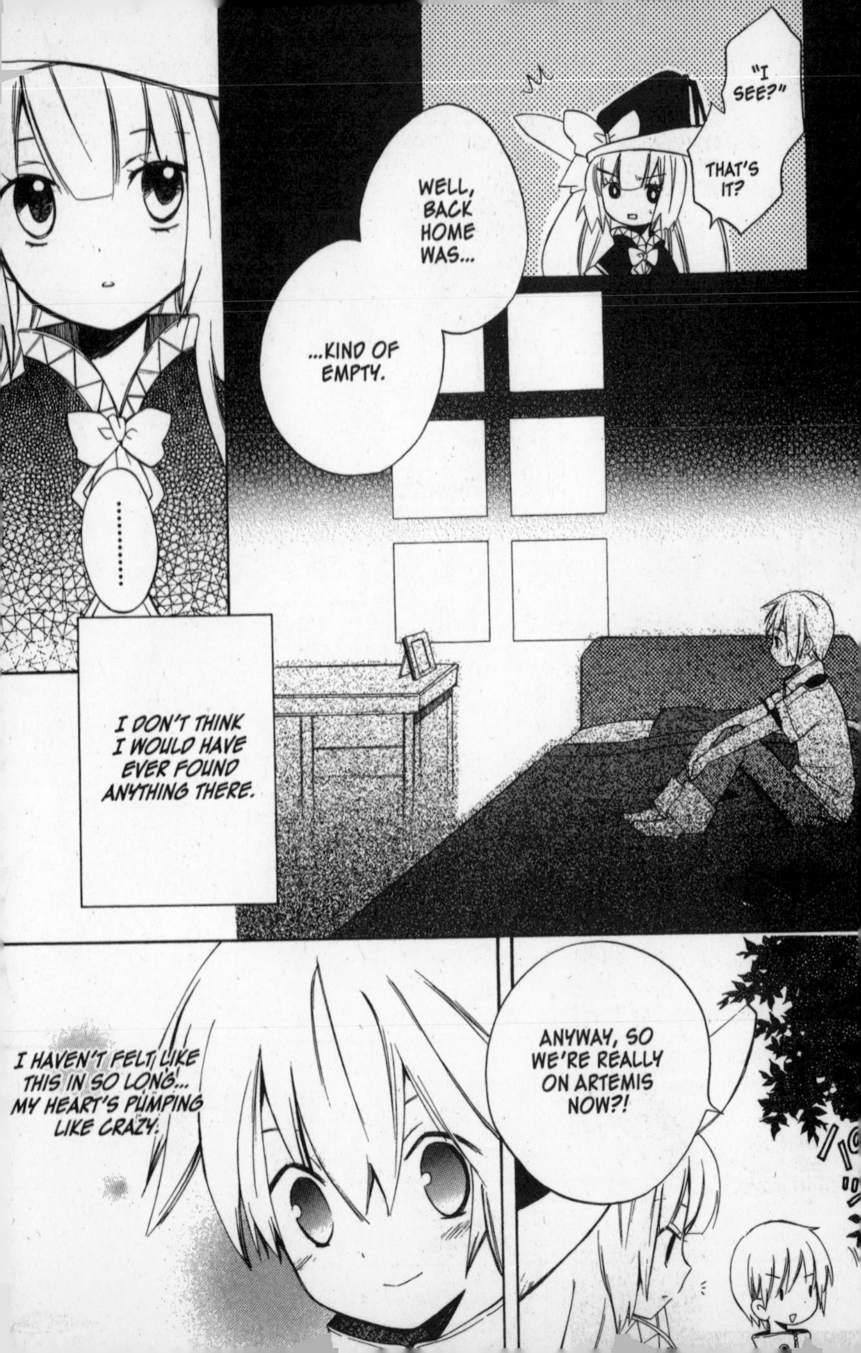
"I SEE?"
THAT'S IT?
WELL, BACK HOME WAS...
...KIND OF EMPTY.
......
I DON'T THINK I WOULD HAVE EVER FOUND ANYTHING THERE.
ANYWAY, SO WE'RE REALLY ON ARTEMIS NOW?!
I HAVEN'T FELT LIKE THIS IN SO LONG... MY HEART'S PUMPING LIKE CRAZY.

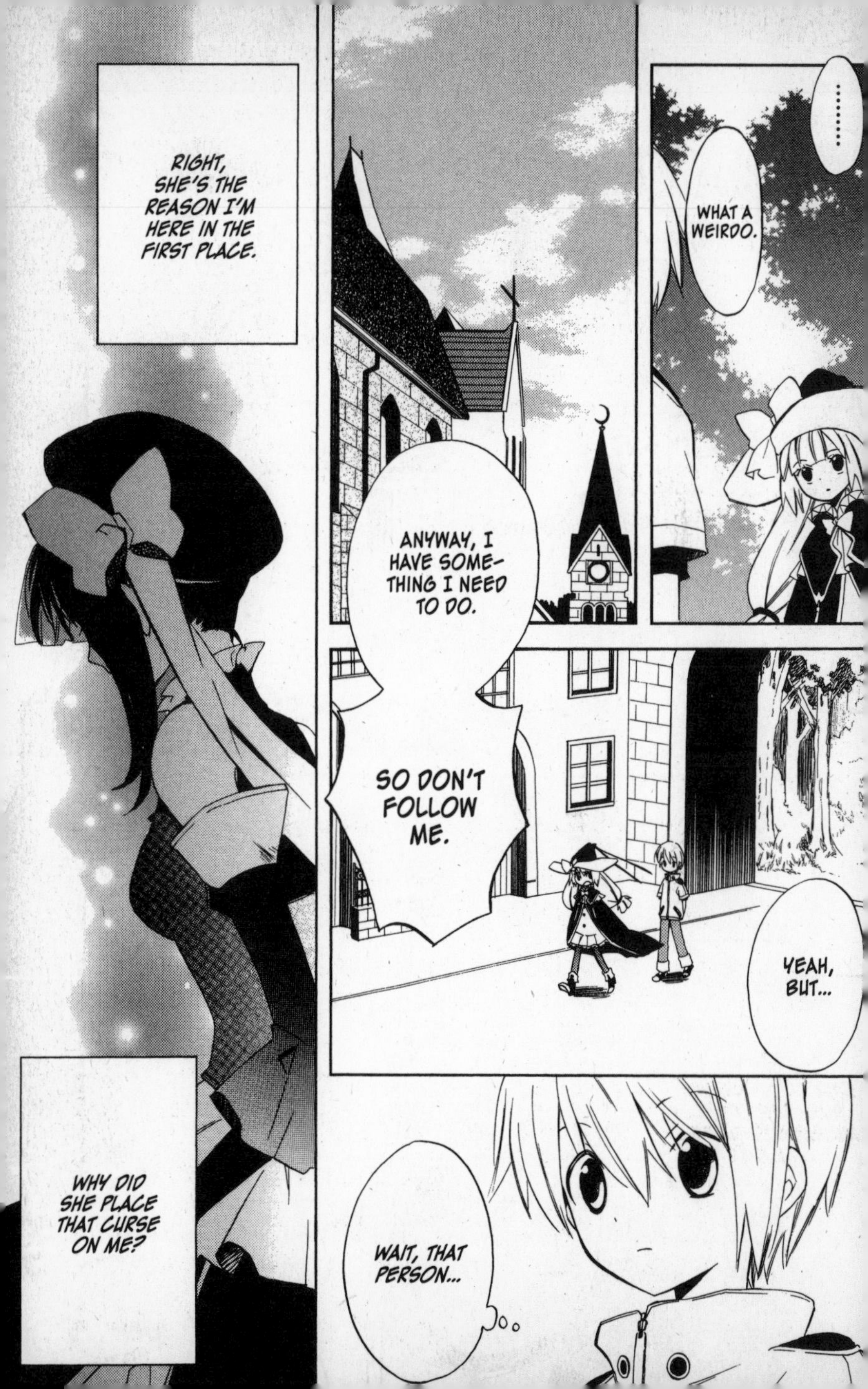
......
WHAT A WEIRDO.
ANYWAY, I HAVE SOMETHING I NEED TO DO.
SO DON'T FOLLOW ME.
YEAH, BUT...
WAIT, THAT PERSON...
RIGHT, SHE'S THE REASON I'M HERE IN THE FIRST PLACE.
WHY DID SHE PLACE THAT CURSE ON ME?

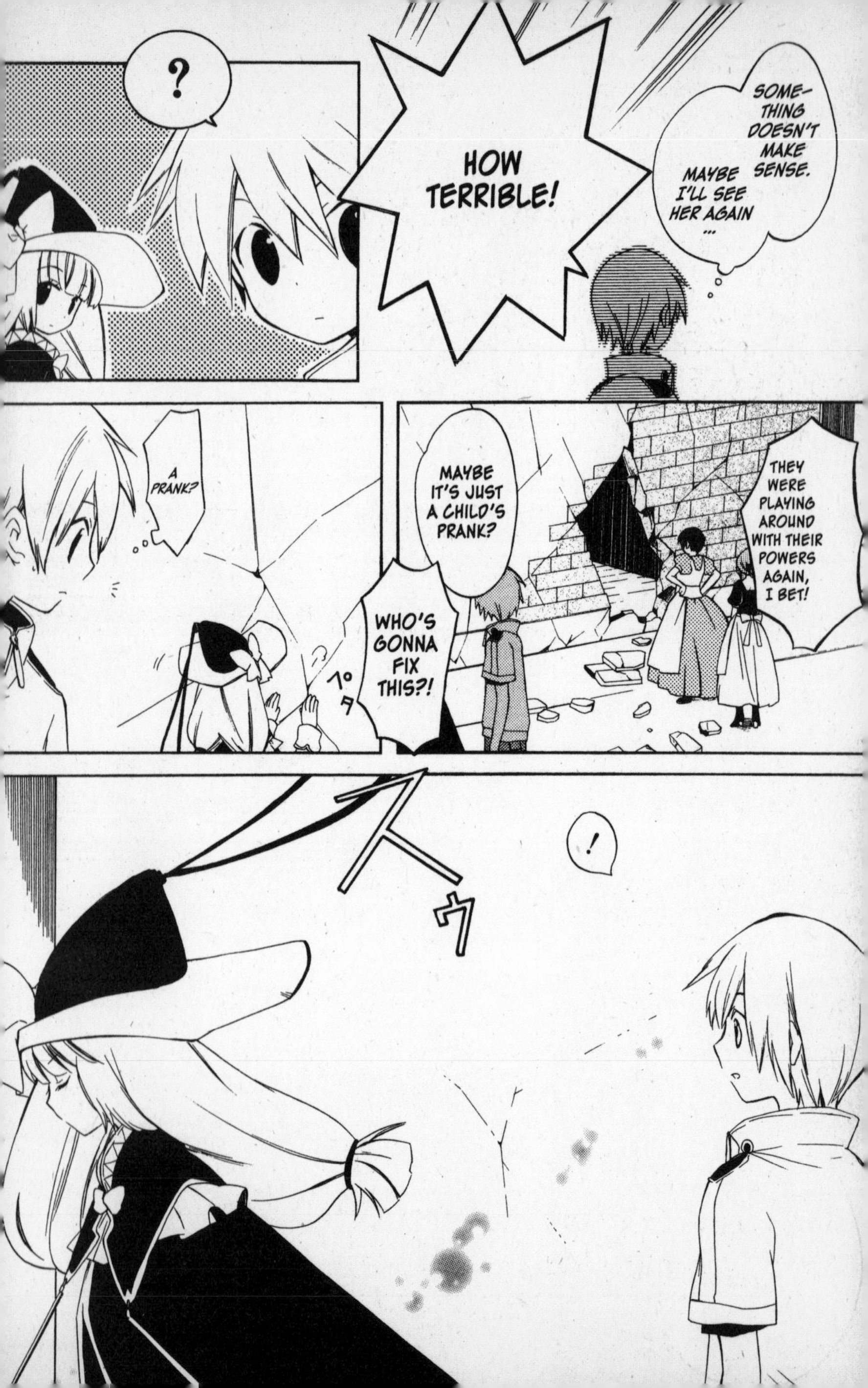
SOME-THING DOESN'T MAKE SENSE.
MAYBE I'LL SEE HER AGAIN...
HOW TERRIBLE!
?
THEY WERE PLAYING AROUND WITH THEIR POWERS AGAIN, I BET!
MAYBE IT'S JUST A CHILD'S PRANK?
WHO'S GONNA FIX THIS?!
ペタ
A PRANK?
!

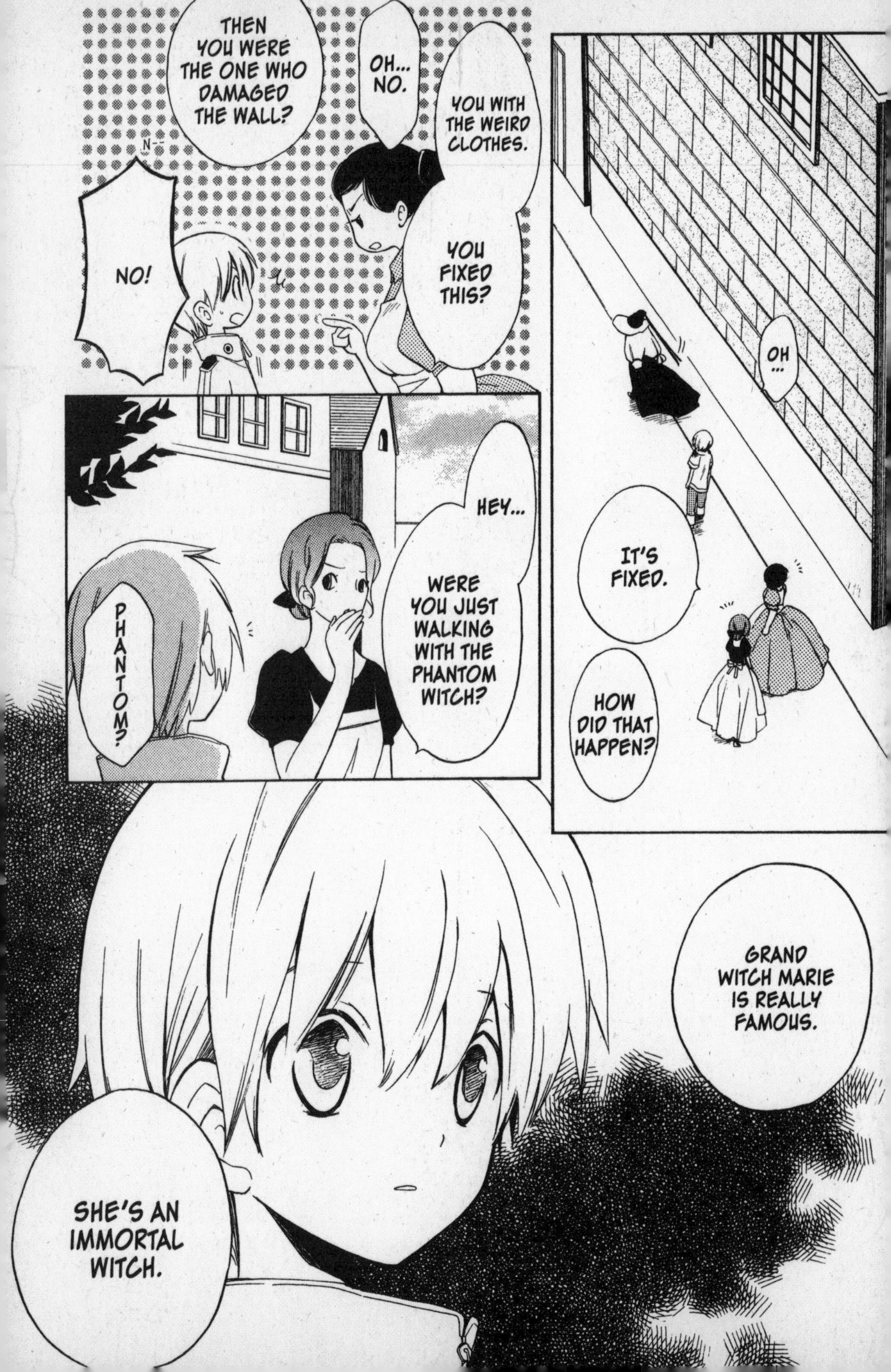

OH...
IT'S FIXED.
HOW DID THAT HAPPEN?
YOU WITH THE WEIRD CLOTHES.
YOU FIXED THIS?
OH... NO.
THEN YOU WERE THE ONE WHO DAMAGED THE WALL?
N--
NO!
HEY...
WERE YOU JUST WALKING WITH THE PHANTOM WITCH?
PHANTOM?
GRAND WITCH MARIE IS REALLY FAMOUS.
SHE'S AN IMMORTAL WITCH.

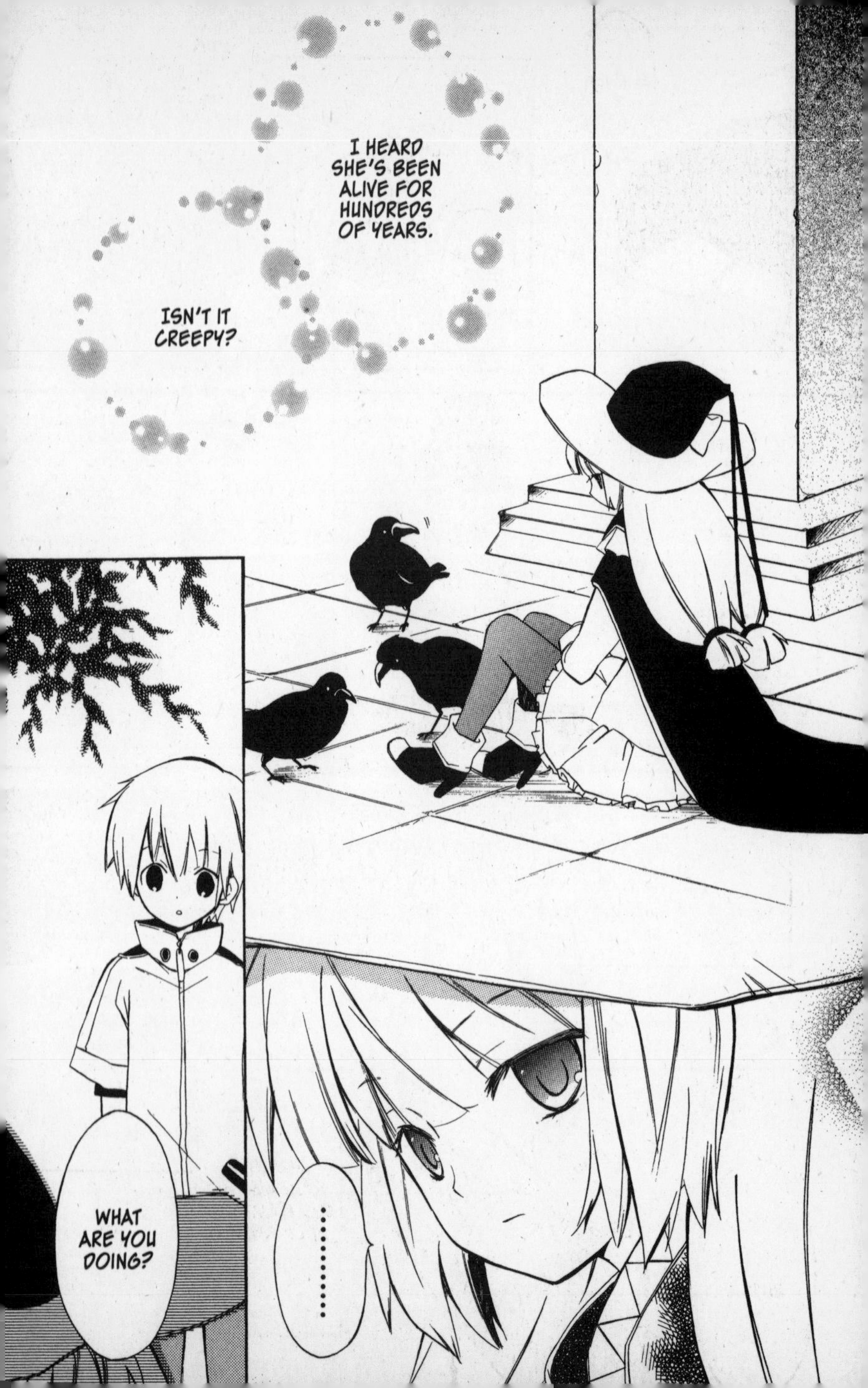
I HEARD SHE'S BEEN ALIVE FOR HUNDREDS OF YEARS.
ISN'T IT CREEPY?
....
WHAT ARE YOU DOING?

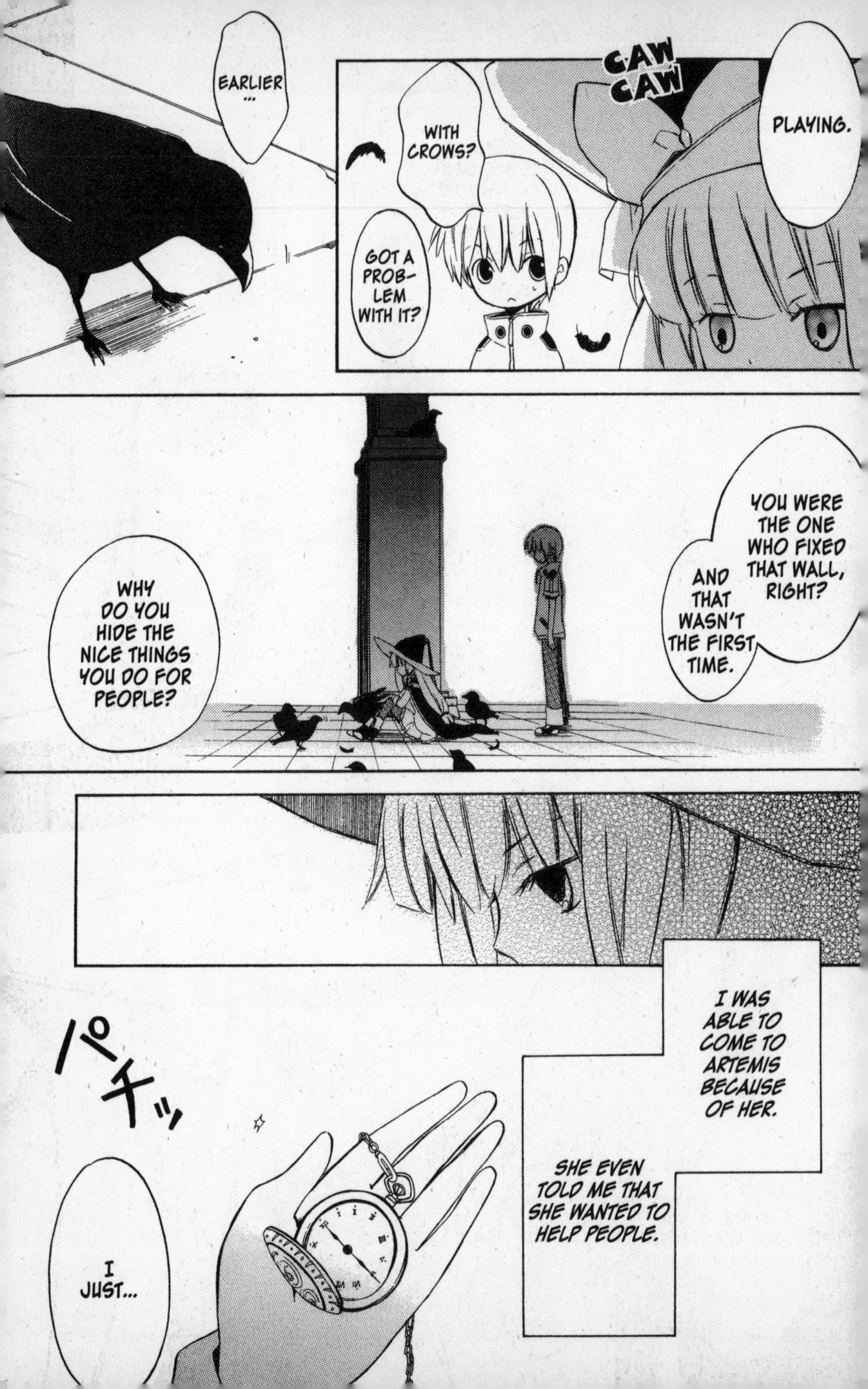
CAW CAW
PLAYING.
WITH CROWS?
GOT A PROB-LEM WITH IT?
EARLIER...
YOU WERE THE ONE WHO FIXED THAT WALL, RIGHT?
AND THAT WASN'T THE FIRST TIME.
WHY DO YOU HIDE THE NICE THINGS YOU DO FOR PEOPLE?
I WAS ABLE TO COME TO ARTEMIS BECAUSE OF HER.
SHE EVEN TOLD ME THAT SHE WANTED TO HELP PEOPLE.
パチッ
I JUST...

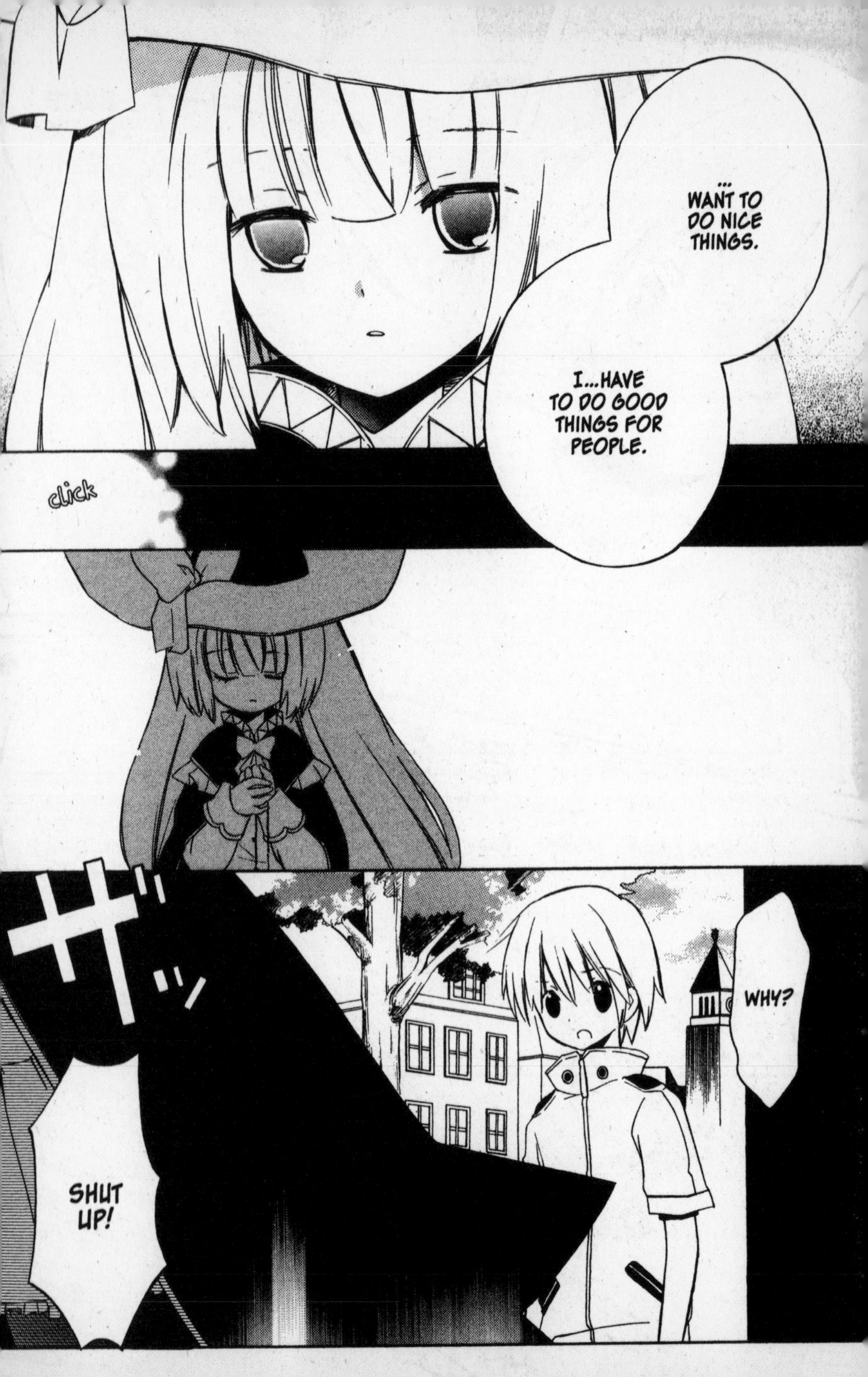
...WANT TO DO NICE THINGS.
I...HAVE TO DO GOOD THINGS FOR PEOPLE.
click
ザッ
WHY?
SHUT UP!

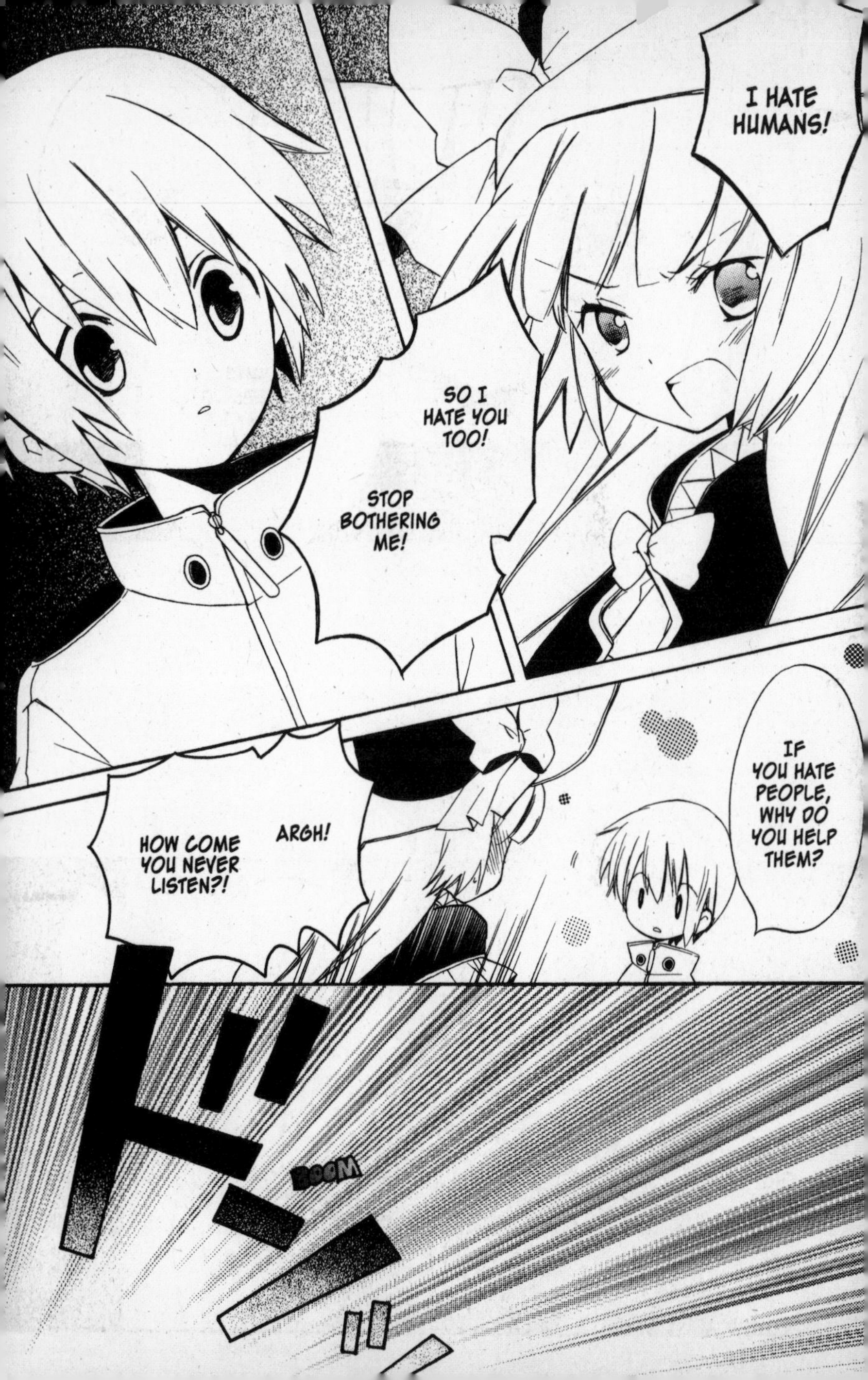
I HATE HUMANS!
SO I HATE YOU TOO!
STOP BOTHERING ME!
IF YOU HATE PEOPLE, WHY DO YOU HELP THEM?
ARGH!
HOW COME YOU NEVER LISTEN?!
BOOM

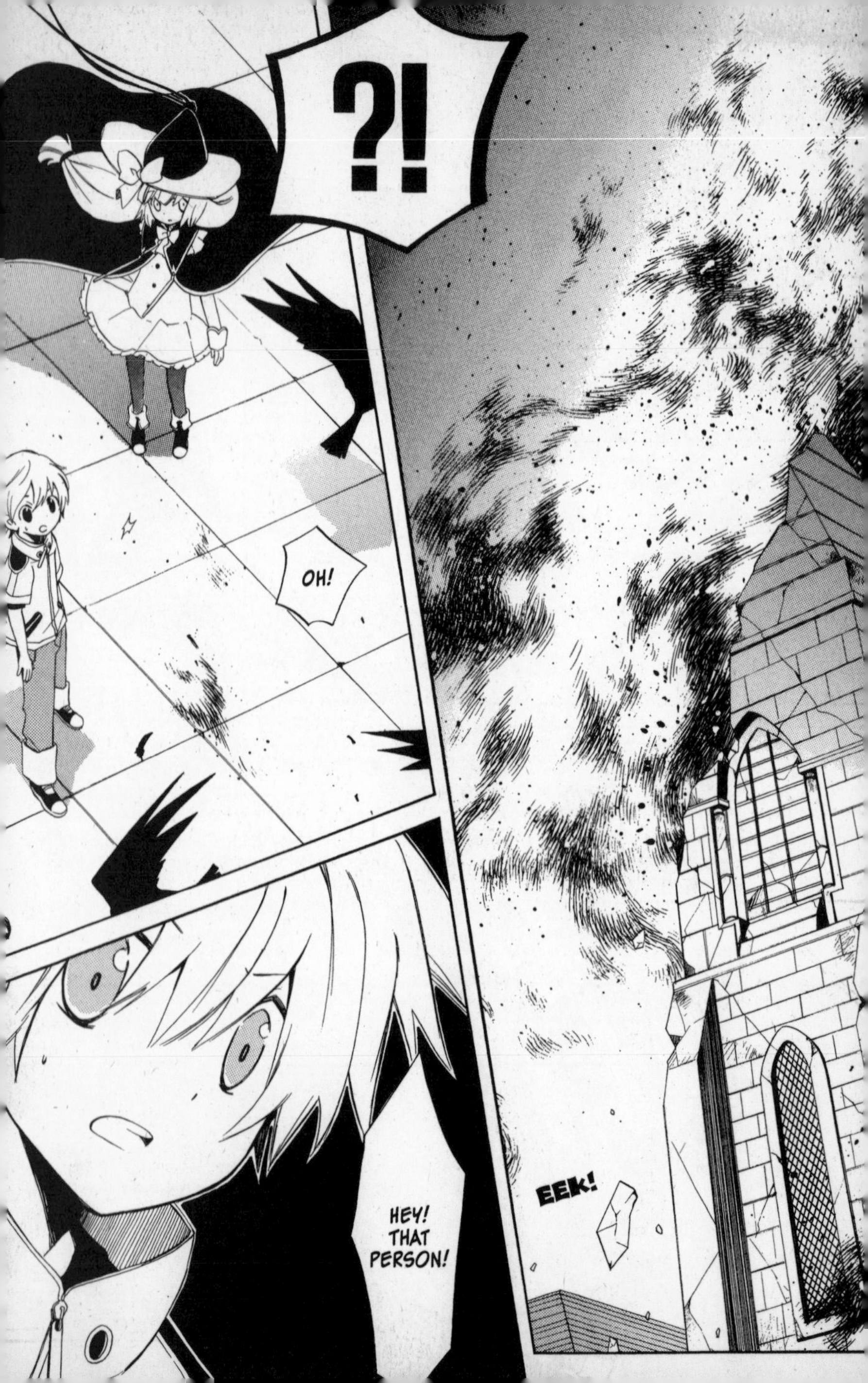
EEK!
?!
OH!
HEY! THAT PERSON!

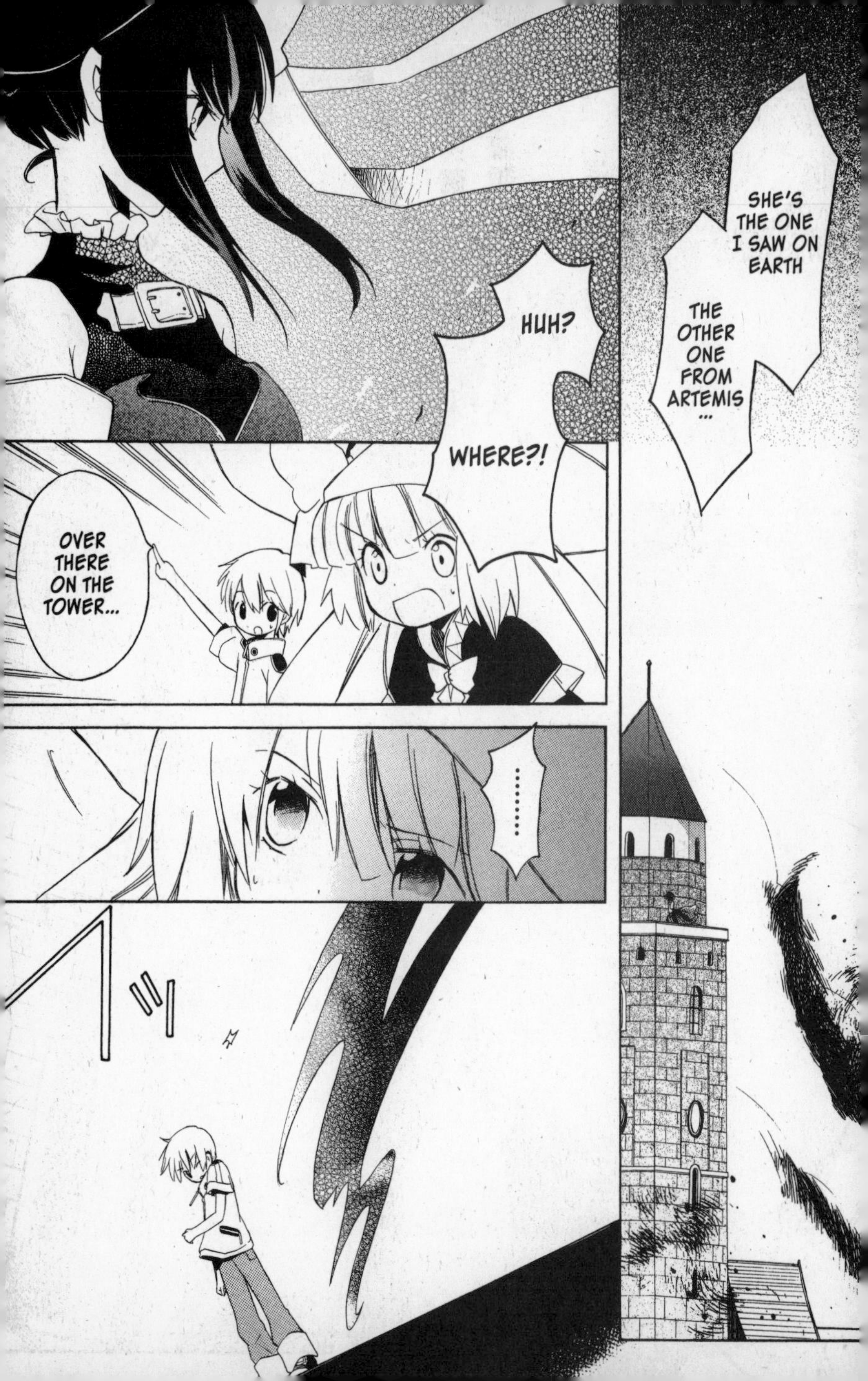
SHE'S THE ONE I SAW ON EARTH
THE OTHER ONE FROM ARTEMIS ...
HUH?
WHERE?!
OVER THERE ON THE TOWER...
......

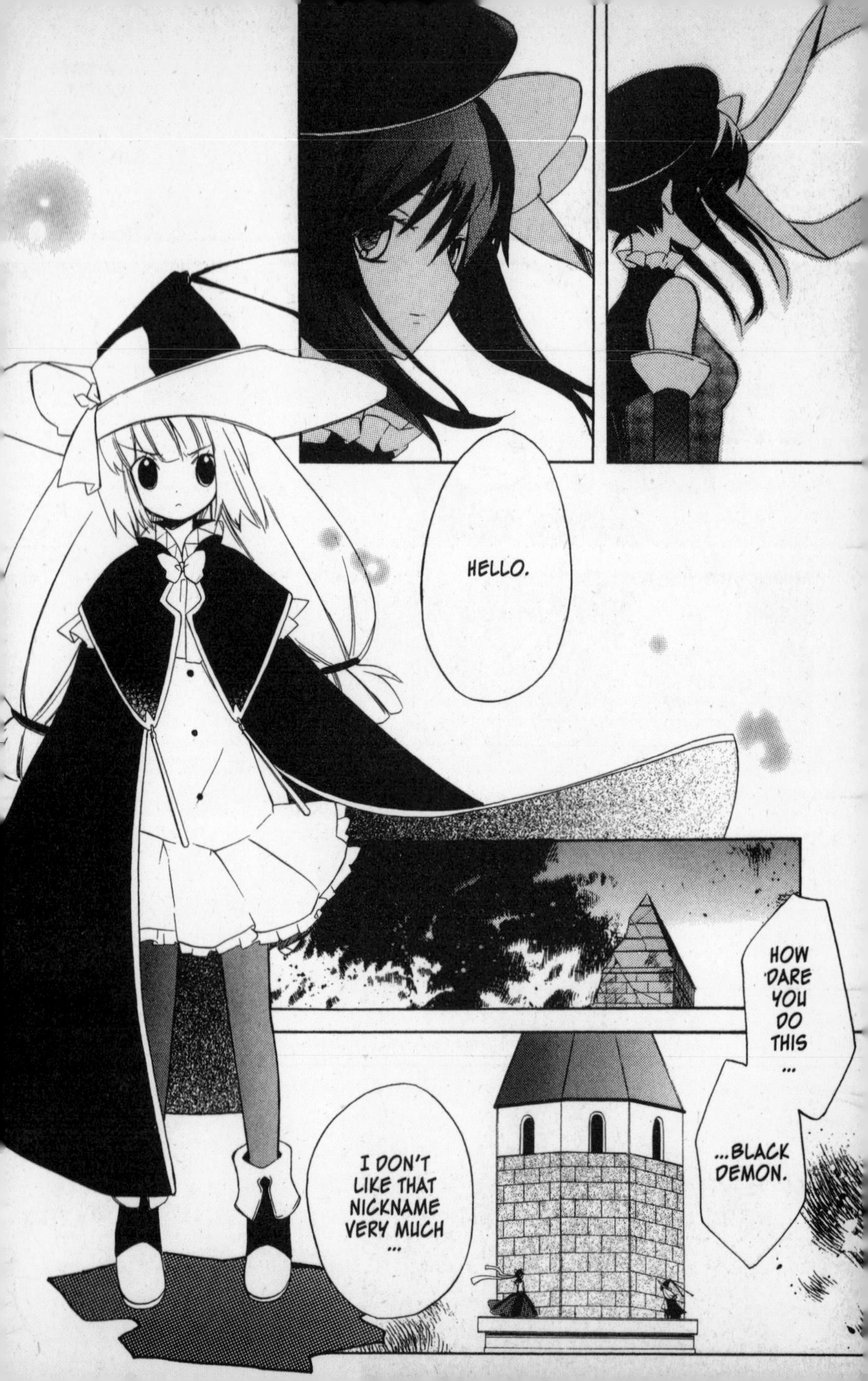
HELLO.
HOW DARE YOU DO THIS ...
...BLACK DEMON.
I DON'T LIKE THAT NICKNAME VERY MUCH ...

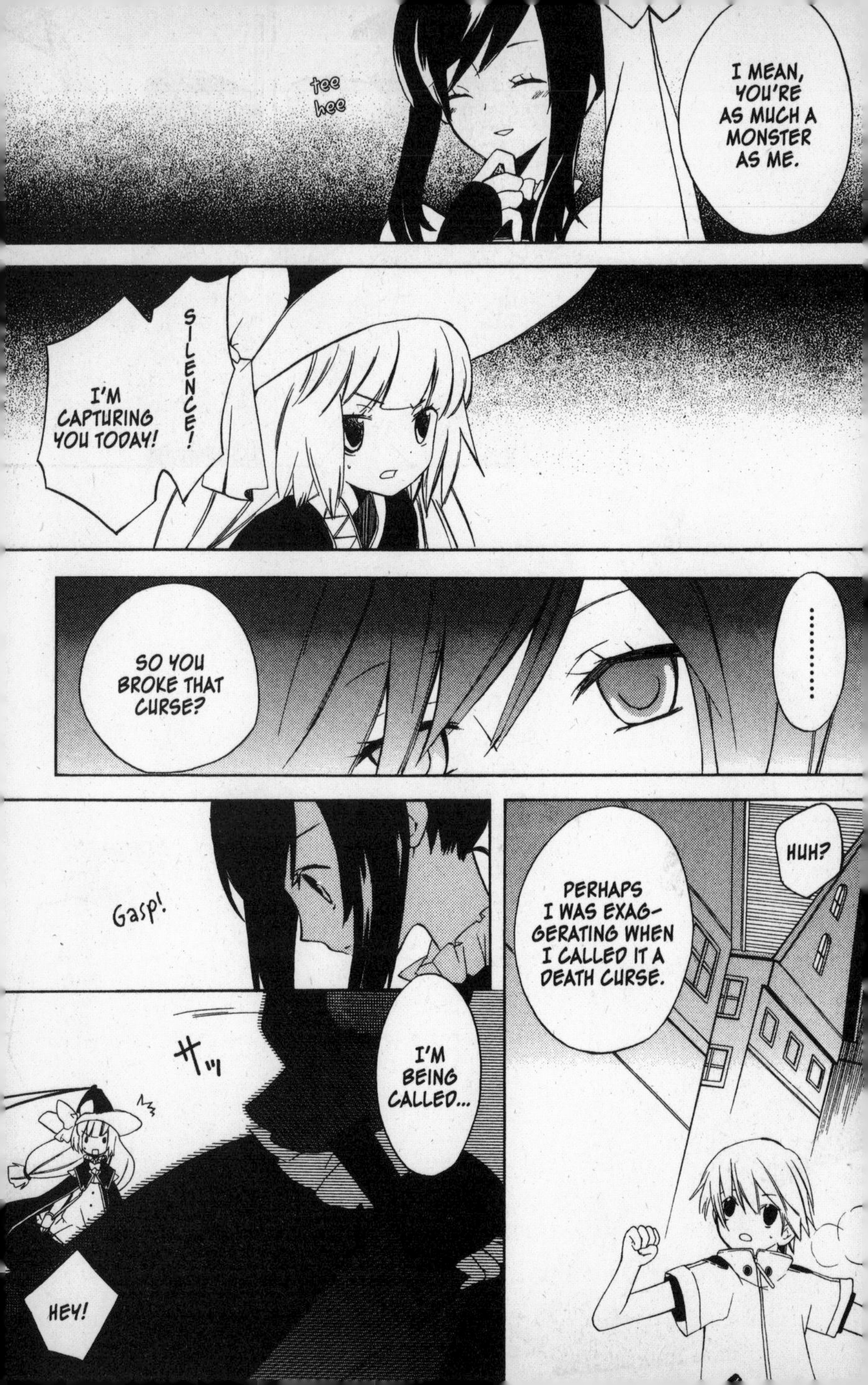
I MEAN, YOU'RE AS MUCH A MONSTER AS ME.
tee hee
SILENCE!
I'M CAPTURING YOU TODAY!
......
SO YOU BROKE THAT CURSE?
HUH?
PERHAPS I WAS EXAG-GERATING WHEN I CALLED IT A DEATH CURSE.
Gasp!
I'M BEING CALLED...
サッ
HEY!

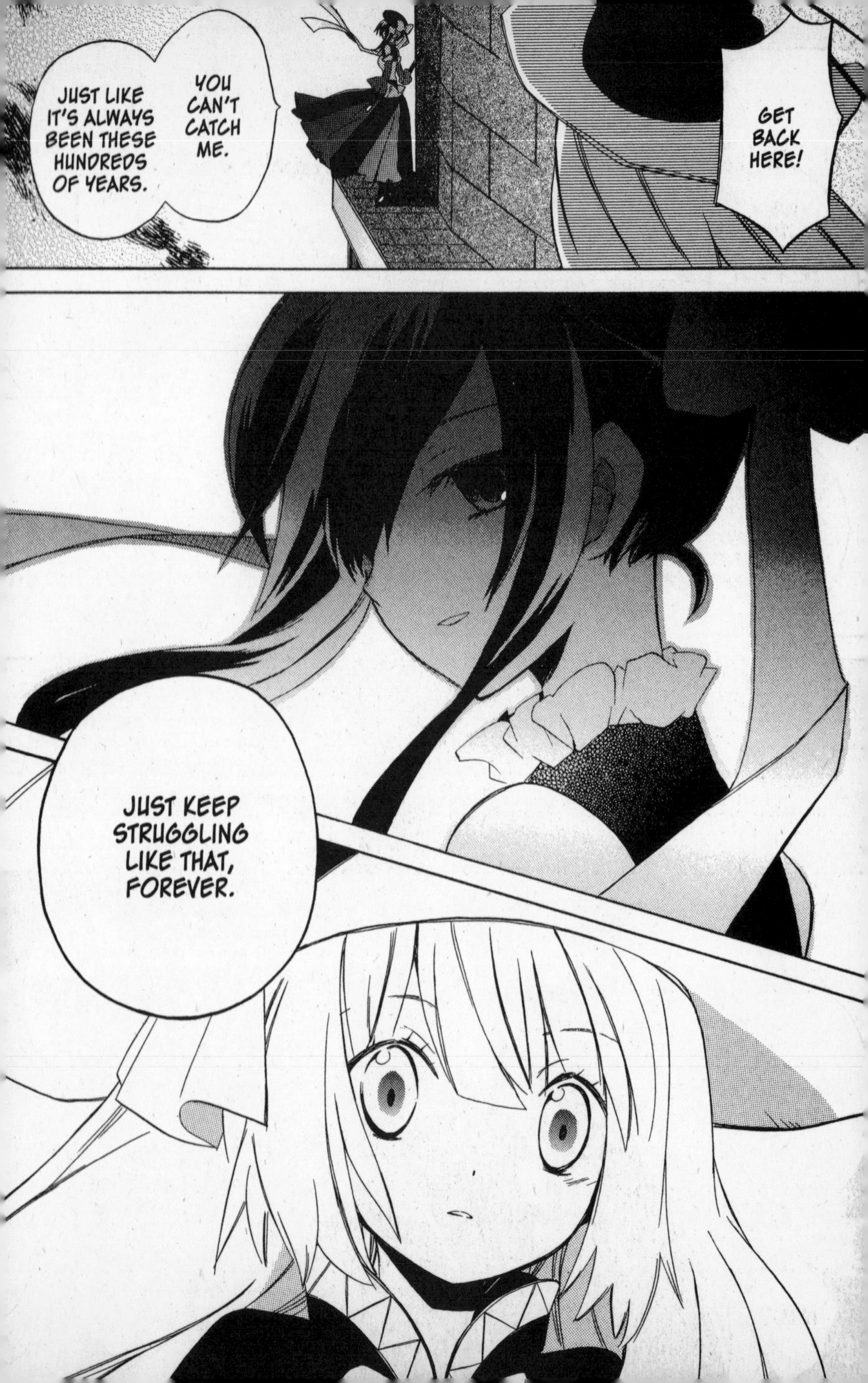
GET BACK HERE!
YOU CAN'T CATCH ME.
JUST LIKE IT'S ALWAYS BEEN THESE HUNDREDS OF YEARS.
JUST KEEP STRUGGLING LIKE THAT, FOREVER.

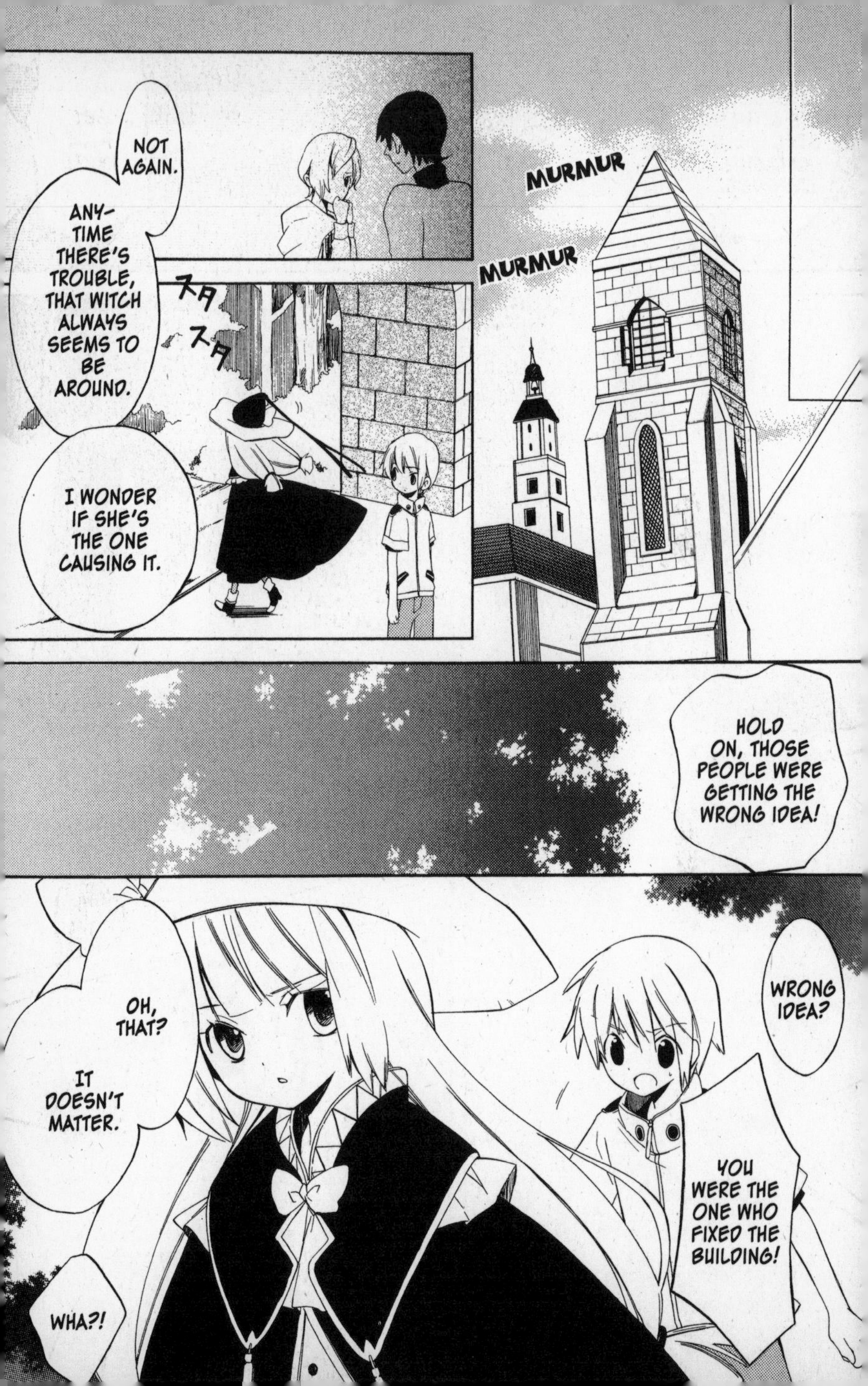
MURMUR
MURMUR
NOT AGAIN.
ANY-TIME THERE'S TROUBLE, THAT WITCH ALWAYS SEEMS TO BE AROUND.
スタ
スタ
I WONDER IF SHE'S THE ONE CAUSING IT.
HOLD ON, THOSE PEOPLE WERE GETTING THE WRONG IDEA!
WRONG IDEA?
OH, THAT?
IT DOESN'T MATTER.
YOU WERE THE ONE WHO FIXED THE BUILDING!
WHA?!

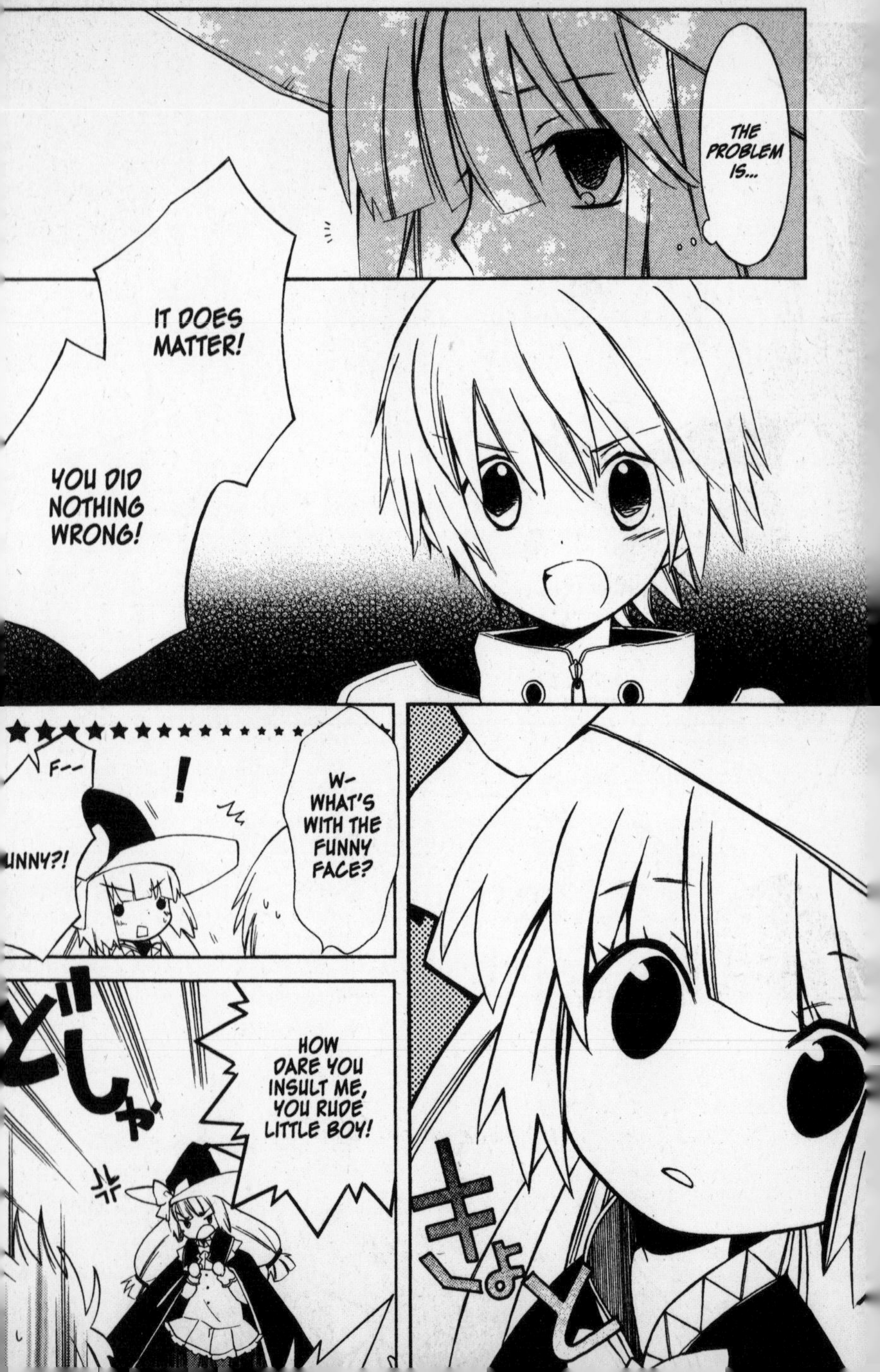
THE PROBLEM IS...
IT DOES MATTER!
YOU DID NOTHING WRONG!
きょと
W- WHAT'S WITH THE FUNNY FACE?
F--
!
UNNY?!
HOW DARE YOU INSULT ME, YOU RUDE LITTLE BOY!
どしゃ

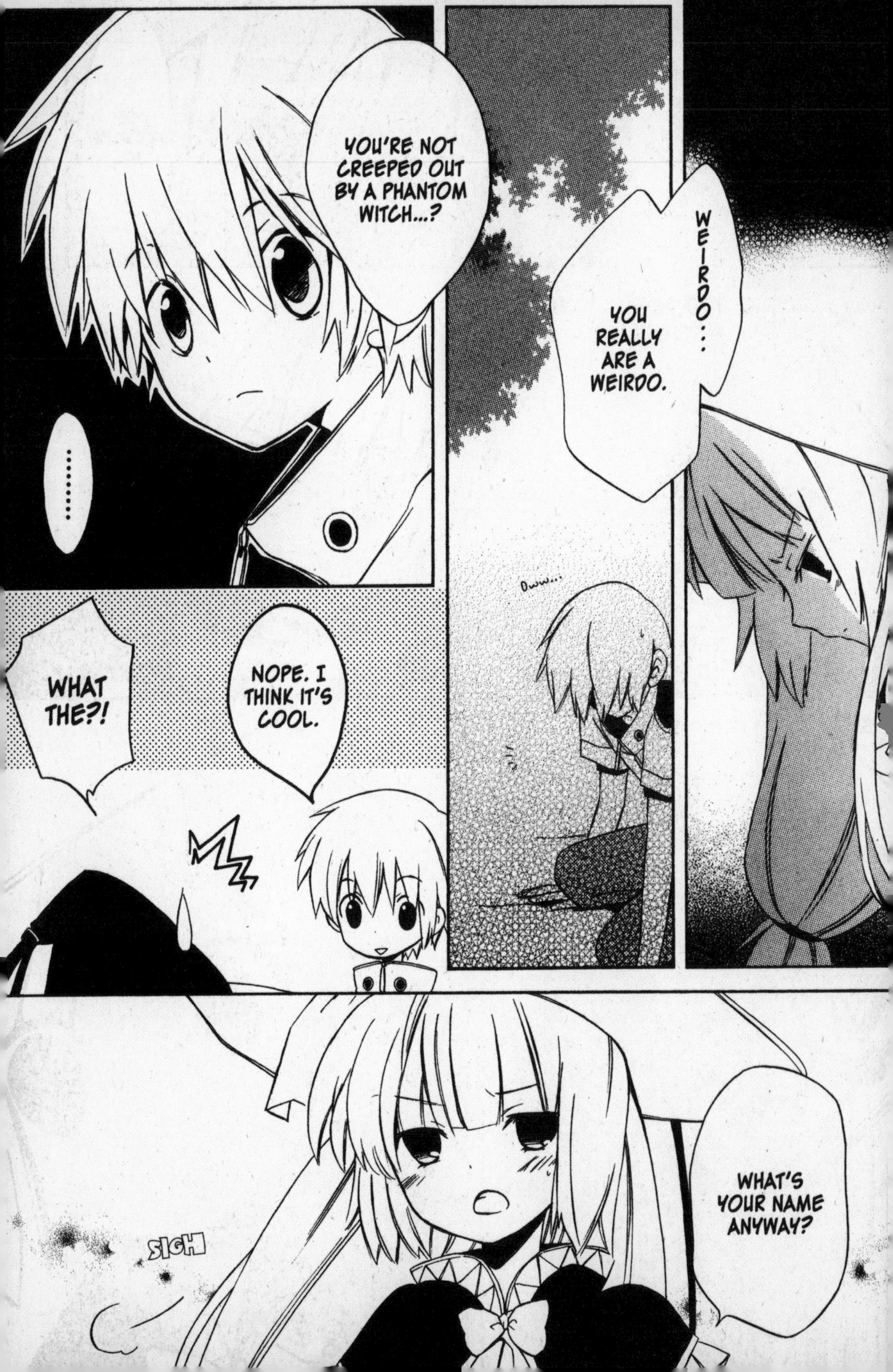
WEIRDO...
YOU REALLY ARE A WEIRDO.
Oww...
YOU'RE NOT CREEPED OUT BY A PHANTOM WITCH...?
......
NOPE. I THINK IT'S COOL.
WHAT THE?!
WHAT'S YOUR NAME ANYWAY?
SIGH

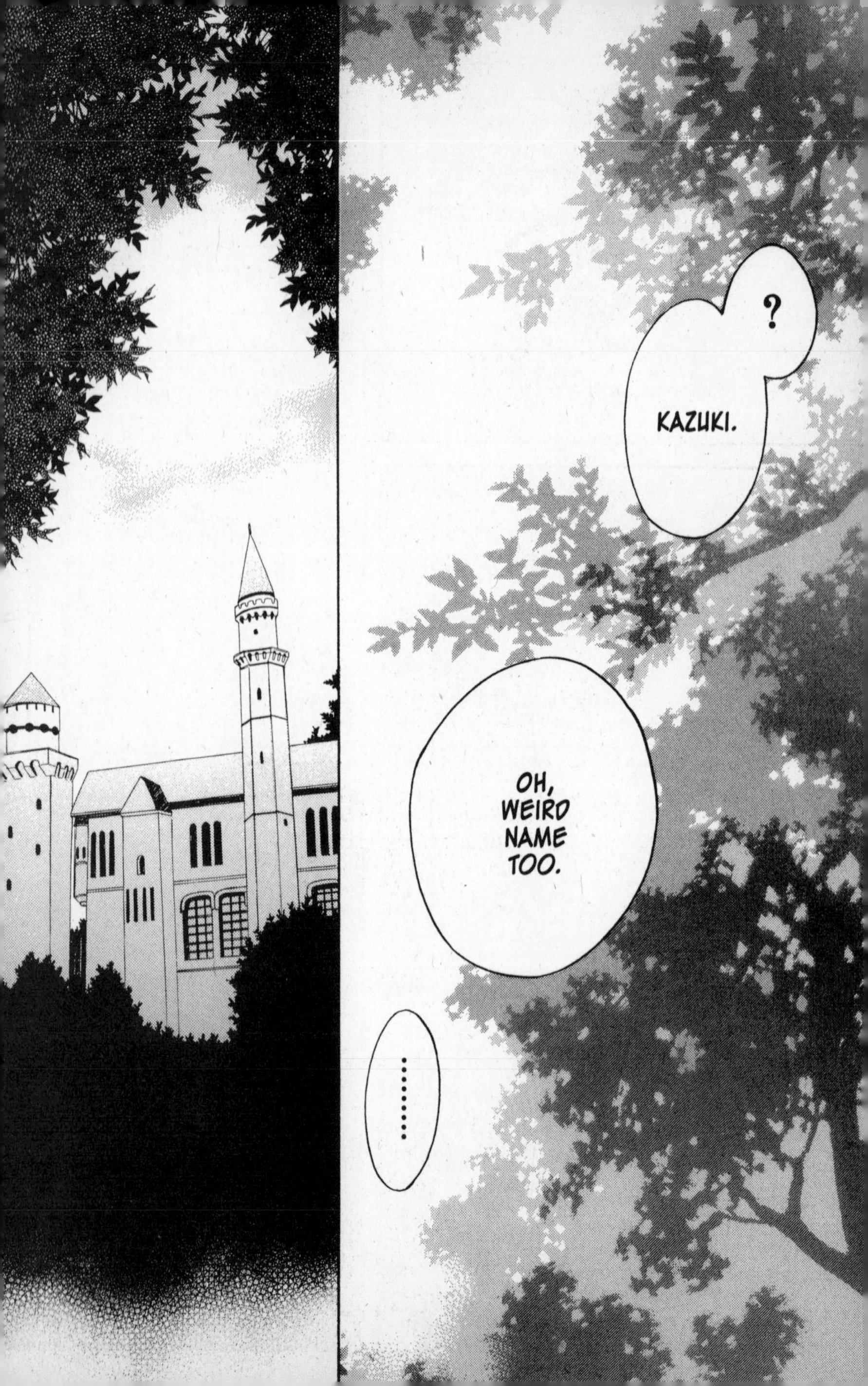
?
KAZUKI.
OH, WEIRD NAME TOO.
....

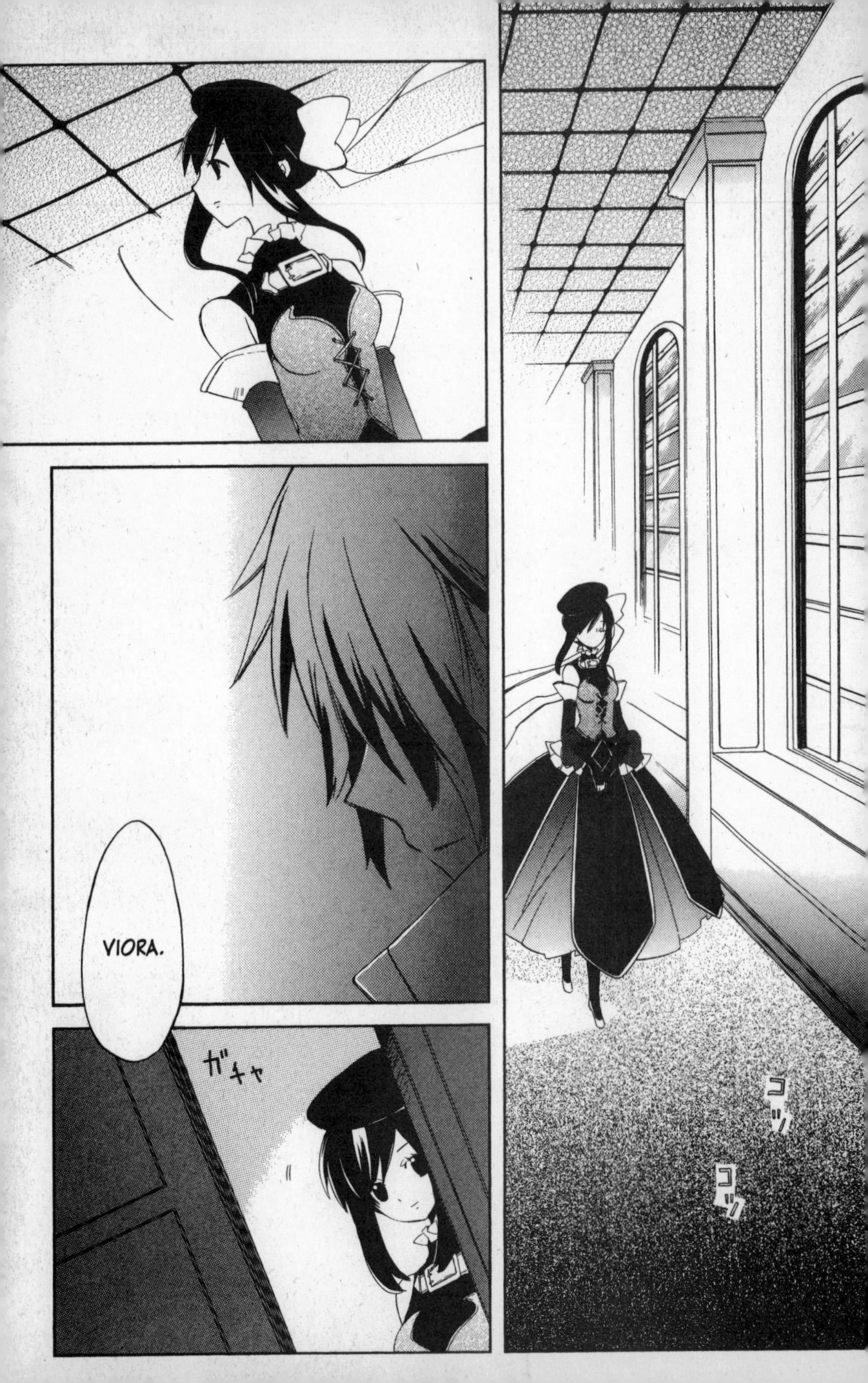
コッ
コッ
VIORA.
ガチャ

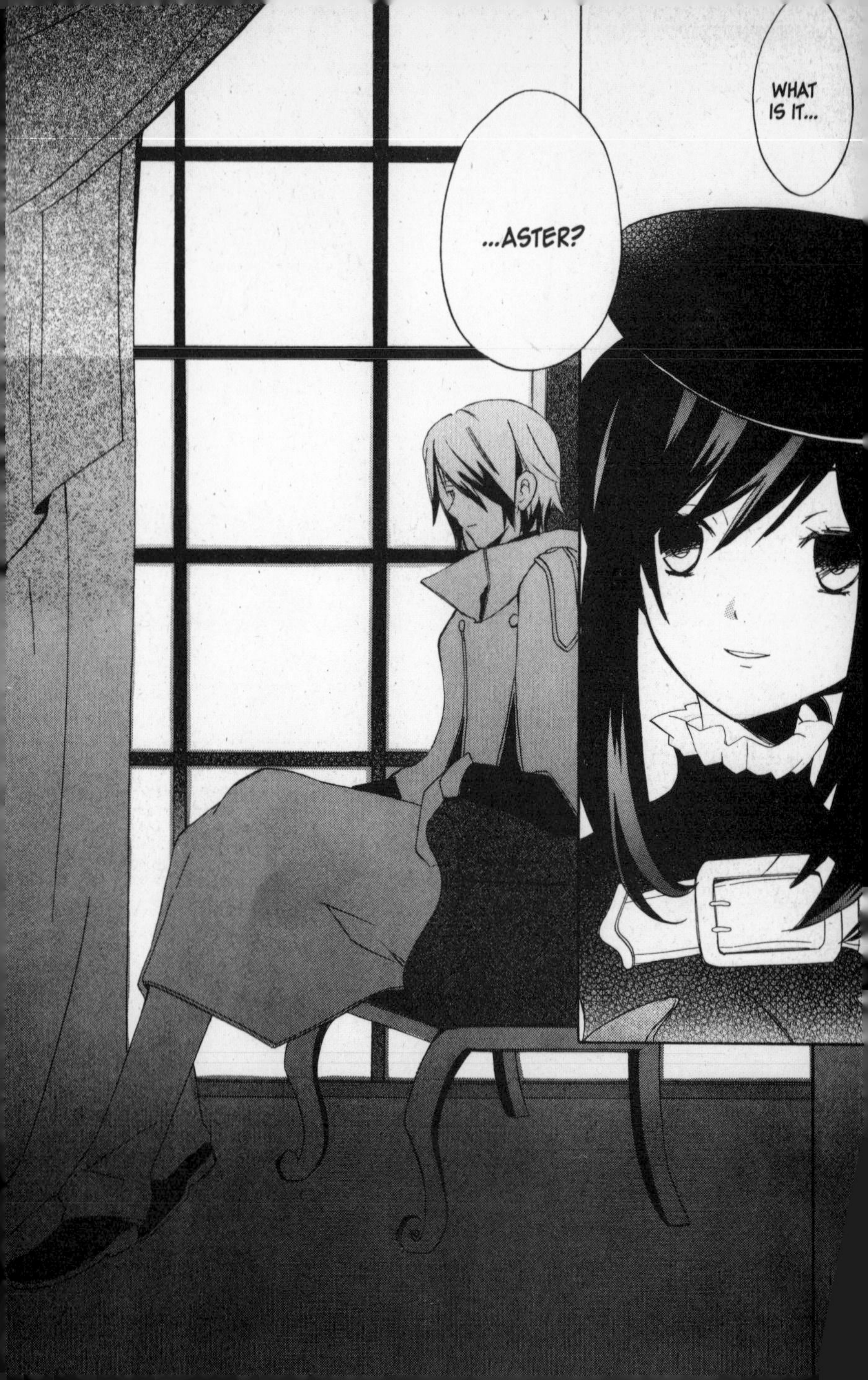
WHAT IS IT...
...ASTER?

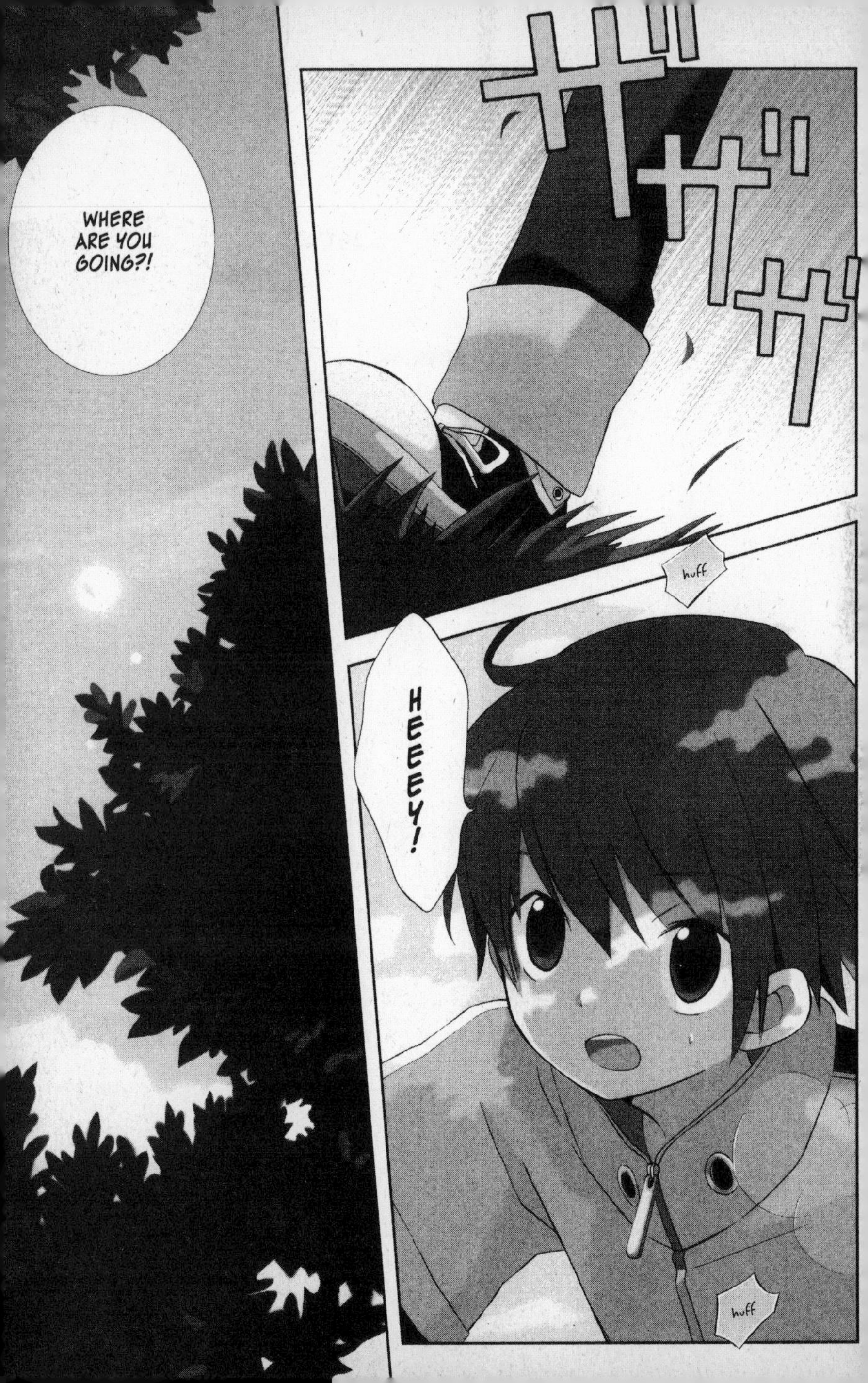
ザザザ
huff
HEEEY!
huff
WHERE ARE YOU GOING?!

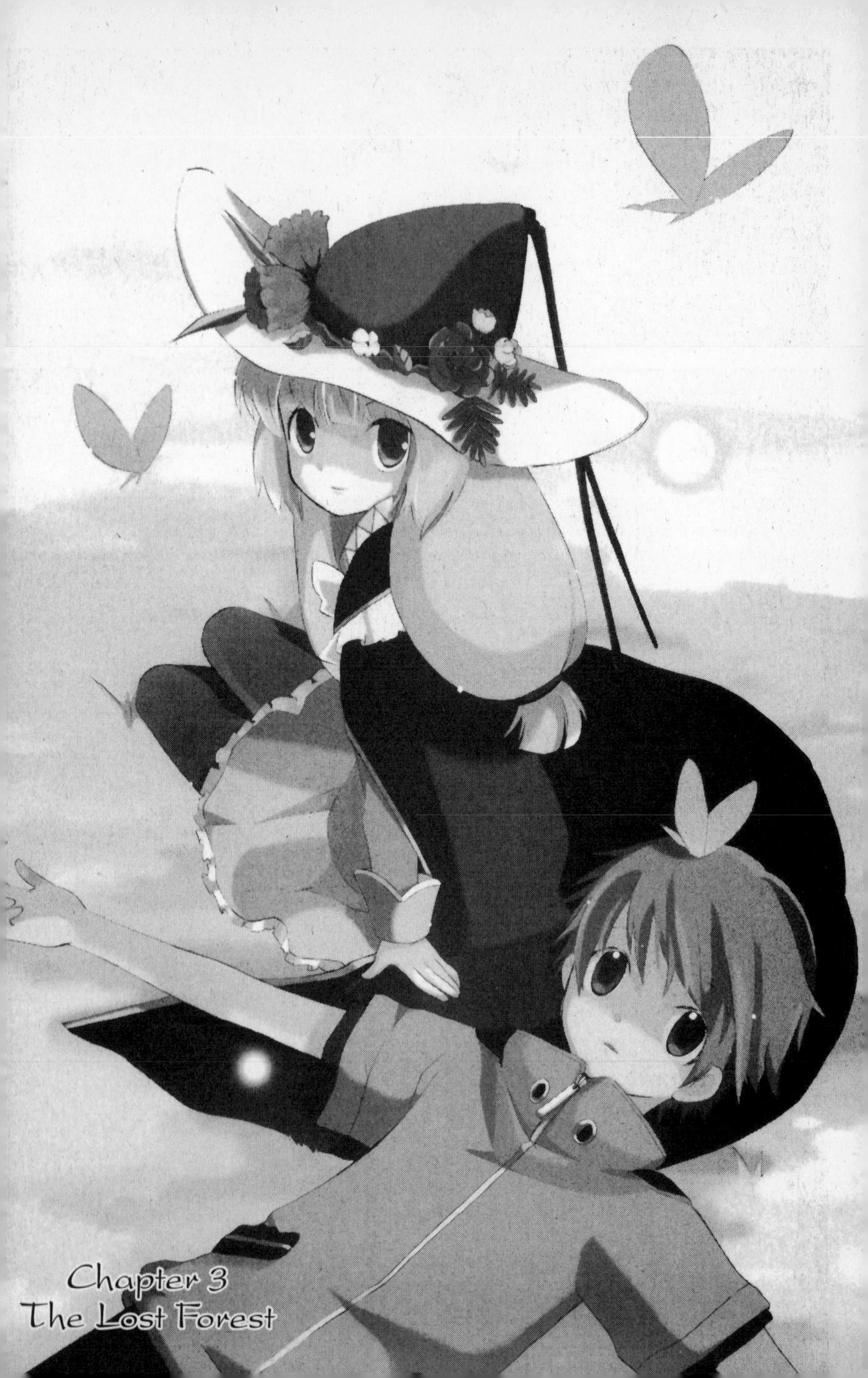

Chapter 3
The Lost Forest

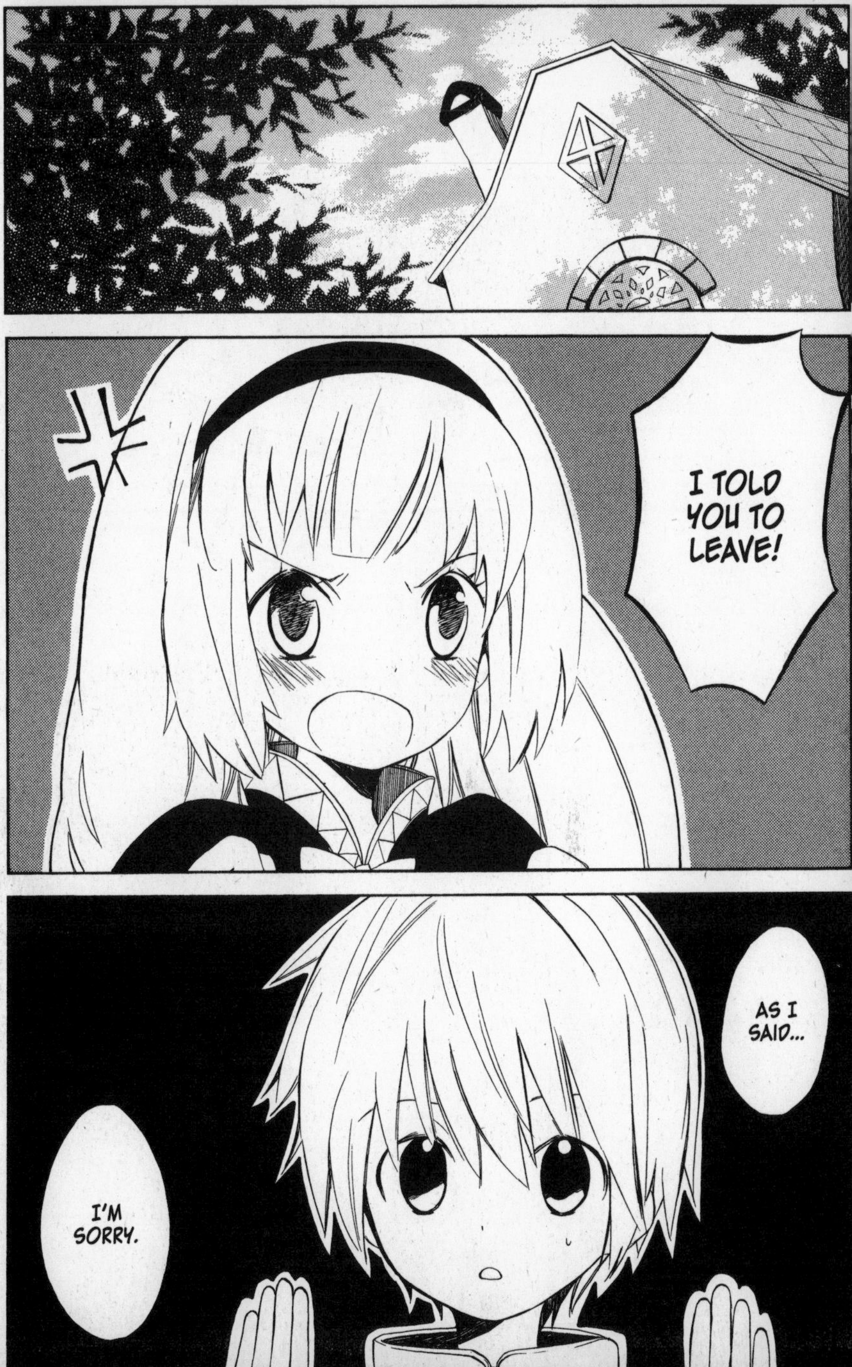
I TOLD YOU TO LEAVE!
AS I SAID...
I'M SORRY.

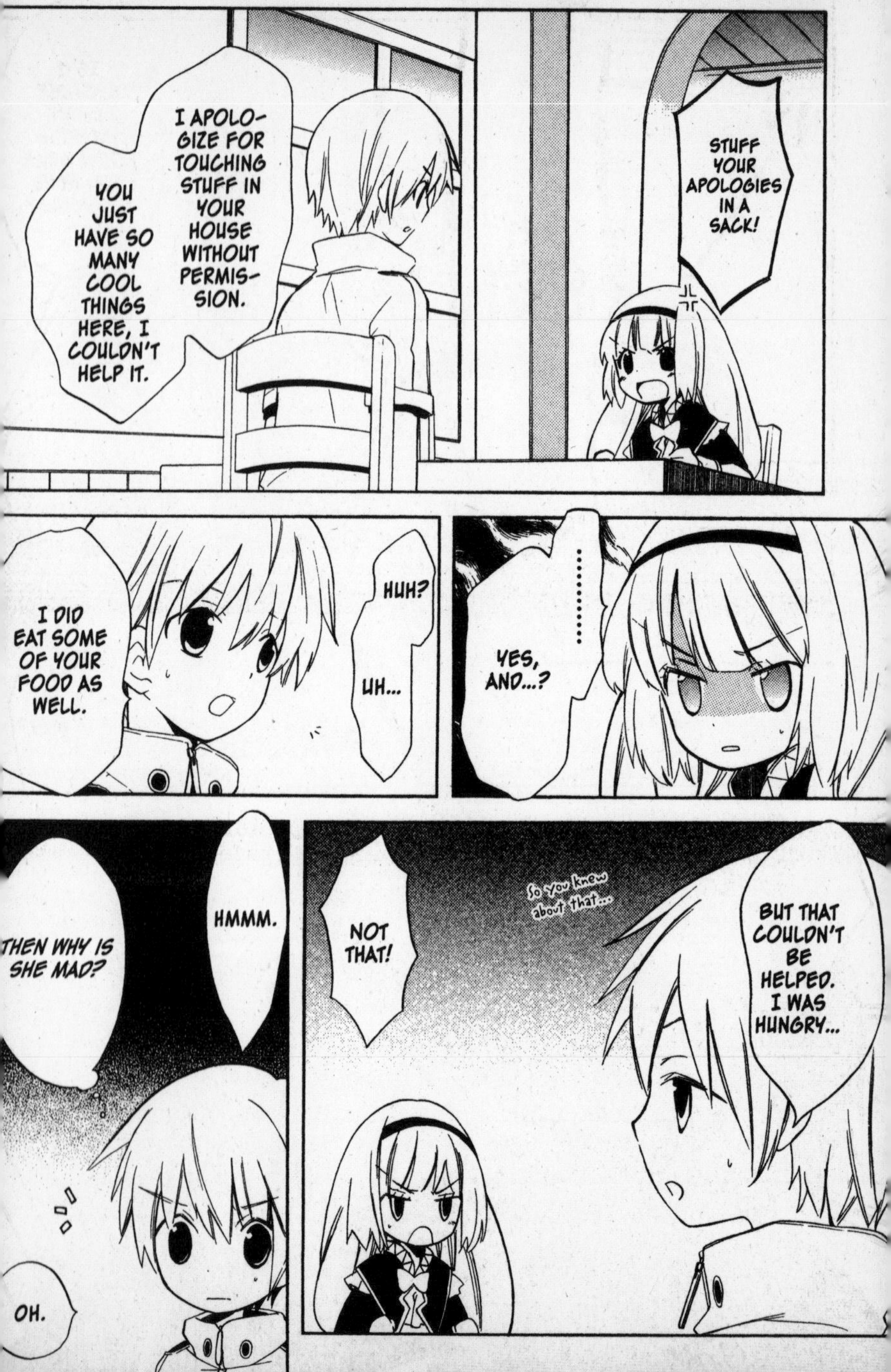
I APOLOGIZE FOR TOUCHING STUFF IN YOUR HOUSE WITHOUT PERMISSION.
YOU JUST HAVE SO MANY COOL THINGS HERE, I COULDN'T HELP IT.
STUFF YOUR APOLOGIES IN A SACK!
I DID EAT SOME OF YOUR FOOD AS WELL.
HUH?
UH...
......
YES, AND...?
HMMM.
THEN WHY IS SHE MAD?
OH.
NOT THAT!
So you knew about that...
BUT THAT COULDN'T BE HELPED. I WAS HUNGRY...

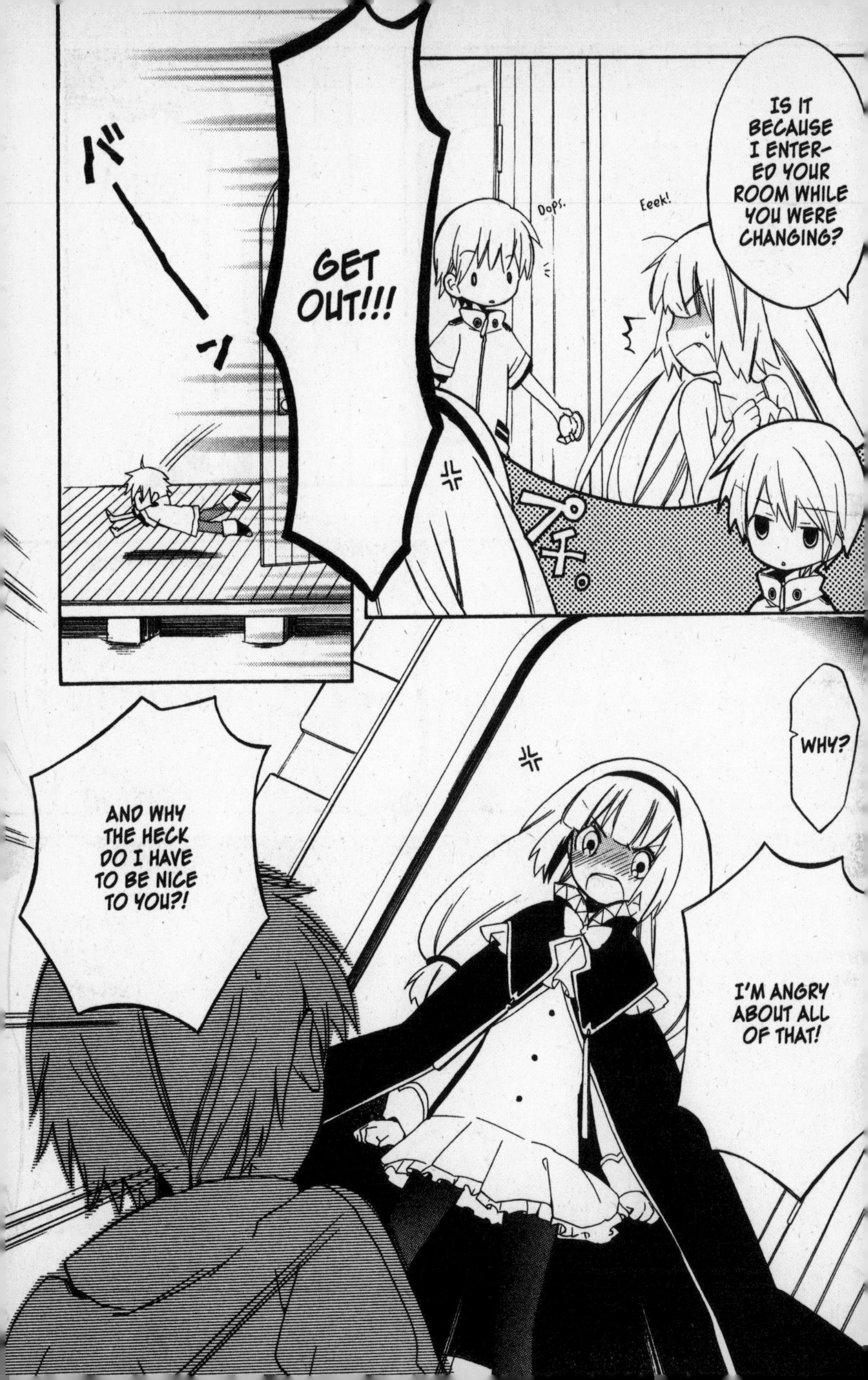

IS IT BECAUSE I ENTER-ED YOUR ROOM WHILE YOU WERE CHANGING?
Eeek!
Oops.
ピキ。
GET OUT!!!
バーーン
WHY?
I'M ANGRY ABOUT ALL OF THAT!
AND WHY THE HECK DO I HAVE TO BE NICE TO YOU?!

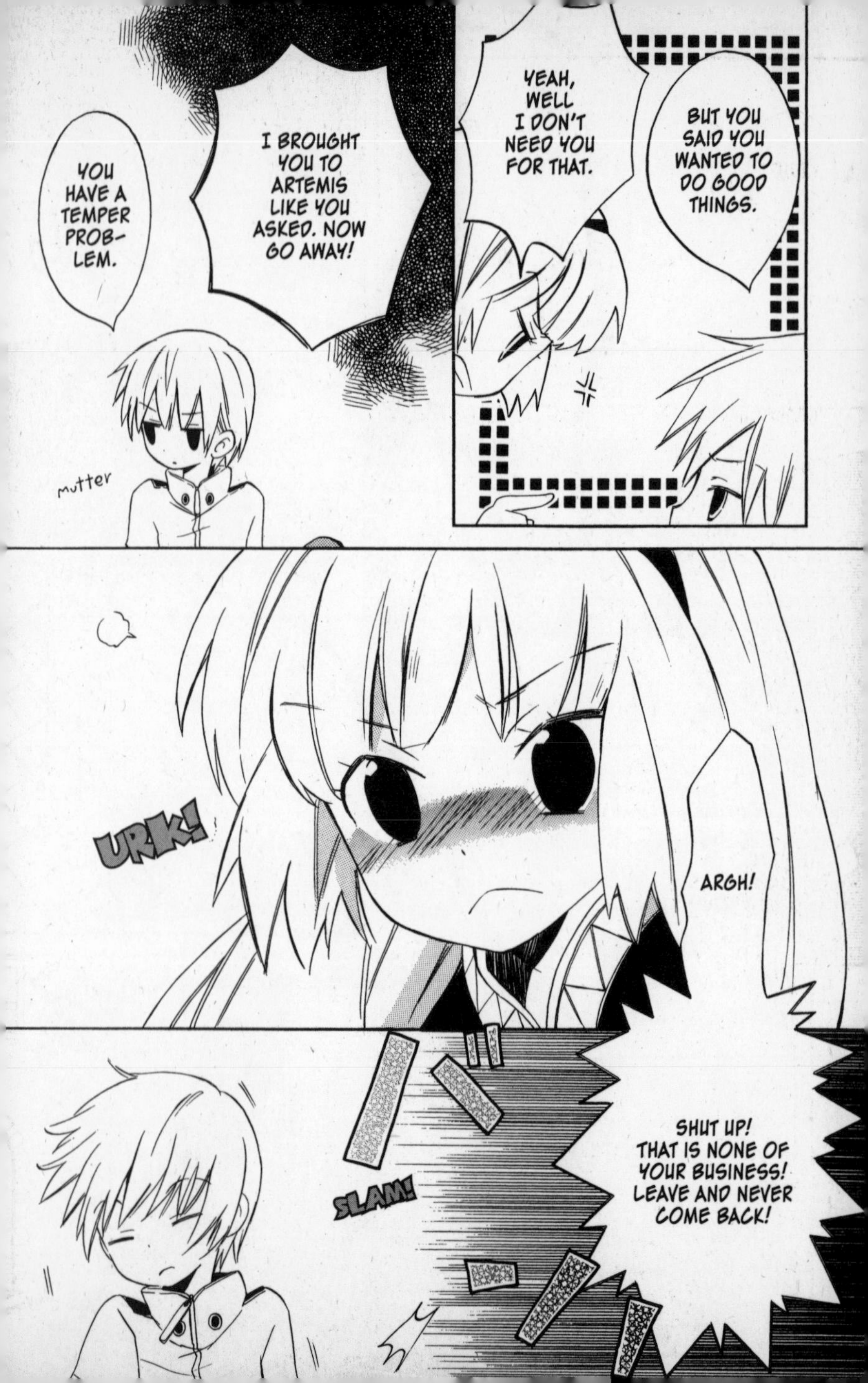
BUT YOU SAID YOU WANTED TO DO GOOD THINGS.
YEAH, WELL I DON'T NEED YOU FOR THAT.
I BROUGHT YOU TO ARTEMIS LIKE YOU ASKED. NOW GO AWAY!
YOU HAVE A TEMPER PROB-LEM.
mutter
ARGH!
URK!
SHUT UP! THAT IS NONE OF YOUR BUSINESS! LEAVE AND NEVER COME BACK!
SLAM!

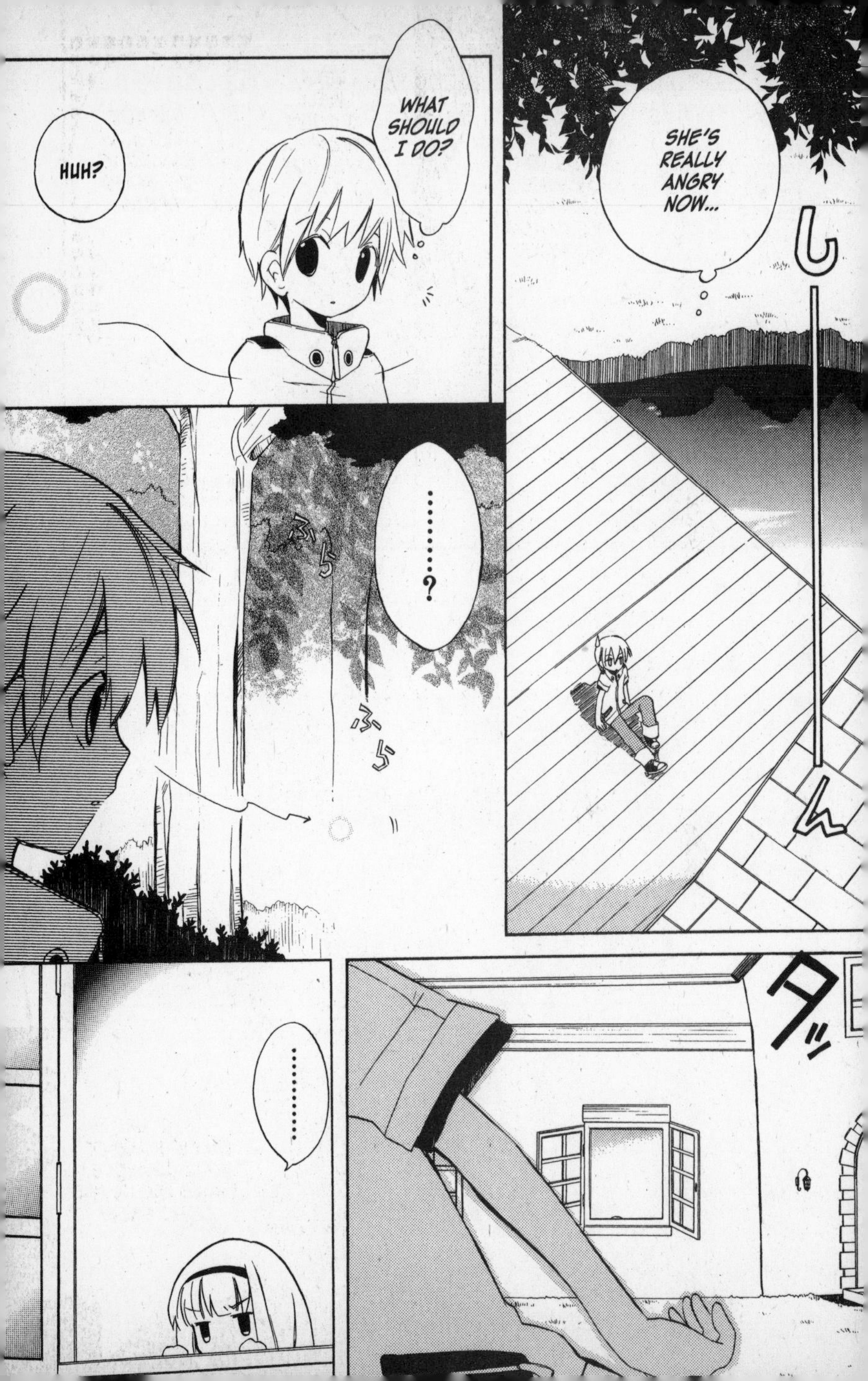
SHE'S REALLY ANGRY NOW...
しーん
WHAT SHOULD I DO?
HUH?
......?
ふら
ふら
タッ
......

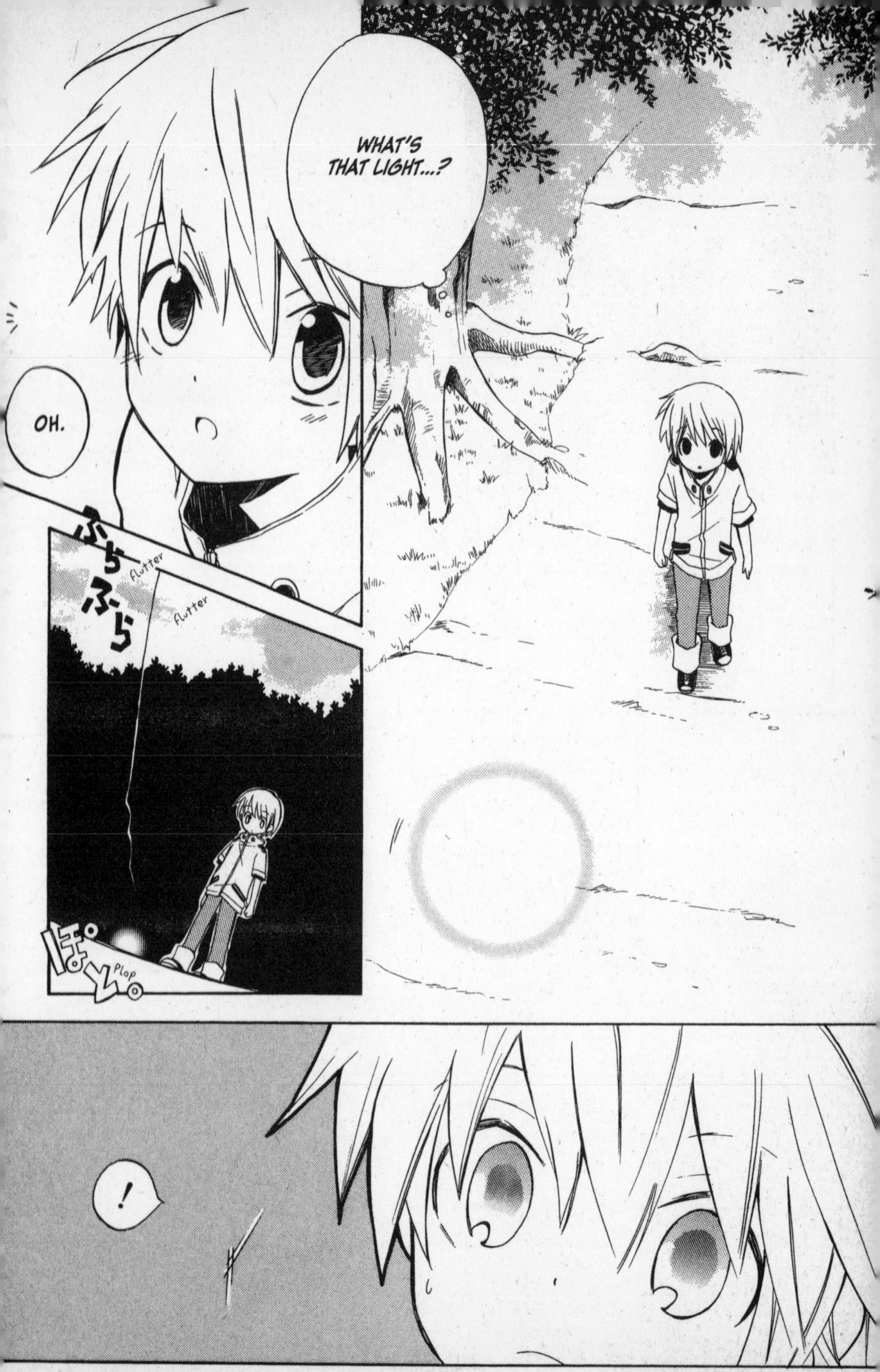
WHAT'S THAT LIGHT...?
OH.
ふらふら
flutter
flutter
ぽと。
Plop
!

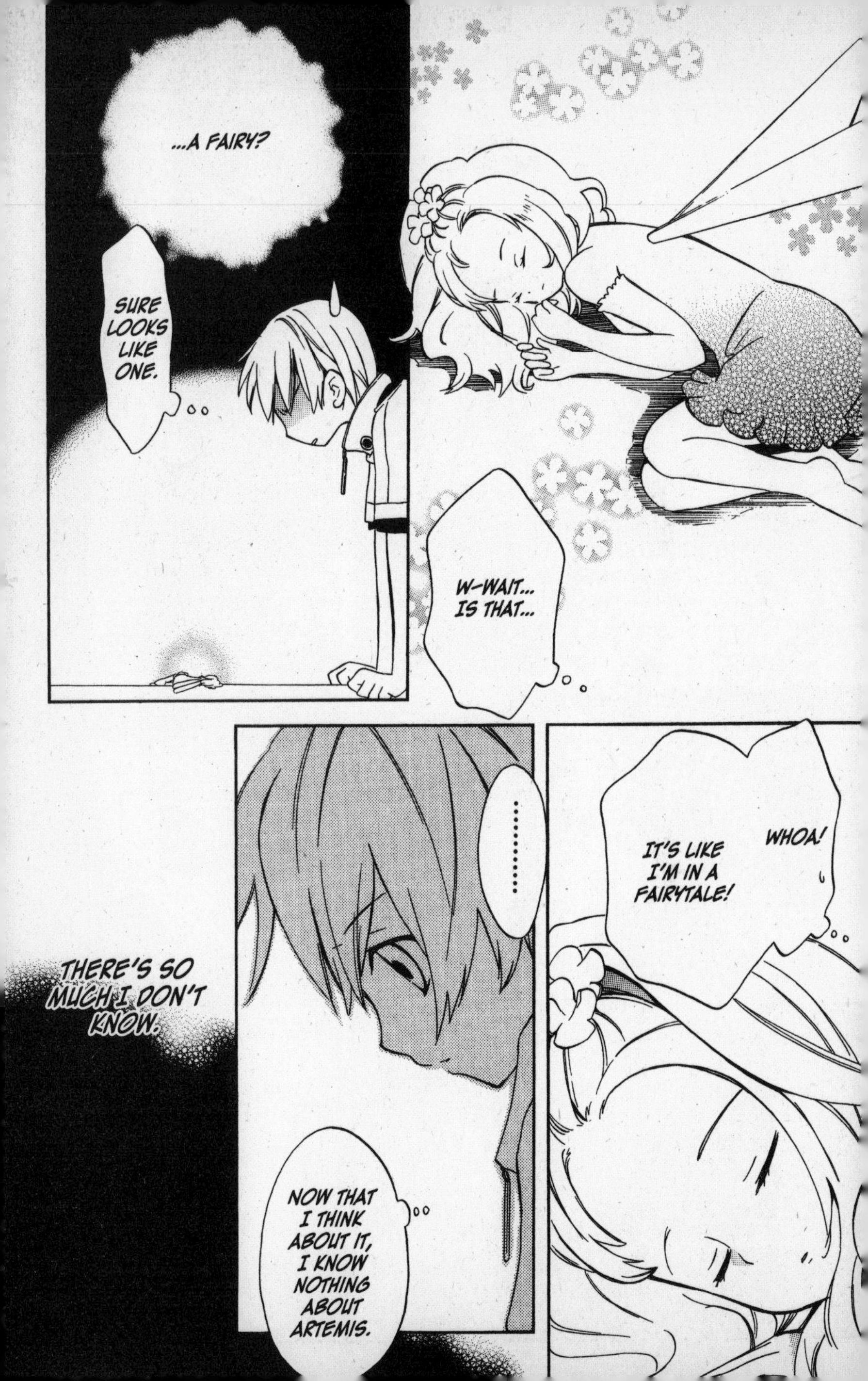
W-WAIT... IS THAT...
...A FAIRY?
SURE LOOKS LIKE ONE.
WHOA!
IT'S LIKE I'M IN A FAIRYTALE!
....
NOW THAT I THINK ABOUT IT, I KNOW NOTHING ABOUT ARTEMIS.
THERE'S SO MUCH I DON'T KNOW.

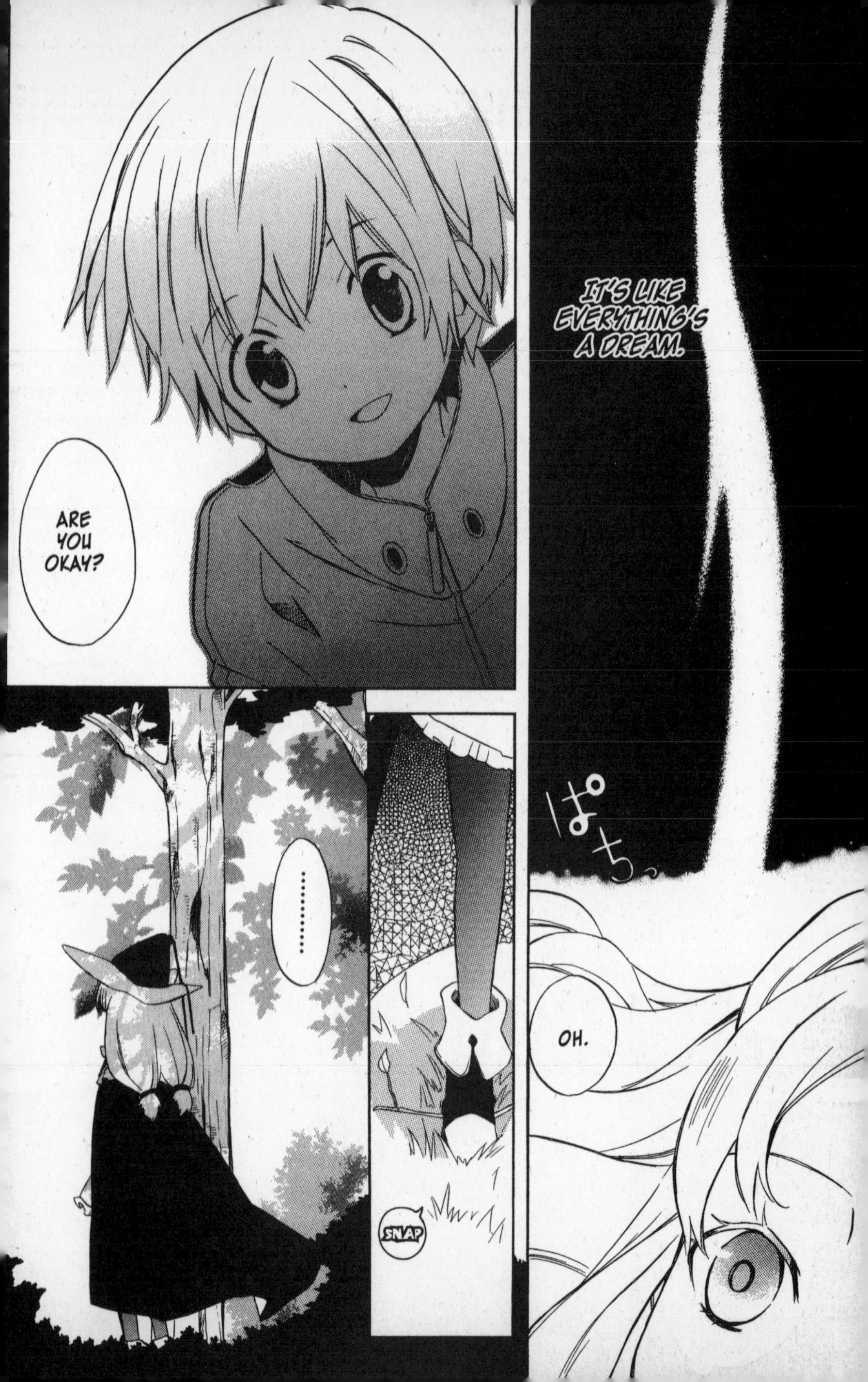
IT'S LIKE EVERYTHING'S A DREAM.
ぱちっ
OH.
ARE YOU OKAY?
SNAP
....

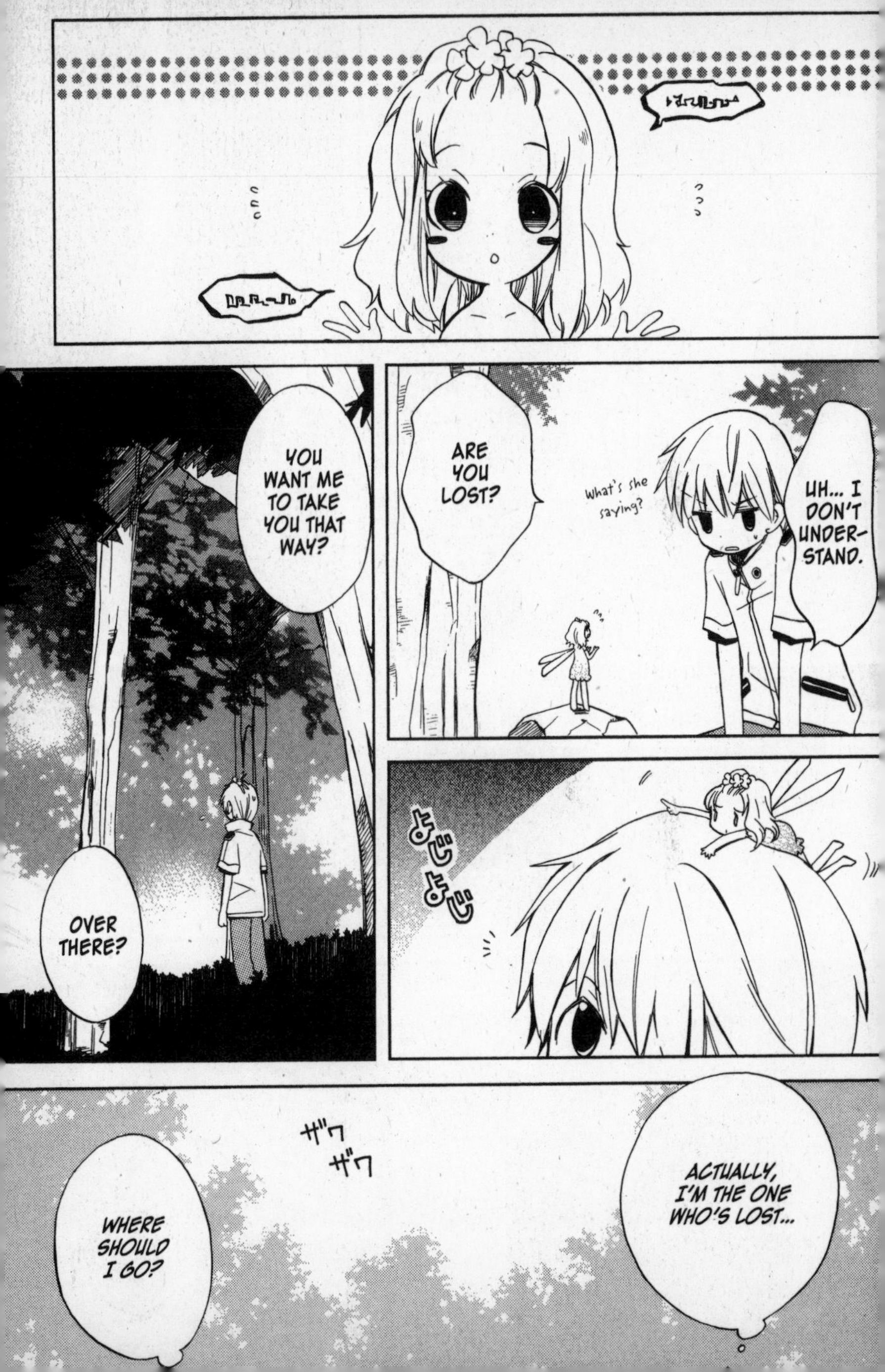
ARE YOU LOST?
What's she saying?
UH... I DON'T UNDER-STAND.
よじよじ
YOU WANT ME TO TAKE YOU THAT WAY?
OVER THERE?
ザワザワ
ACTUALLY, I'M THE ONE WHO'S LOST...
WHERE SHOULD I GO?

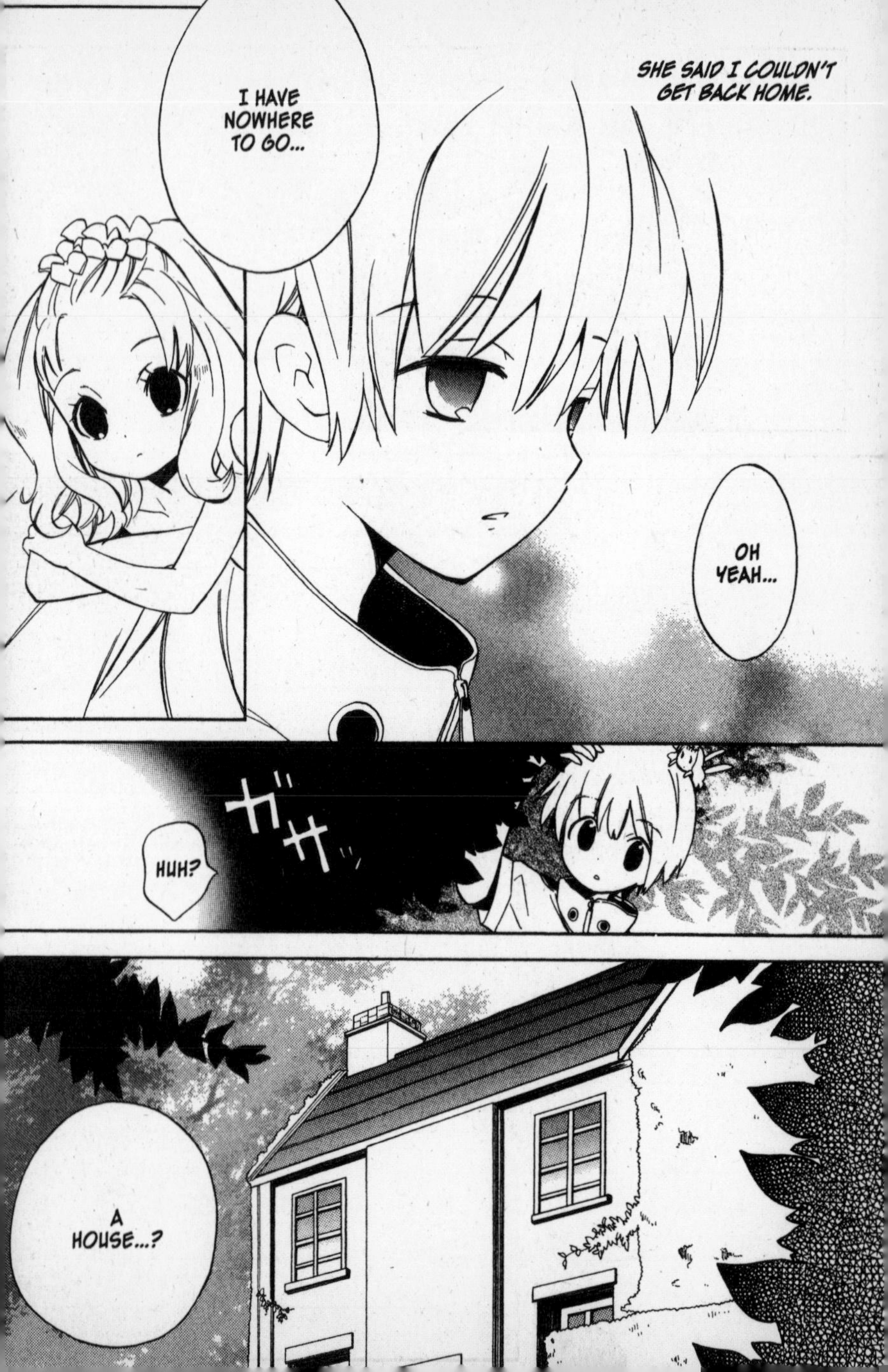

SHE SAID I COULDN'T GET BACK HOME.
I HAVE NOWHERE TO GO...
OH YEAH...
ガサッ
HUH?
A HOUSE...?

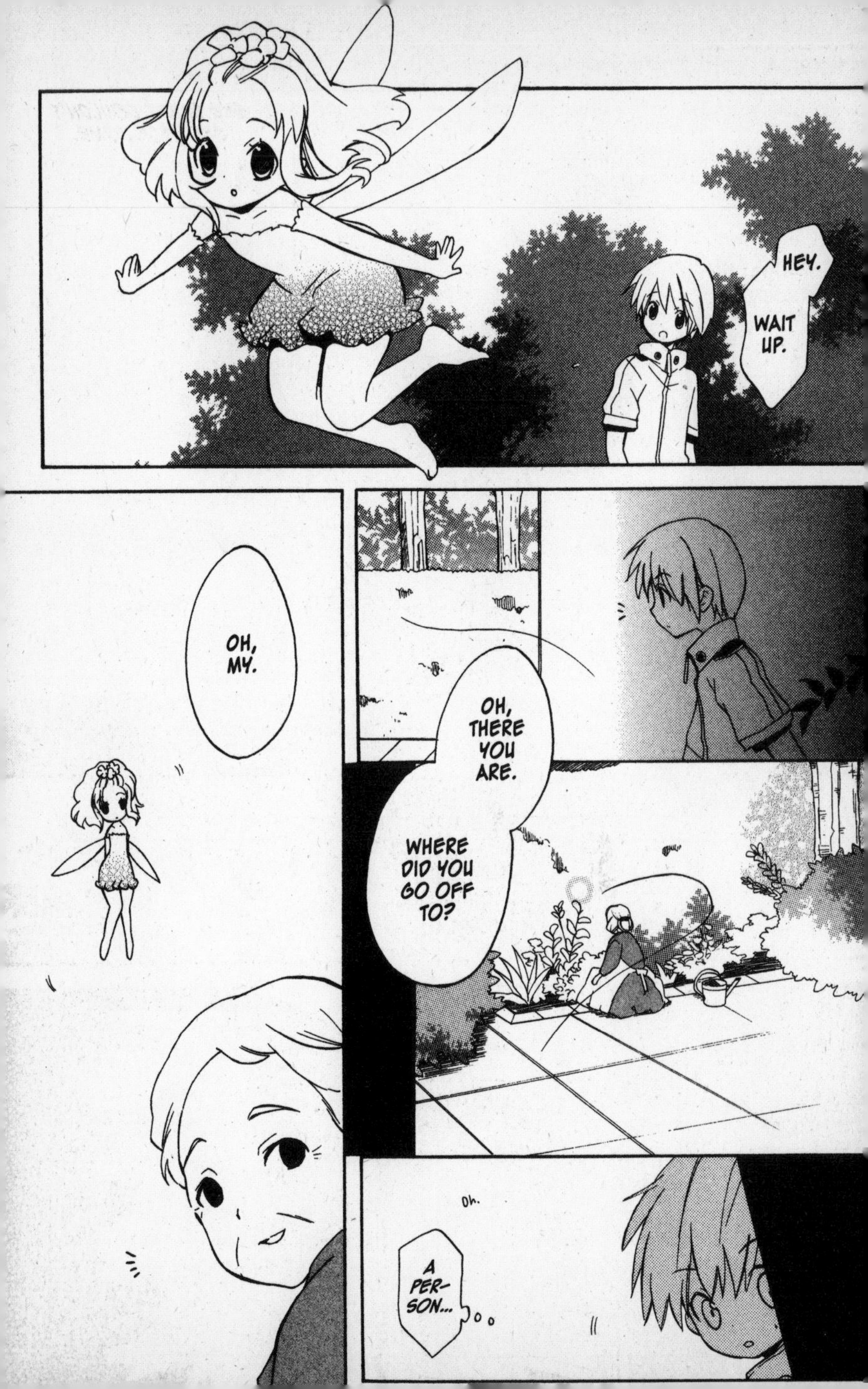
HEY.
WAIT UP.
OH, THERE YOU ARE.
WHERE DID YOU GO OFF TO?
Oh.
A PERSON...
OH, MY.

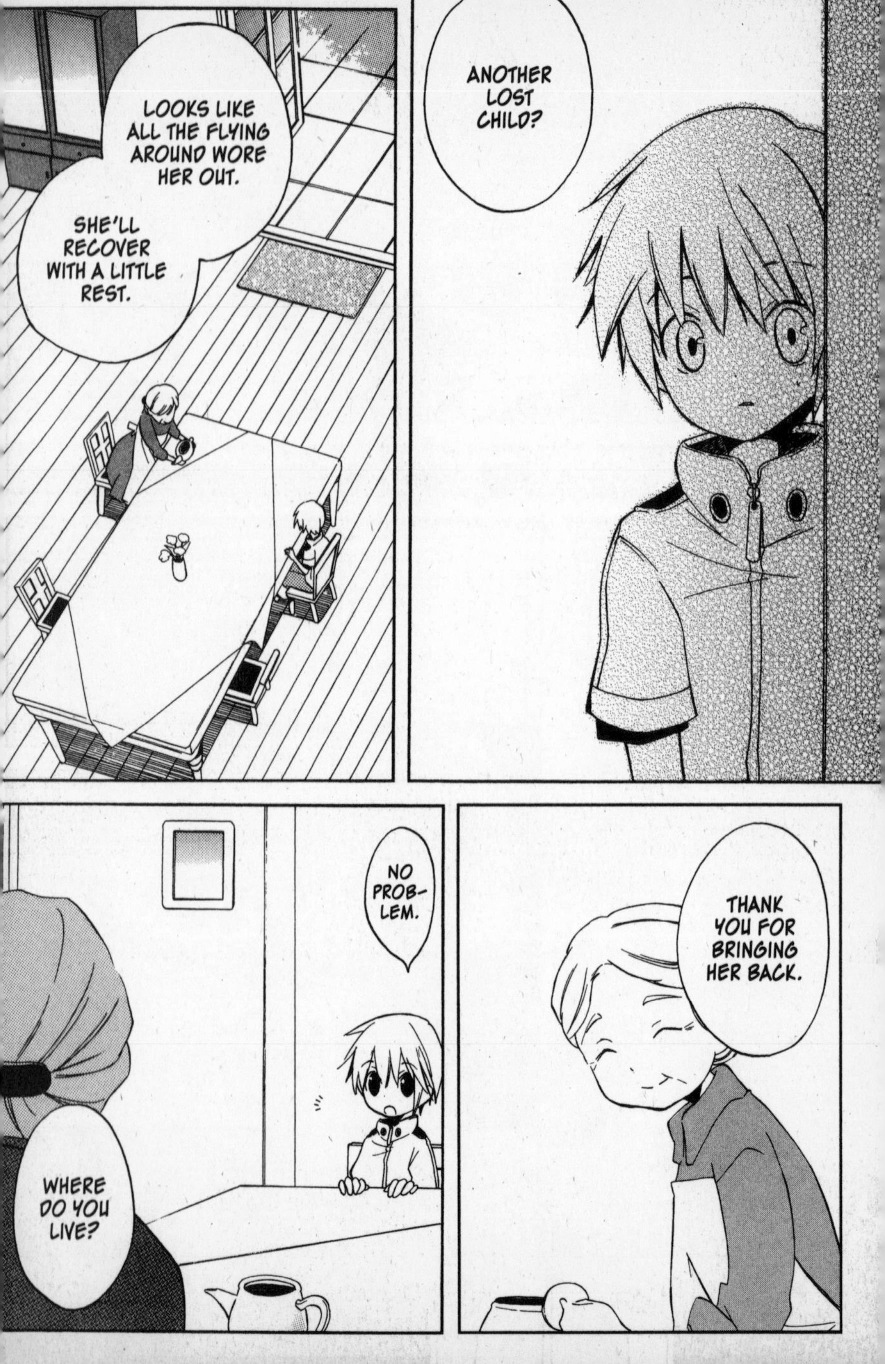
ANOTHER LOST CHILD?
LOOKS LIKE ALL THE FLYING AROUND WORE HER OUT.
SHE'LL RECOVER WITH A LITTLE REST.
THANK YOU FOR BRINGING HER BACK.
NO PROB-LEM.
WHERE DO YOU LIVE?

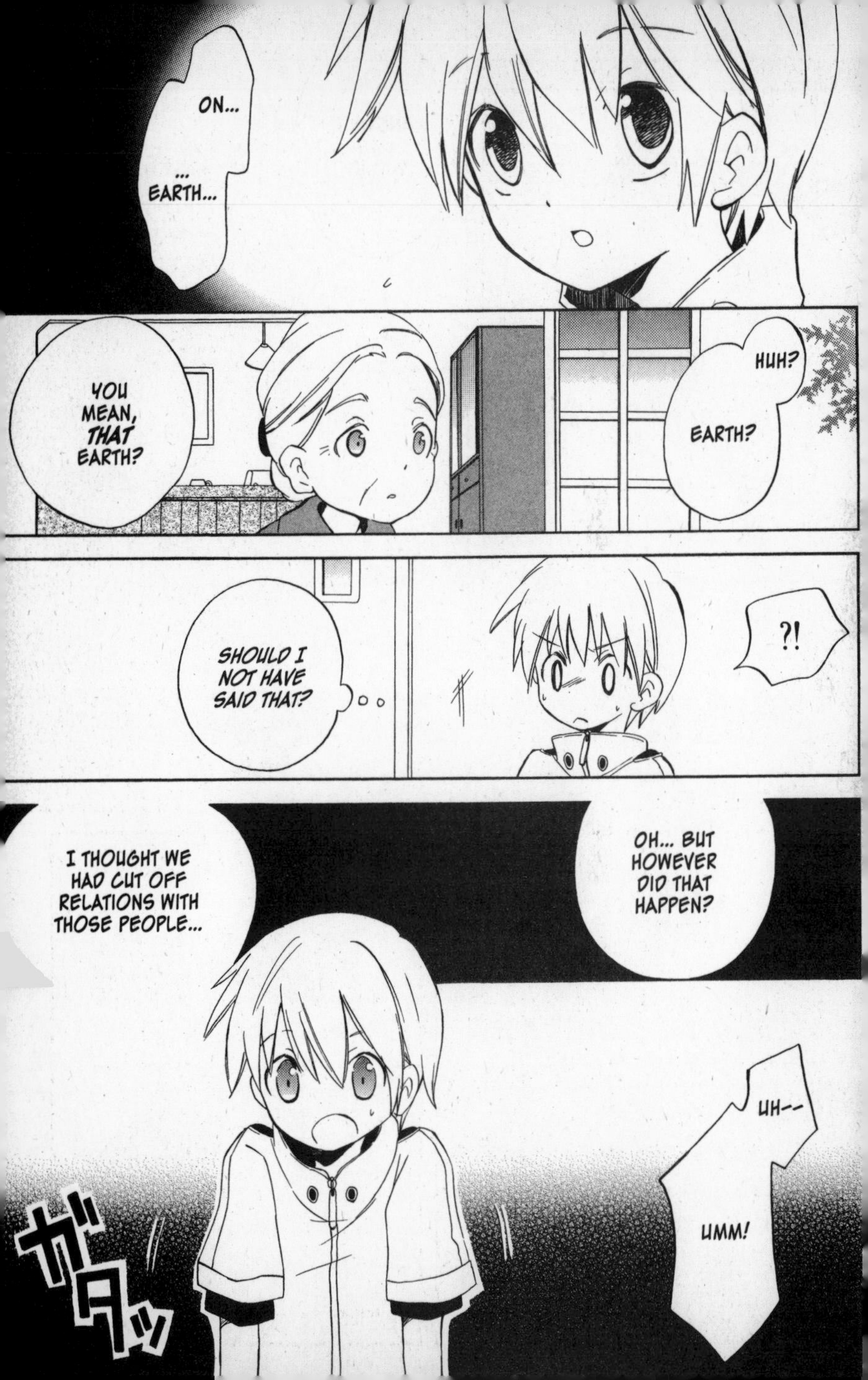
ON... ...EARTH...
HUH? EARTH?
YOU MEAN, *THAT* EARTH?
?!
SHOULD I NOT HAVE SAID THAT?
OH... BUT HOWEVER DID THAT HAPPEN?
I THOUGHT WE HAD CUT OFF RELATIONS WITH THOSE PEOPLE...
UH-- UMM!
ガタッ

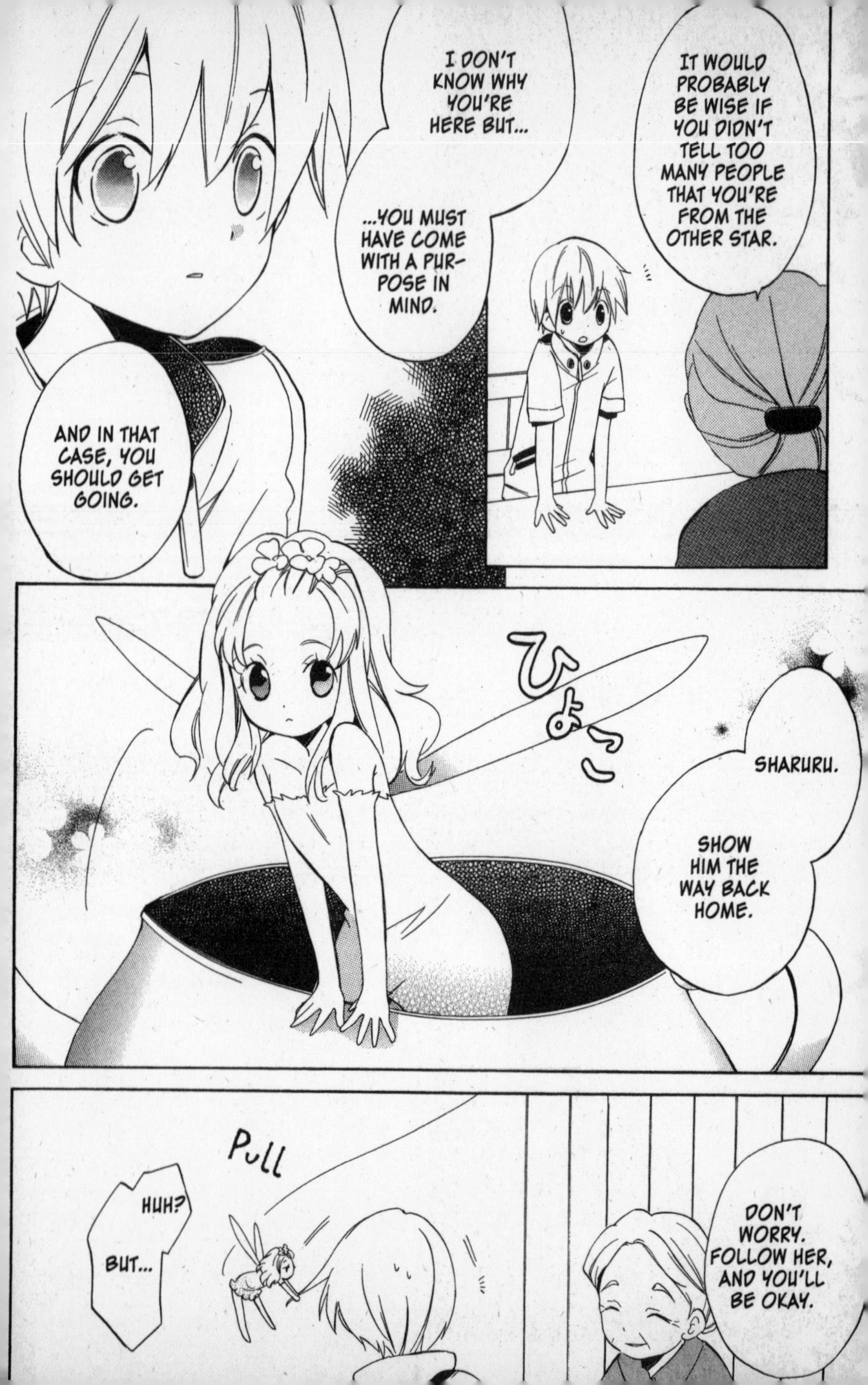
IT WOULD PROBABLY BE WISE IF YOU DIDN'T TELL TOO MANY PEOPLE THAT YOU'RE FROM THE OTHER STAR.
I DON'T KNOW WHY YOU'RE HERE BUT...
...YOU MUST HAVE COME WITH A PUR-POSE IN MIND.
AND IN THAT CASE, YOU SHOULD GET GOING.
SHARURU.
SHOW HIM THE WAY BACK HOME.
ひょっこ
DON'T WORRY. FOLLOW HER, AND YOU'LL BE OKAY.
Pull
HUH?
BUT...

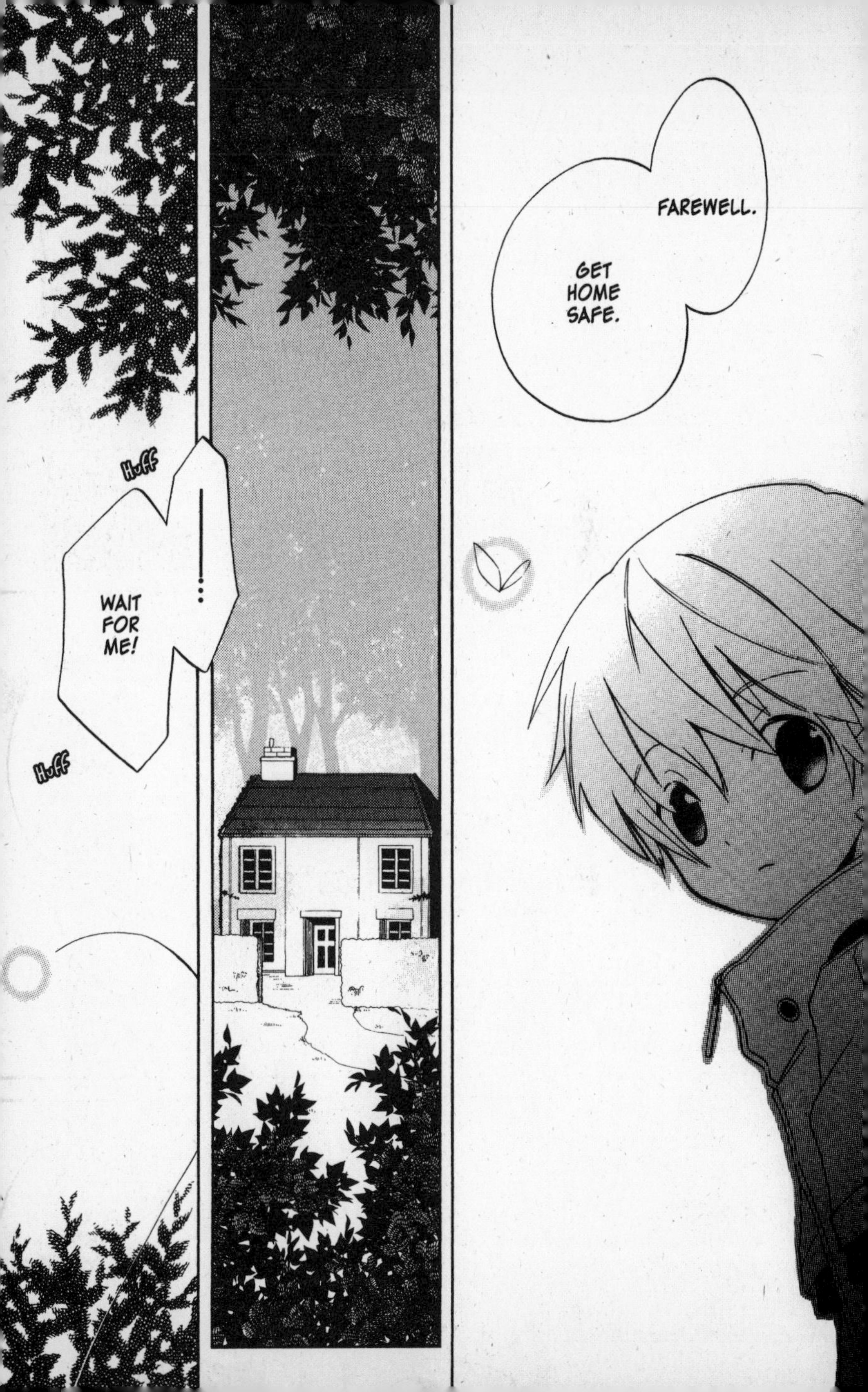
FAREWELL.
GET HOME SAFE.
Huff
......
WAIT FOR ME!
Huff

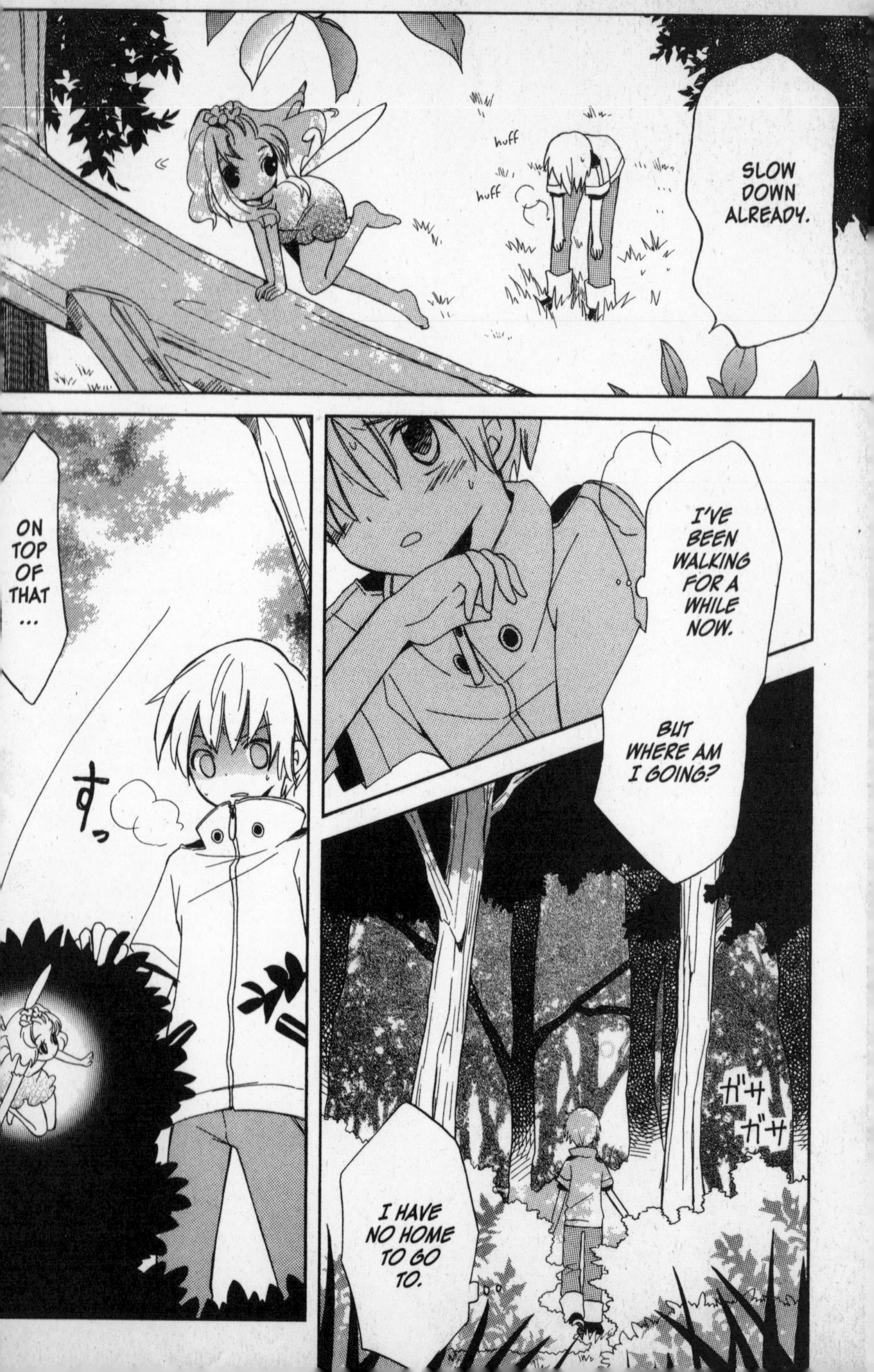
SLOW DOWN ALREADY.
huff
huff
I'VE BEEN WALKING FOR A WHILE NOW.
BUT WHERE AM I GOING?
ガサ
ガサ
I HAVE NO HOME TO GO TO.
ON TOP OF THAT ...
すっ

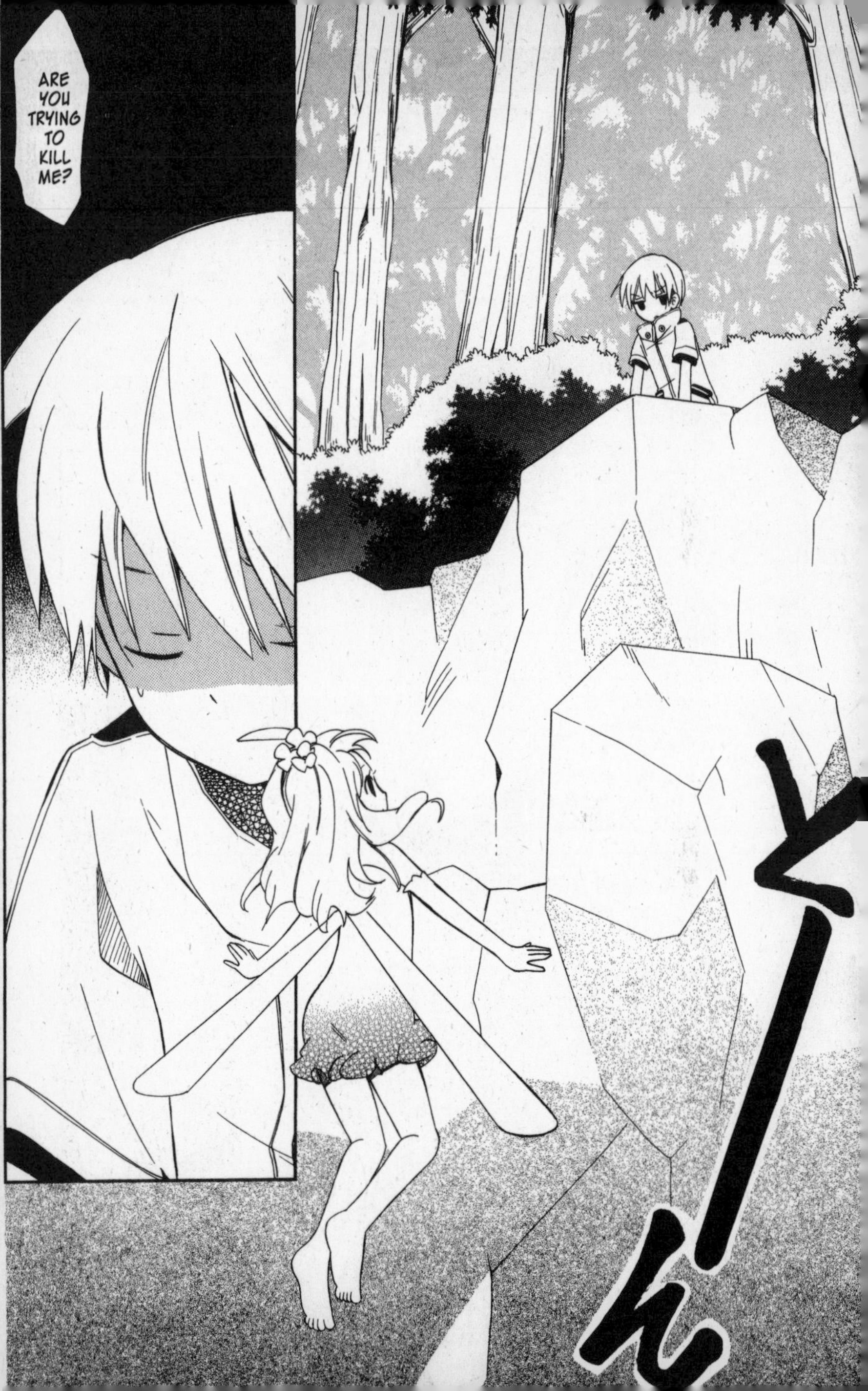
ARE YOU TRYING TO KILL ME?

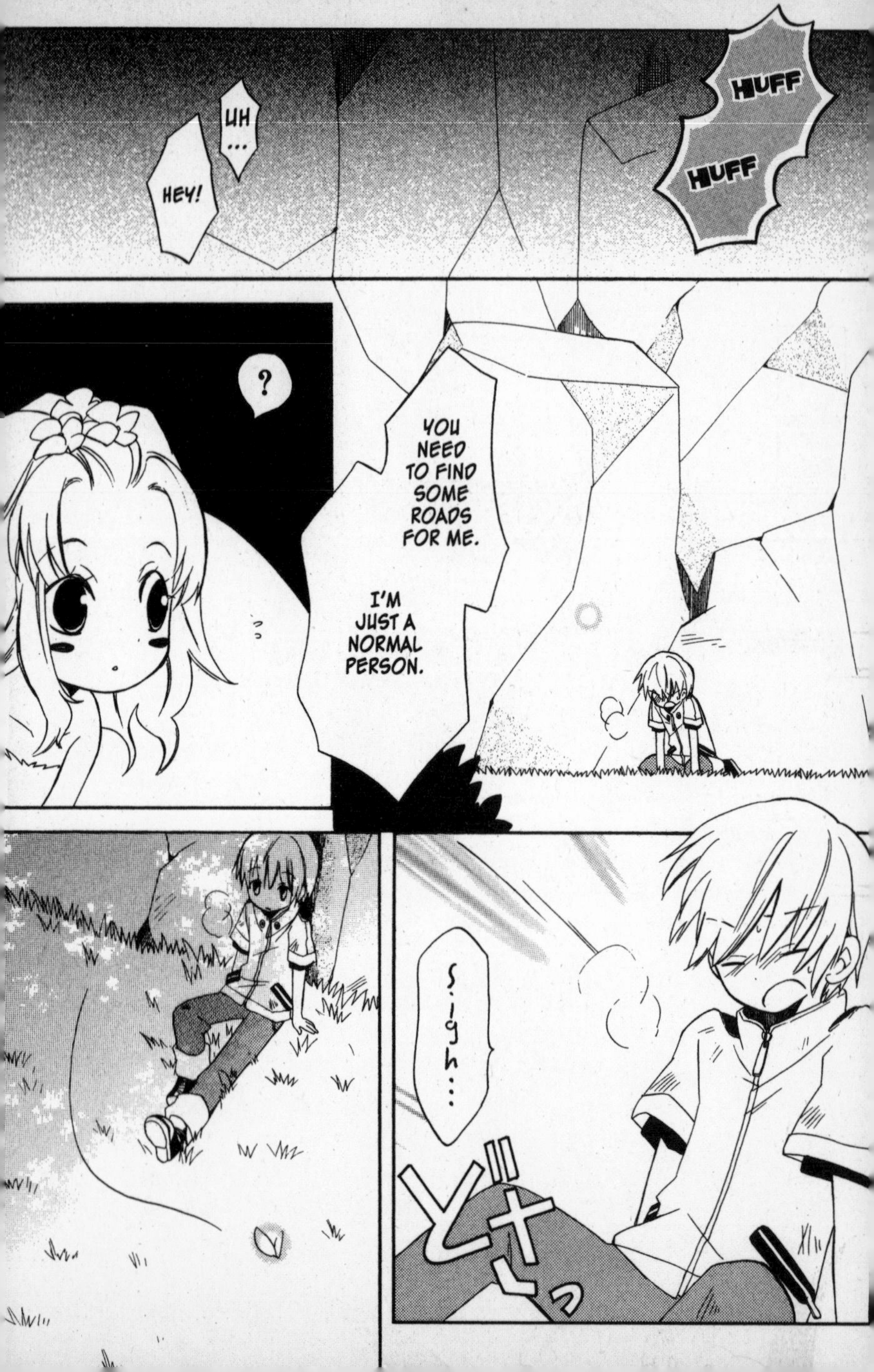
HUFF
HUFF
UH...
HEY!
YOU NEED TO FIND SOME ROADS FOR ME.
I'M JUST A NORMAL PERSON.
?
sigh...
どさっ

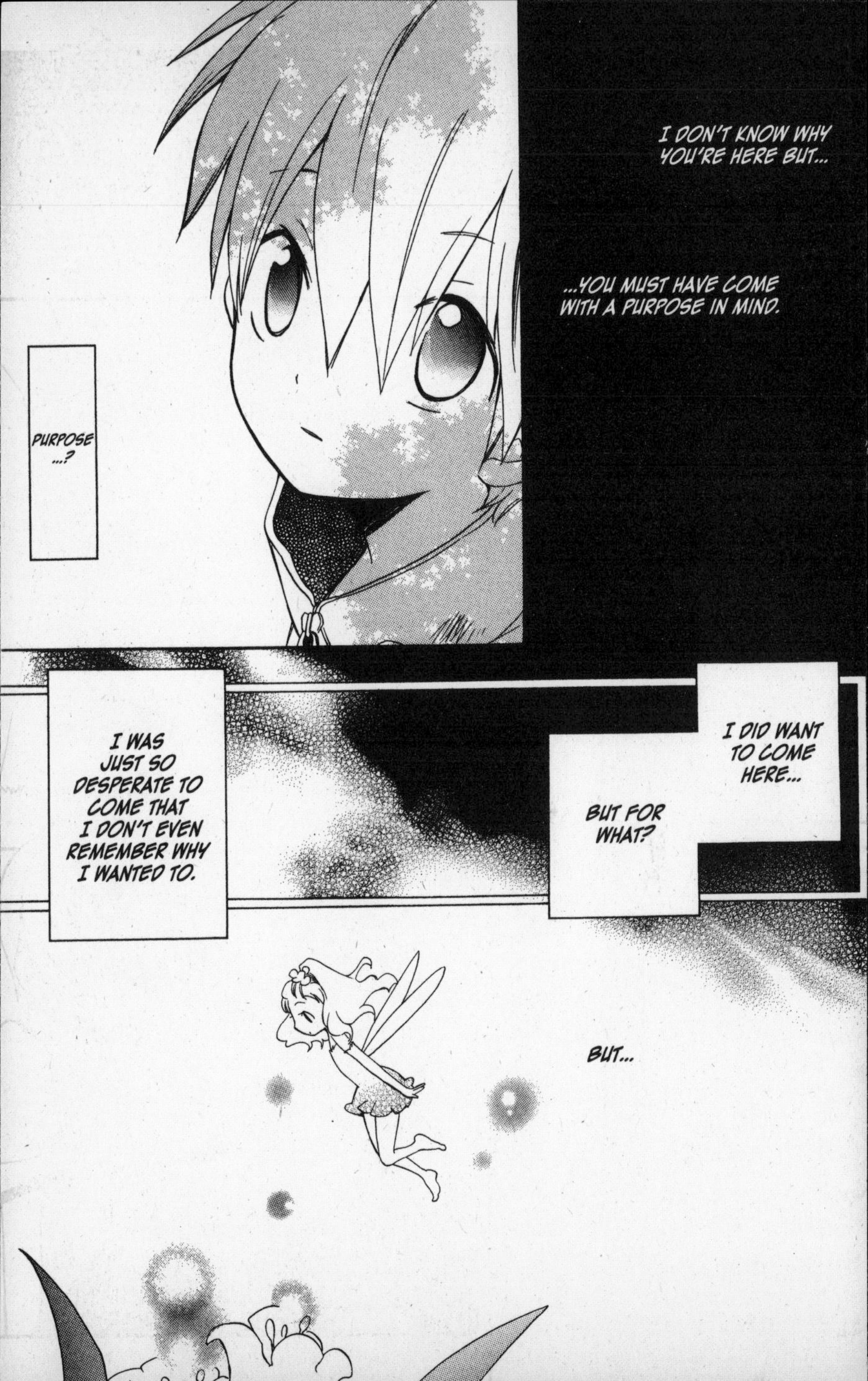
I DON'T KNOW WHY YOU'RE HERE BUT...
...YOU MUST HAVE COME WITH A PURPOSE IN MIND.
PURPOSE ...?
I DID WANT TO COME HERE...
BUT FOR WHAT?
I WAS JUST SO DESPERATE TO COME THAT I DON'T EVEN REMEMBER WHY I WANTED TO.
BUT...

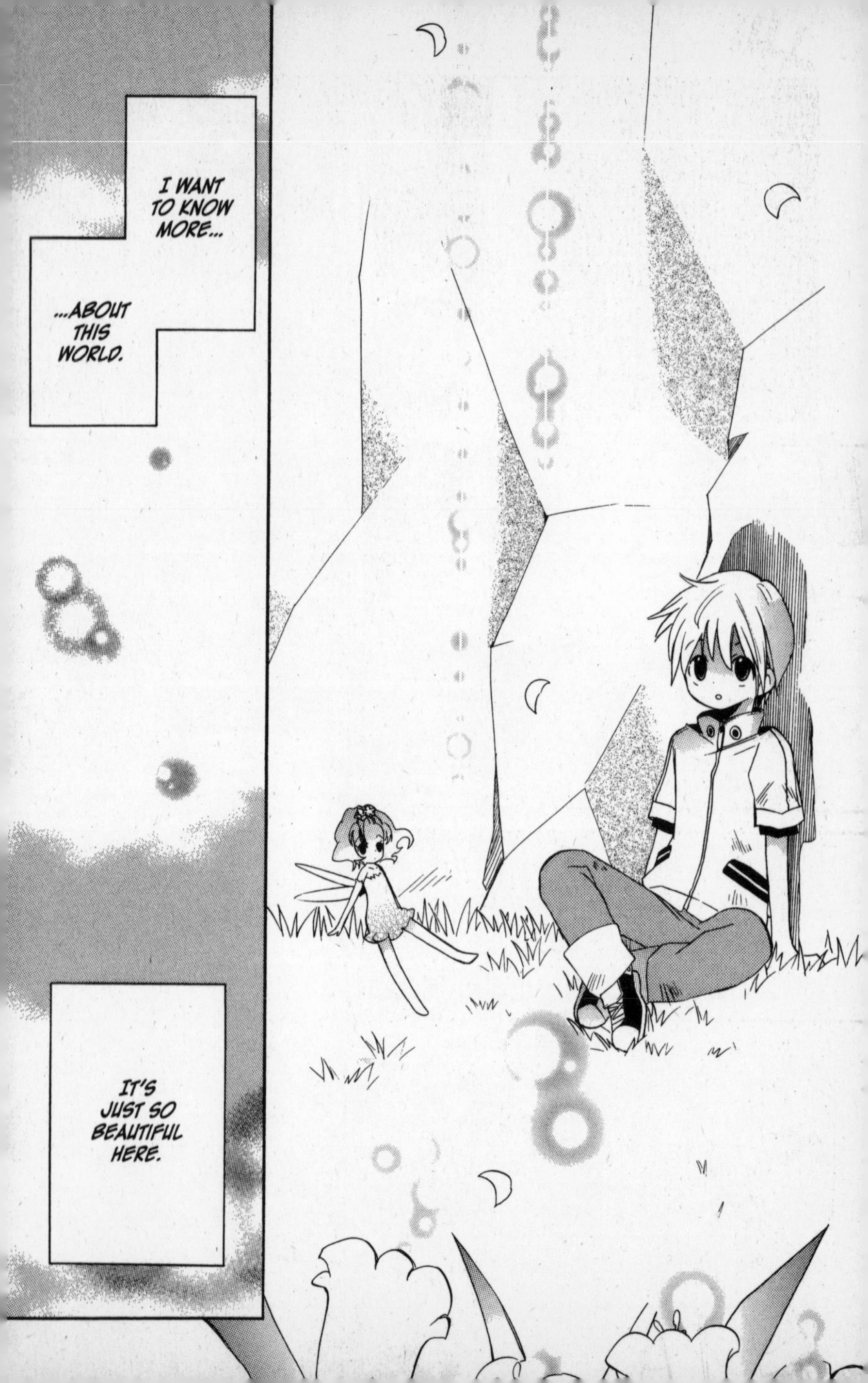
I WANT TO KNOW MORE...
...ABOUT THIS WORLD.
IT'S JUST SO BEAUTIFUL HERE.

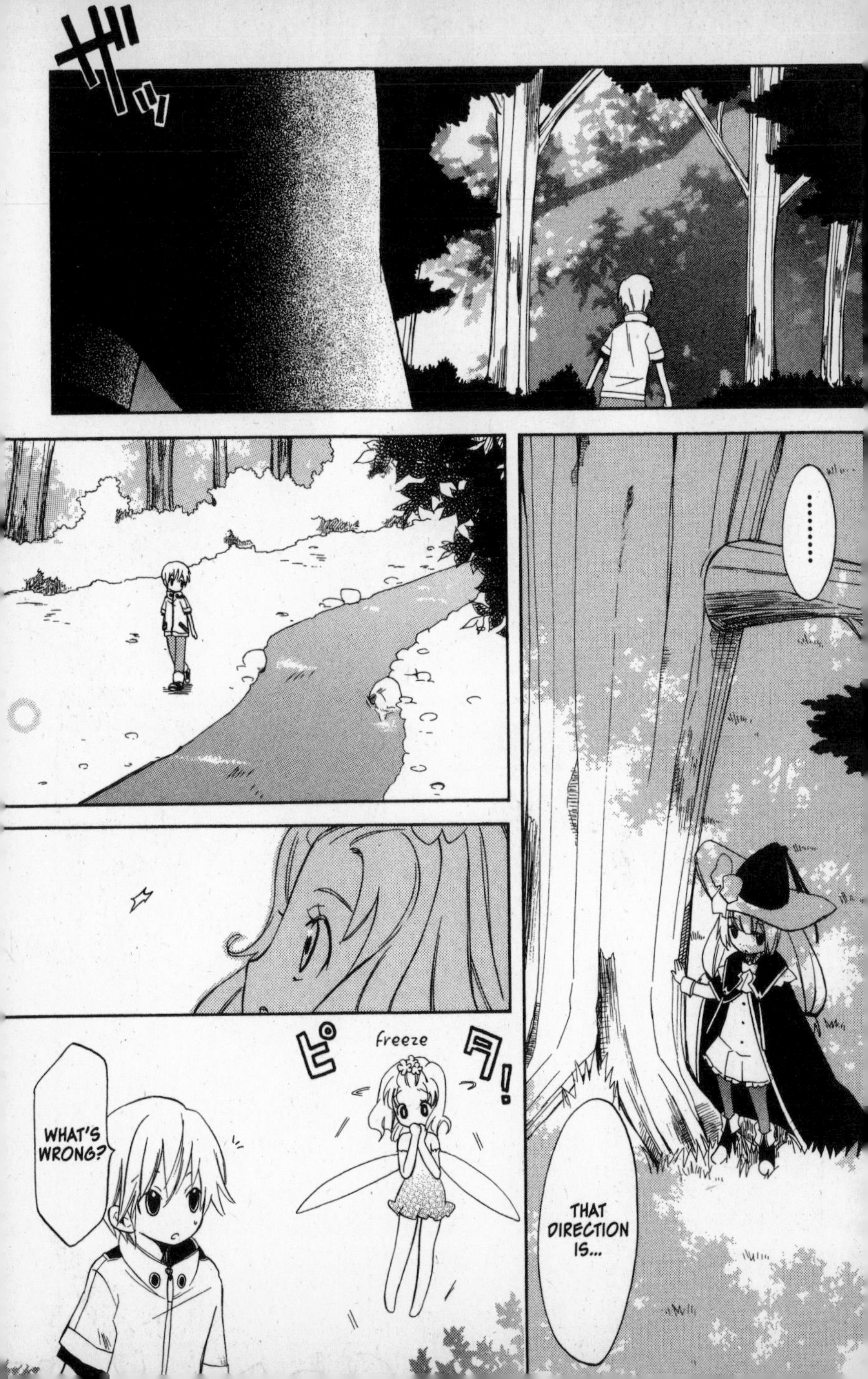
ザッ
......
THAT DIRECTION IS...
ピタ!
freeze
WHAT'S WRONG?

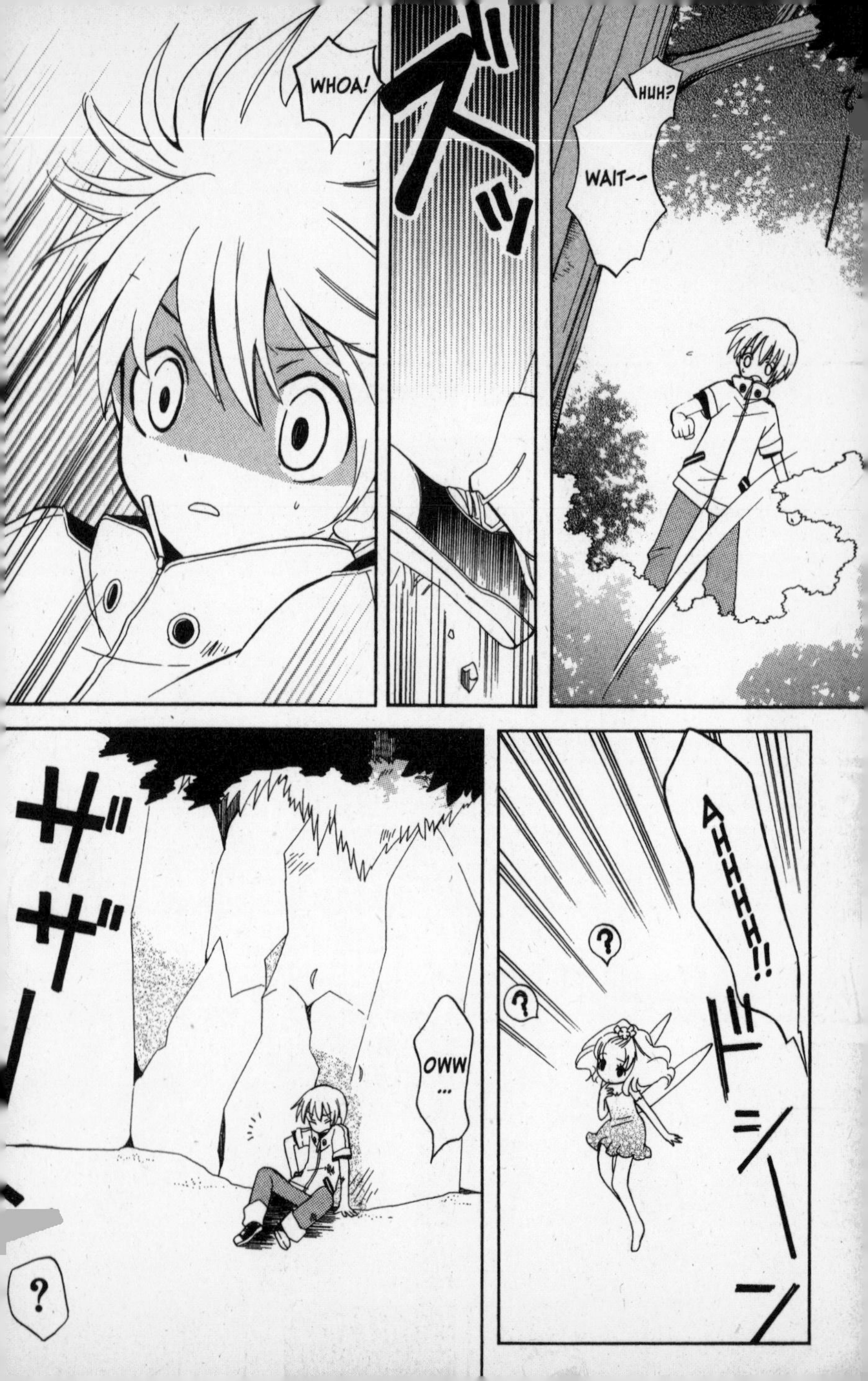
HUH?
WAIT--
WHOA!
AHHHHH!!
?
?
OWW ...
?

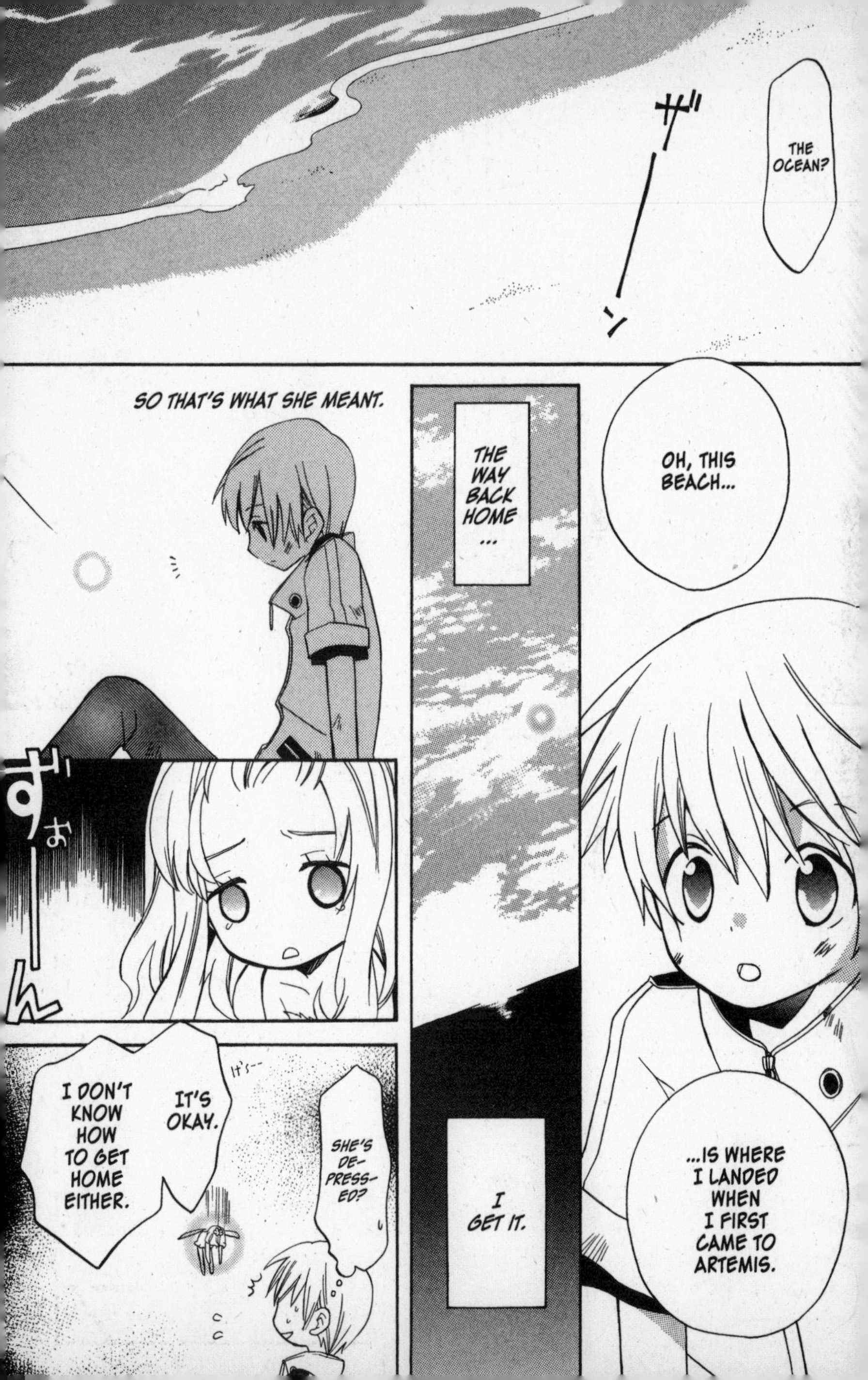
THE OCEAN?
OH, THIS BEACH...
...IS WHERE I LANDED WHEN I FIRST CAME TO ARTEMIS.
THE WAY BACK HOME ...
I GET IT.
SO THAT'S WHAT SHE MEANT.
SHE'S DE-PRESS-ED?
IT'S OKAY.
I DON'T KNOW HOW TO GET HOME EITHER.

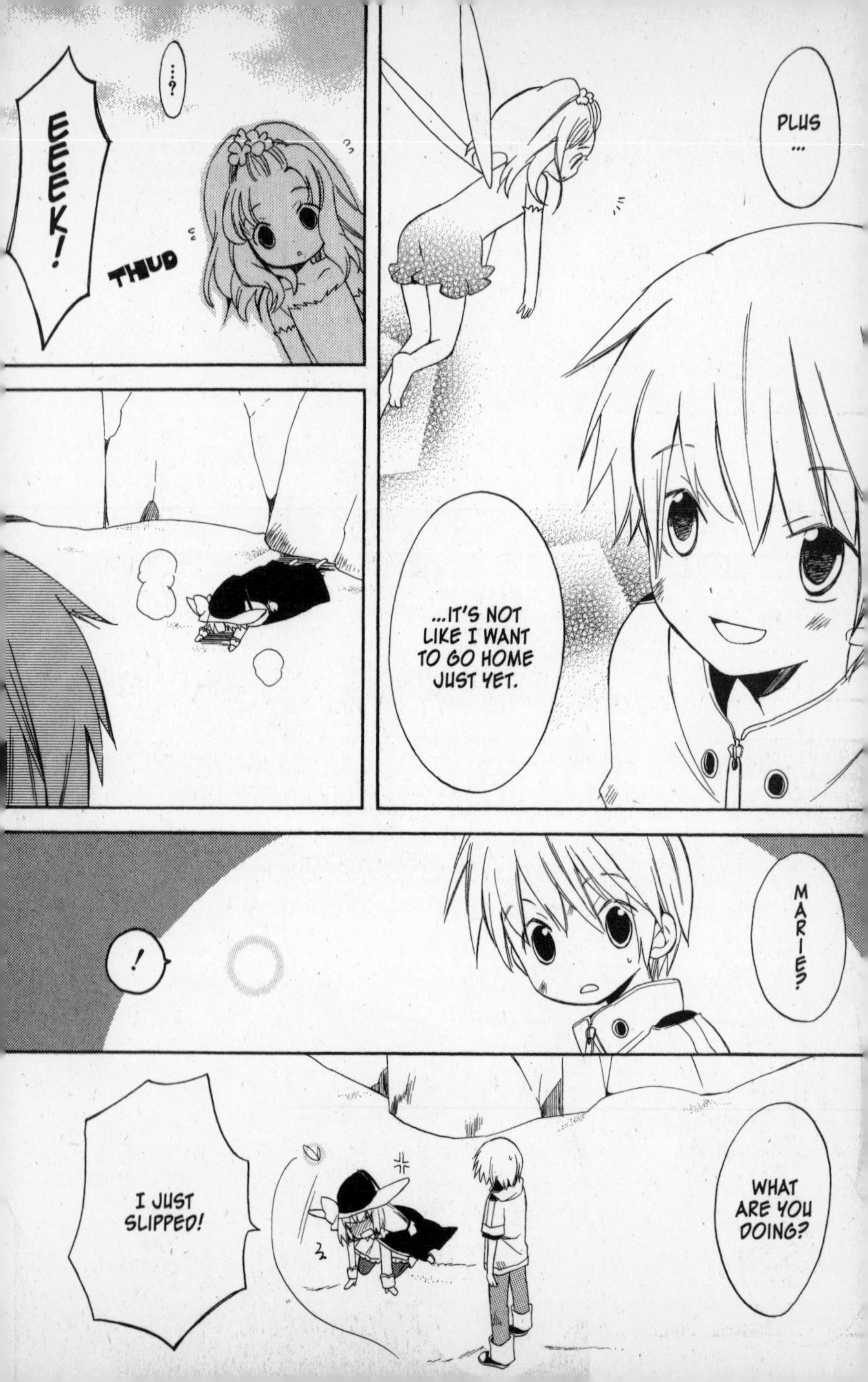
PLUS ...
...IT'S NOT LIKE I WANT TO GO HOME JUST YET.
...?
EEEK!
THUD
MARIE?
!
WHAT ARE YOU DOING?
I JUST SLIPPED!

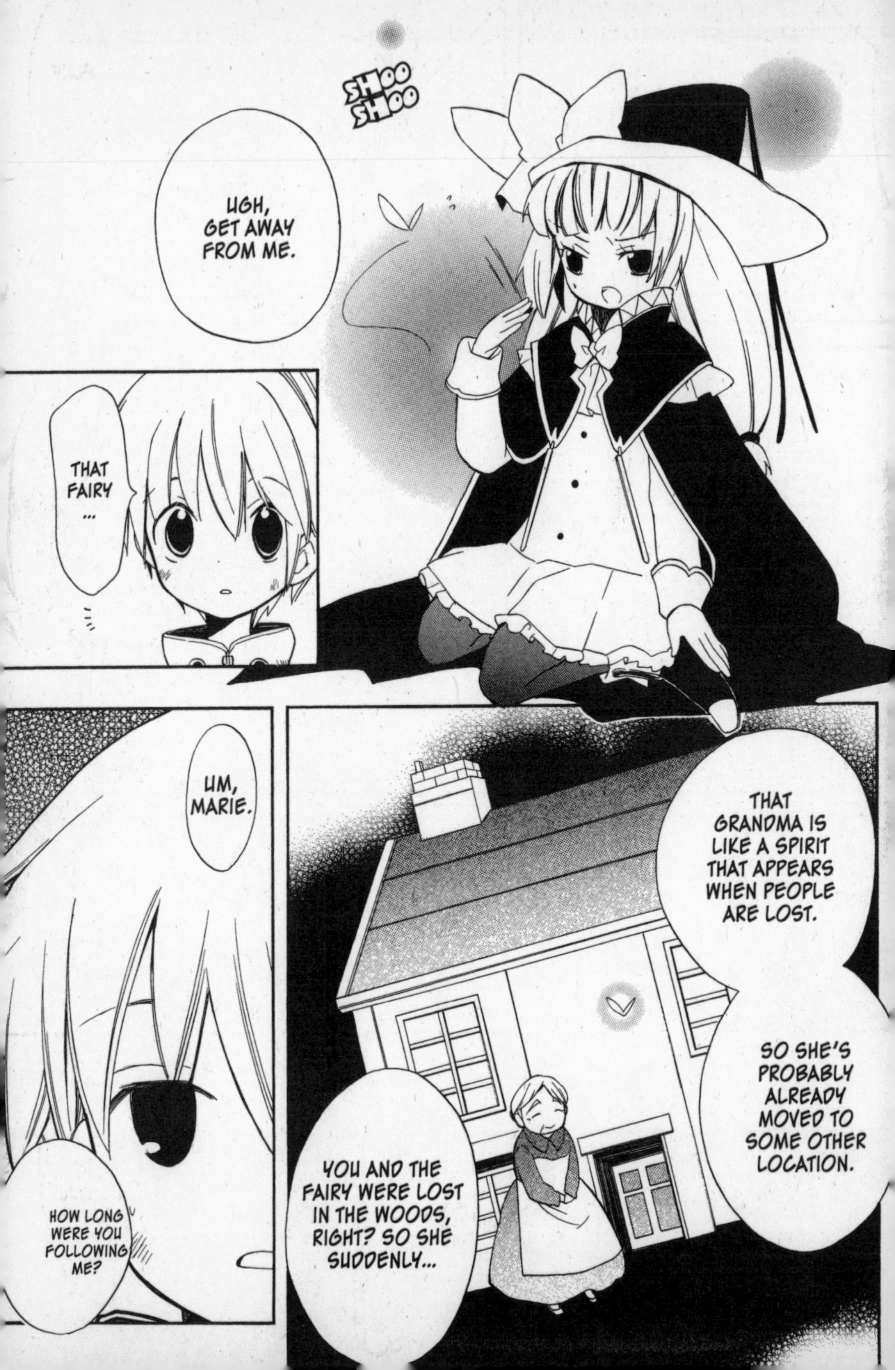
SHOO SHOO
UGH, GET AWAY FROM ME.
THAT FAIRY ...
THAT GRANDMA IS LIKE A SPIRIT THAT APPEARS WHEN PEOPLE ARE LOST.
SO SHE'S PROBABLY ALREADY MOVED TO SOME OTHER LOCATION.
YOU AND THE FAIRY WERE LOST IN THE WOODS, RIGHT? SO SHE SUDDENLY...
UM, MARIE.
HOW LONG WERE YOU FOLLOWING ME?

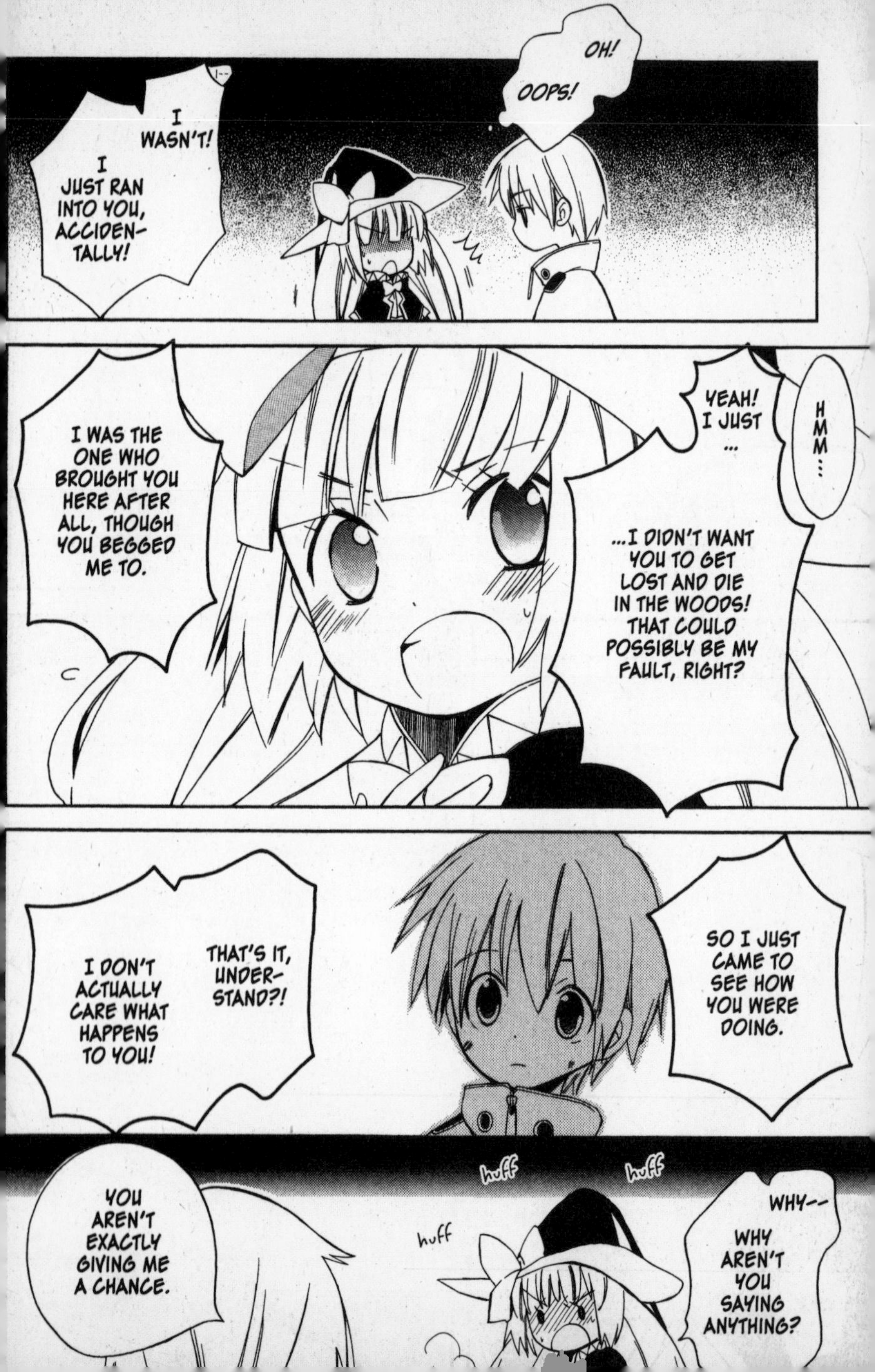
OH!
OOPS!
I--
I WASN'T!
I JUST RAN INTO YOU, ACCIDENTALLY!
HMM...
YEAH! I JUST ...
...I DIDN'T WANT YOU TO GET LOST AND DIE IN THE WOODS! THAT COULD POSSIBLY BE MY FAULT, RIGHT?
I WAS THE ONE WHO BROUGHT YOU HERE AFTER ALL, THOUGH YOU BEGGED ME TO.
SO I JUST CAME TO SEE HOW YOU WERE DOING.
THAT'S IT, UNDERSTAND?!
I DON'T ACTUALLY CARE WHAT HAPPENS TO YOU!
huff
huff
huff
WHY--
WHY AREN'T YOU SAYING ANYTHING?
YOU AREN'T EXACTLY GIVING ME A CHANCE.

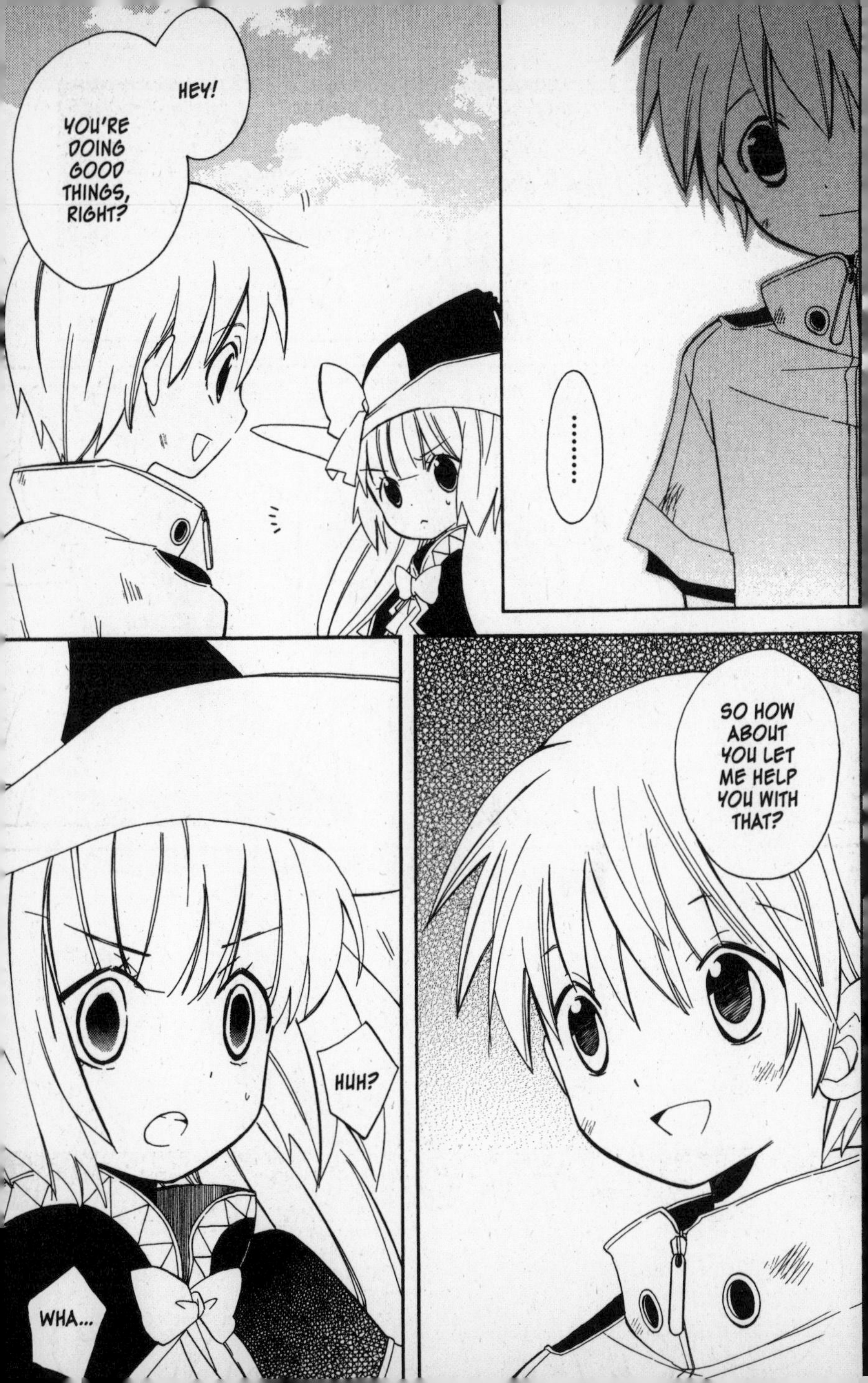

......
HEY!
YOU'RE DOING GOOD THINGS, RIGHT?
SO HOW ABOUT YOU LET ME HELP YOU WITH THAT?
HUH?
WHA...

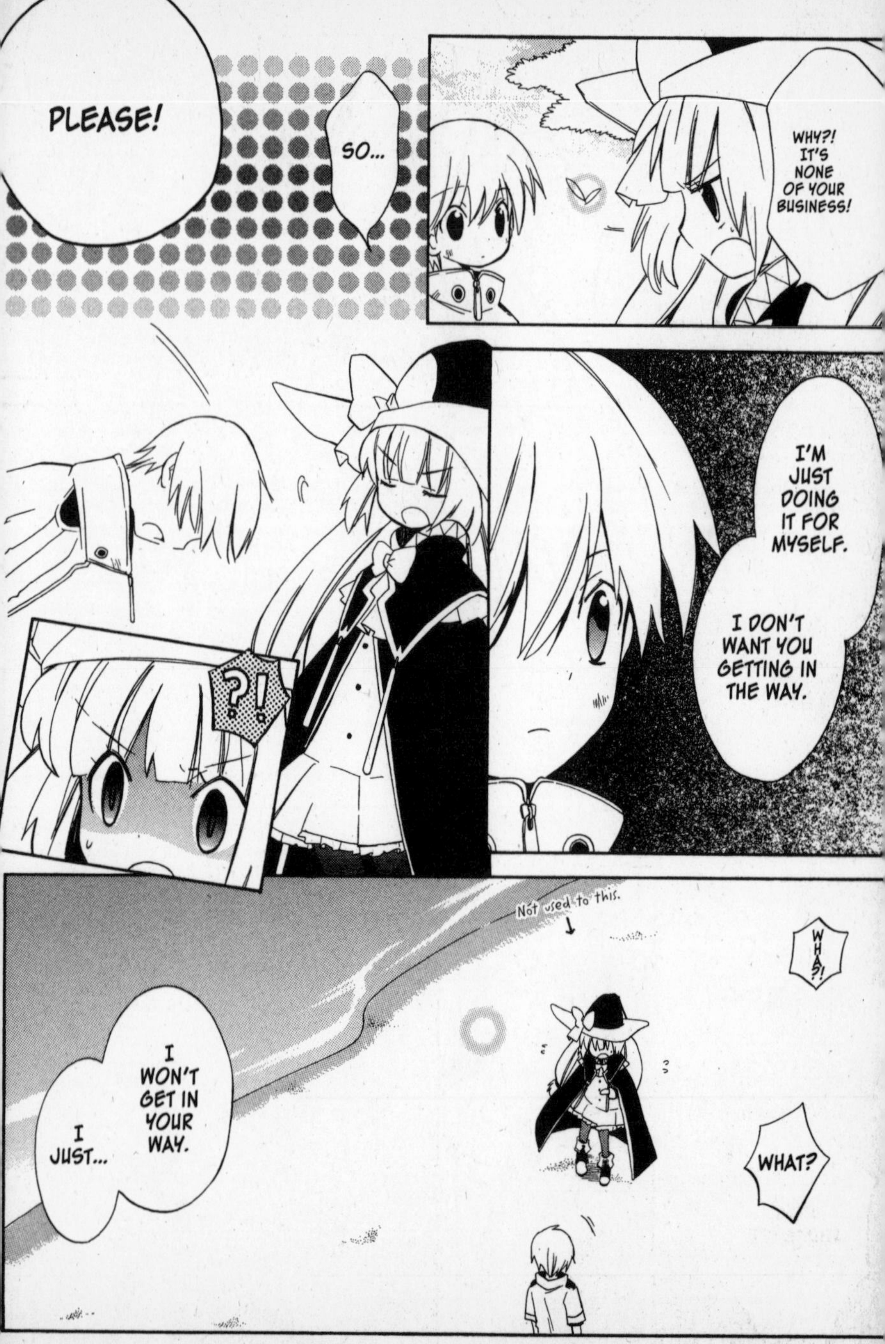
WHY?! IT'S NONE OF YOUR BUSINESS!
SO...
PLEASE!
I'M JUST DOING IT FOR MYSELF.
I DON'T WANT YOU GETTING IN THE WAY.
?!
WHA?!
WHAT?
Not used to this.
I WON'T GET IN YOUR WAY.
I JUST...

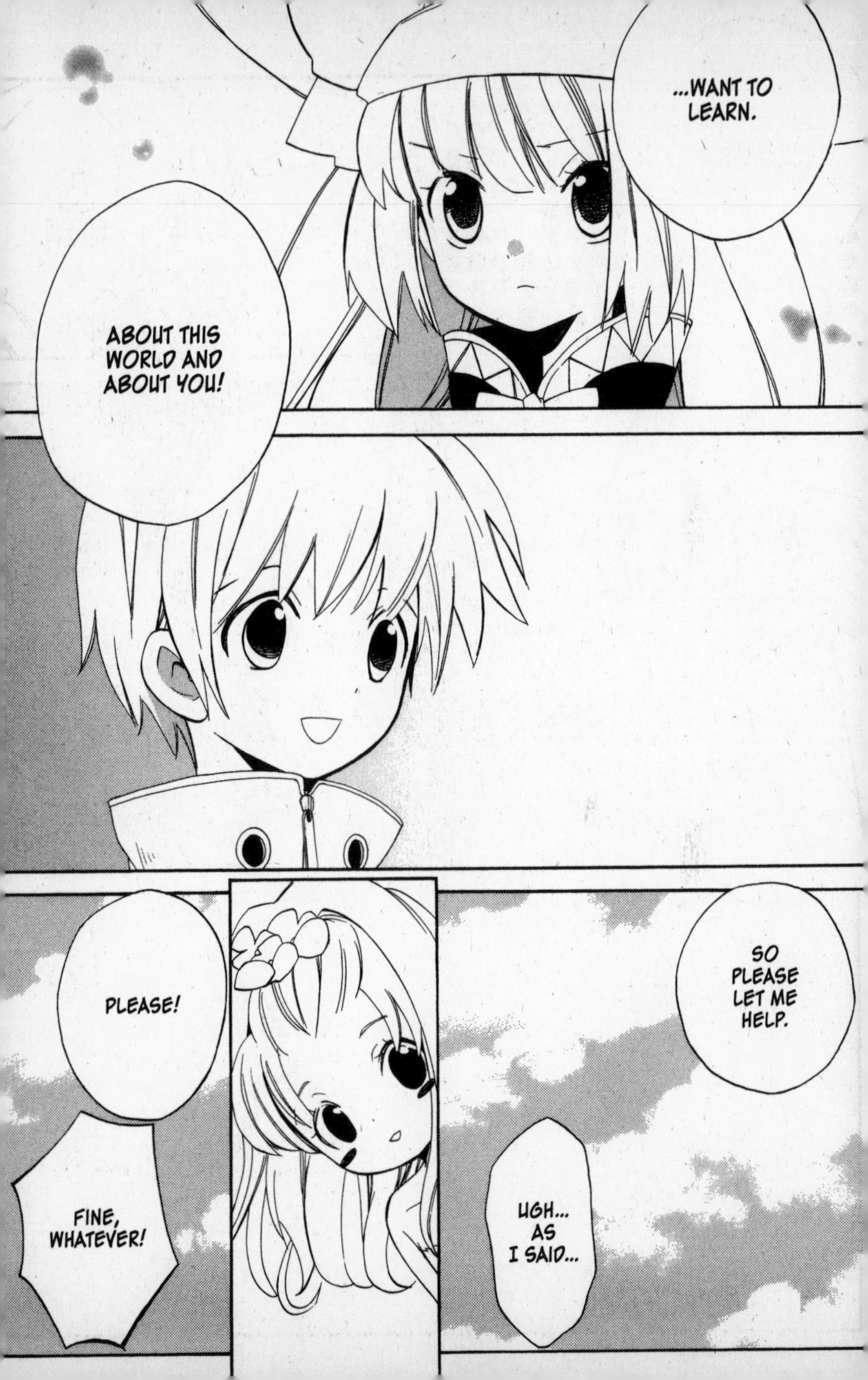
...WANT TO LEARN.
ABOUT THIS WORLD AND ABOUT YOU!
SO PLEASE LET ME HELP.
UGH... AS I SAID...
PLEASE!
FINE, WHATEVER!

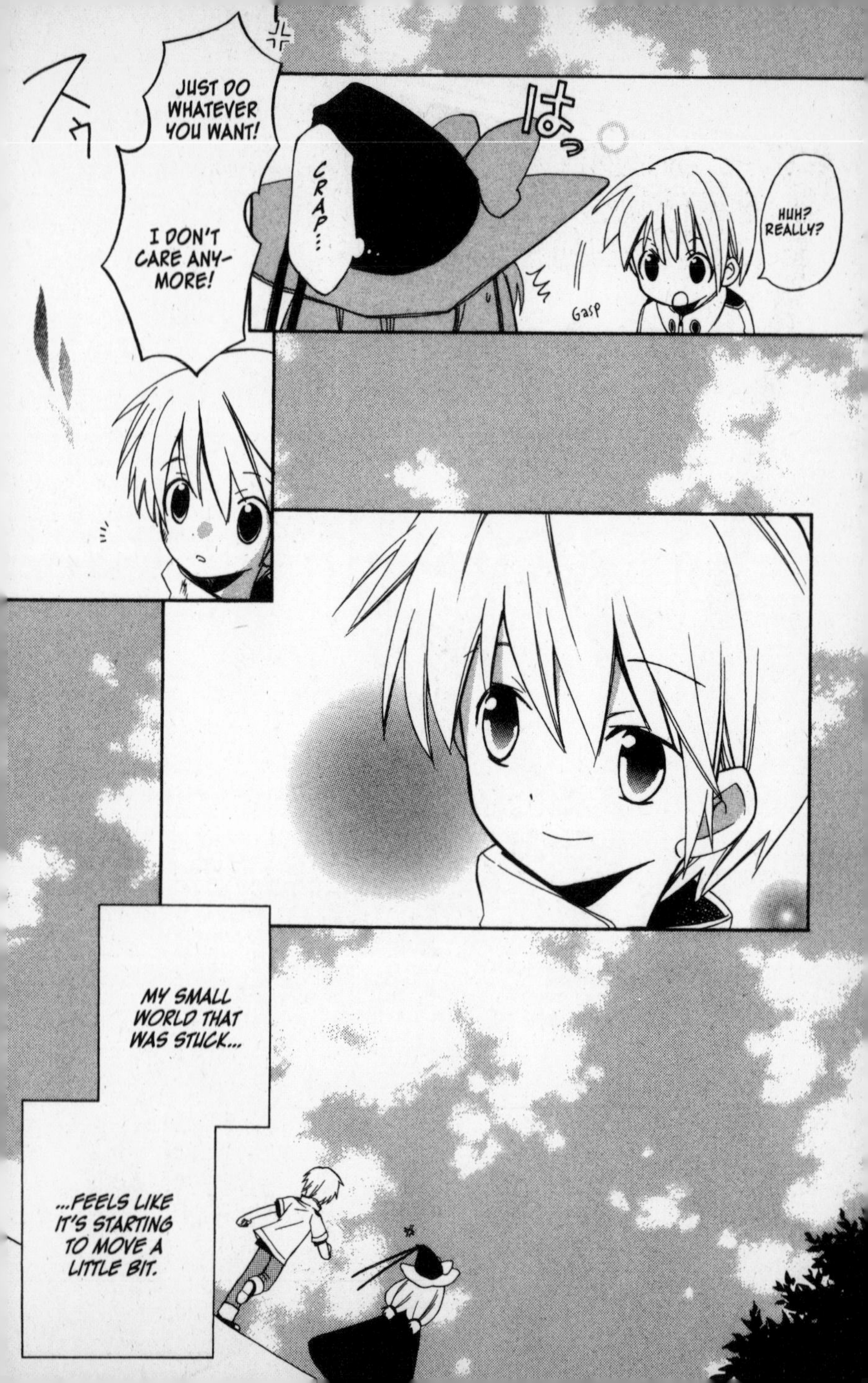
はっ
HUH? REALLY?
Gasp
CRAP...
JUST DO WHATEVER YOU WANT!
I DON'T CARE ANY-MORE!
MY SMALL WORLD THAT WAS STUCK...
...FEELS LIKE IT'S STARTING TO MOVE A LITTLE BIT.

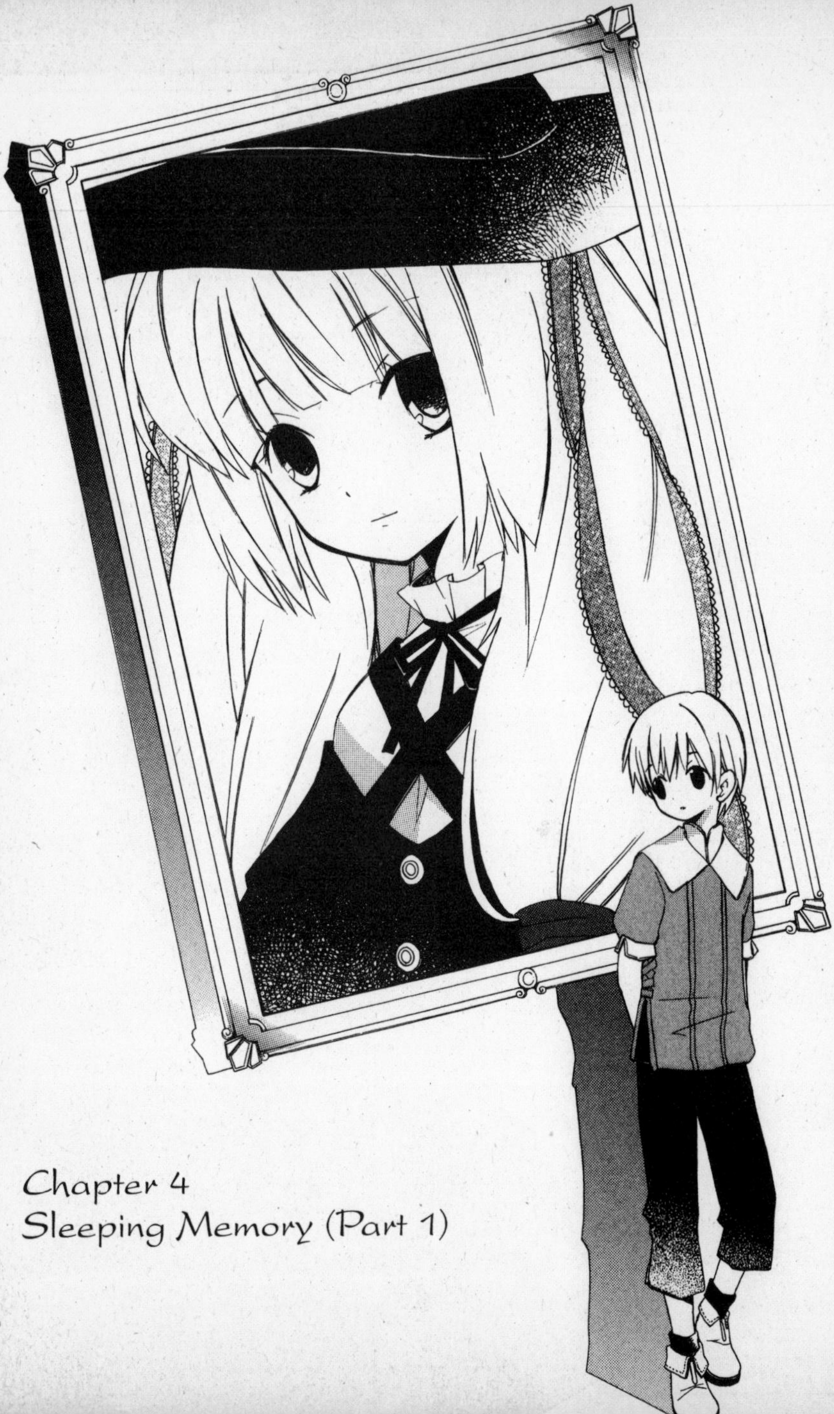

Chapter 4
Sleeping Memory (Part 1)

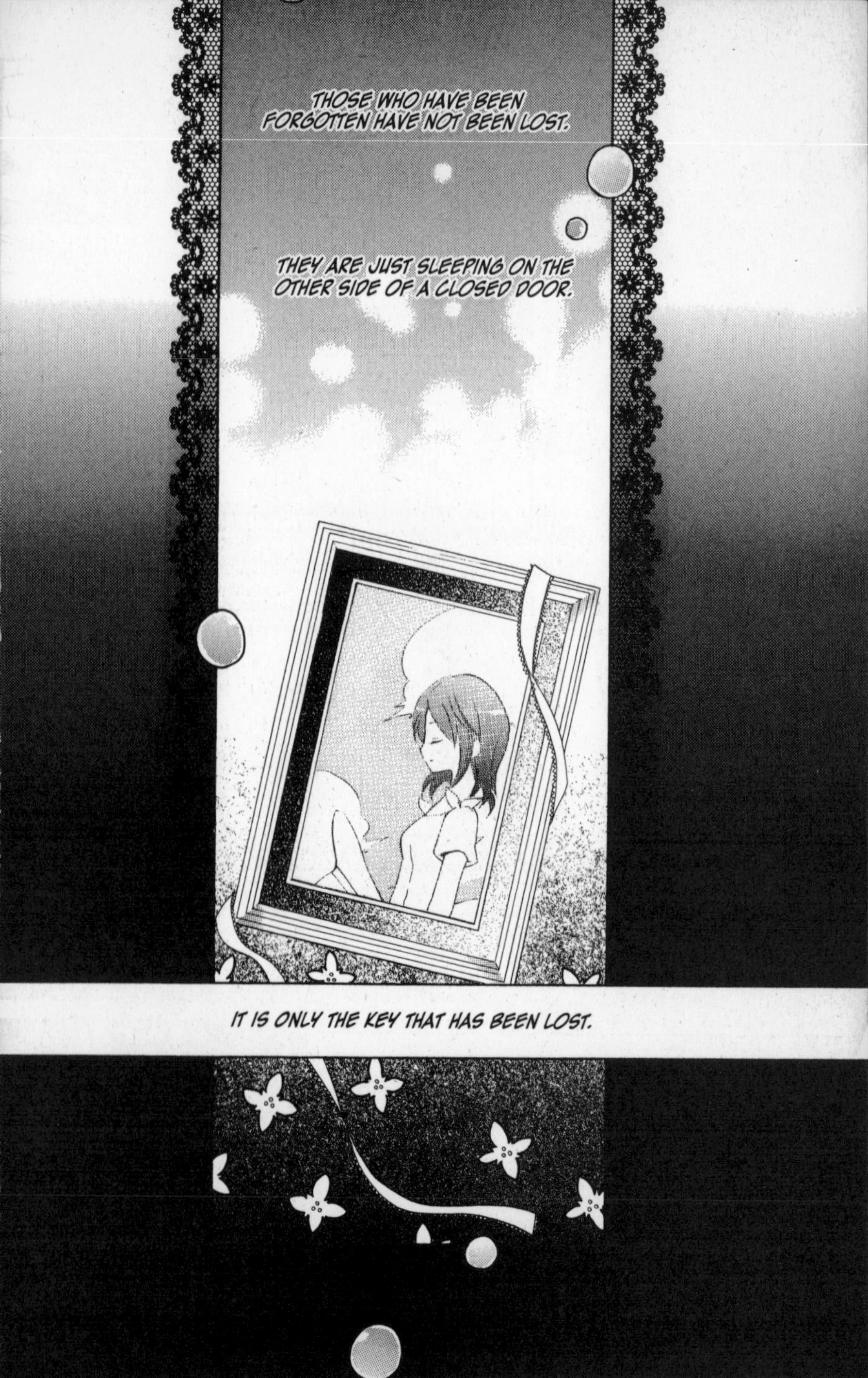
THOSE WHO HAVE BEEN FORGOTTEN HAVE NOT BEEN LOST.
THEY ARE JUST SLEEPING ON THE OTHER SIDE OF A CLOSED DOOR.
IT IS ONLY THE KEY THAT HAS BEEN LOST.

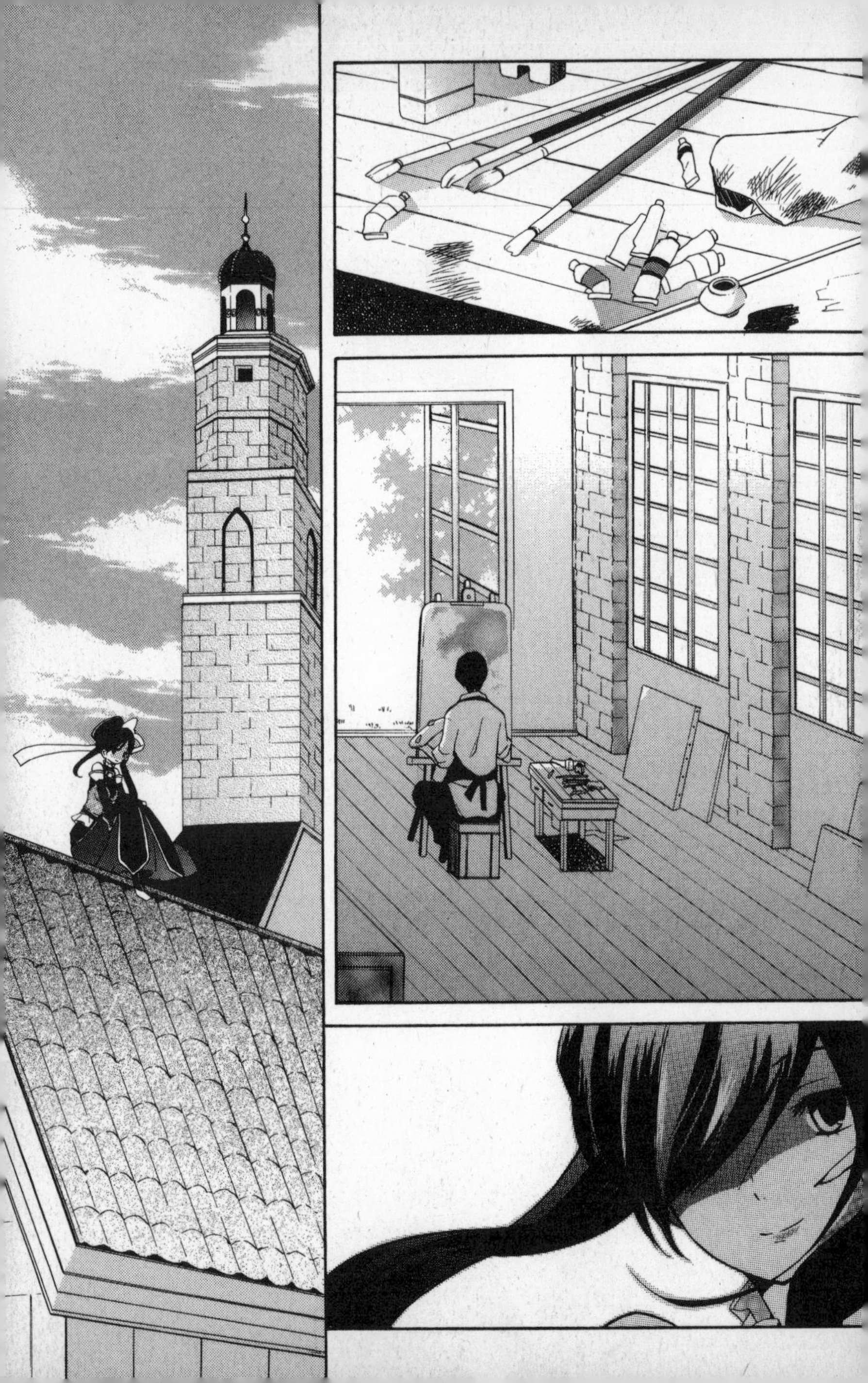

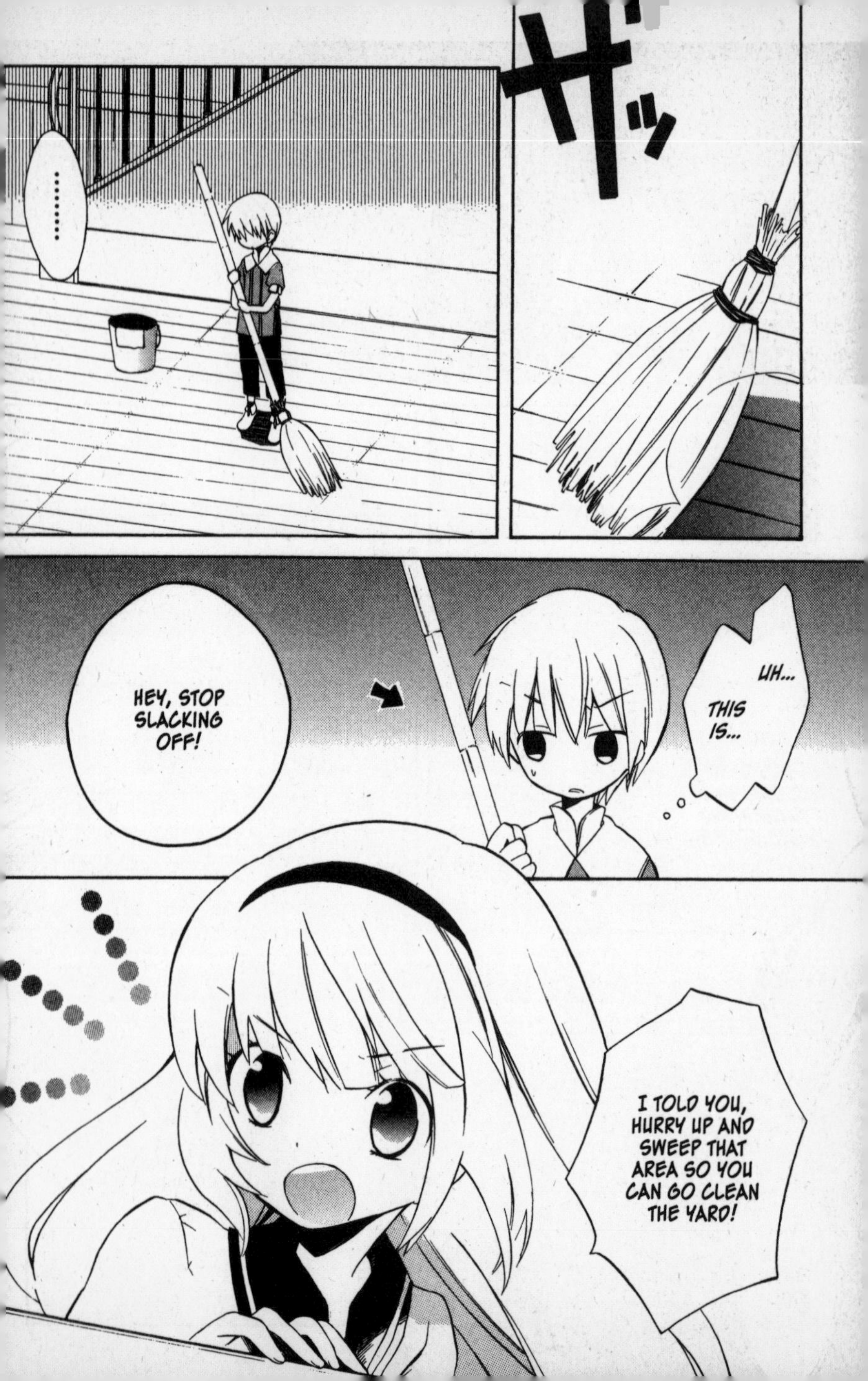
ザッ
......
UH... THIS IS...
HEY, STOP SLACKING OFF!
I TOLD YOU, HURRY UP AND SWEEP THAT AREA SO YOU CAN GO CLEAN THE YARD!

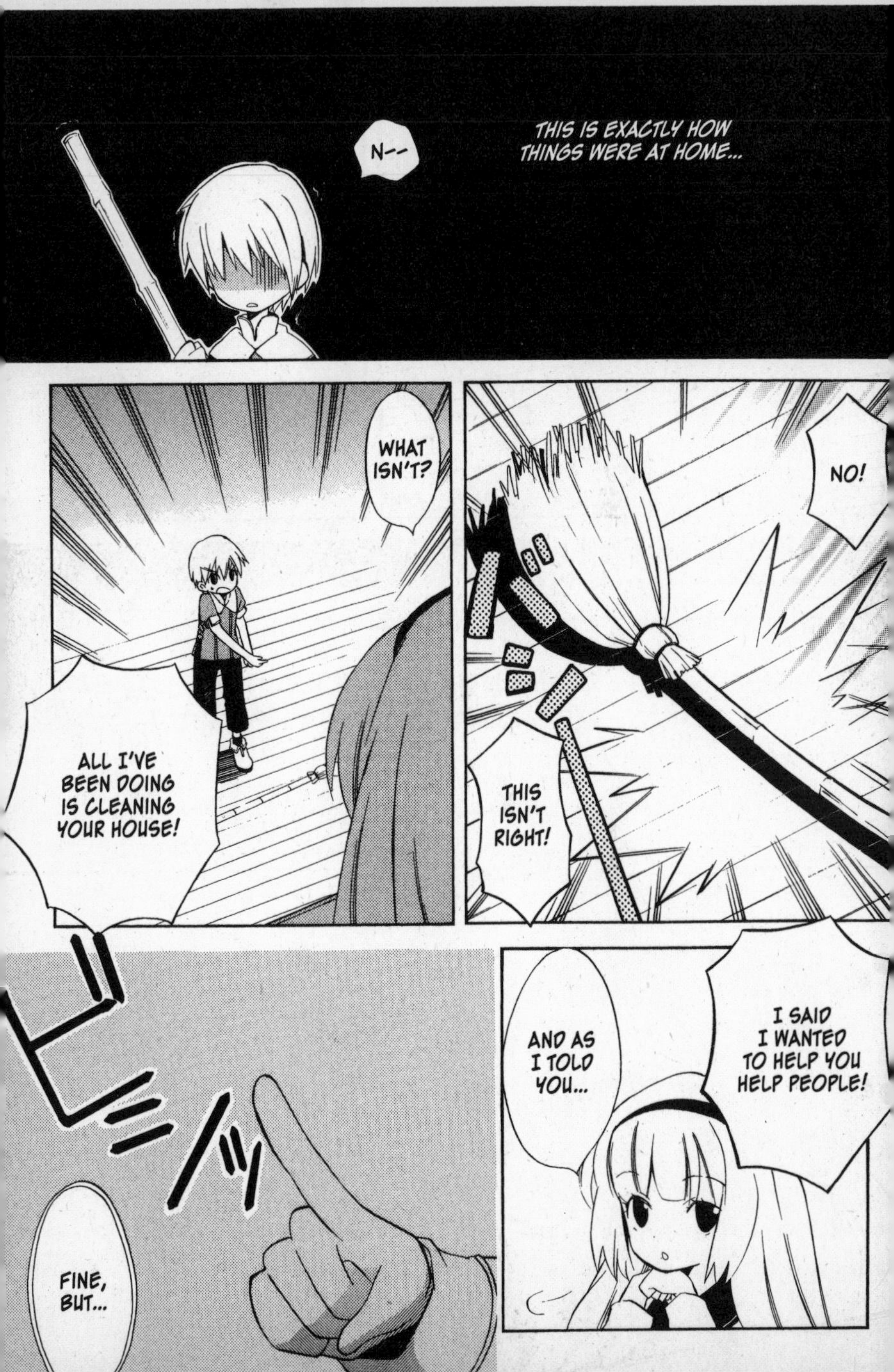
THIS IS EXACTLY HOW THINGS WERE AT HOME...
N--
NO!
THIS ISN'T RIGHT!
WHAT ISN'T?
ALL I'VE BEEN DOING IS CLEANING YOUR HOUSE!
I SAID I WANTED TO HELP YOU HELP PEOPLE!
AND AS I TOLD YOU...
FINE, BUT...

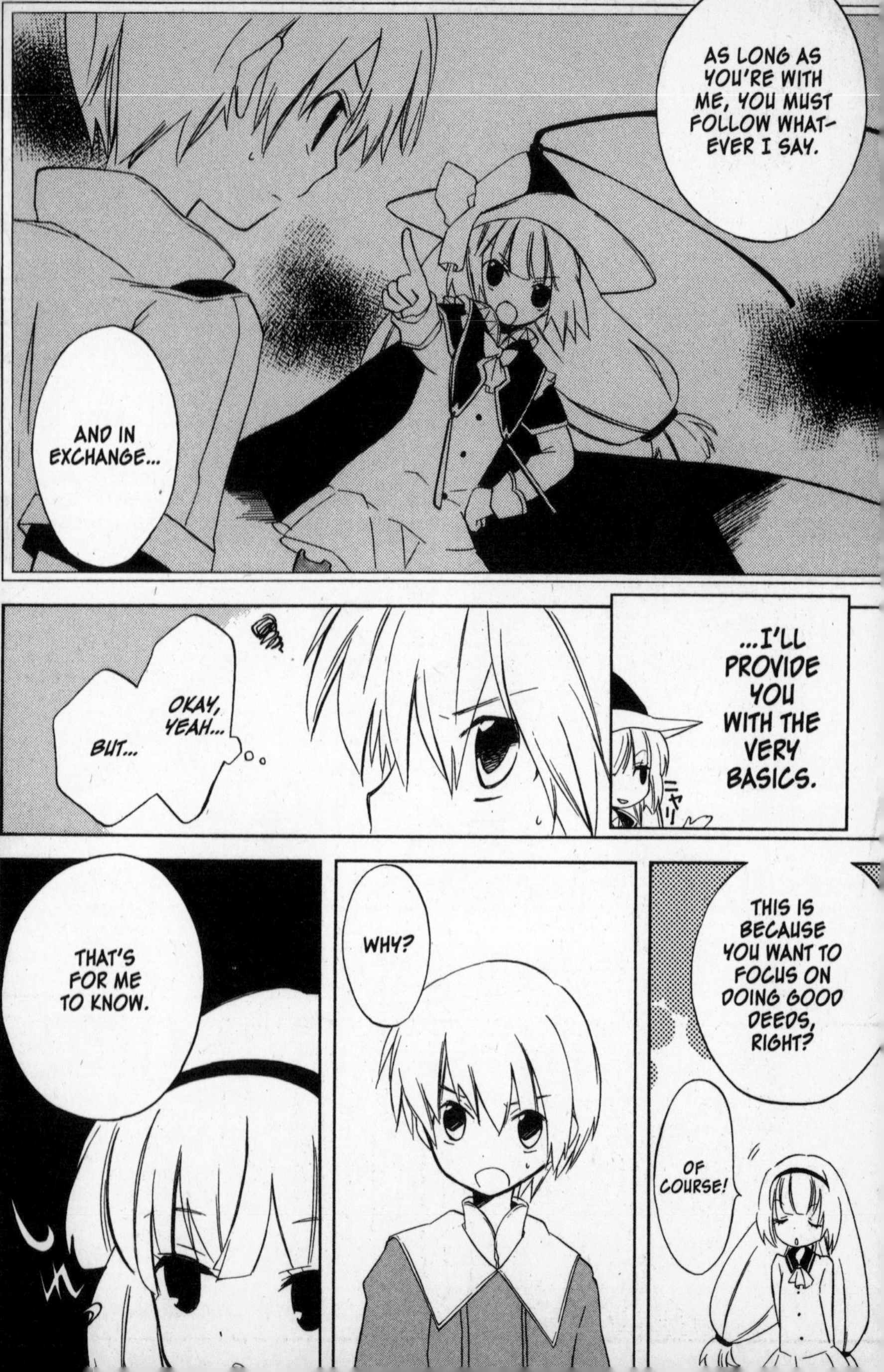
AS LONG AS YOU'RE WITH ME, YOU MUST FOLLOW WHAT-EVER I SAY.
AND IN EXCHANGE...
...I'LL PROVIDE YOU WITH THE VERY BASICS.
ニヤリ
OKAY, YEAH... BUT...
THIS IS BECAUSE YOU WANT TO FOCUS ON DOING GOOD DEEDS, RIGHT?
OF COURSE!
WHY?
THAT'S FOR ME TO KNOW.

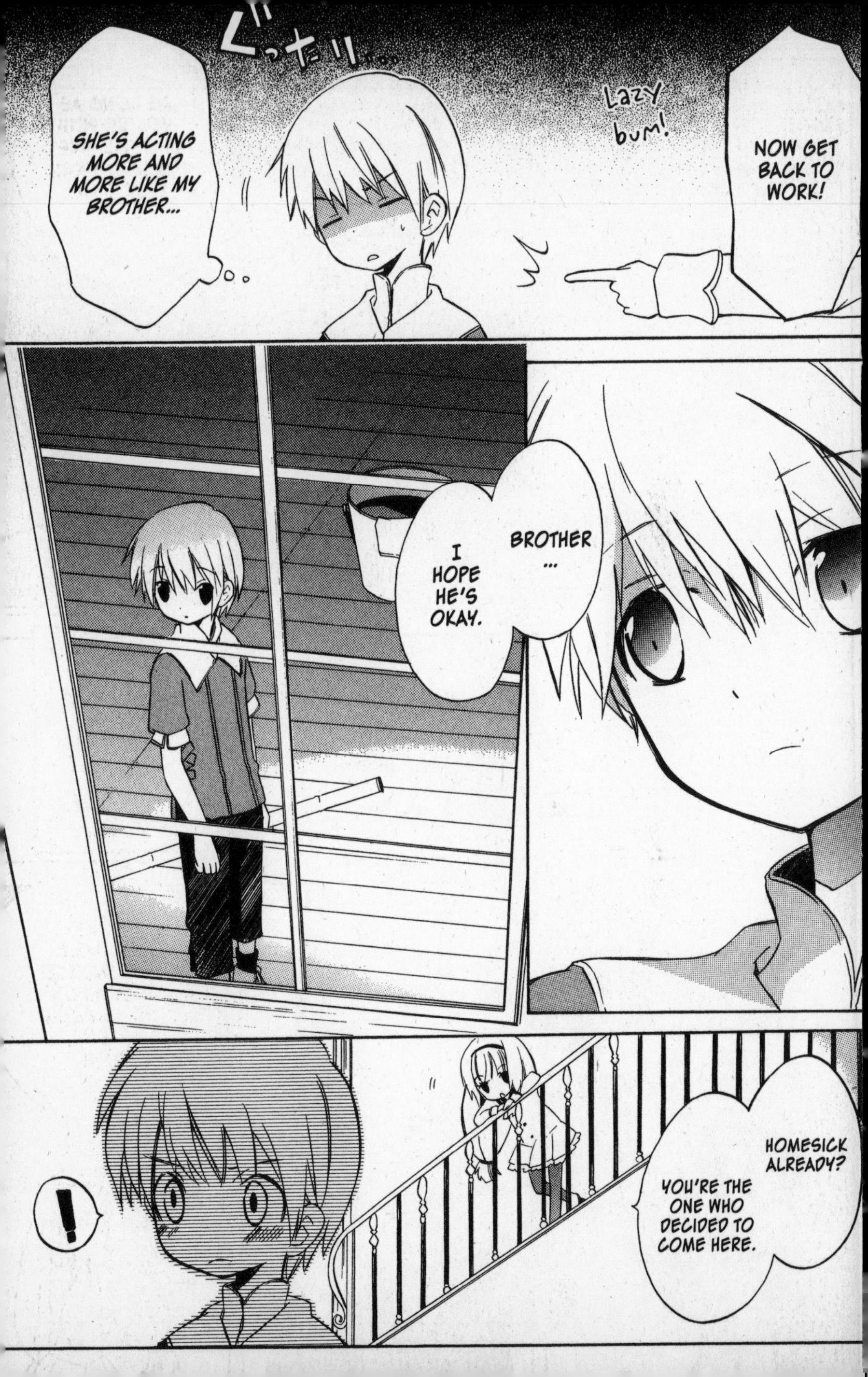
NOW GET BACK TO WORK!
Lazy bum!
ぐったり
SHE'S ACTING MORE AND MORE LIKE MY BROTHER...
BROTHER ...
I HOPE HE'S OKAY.
HOMESICK ALREADY?
YOU'RE THE ONE WHO DECIDED TO COME HERE.
!

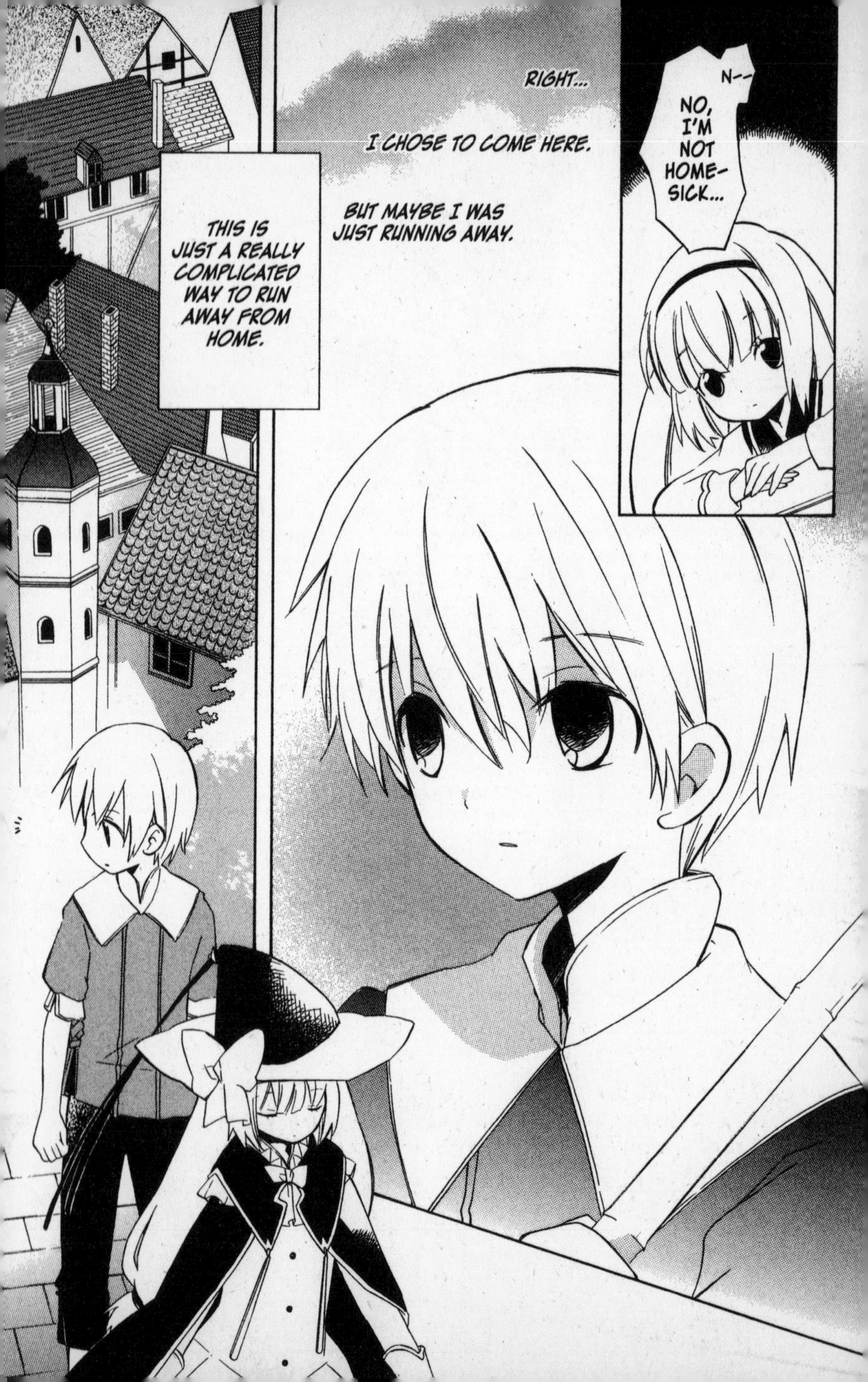
N--
NO, I'M NOT HOME-SICK...
RIGHT...
I CHOSE TO COME HERE.
BUT MAYBE I WAS JUST RUNNING AWAY.
THIS IS JUST A REALLY COMPLICATED WAY TO RUN AWAY FROM HOME.

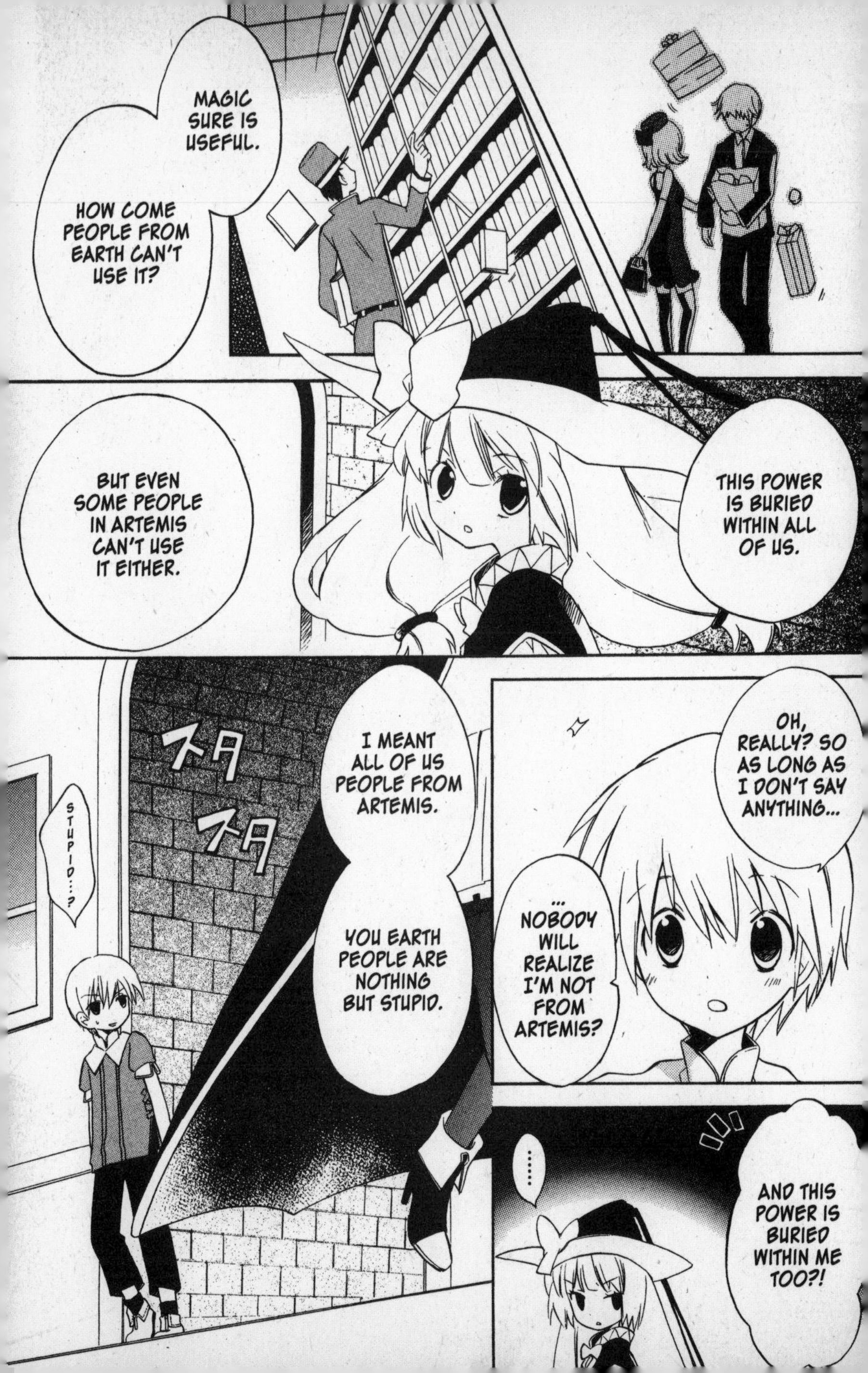
MAGIC SURE IS USEFUL.
HOW COME PEOPLE FROM EARTH CAN'T USE IT?
BUT EVEN SOME PEOPLE IN ARTEMIS CAN'T USE IT EITHER.
THIS POWER IS BURIED WITHIN ALL OF US.
OH, REALLY? SO AS LONG AS I DON'T SAY ANYTHING...
...NOBODY WILL REALIZE I'M NOT FROM ARTEMIS?
AND THIS POWER IS BURIED WITHIN ME TOO?!
......
I MEANT ALL OF US PEOPLE FROM ARTEMIS.
YOU EARTH PEOPLE ARE NOTHING BUT STUPID.
スタ
スタ
STUPID...?

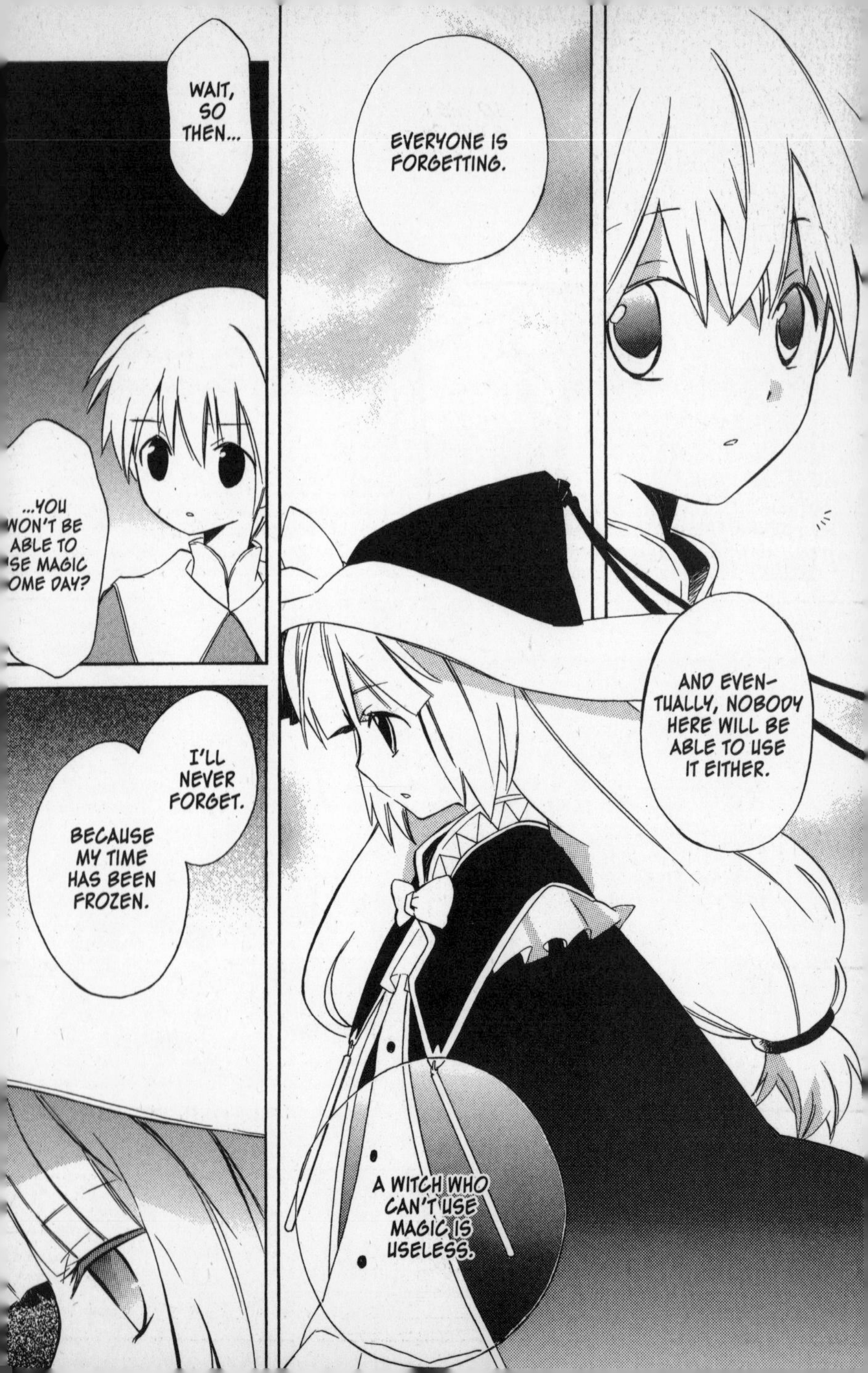
EVERYONE IS FORGETTING.
AND EVEN-TUALLY, NOBODY HERE WILL BE ABLE TO USE IT EITHER.
A WITCH WHO CAN'T USE MAGIC IS USELESS.
WAIT, SO THEN...
...YOU WON'T BE ABLE TO SE MAGIC OME DAY?
I'LL NEVER FORGET.
BECAUSE MY TIME HAS BEEN FROZEN.

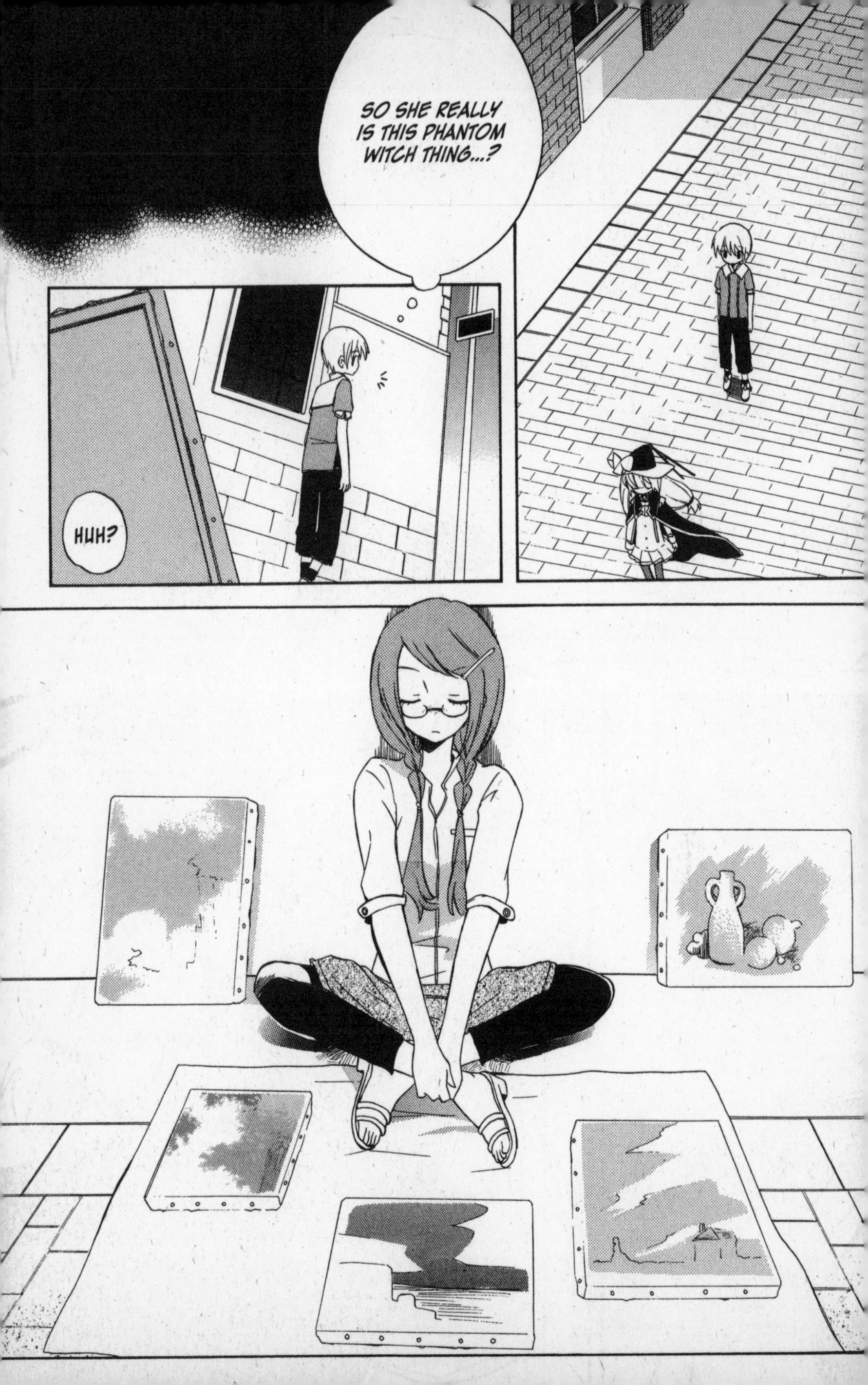
SO SHE REALLY IS THIS PHANTOM WITCH THING...?
HUH?

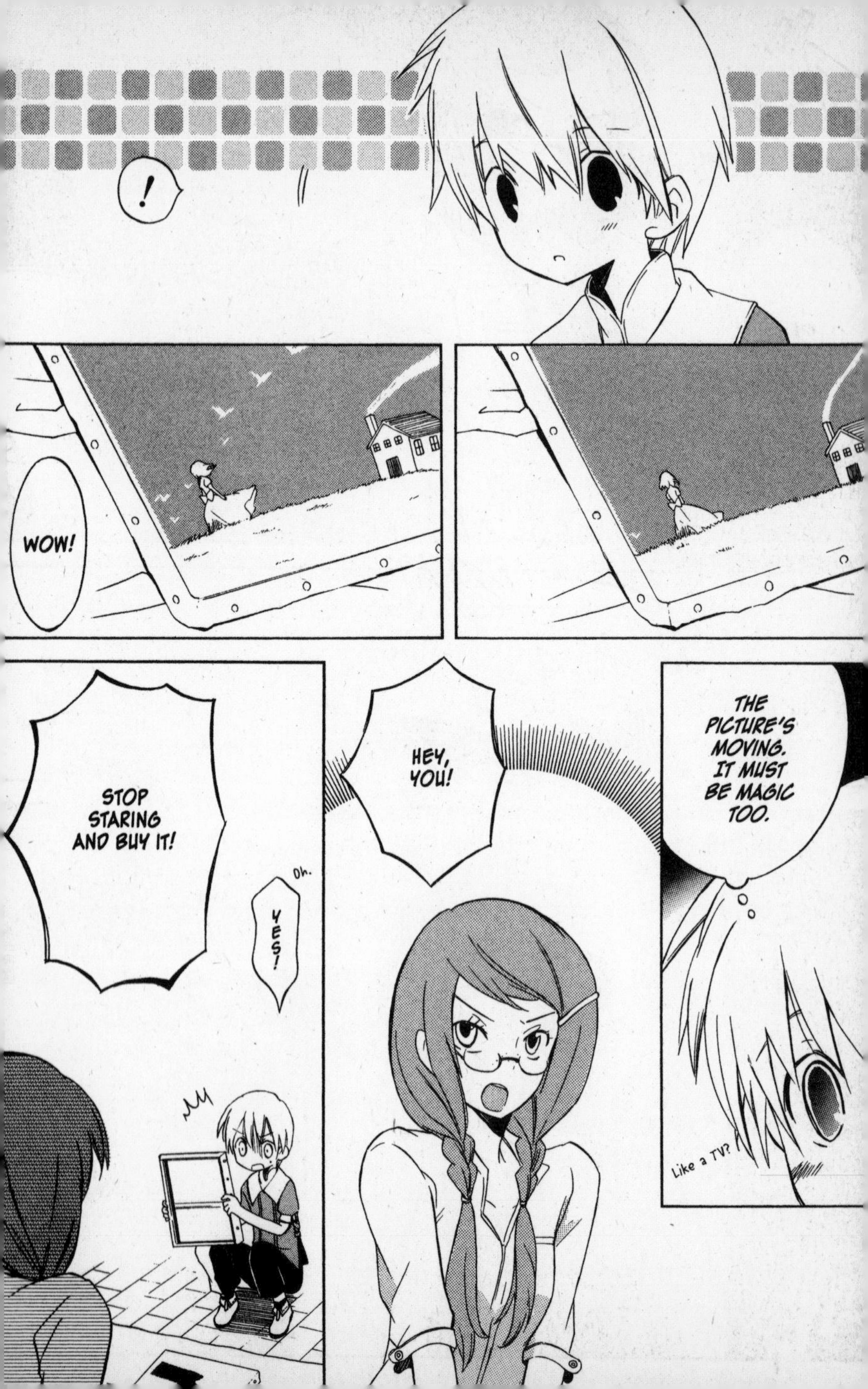
!
WOW!
THE PICTURE'S MOVING. IT MUST BE MAGIC TOO.
Like a TV?
HEY, YOU!
STOP STARING AND BUY IT!
Oh.
YES!

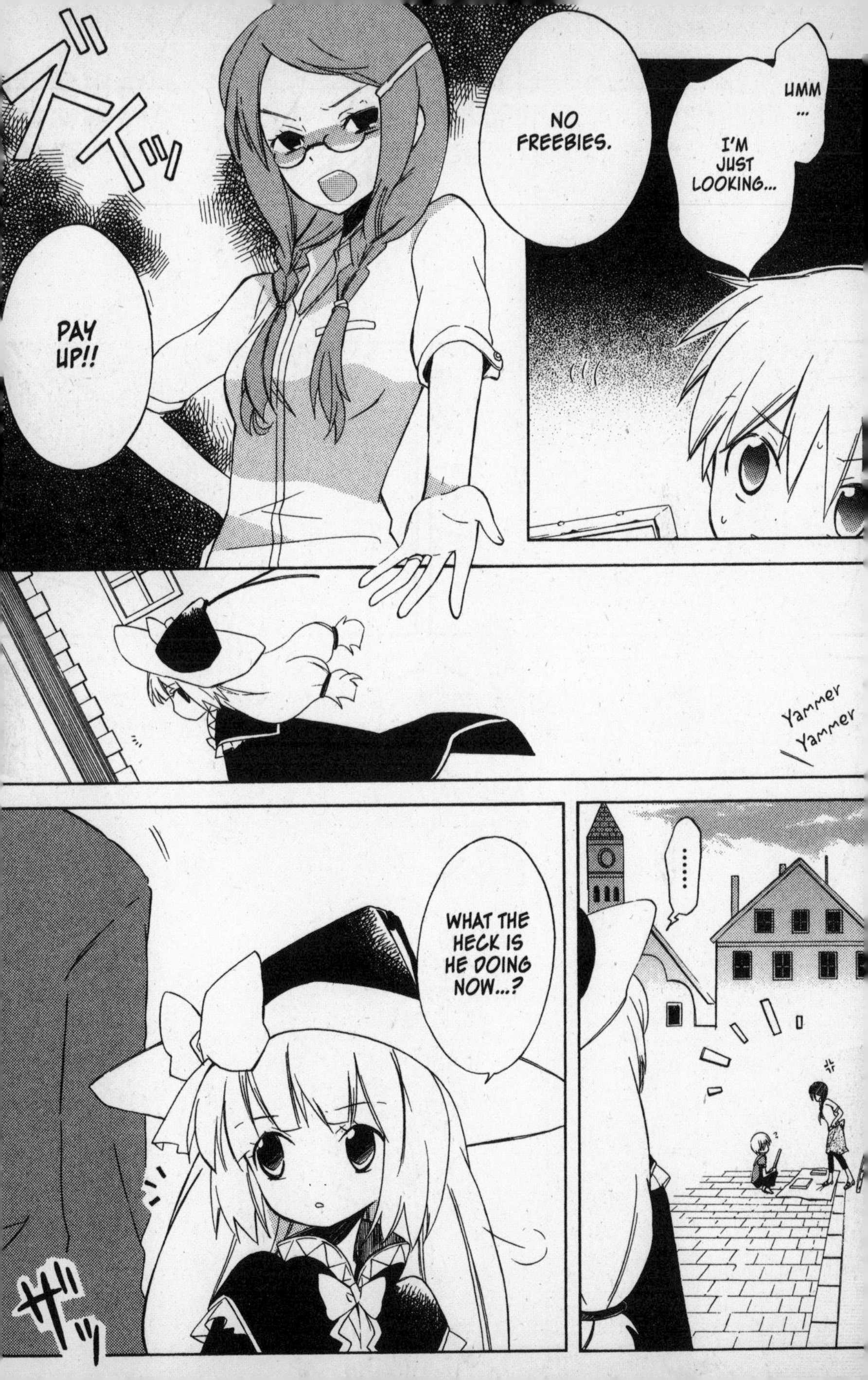
UMM... I'M JUST LOOKING...
NO FREEBIES.
PAY UP!!
ズイッ
Yammer Yammer
......
WHAT THE HECK IS HE DOING NOW...?
ザッ

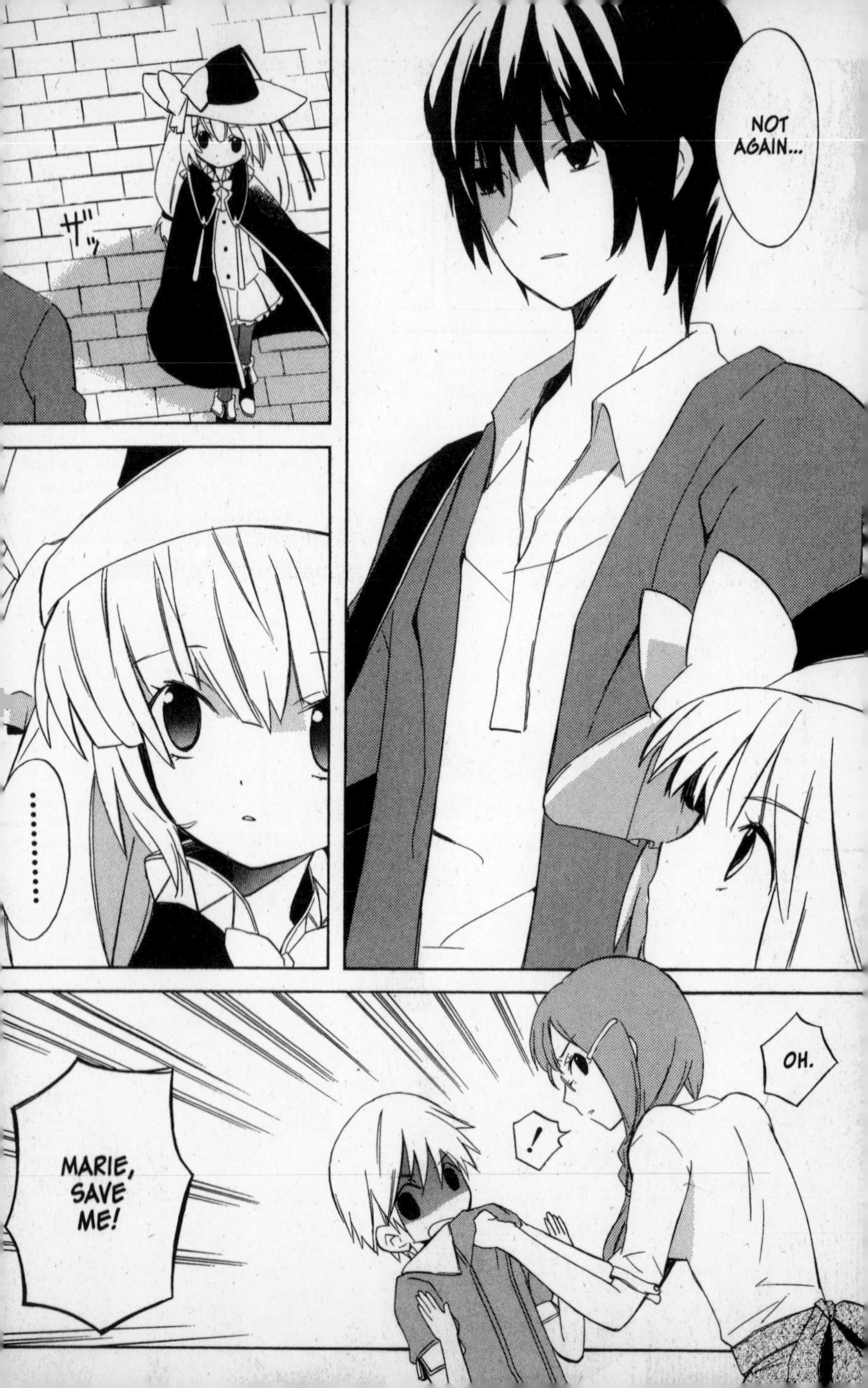
NOT AGAIN...
ザッ
....
OH.
!
MARIE, SAVE ME!

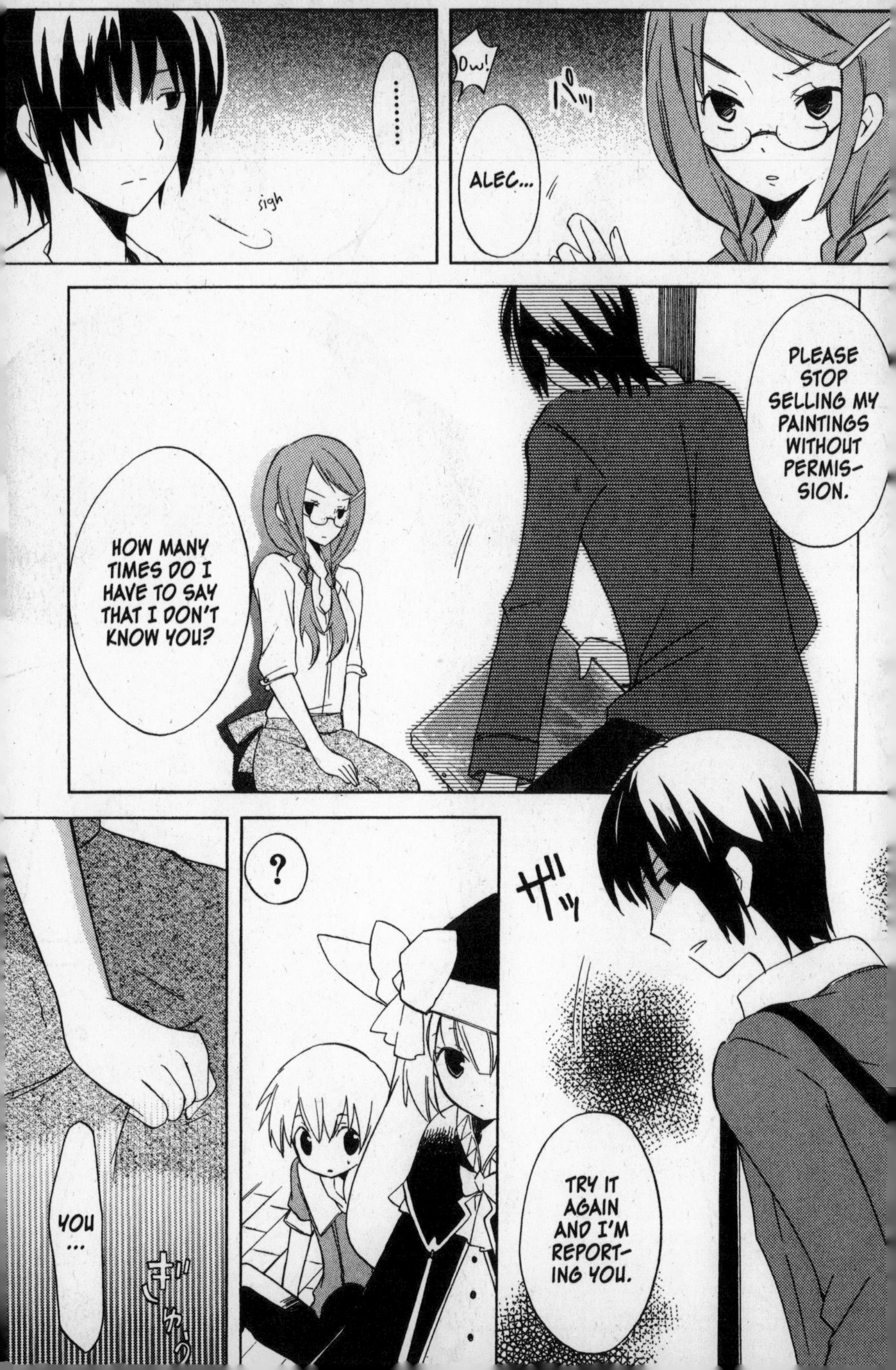
Ow!
パッ
ALEC...
......
sigh
PLEASE STOP SELLING MY PAINTINGS WITHOUT PERMIS-SION.
HOW MANY TIMES DO I HAVE TO SAY THAT I DON'T KNOW YOU?
ザッ
TRY IT AGAIN AND I'M REPORT-ING YOU.
?
YOU ...
ぎゅっ

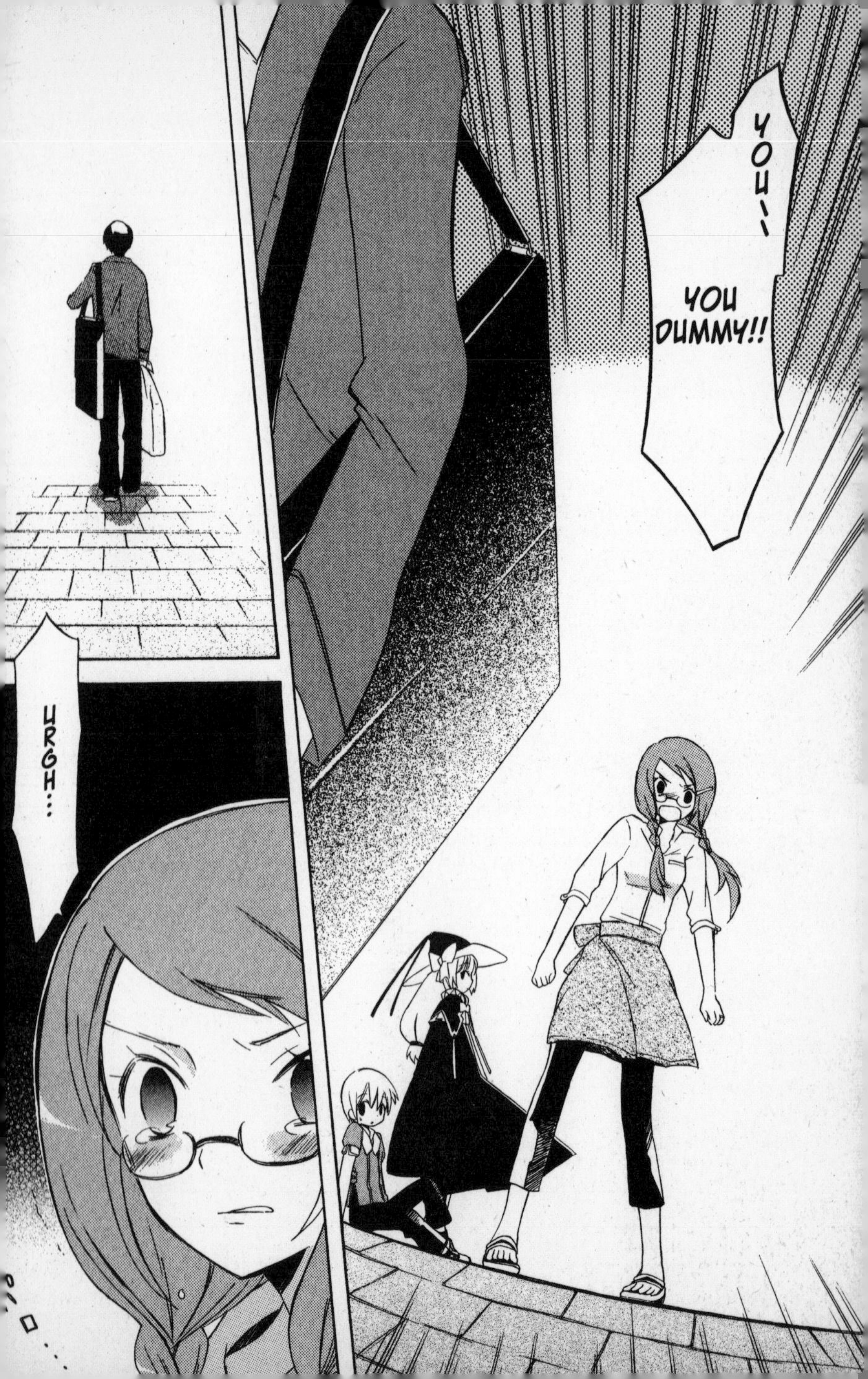
YOU~~
YOU DUMMY!!
URGH...

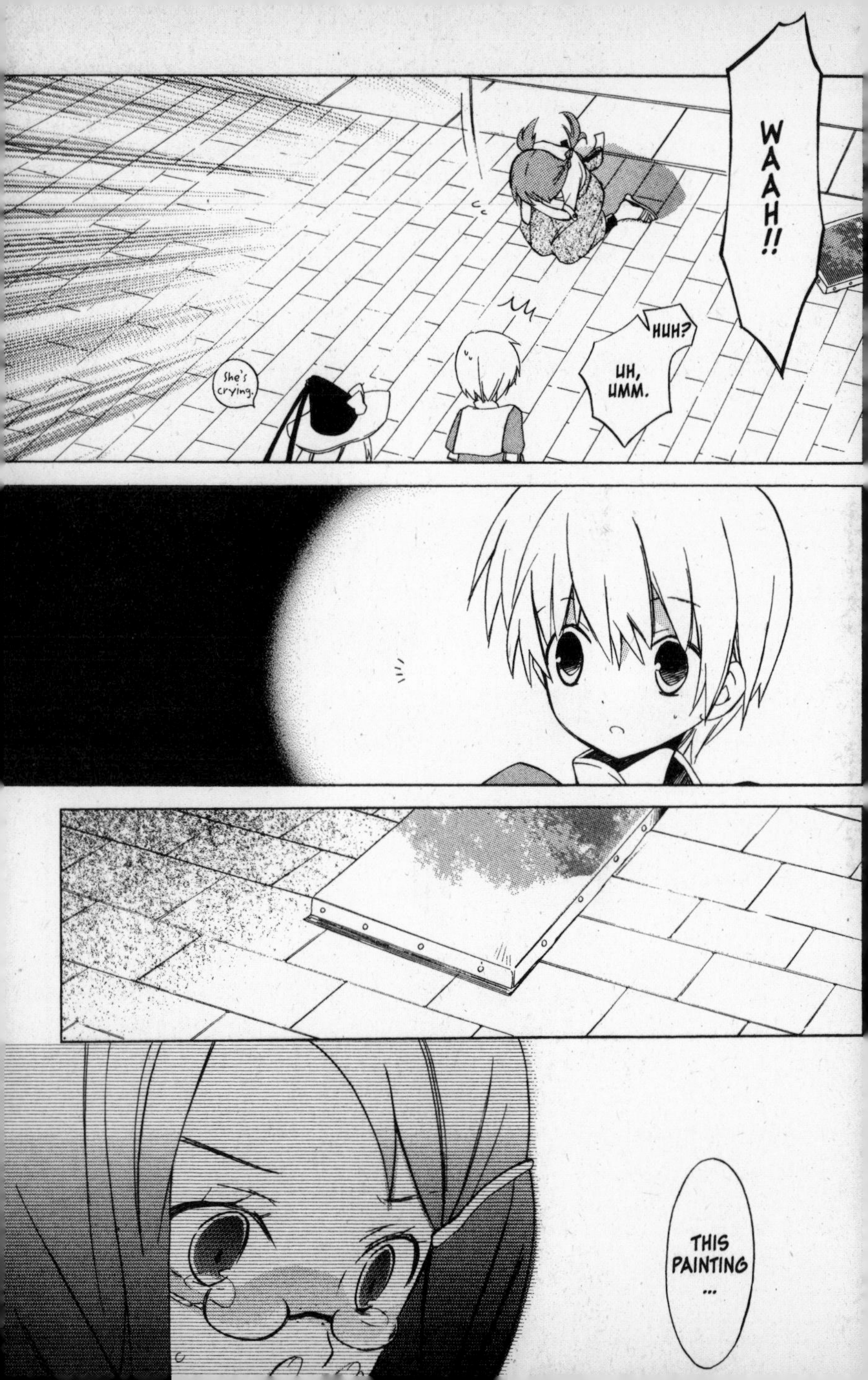
WAAH!!
HUH?
UH, UMM.
She's crying.
THIS PAINTING ...

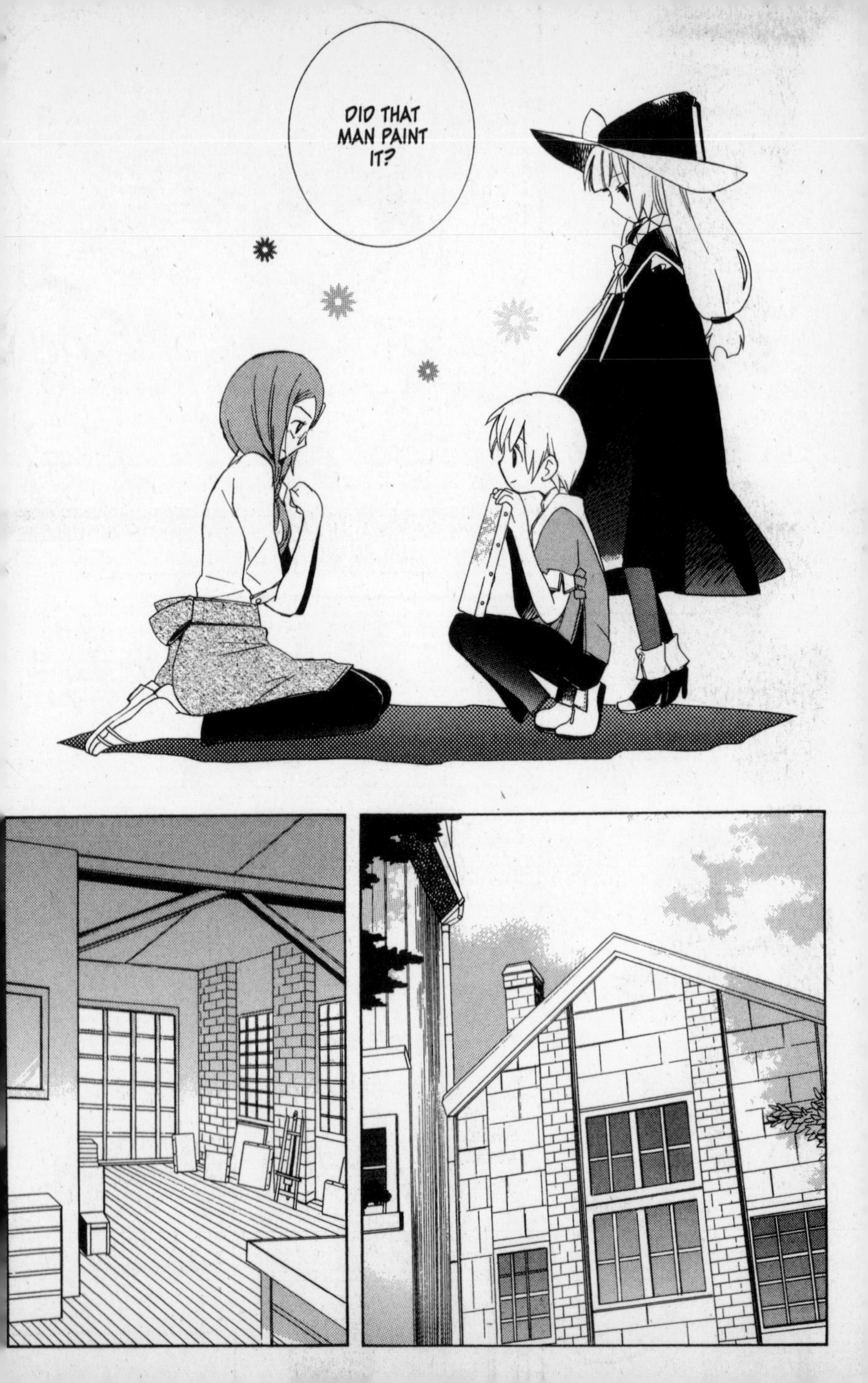
DID THAT MAN PAINT IT?

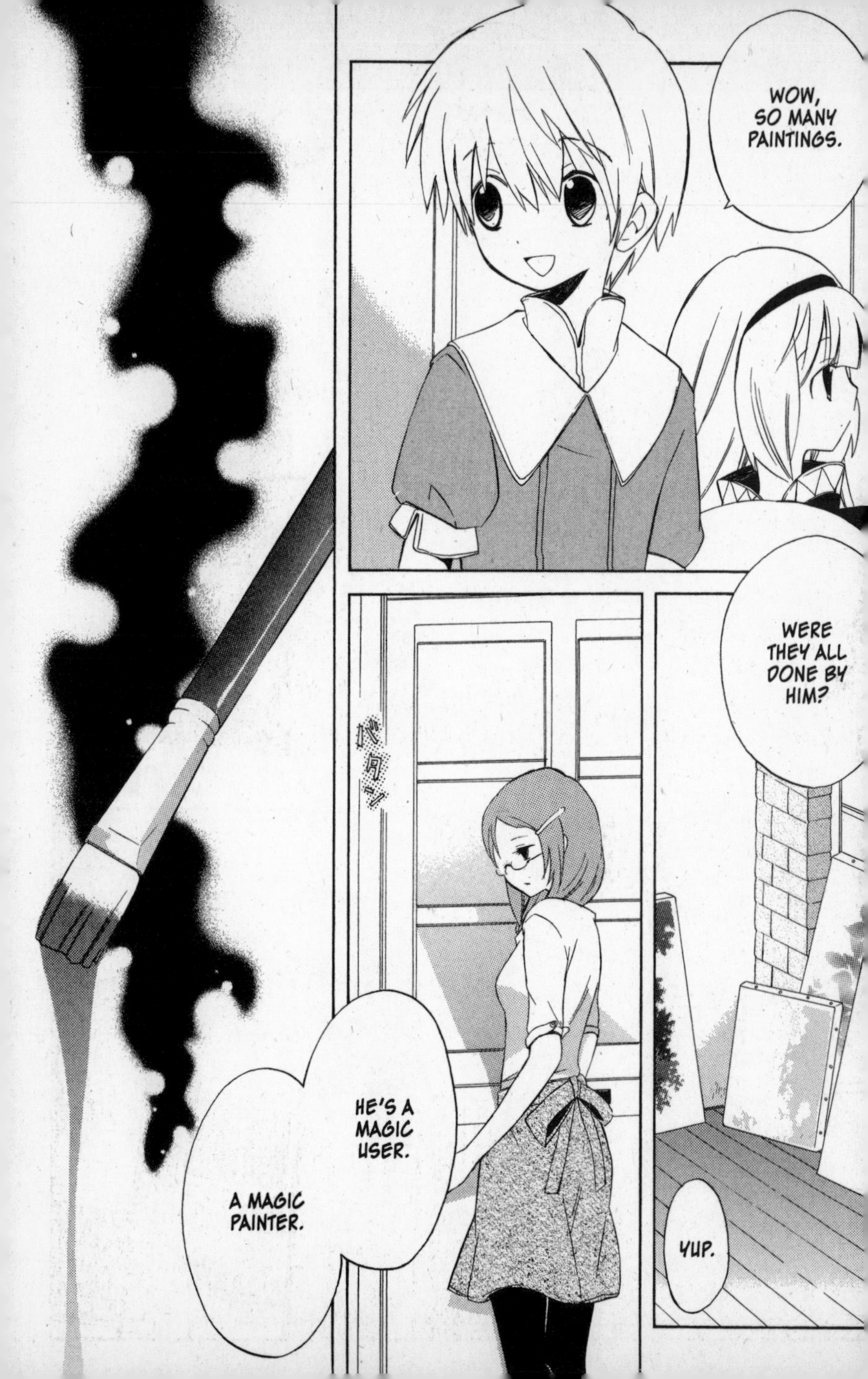
WOW, SO MANY PAINTINGS.
WERE THEY ALL DONE BY HIM?
YUP.
バタン!
HE'S A MAGIC USER.
A MAGIC PAINTER.

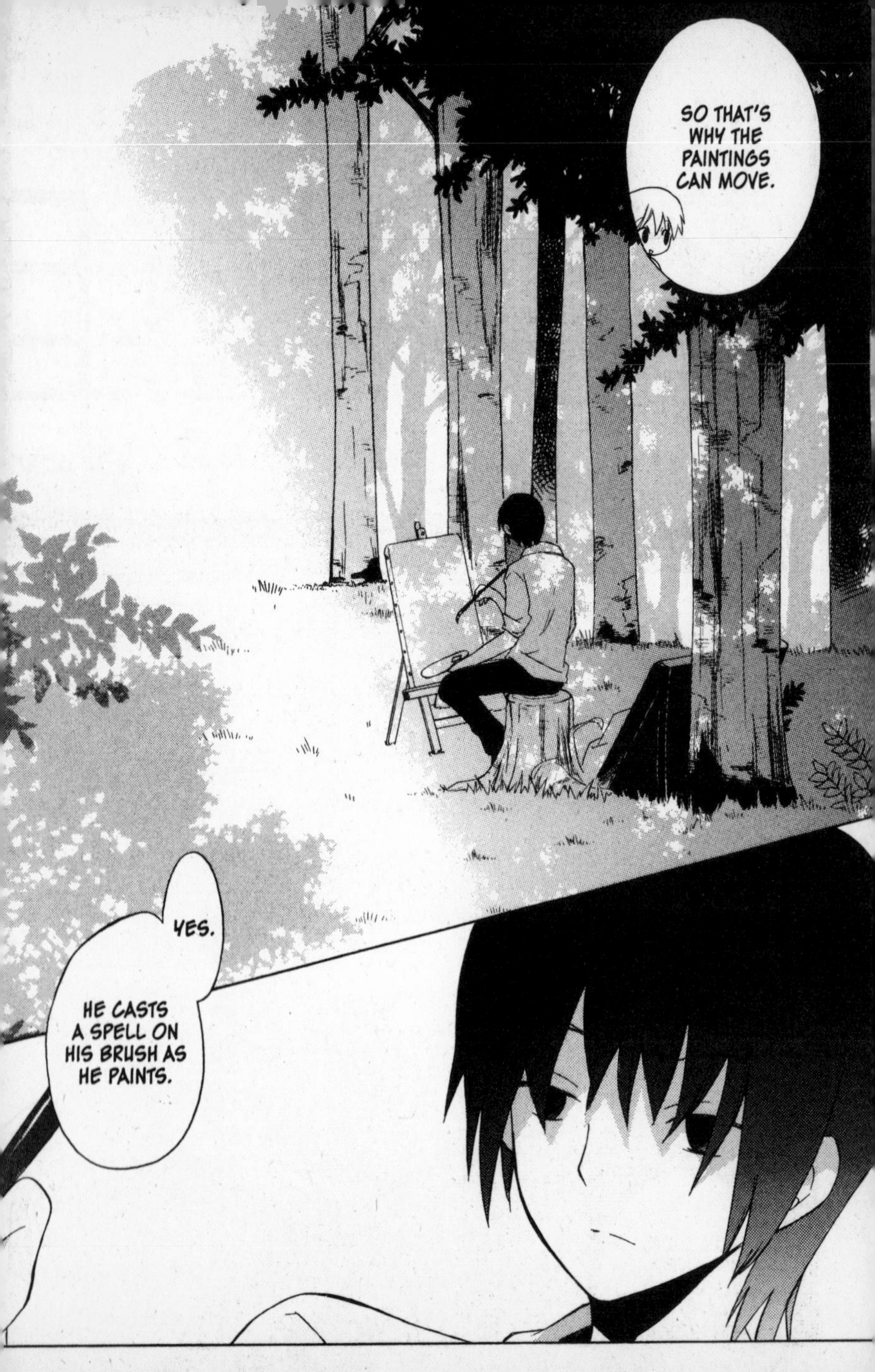
SO THAT'S WHY THE PAINTINGS CAN MOVE.
YES.
HE CASTS A SPELL ON HIS BRUSH AS HE PAINTS.

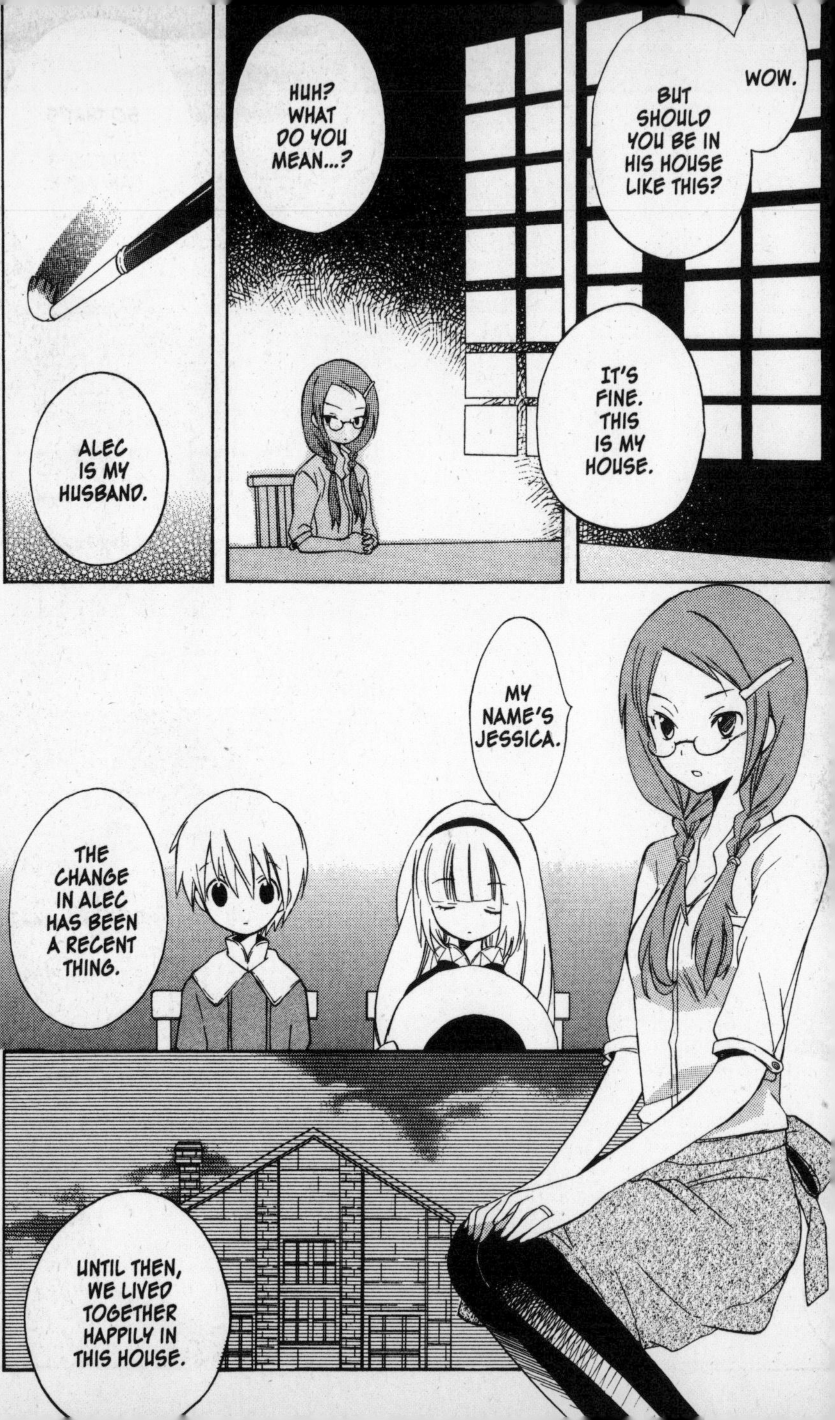
WOW.
BUT SHOULD YOU BE IN HIS HOUSE LIKE THIS?
IT'S FINE. THIS IS MY HOUSE.
HUH? WHAT DO YOU MEAN...?
ALEC IS MY HUSBAND.
MY NAME'S JESSICA.
THE CHANGE IN ALEC HAS BEEN A RECENT THING.
UNTIL THEN, WE LIVED TOGETHER HAPPILY IN THIS HOUSE.

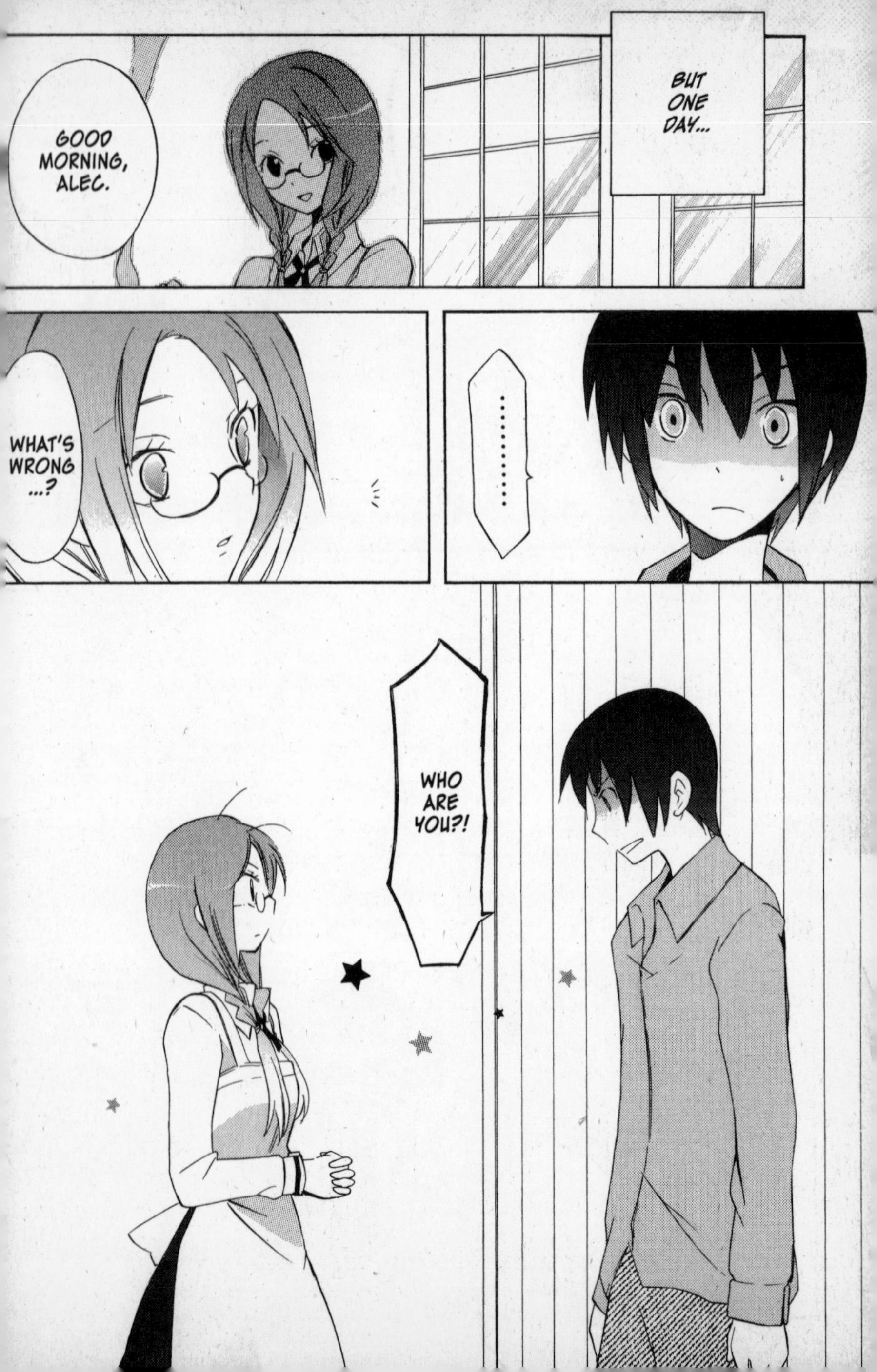
BUT ONE DAY...
GOOD MORNING, ALEC.
....
WHAT'S WRONG ...?
WHO ARE YOU?!

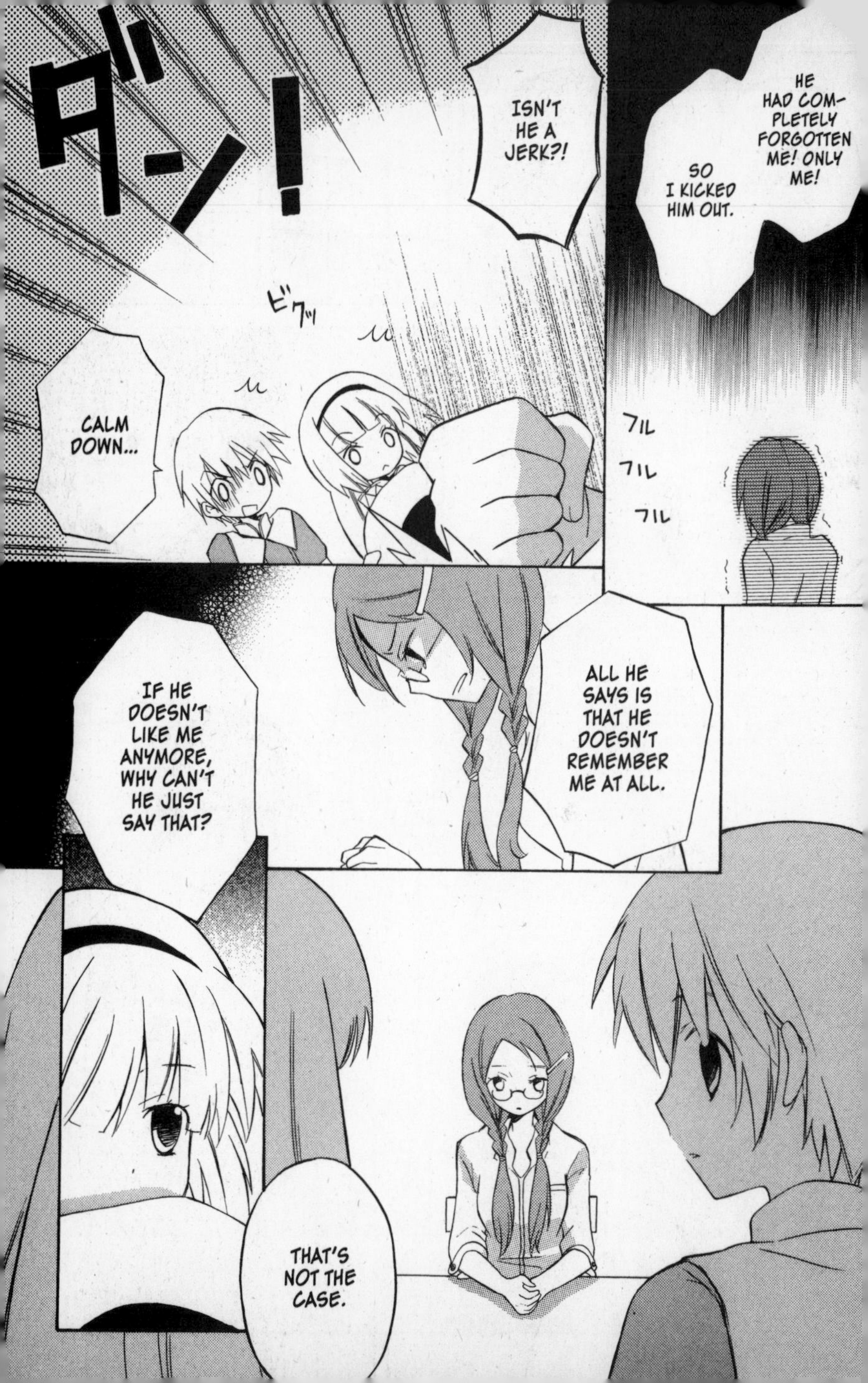
HE HAD COM-PLETELY FORGOTTEN ME! ONLY ME!
SO I KICKED HIM OUT.
フル
フル
フル
ダーン!
ISN'T HE A JERK?!
ビクッ
CALM DOWN...
ALL HE SAYS IS THAT HE DOESN'T REMEMBER ME AT ALL.
IF HE DOESN'T LIKE ME ANYMORE, WHY CAN'T HE JUST SAY THAT?
THAT'S NOT THE CASE.

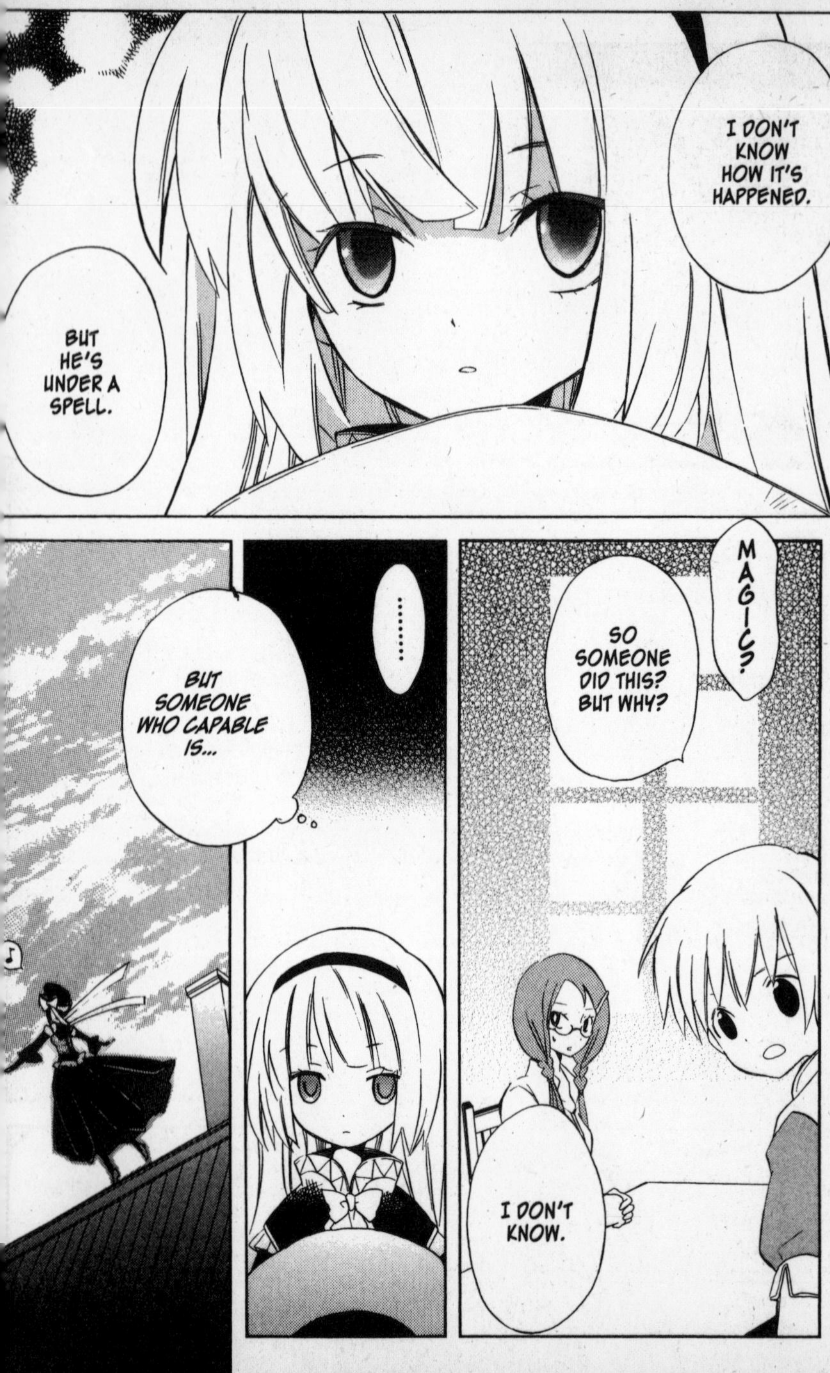
I DON'T KNOW HOW IT'S HAPPENED.
BUT HE'S UNDER A SPELL.
MAGIC?
SO SOMEONE DID THIS? BUT WHY?
I DON'T KNOW.
....
BUT SOMEONE WHO CAPABLE IS...
♪

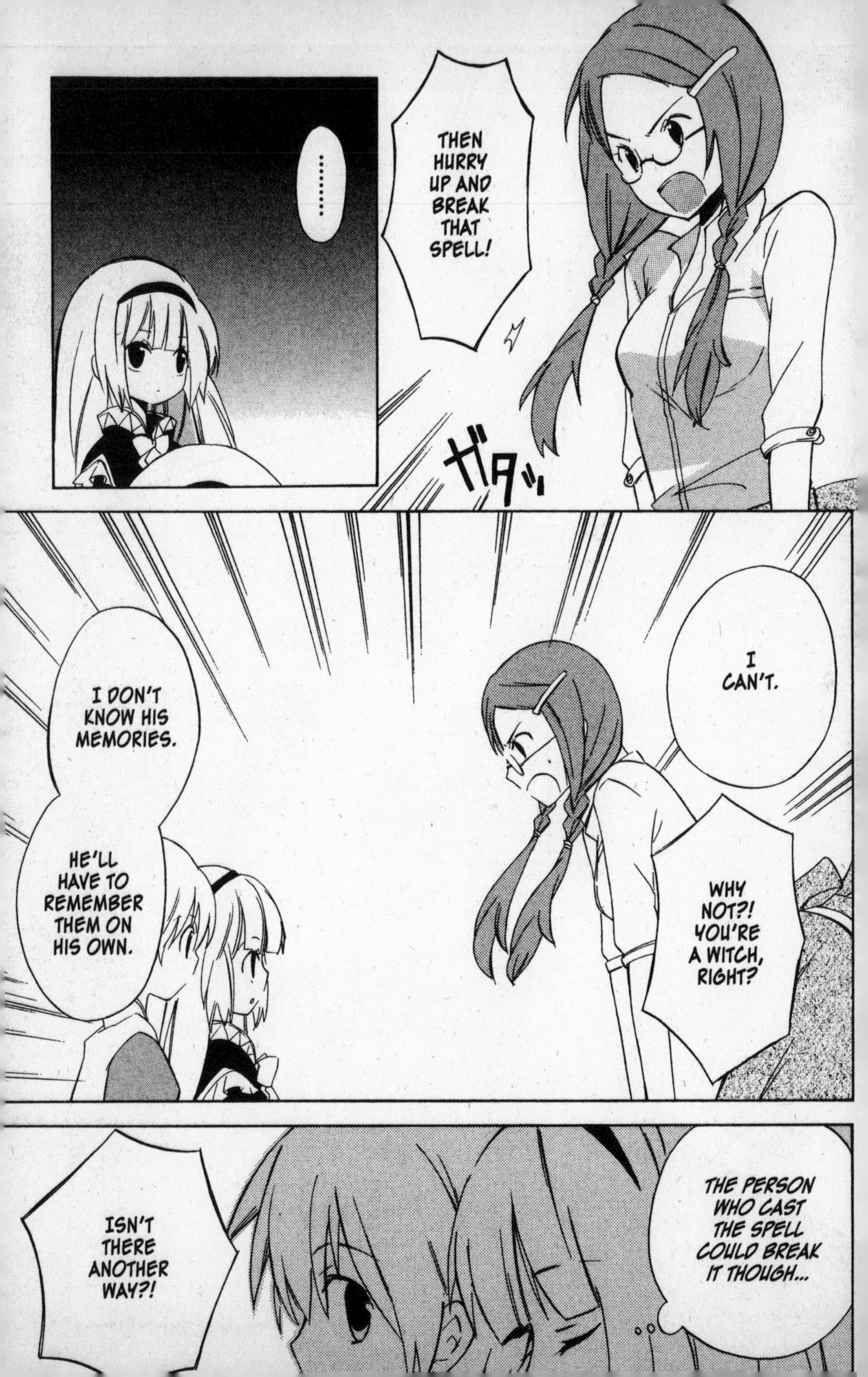
THEN HURRY UP AND BREAK THAT SPELL!
ガタッ
......
I CAN'T.
WHY NOT?! YOU'RE A WITCH, RIGHT?
I DON'T KNOW HIS MEMORIES.
HE'LL HAVE TO REMEMBER THEM ON HIS OWN.
THE PERSON WHO CAST THE SPELL COULD BREAK IT THOUGH...
ISN'T THERE ANOTHER WAY?!

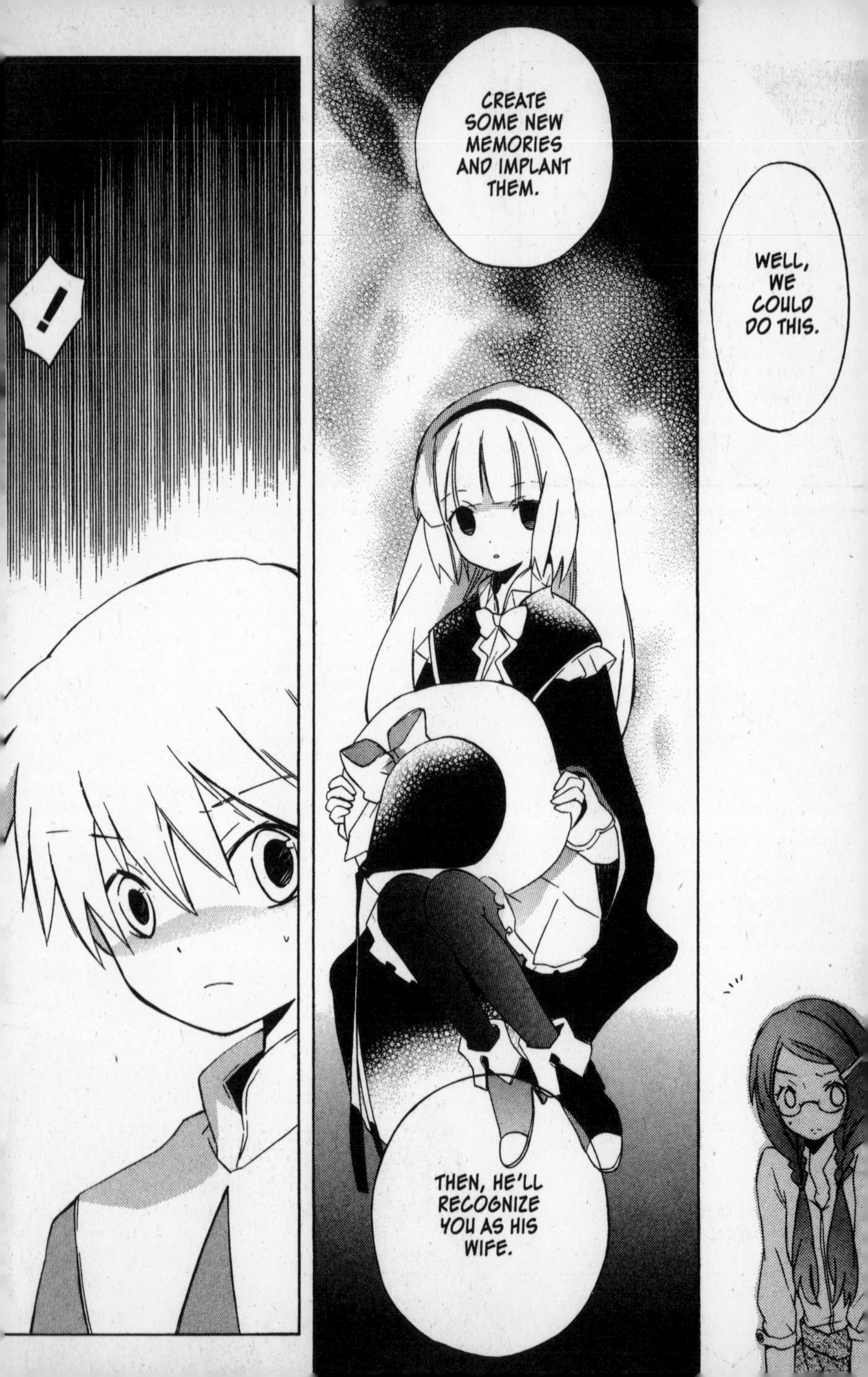
WELL, WE COULD DO THIS.
CREATE SOME NEW MEMORIES AND IMPLANT THEM.
THEN, HE'LL RECOGNIZE YOU AS HIS WIFE.
!

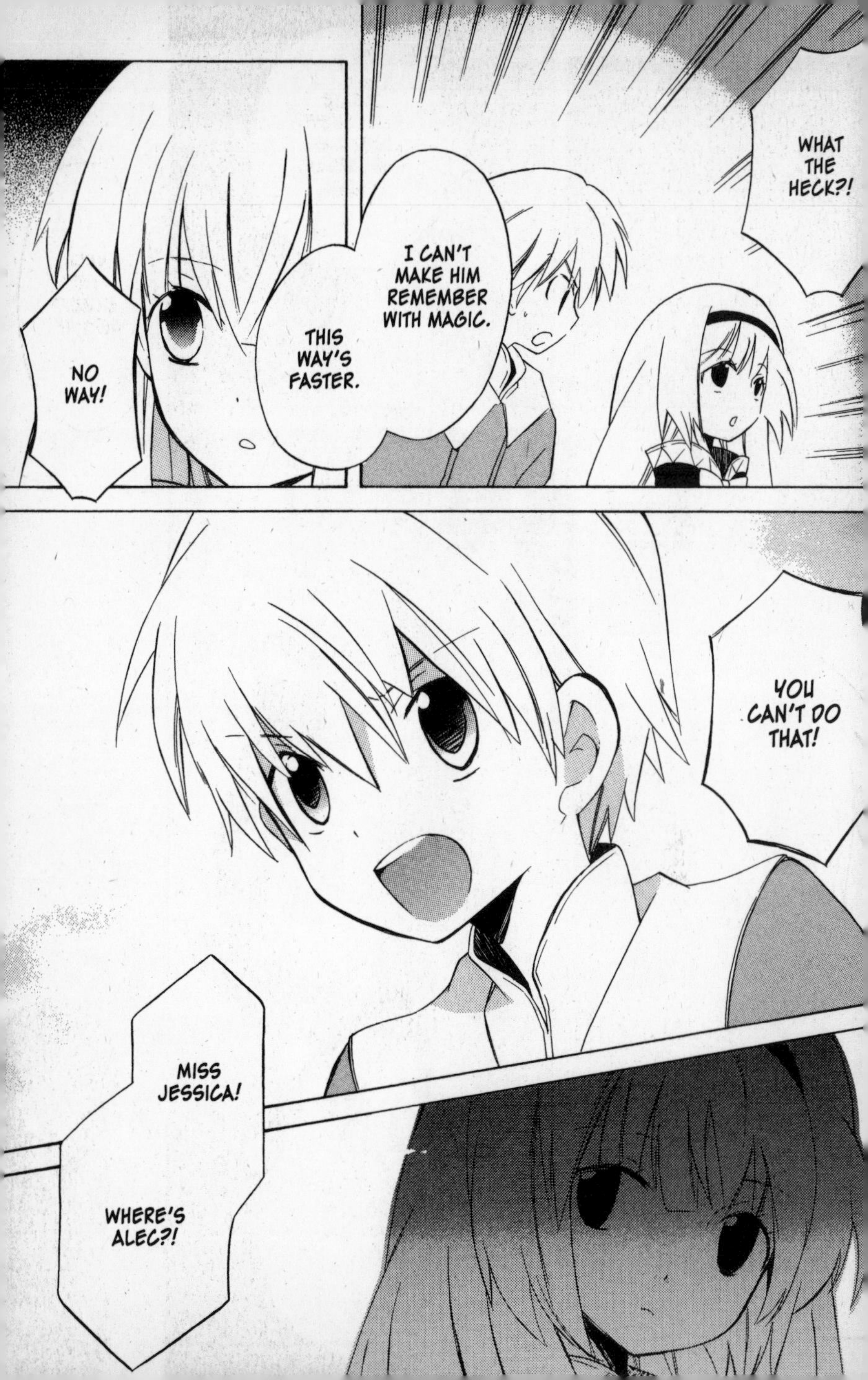
WHAT THE HECK?!
I CAN'T MAKE HIM REMEMBER WITH MAGIC.
THIS WAY'S FASTER.
NO WAY!
YOU CAN'T DO THAT!
MISS JESSICA!
WHERE'S ALEC?!

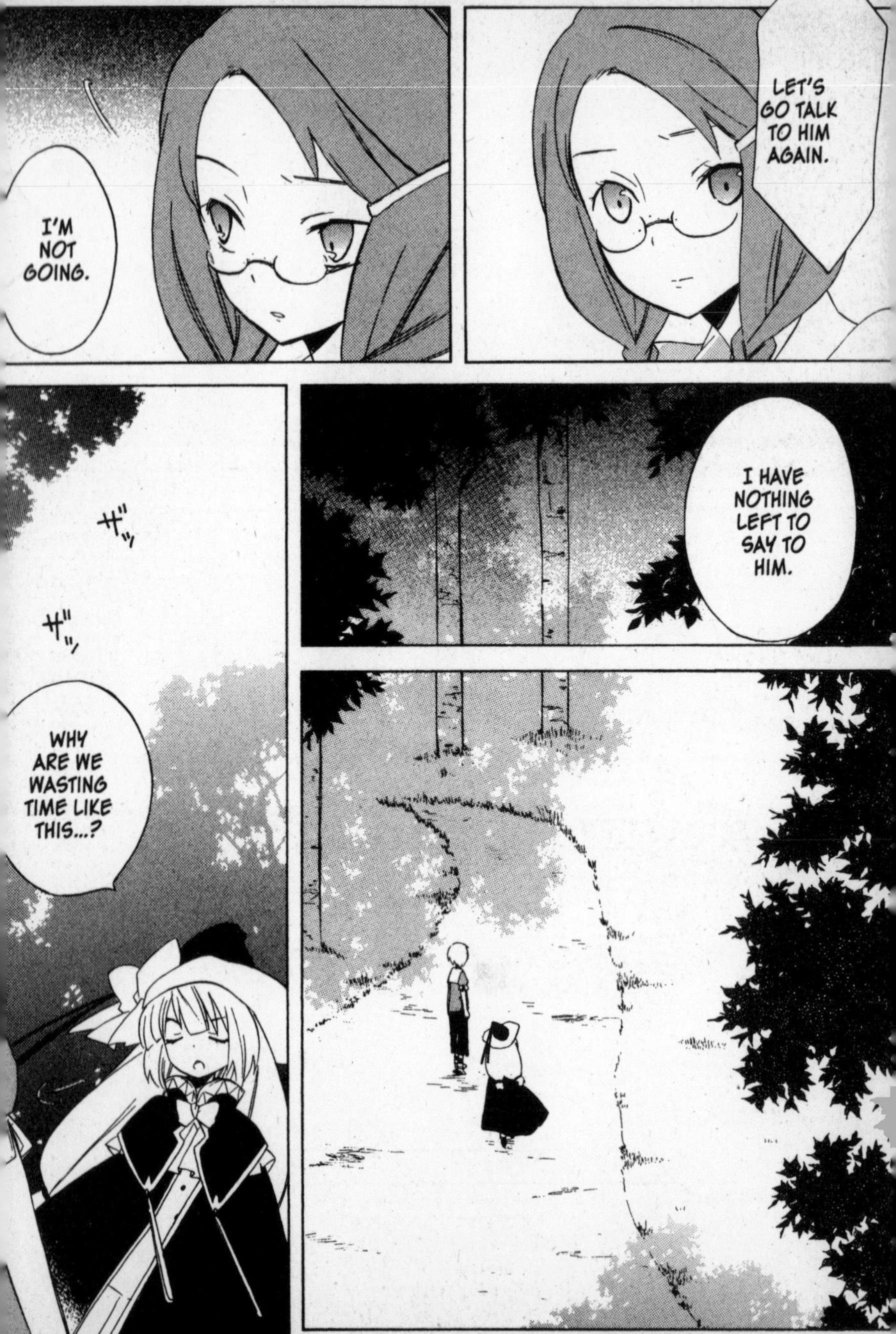
LET'S GO TALK TO HIM AGAIN.
I'M NOT GOING.
I HAVE NOTHING LEFT TO SAY TO HIM.
ザッ
ザッ
WHY ARE WE WASTING TIME LIKE THIS...?

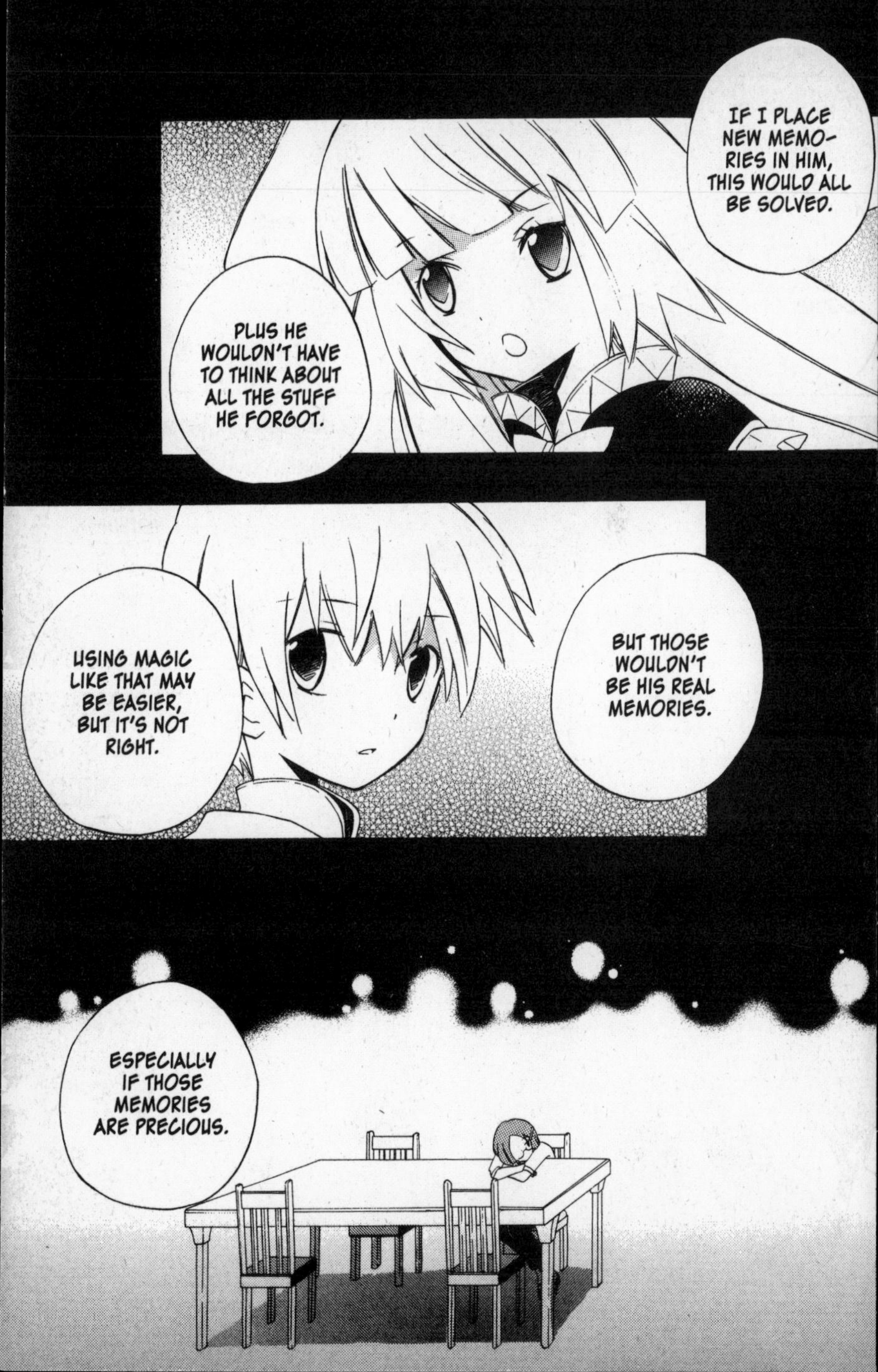
IF I PLACE NEW MEMORIES IN HIM, THIS WOULD ALL BE SOLVED.
PLUS HE WOULDN'T HAVE TO THINK ABOUT ALL THE STUFF HE FORGOT.
BUT THOSE WOULDN'T BE HIS REAL MEMORIES.
USING MAGIC LIKE THAT MAY BE EASIER, BUT IT'S NOT RIGHT.
ESPECIALLY IF THOSE MEMORIES ARE PRECIOUS.

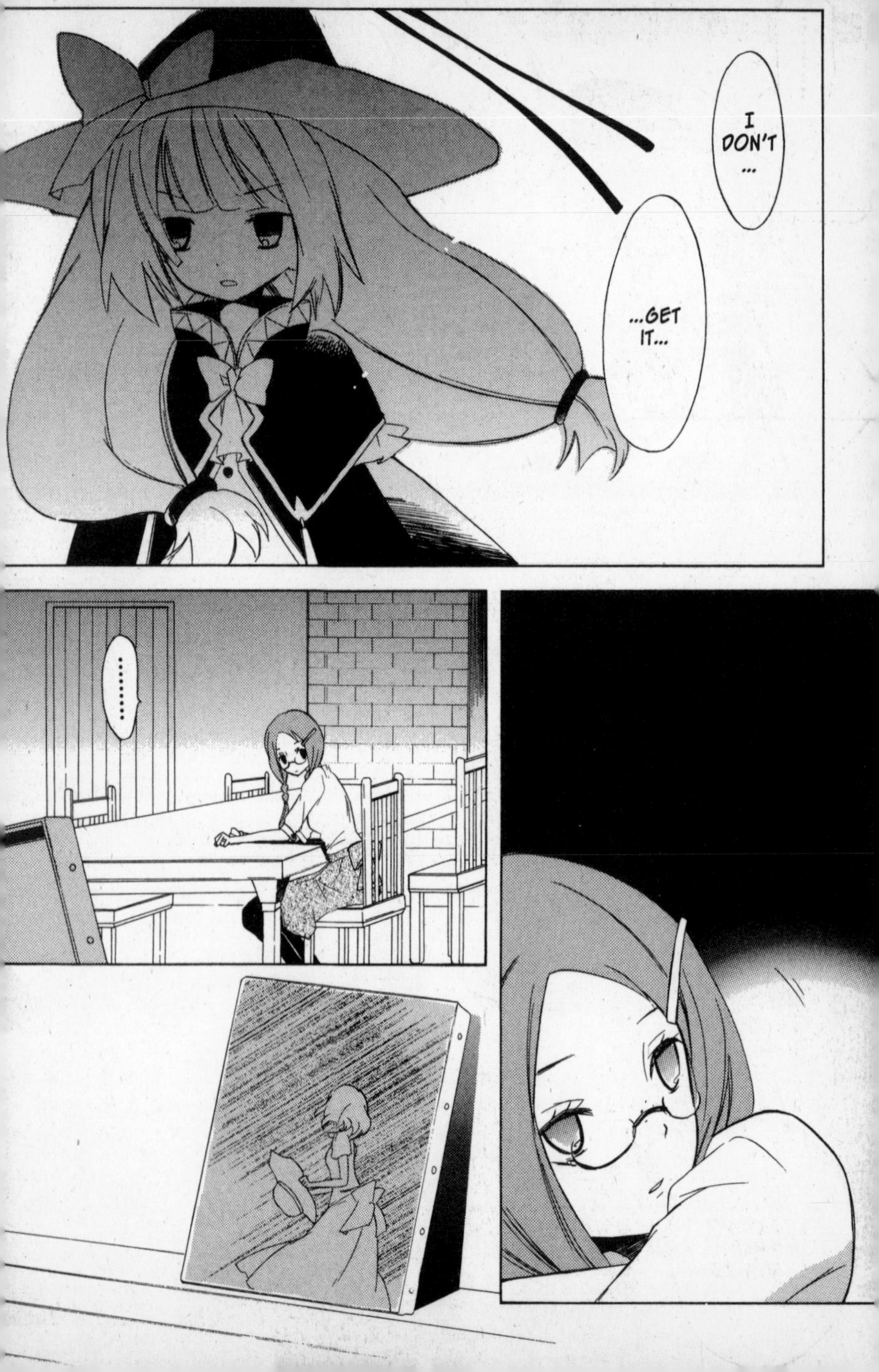
I DON'T ...
...GET IT...
....

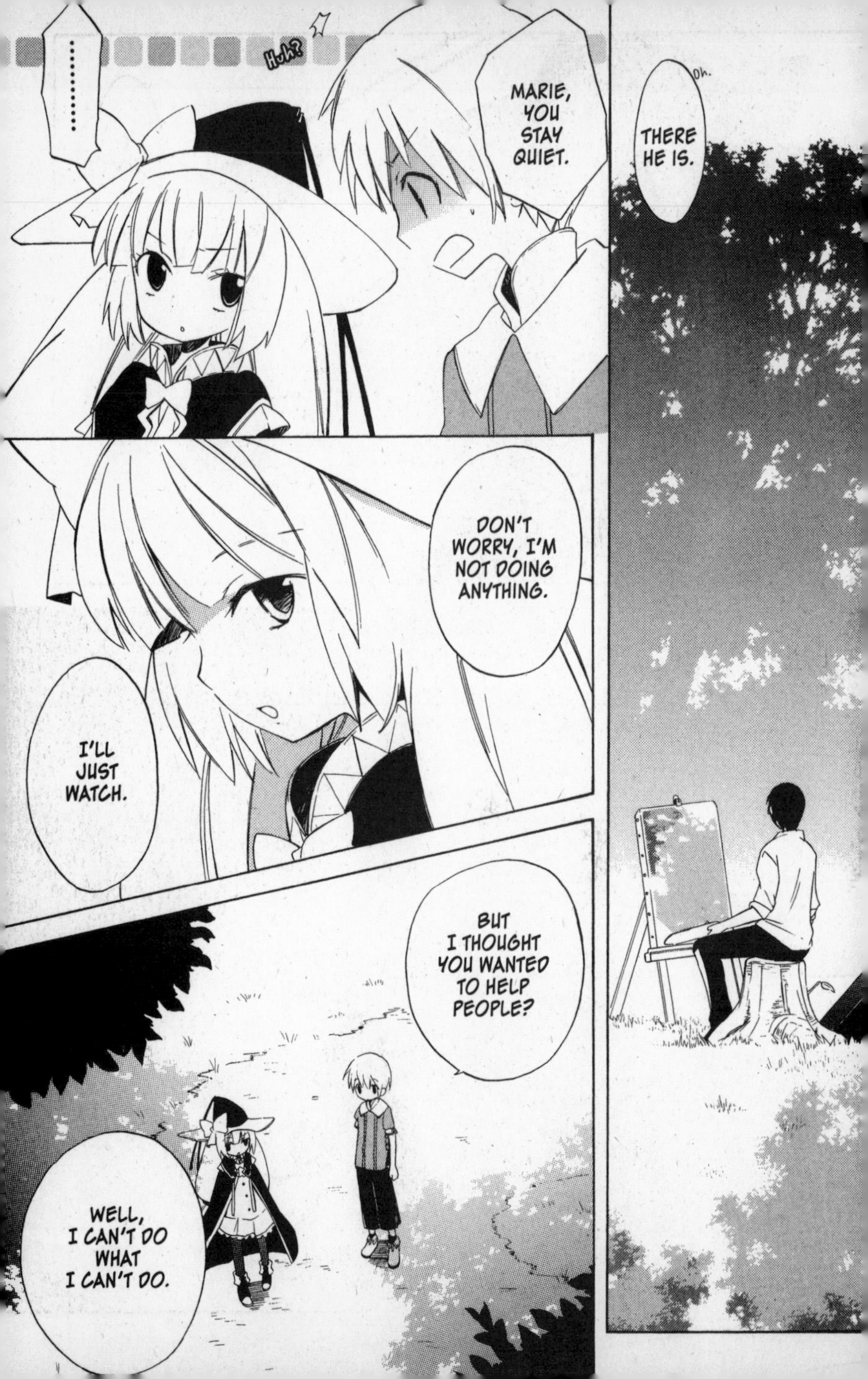
Oh.
THERE HE IS.
MARIE, YOU STAY QUIET.
Huh?
......
DON'T WORRY, I'M NOT DOING ANYTHING.
I'LL JUST WATCH.
BUT I THOUGHT YOU WANTED TO HELP PEOPLE?
WELL, I CAN'T DO WHAT I CAN'T DO.

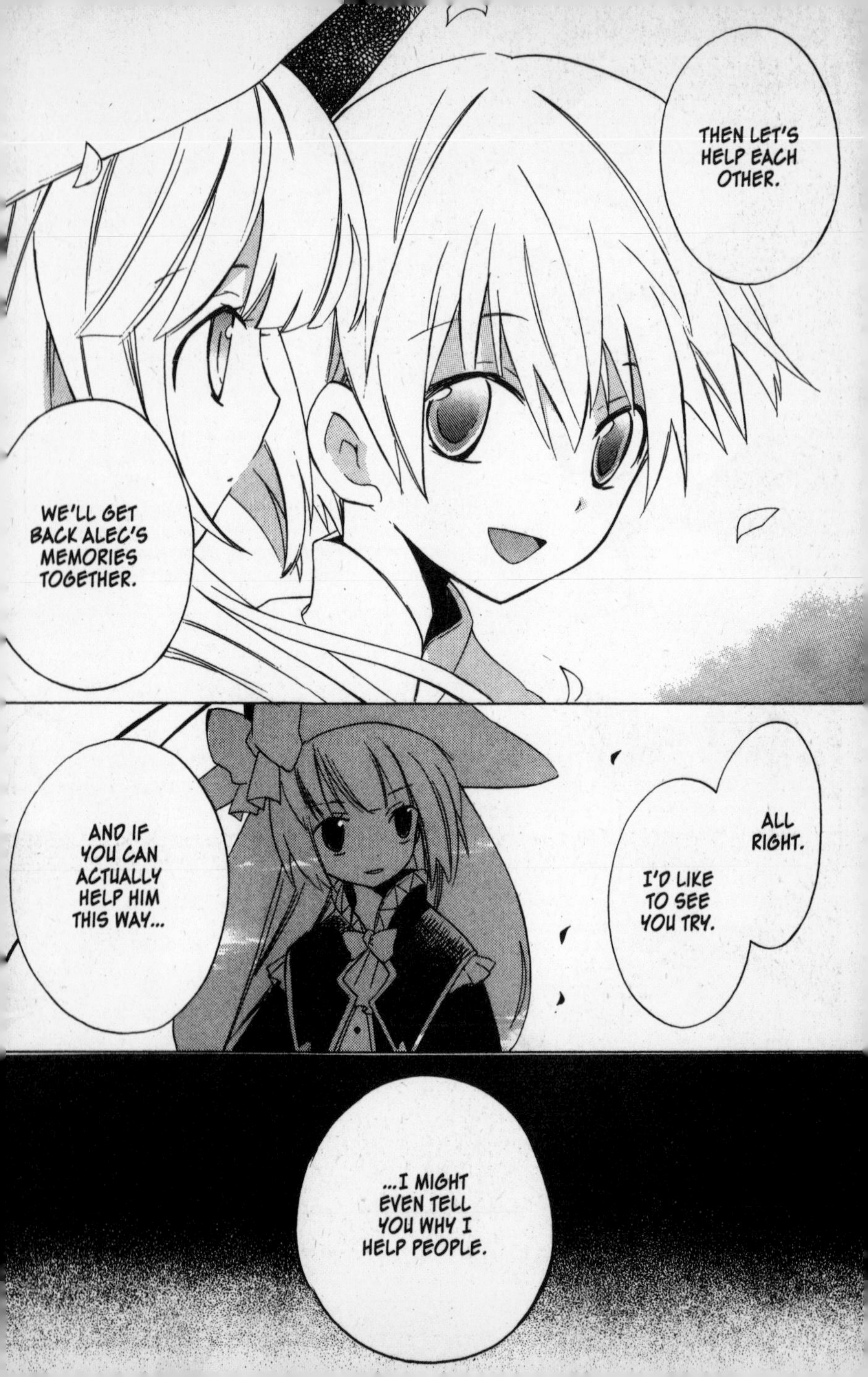
THEN LET'S HELP EACH OTHER.
WE'LL GET BACK ALEC'S MEMORIES TOGETHER.
ALL RIGHT.
I'D LIKE TO SEE YOU TRY.
AND IF YOU CAN ACTUALLY HELP HIM THIS WAY...
...I MIGHT EVEN TELL YOU WHY I HELP PEOPLE.

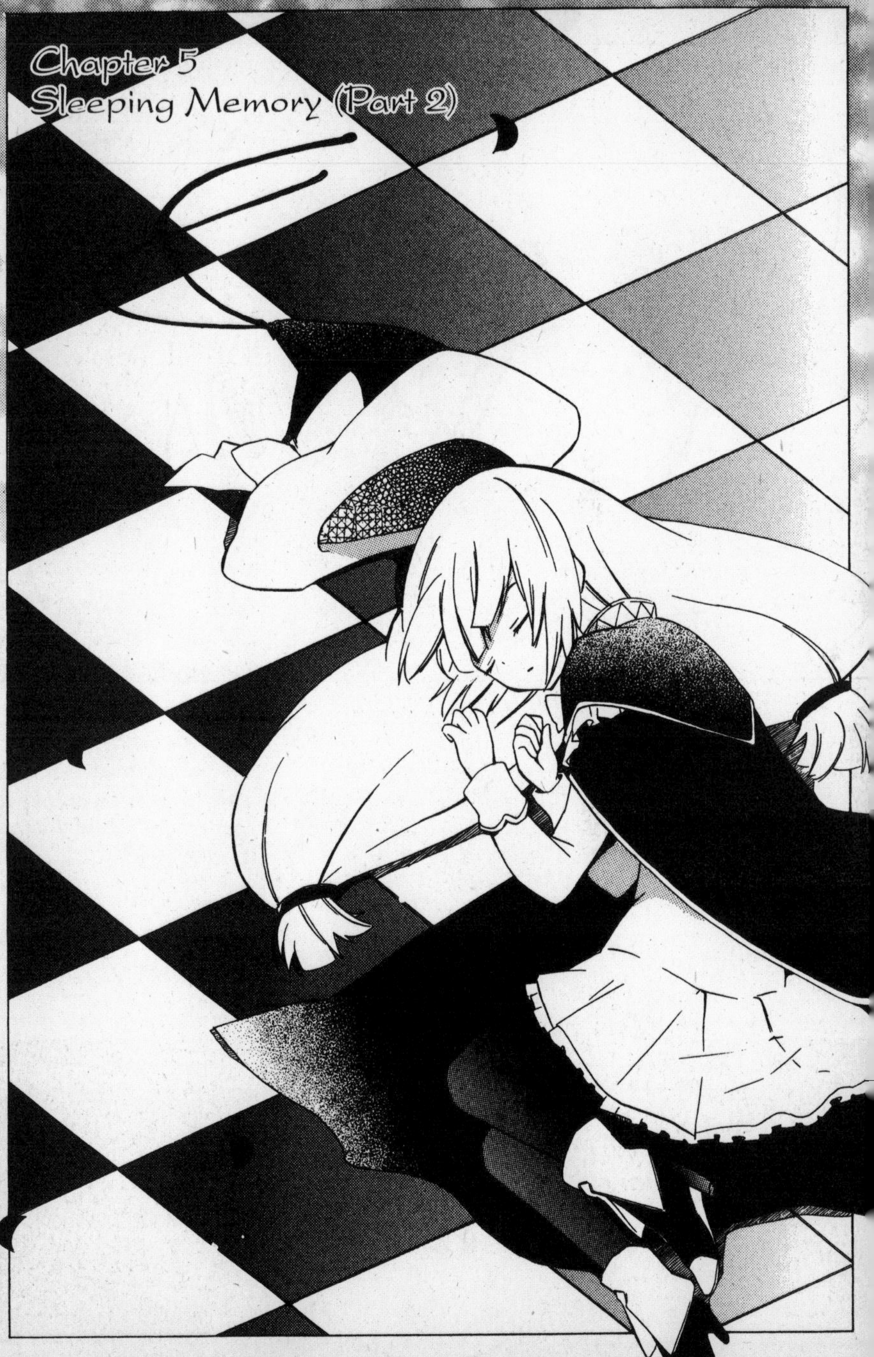
Chapter 5
Sleeping Memory (Part 2)

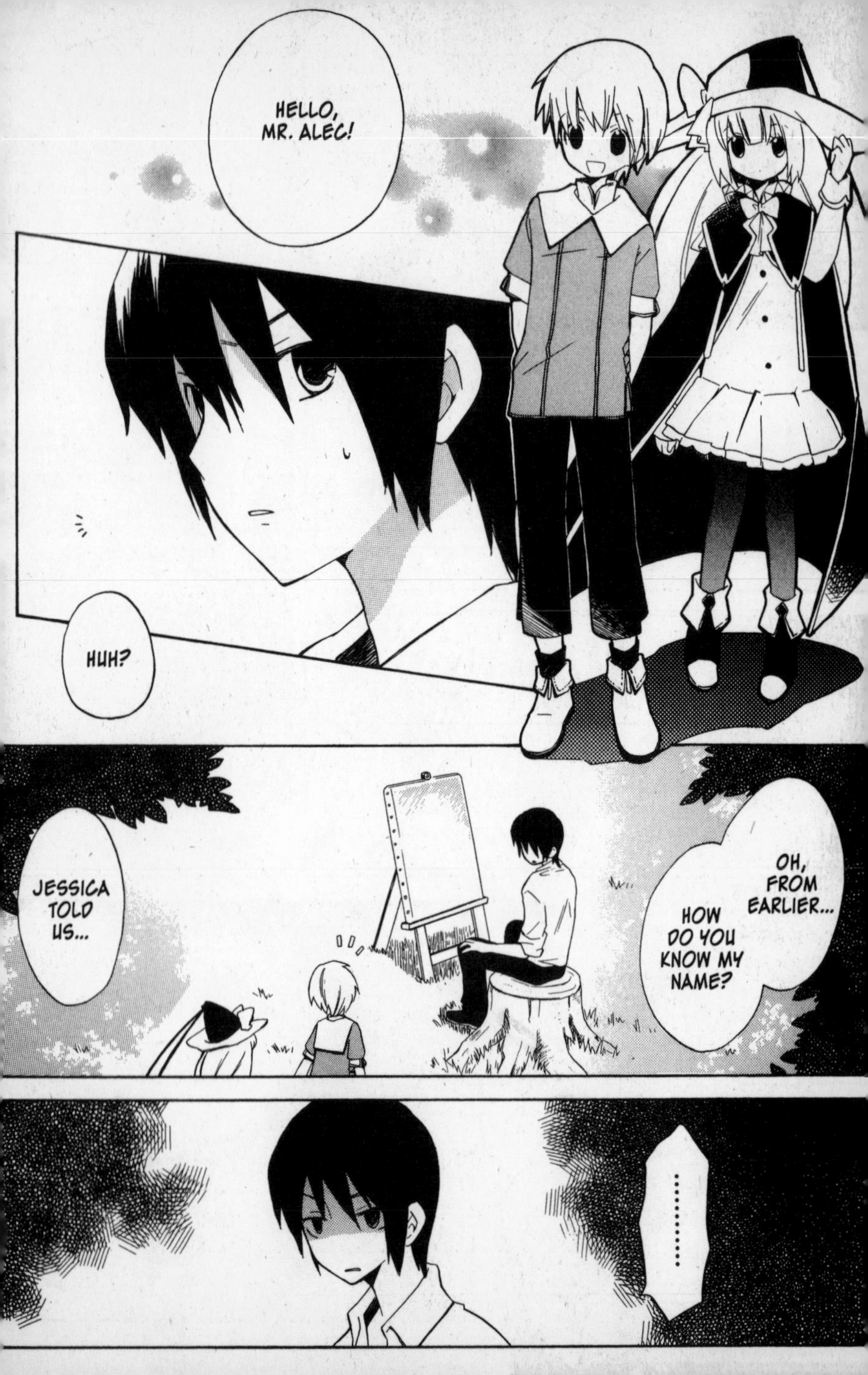
HELLO, MR. ALEC!
HUH?
OH, FROM EARLIER...
HOW DO YOU KNOW MY NAME?
JESSICA TOLD US...
....

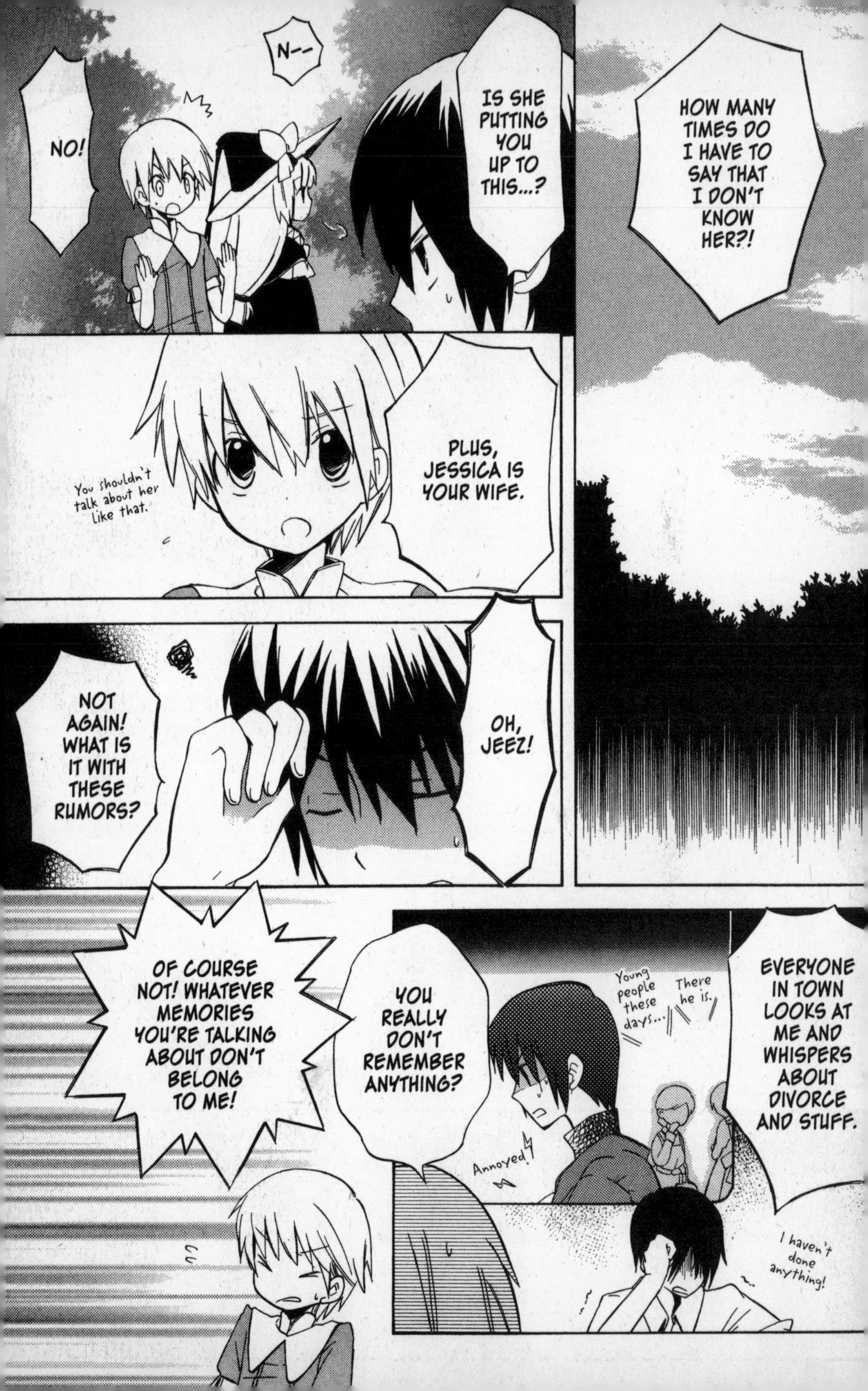
HOW MANY TIMES DO I HAVE TO SAY THAT I DON'T KNOW HER?!
IS SHE PUTTING YOU UP TO THIS...?
N--
NO!
PLUS, JESSICA IS YOUR WIFE.
You shouldn't talk about her like that.
OH, JEEZ!
NOT AGAIN! WHAT IS IT WITH THESE RUMORS?
EVERYONE IN TOWN LOOKS AT ME AND WHISPERS ABOUT DIVORCE AND STUFF.
There he is.
Young people these days...
Annoyed!
I haven't done anything!
YOU REALLY DON'T REMEMBER ANYTHING?
OF COURSE NOT! WHATEVER MEMORIES YOU'RE TALKING ABOUT DON'T BELONG TO ME!

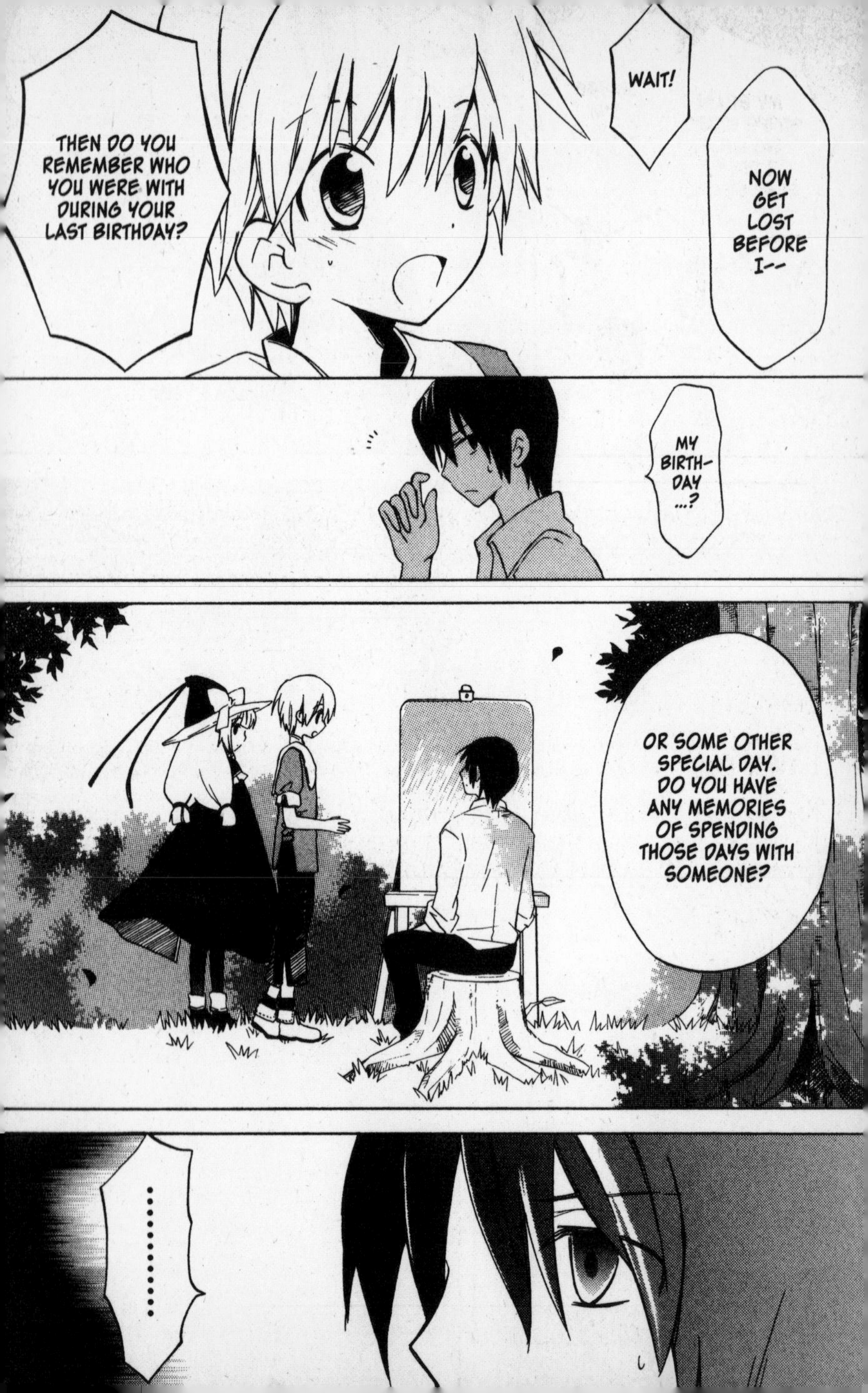
NOW GET LOST BEFORE I--
WAIT!
THEN DO YOU REMEMBER WHO YOU WERE WITH DURING YOUR LAST BIRTHDAY?
MY BIRTH-DAY ...?
OR SOME OTHER SPECIAL DAY. DO YOU HAVE ANY MEMORIES OF SPENDING THOSE DAYS WITH SOMEONE?
....

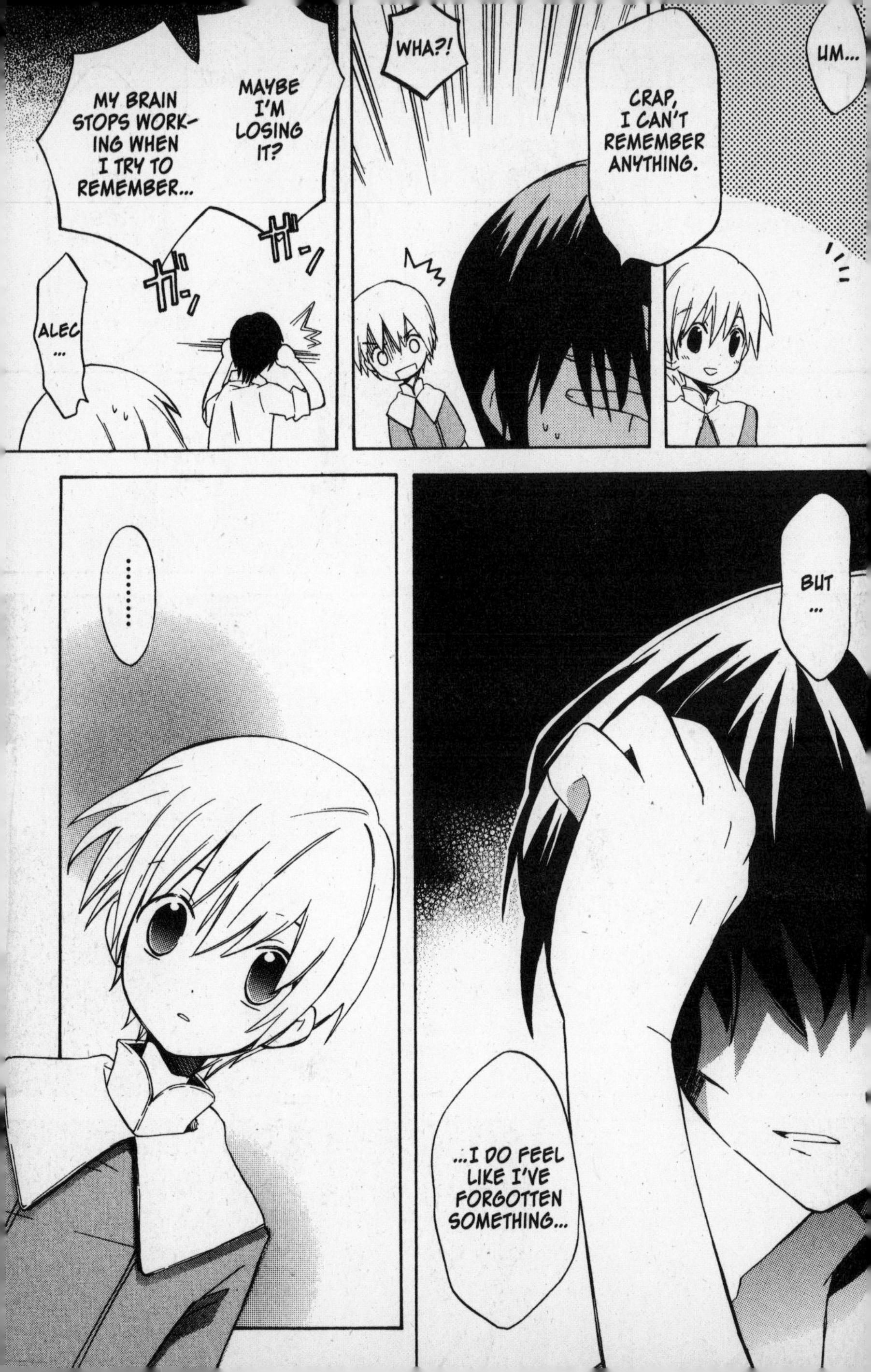

UM...
WHA?!
CRAP, I CAN'T REMEMBER ANYTHING.
MAYBE I'M LOSING IT?
MY BRAIN STOPS WORKING WHEN I TRY TO REMEMBER...
ALEC...
BUT...
...I DO FEEL LIKE I'VE FORGOTTEN SOMETHING...
....

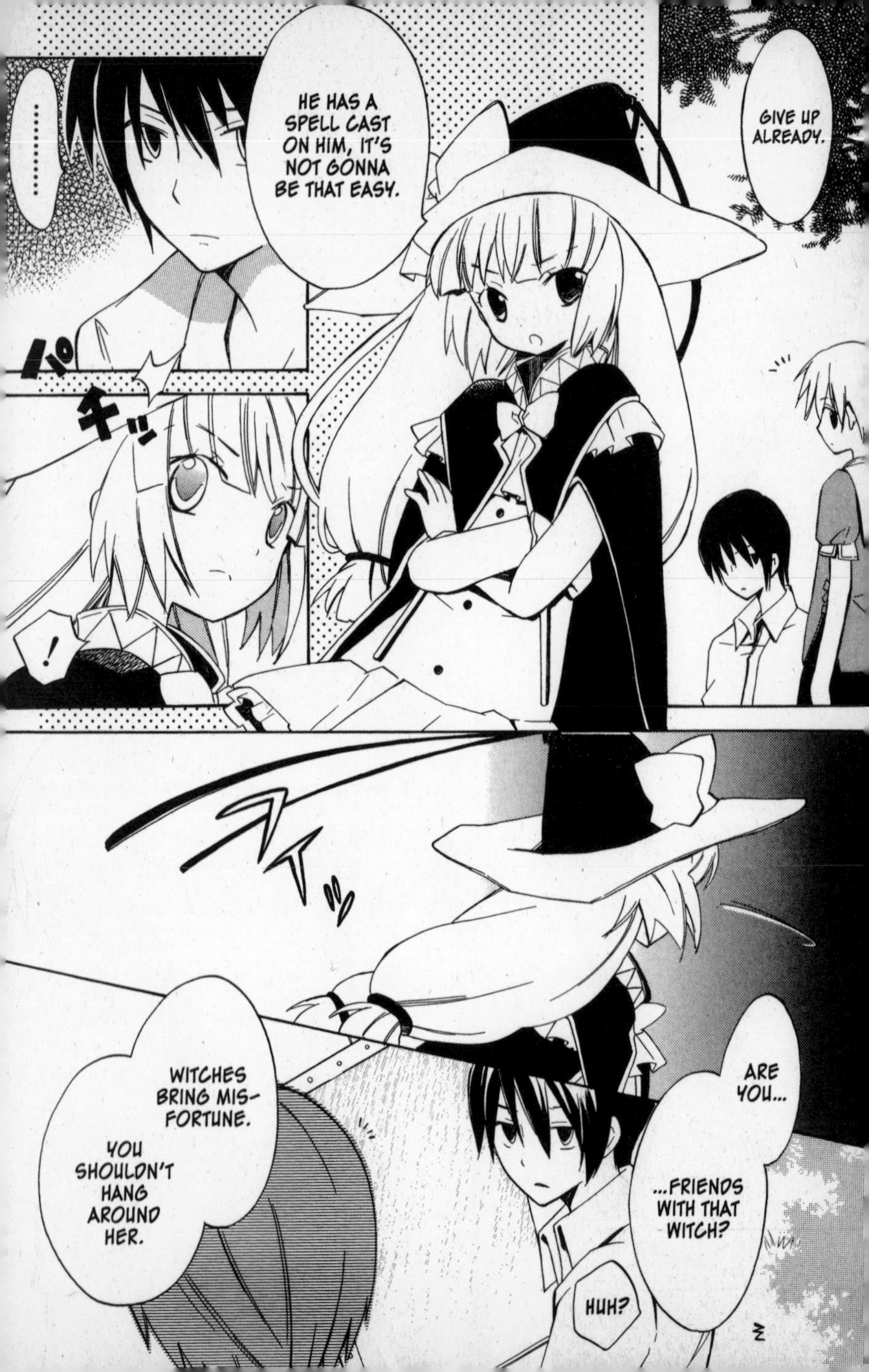
GIVE UP ALREADY.
HE HAS A SPELL CAST ON HIM, IT'S NOT GONNA BE THAT EASY.
......
パチッ
!
スッ
ARE YOU...
...FRIENDS WITH THAT WITCH?
HUH?
WITCHES BRING MIS-FORTUNE.
YOU SHOULDN'T HANG AROUND HER.

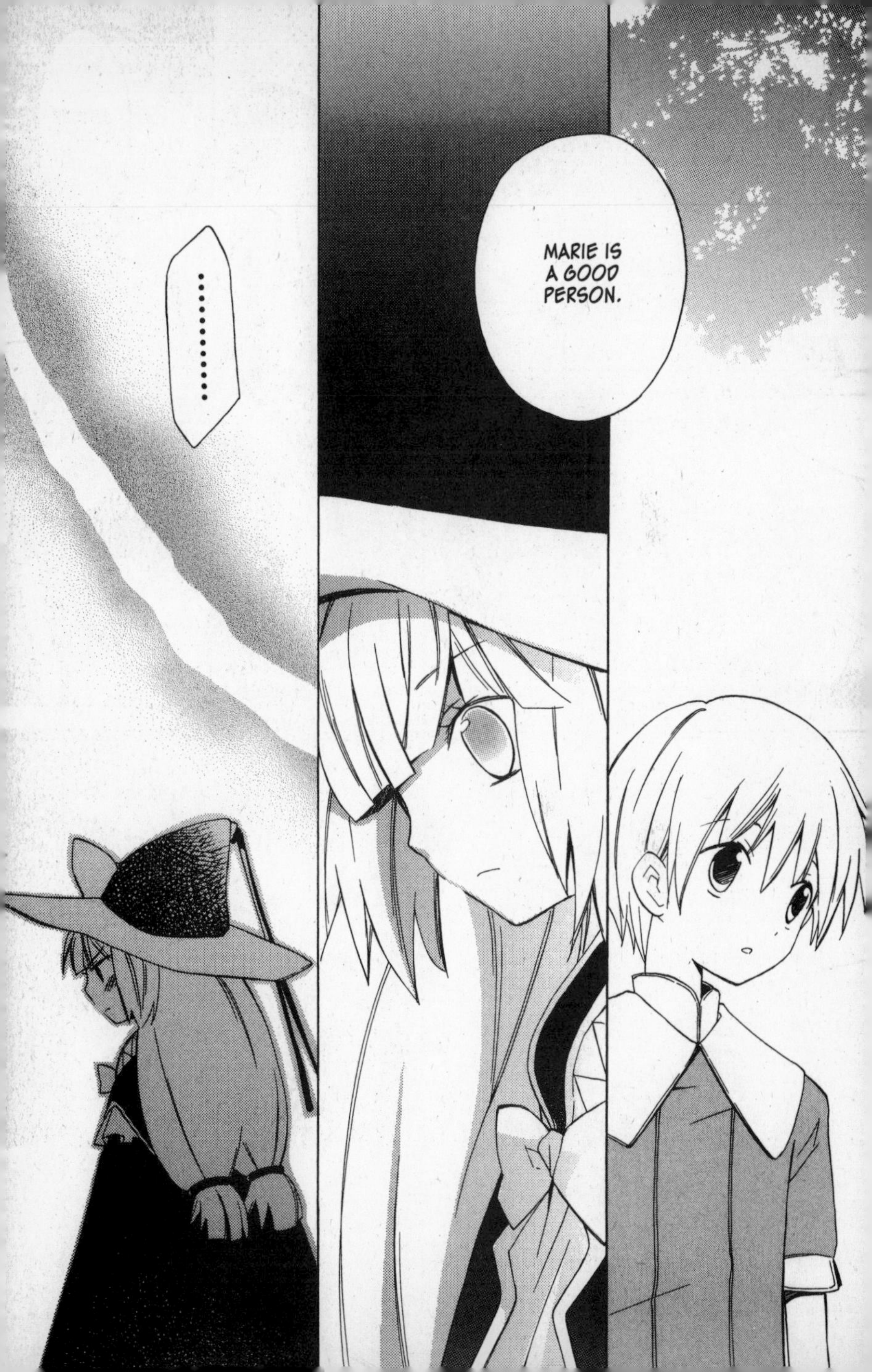
MARIE IS A GOOD PERSON.
....

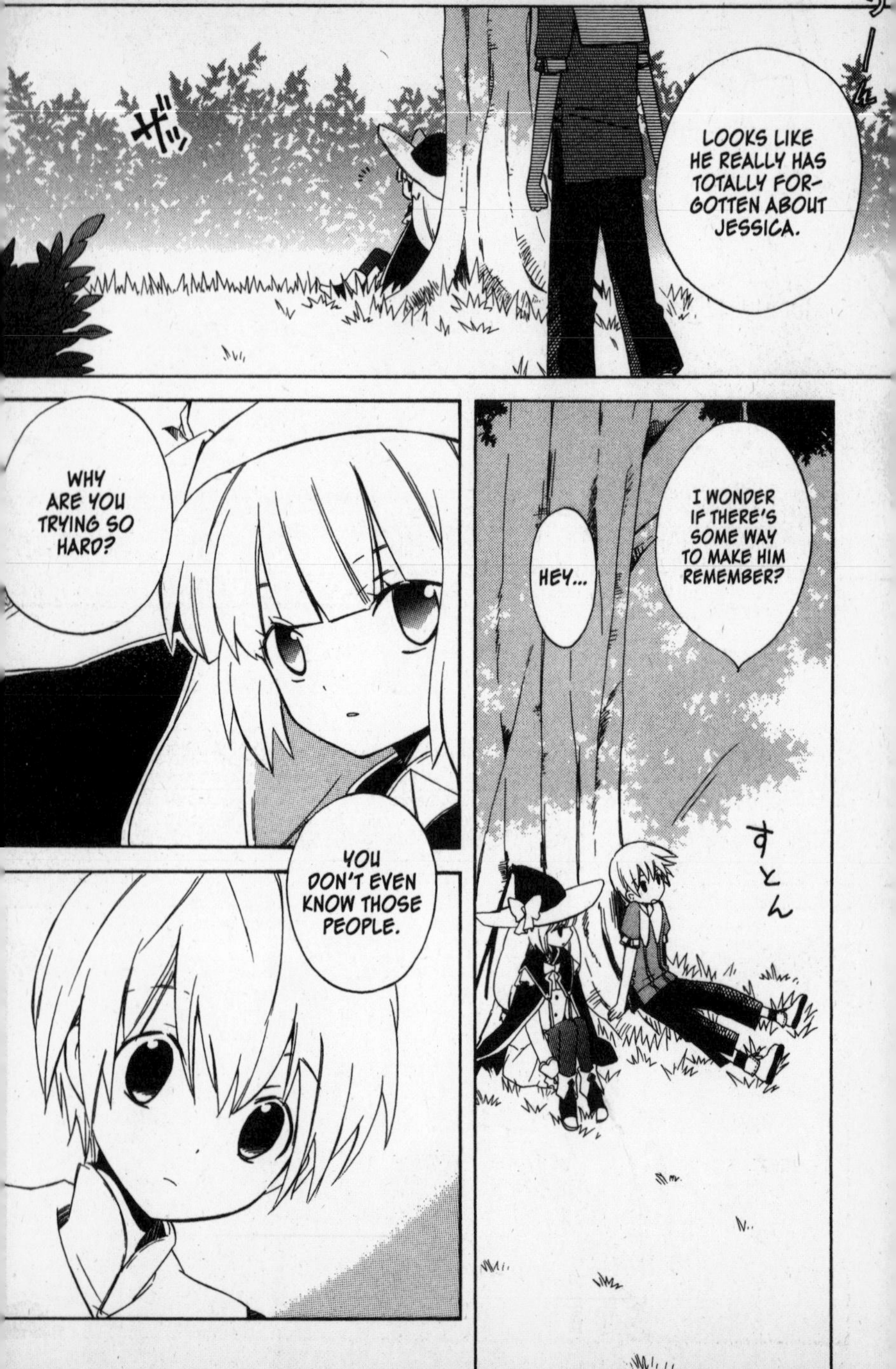
うーん
LOOKS LIKE HE REALLY HAS TOTALLY FOR-GOTTEN ABOUT JESSICA.
ザッ
I WONDER IF THERE'S SOME WAY TO MAKE HIM REMEMBER?
HEY...
すとん
WHY ARE YOU TRYING SO HARD?
YOU DON'T EVEN KNOW THOSE PEOPLE.

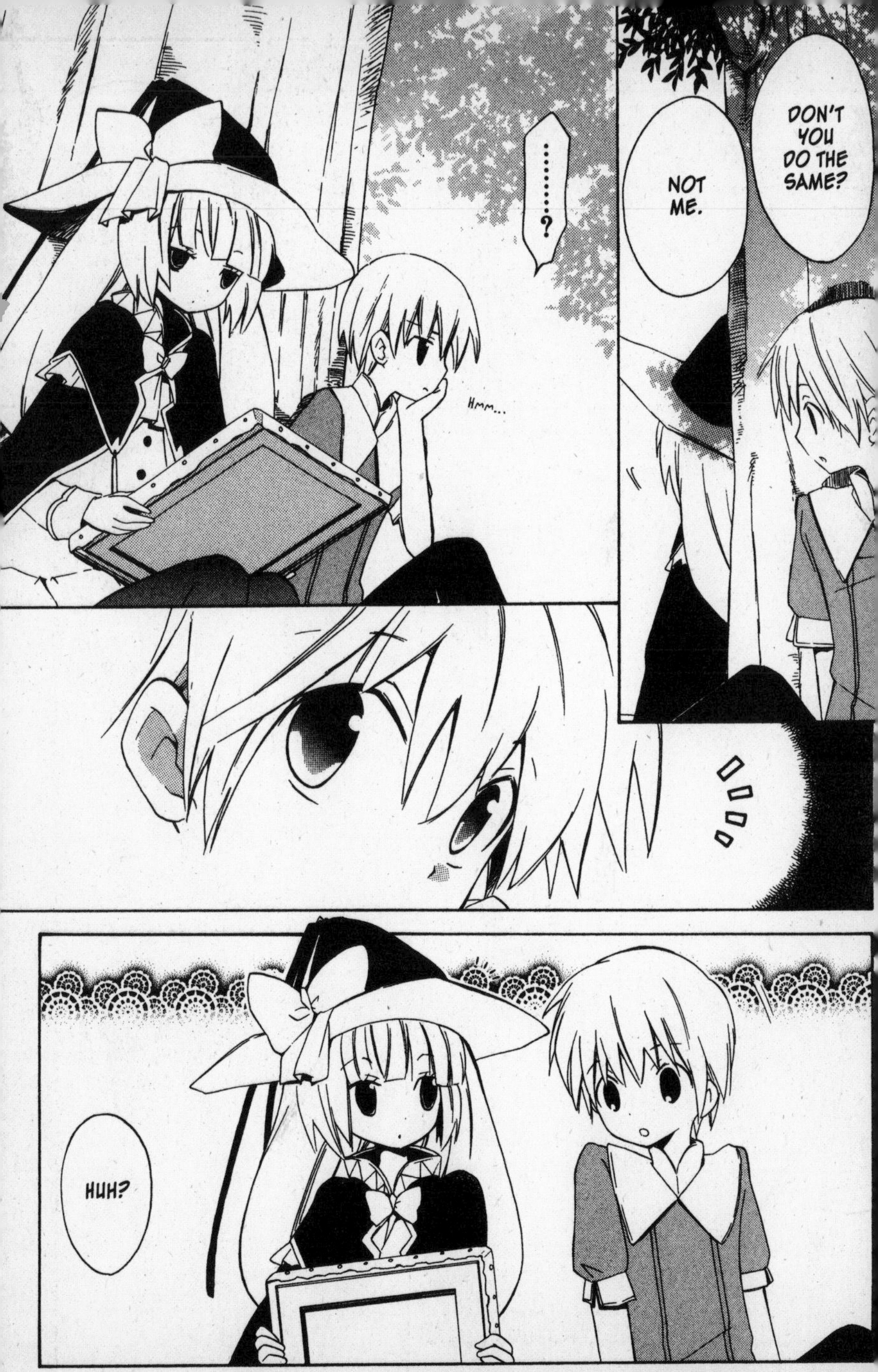
DON'T YOU DO THE SAME?
NOT ME.
......?
HMM...
HUH?

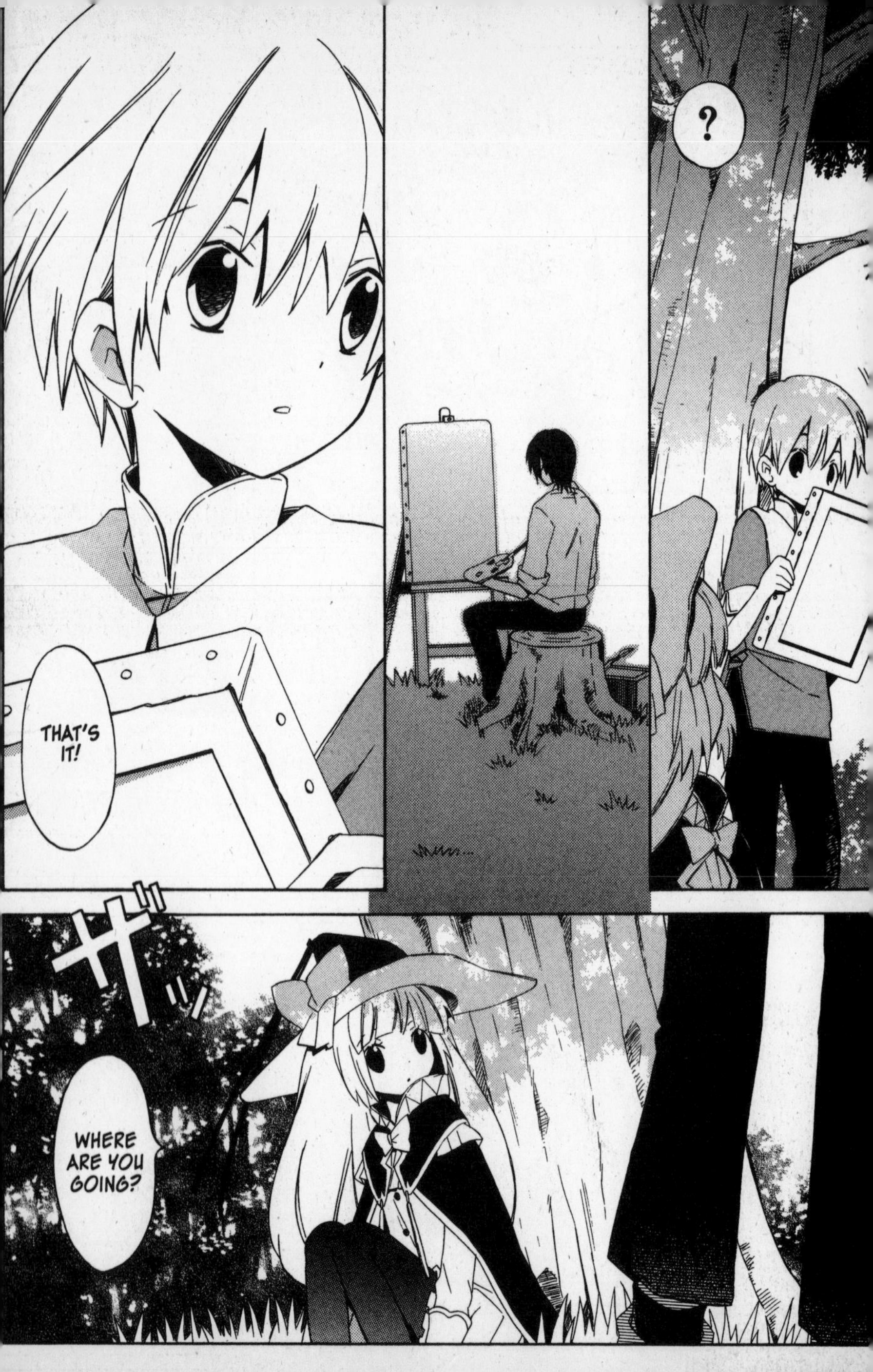
?
THAT'S IT!
ザッ
WHERE ARE YOU GOING?

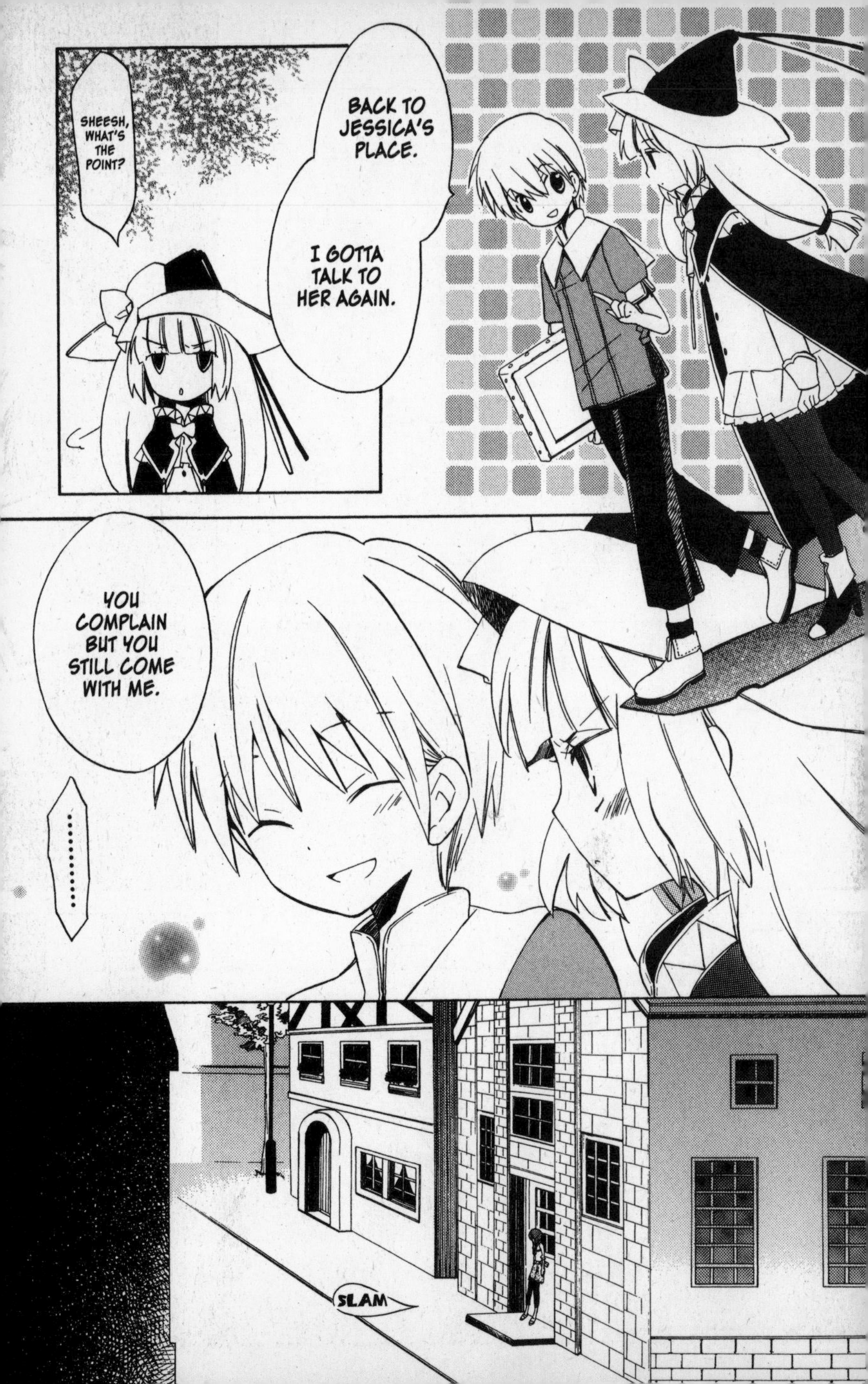
BACK TO JESSICA'S PLACE.
I GOTTA TALK TO HER AGAIN.
SHEESH, WHAT'S THE POINT?
YOU COMPLAIN BUT YOU STILL COME WITH ME.
....
SLAM

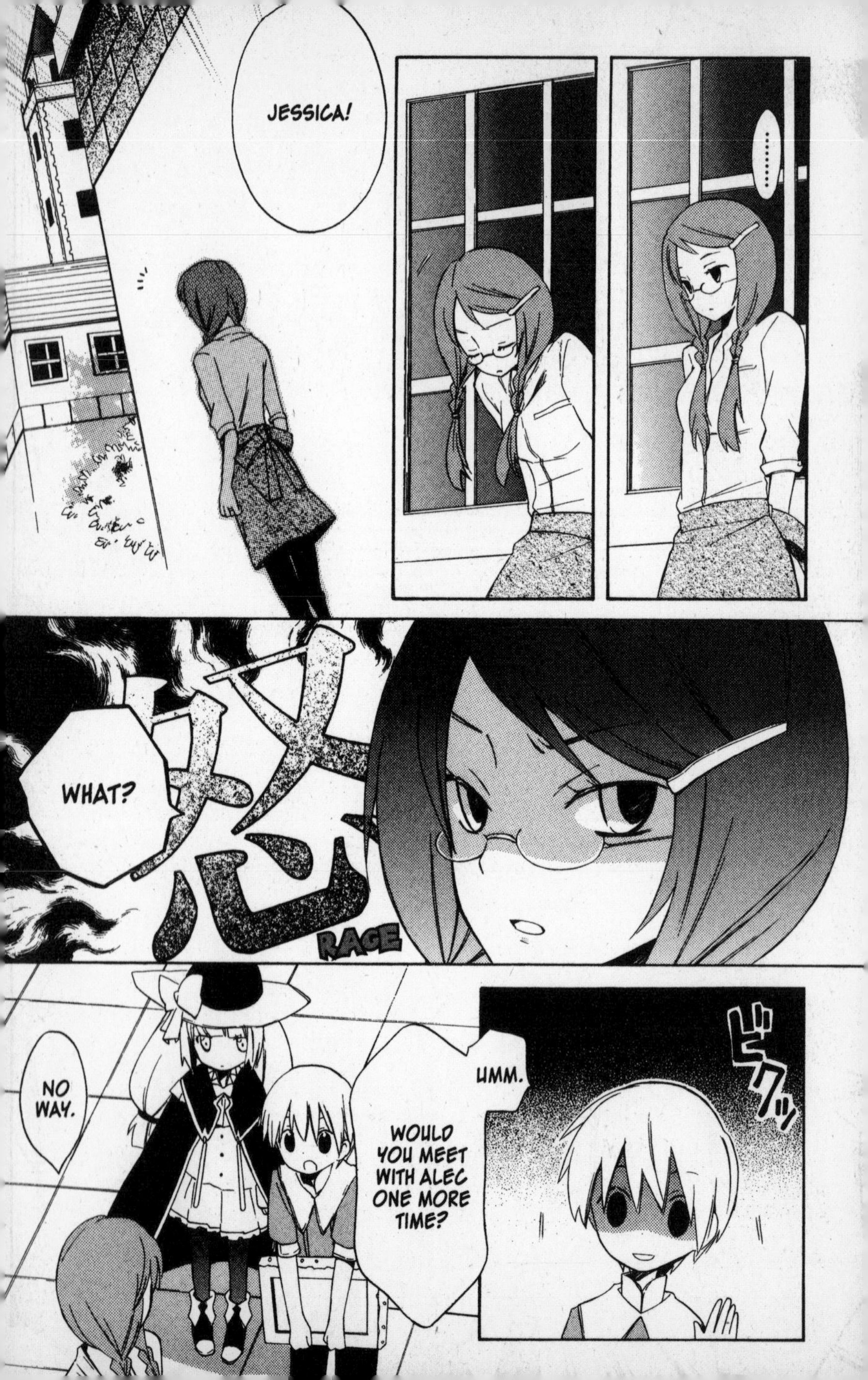
......
JESSICA!
WHAT?
RAGE
ビクッ
UMM.
WOULD YOU MEET WITH ALEC ONE MORE TIME?
NO WAY.

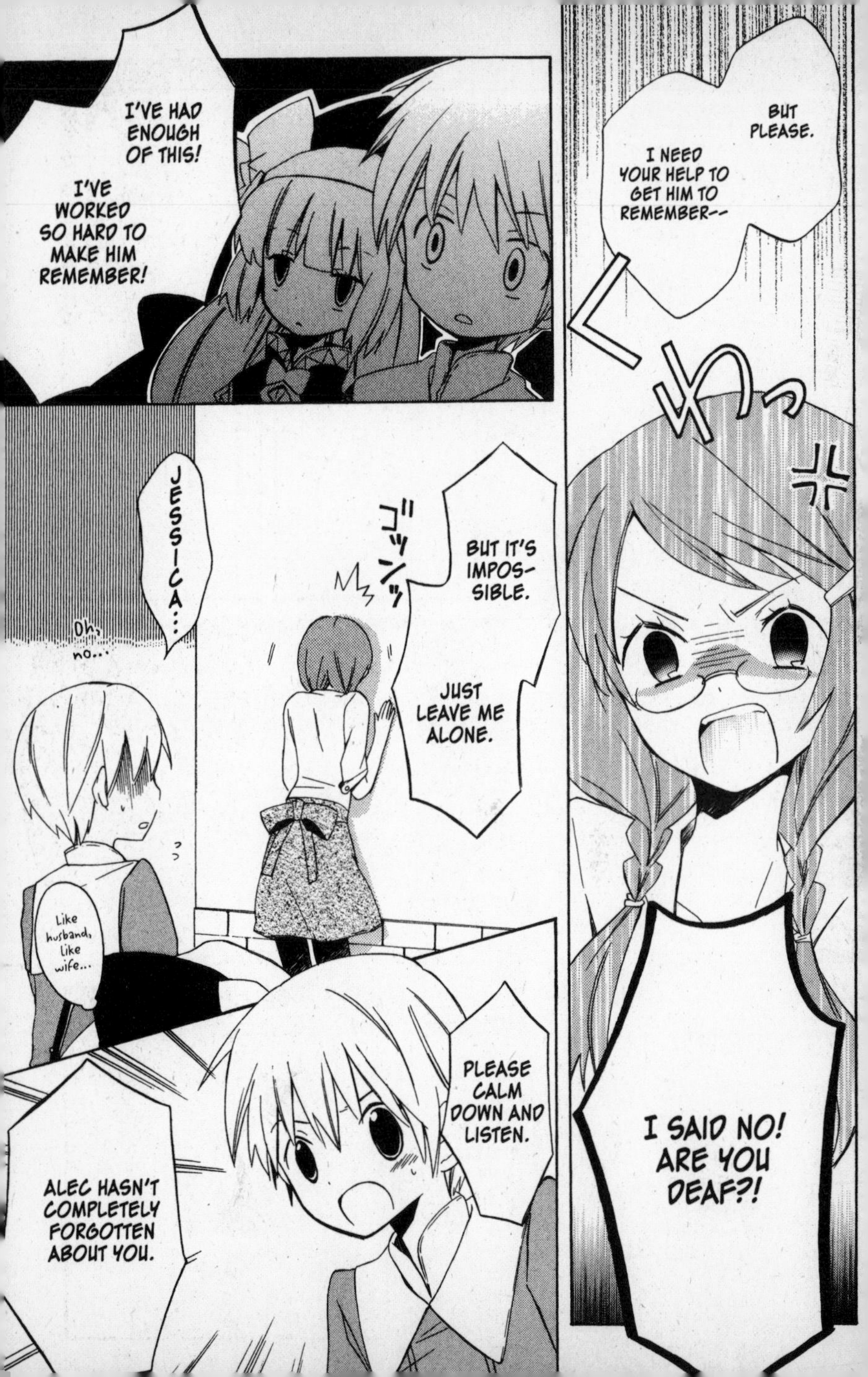
BUT PLEASE.
I NEED YOUR HELP TO GET HIM TO REMEMBER--
むっ
I SAID NO! ARE YOU DEAF?!
I'VE HAD ENOUGH OF THIS!
I'VE WORKED SO HARD TO MAKE HIM REMEMBER!
BUT IT'S IMPOS-SIBLE.
ゴツンッ
JUST LEAVE ME ALONE.
JESSICA...
Oh, no...
Like husband, like wife...
PLEASE CALM DOWN AND LISTEN.
ALEC HASN'T COMPLETELY FORGOTTEN ABOUT YOU.

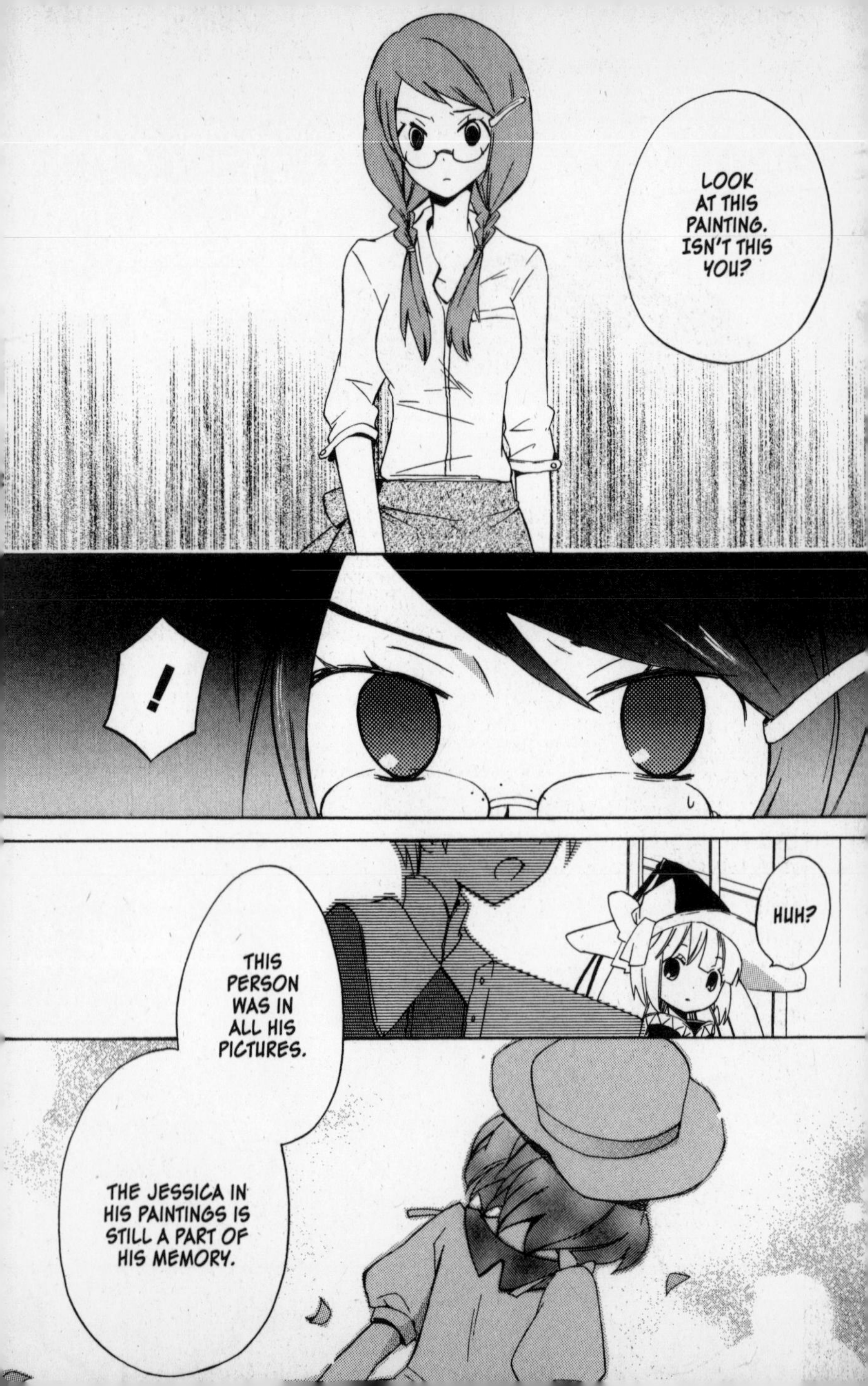
LOOK AT THIS PAINTING. ISN'T THIS YOU?
!
HUH?
THIS PERSON WAS IN ALL HIS PICTURES.
THE JESSICA IN HIS PAINTINGS IS STILL A PART OF HIS MEMORY.

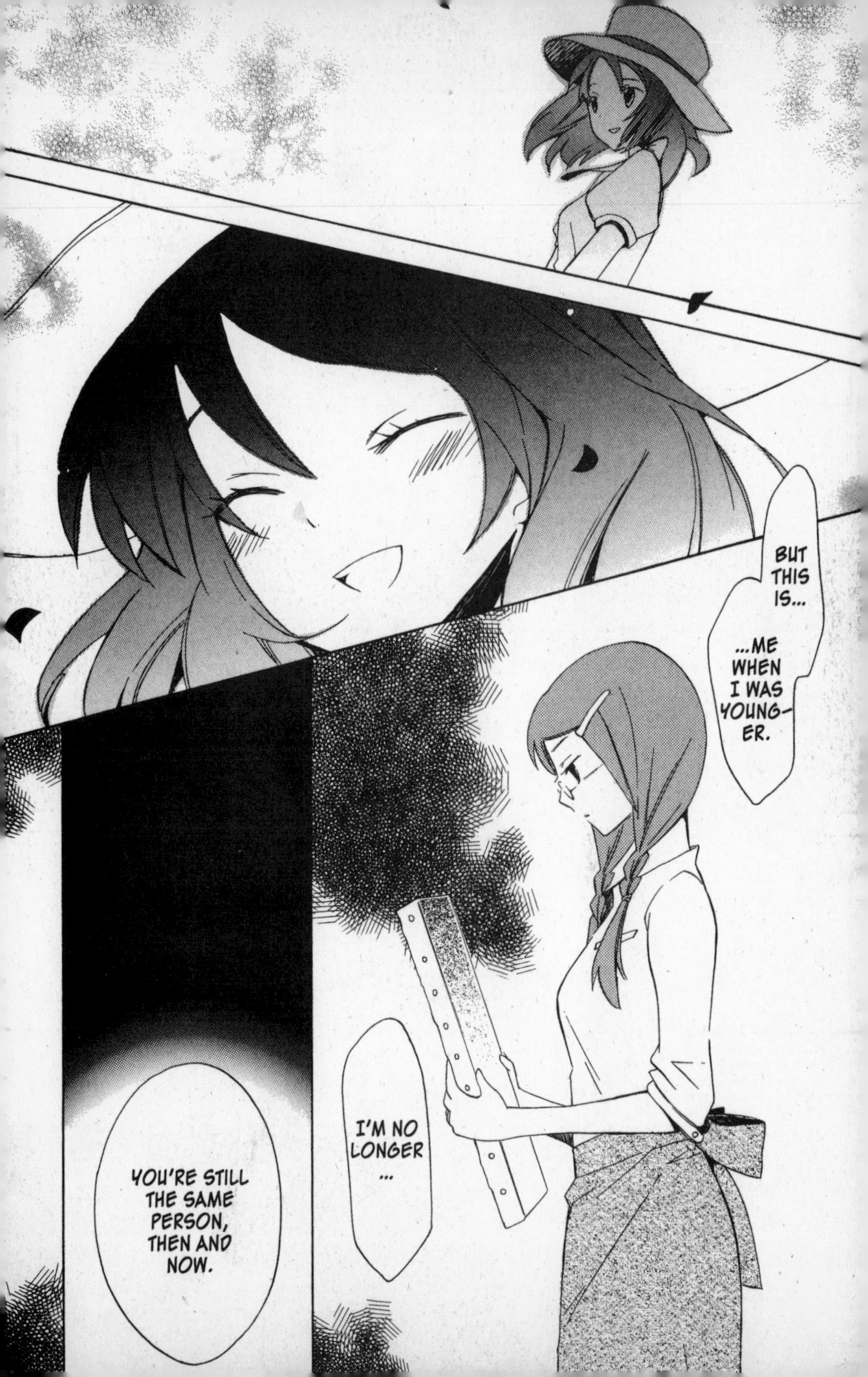
BUT THIS IS... ...ME WHEN I WAS YOUNG-ER.
I'M NO LONGER ...
YOU'RE STILL THE SAME PERSON, THEN AND NOW.

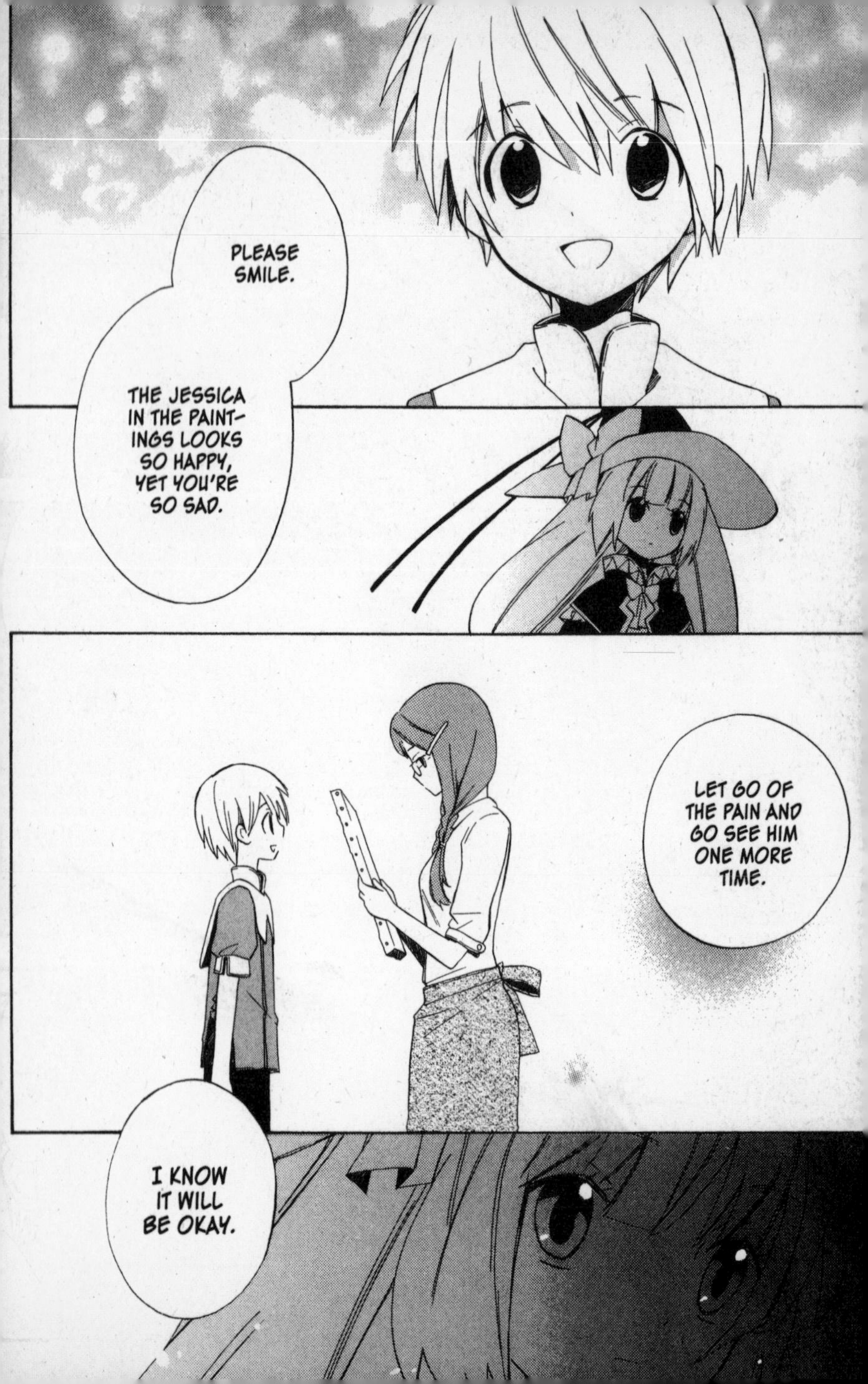
PLEASE SMILE.
THE JESSICA IN THE PAINT-INGS LOOKS SO HAPPY, YET YOU'RE SO SAD.
LET GO OF THE PAIN AND GO SEE HIM ONE MORE TIME.
I KNOW IT WILL BE OKAY.

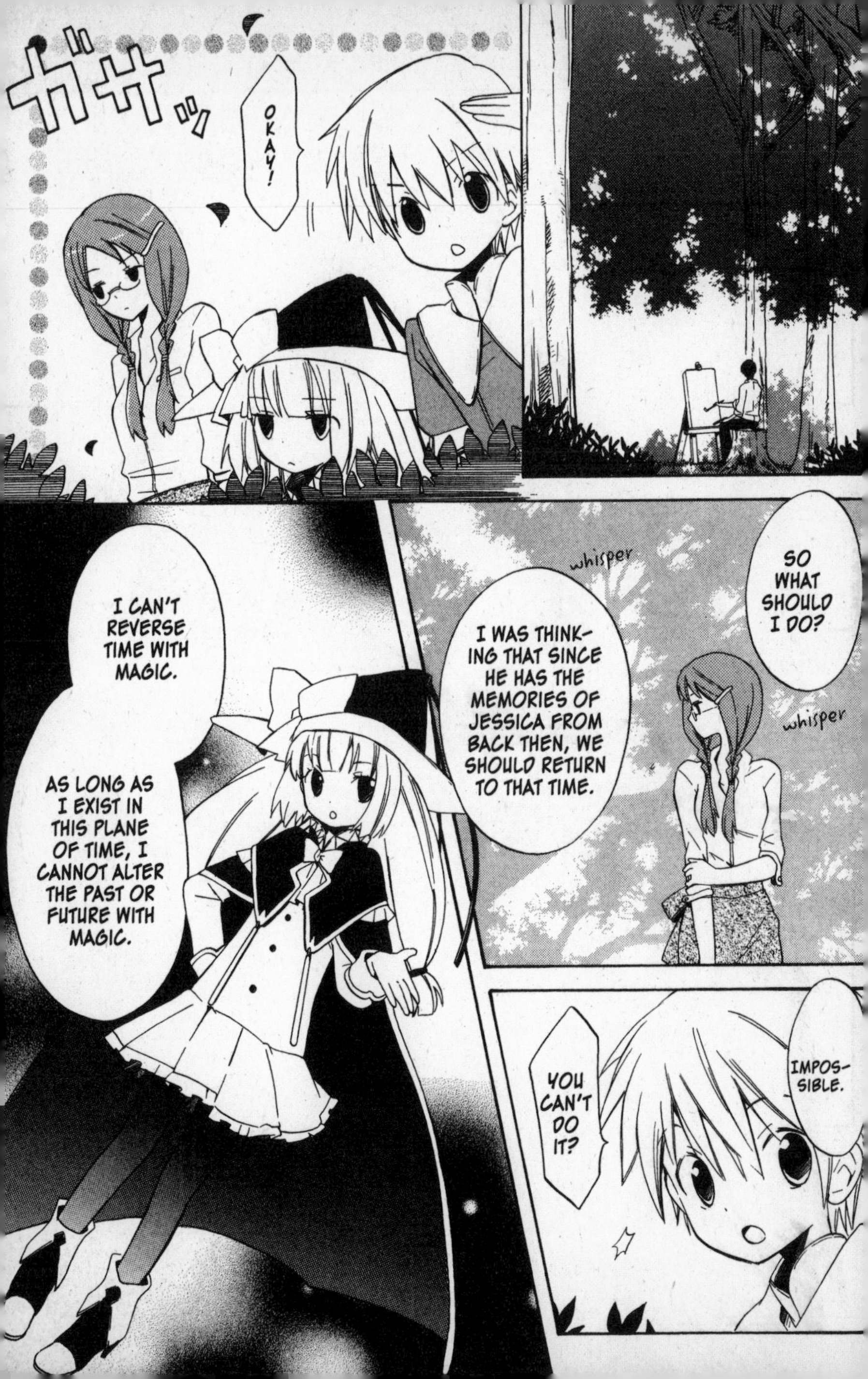
ガサッ
OKAY!
SO WHAT SHOULD I DO?
whisper
I WAS THINKING THAT SINCE HE HAS THE MEMORIES OF JESSICA FROM BACK THEN, WE SHOULD RETURN TO THAT TIME.
whisper
IMPOSSIBLE.
YOU CAN'T DO IT?
I CAN'T REVERSE TIME WITH MAGIC.
AS LONG AS I EXIST IN THIS PLANE OF TIME, I CANNOT ALTER THE PAST OR FUTURE WITH MAGIC.

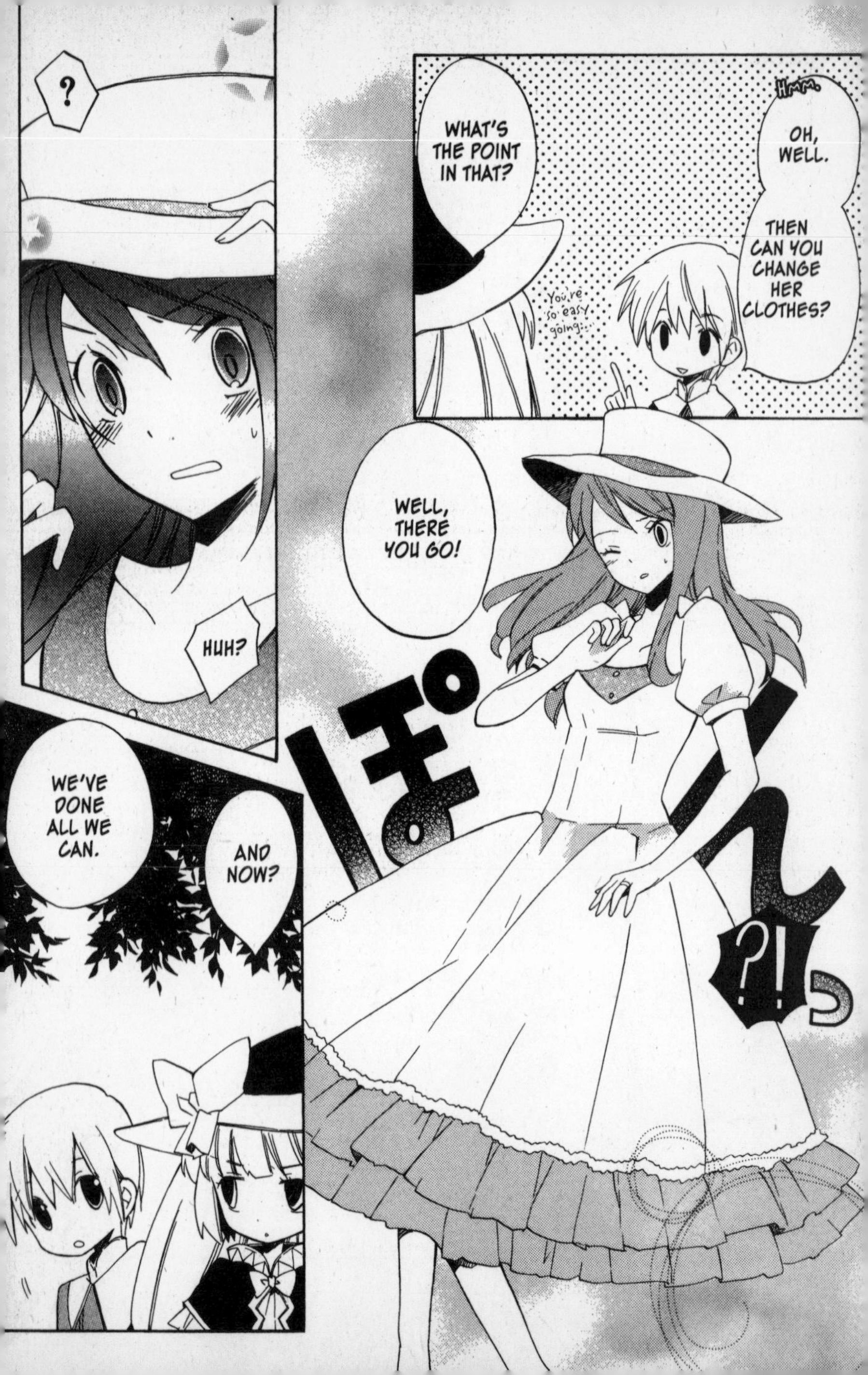
HMM.
OH, WELL.
THEN CAN YOU CHANGE HER CLOTHES?
You're so easy going...
WHAT'S THE POINT IN THAT?
WELL, THERE YOU GO!
ぽん
?!
?
HUH?
WE'VE DONE ALL WE CAN.
AND NOW?

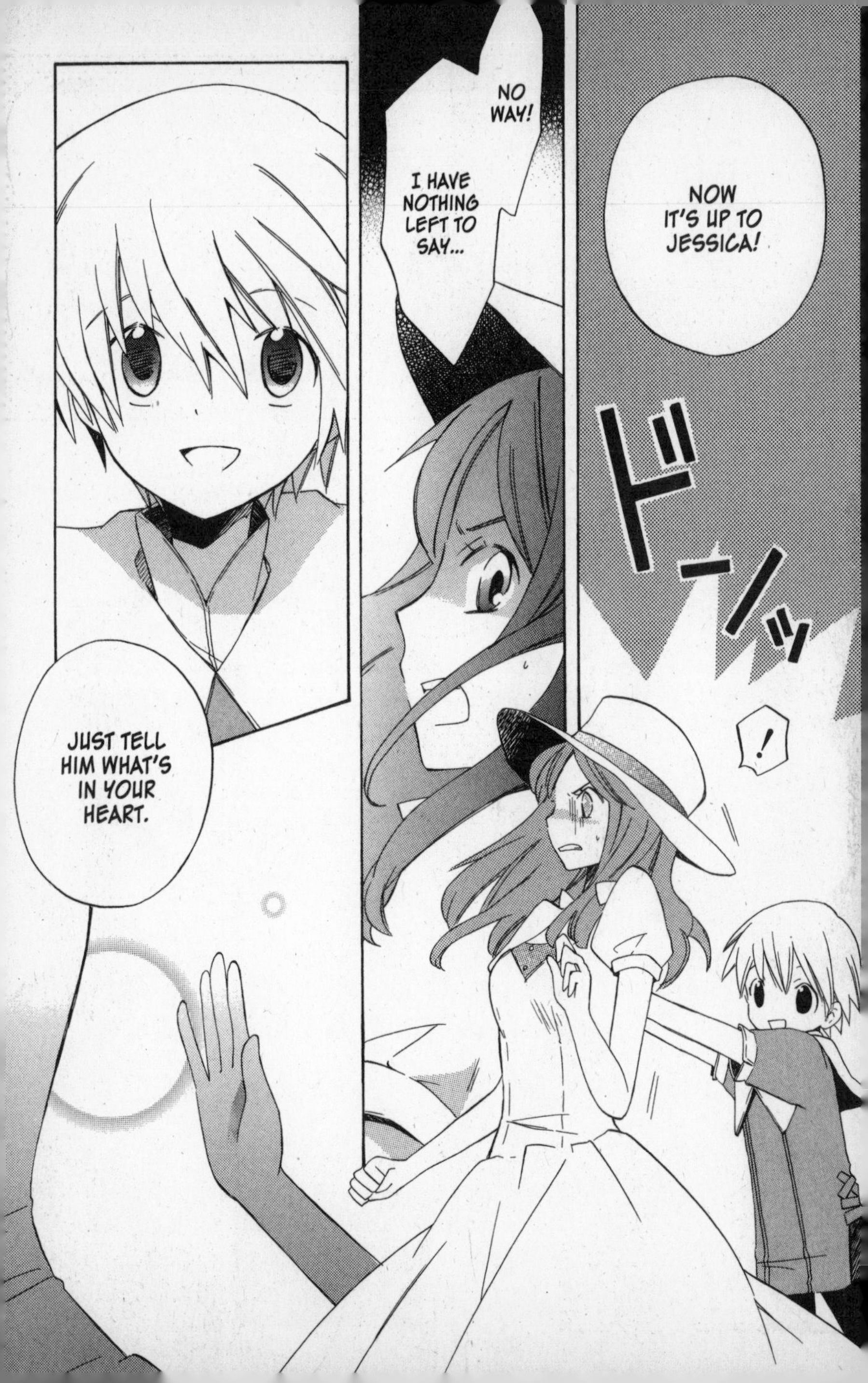
NOW IT'S UP TO JESSICA!
ドーンッ
!
NO WAY!
I HAVE NOTHING LEFT TO SAY...
JUST TELL HIM WHAT'S IN YOUR HEART.

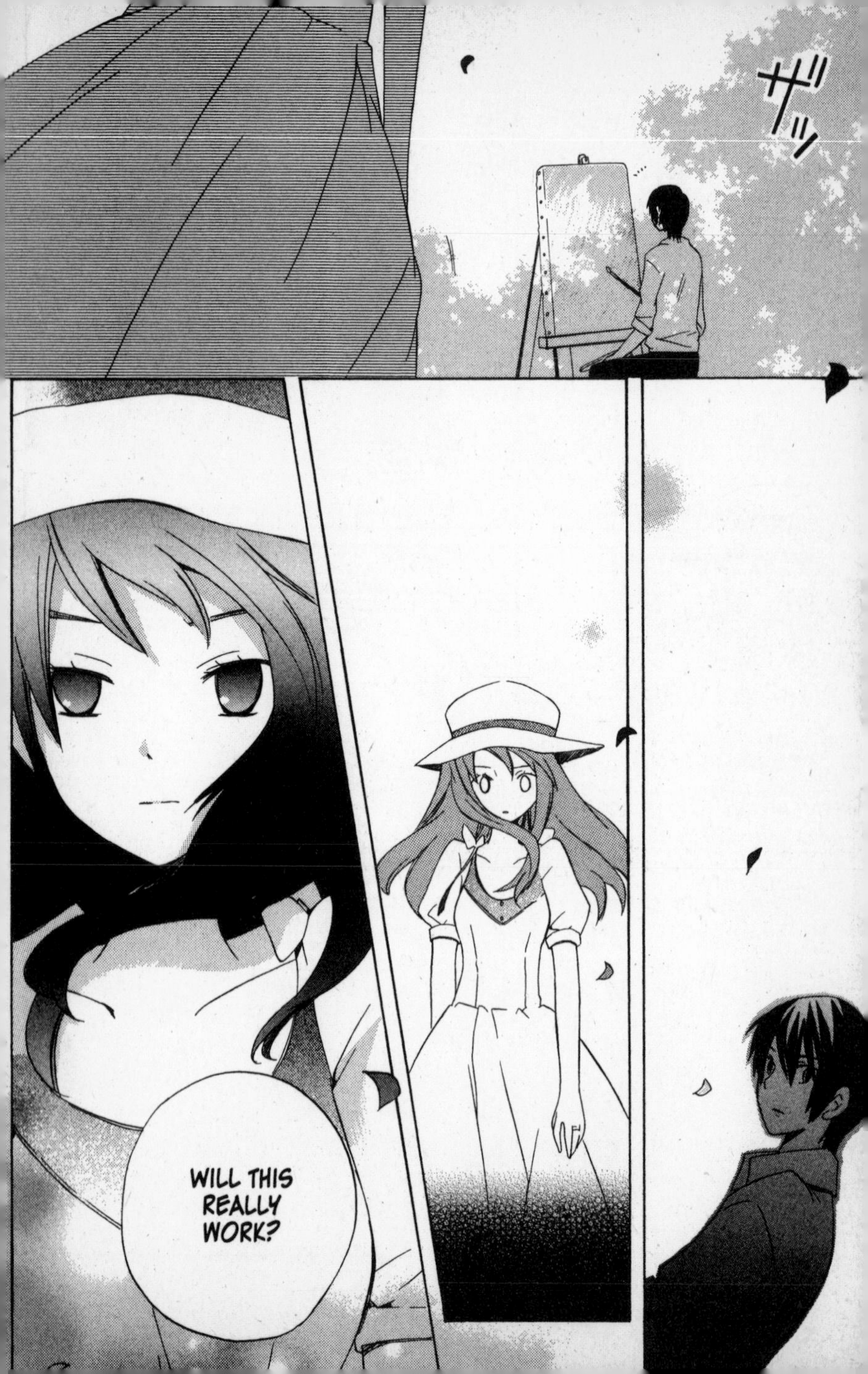
ザッ
WILL THIS REALLY WORK?

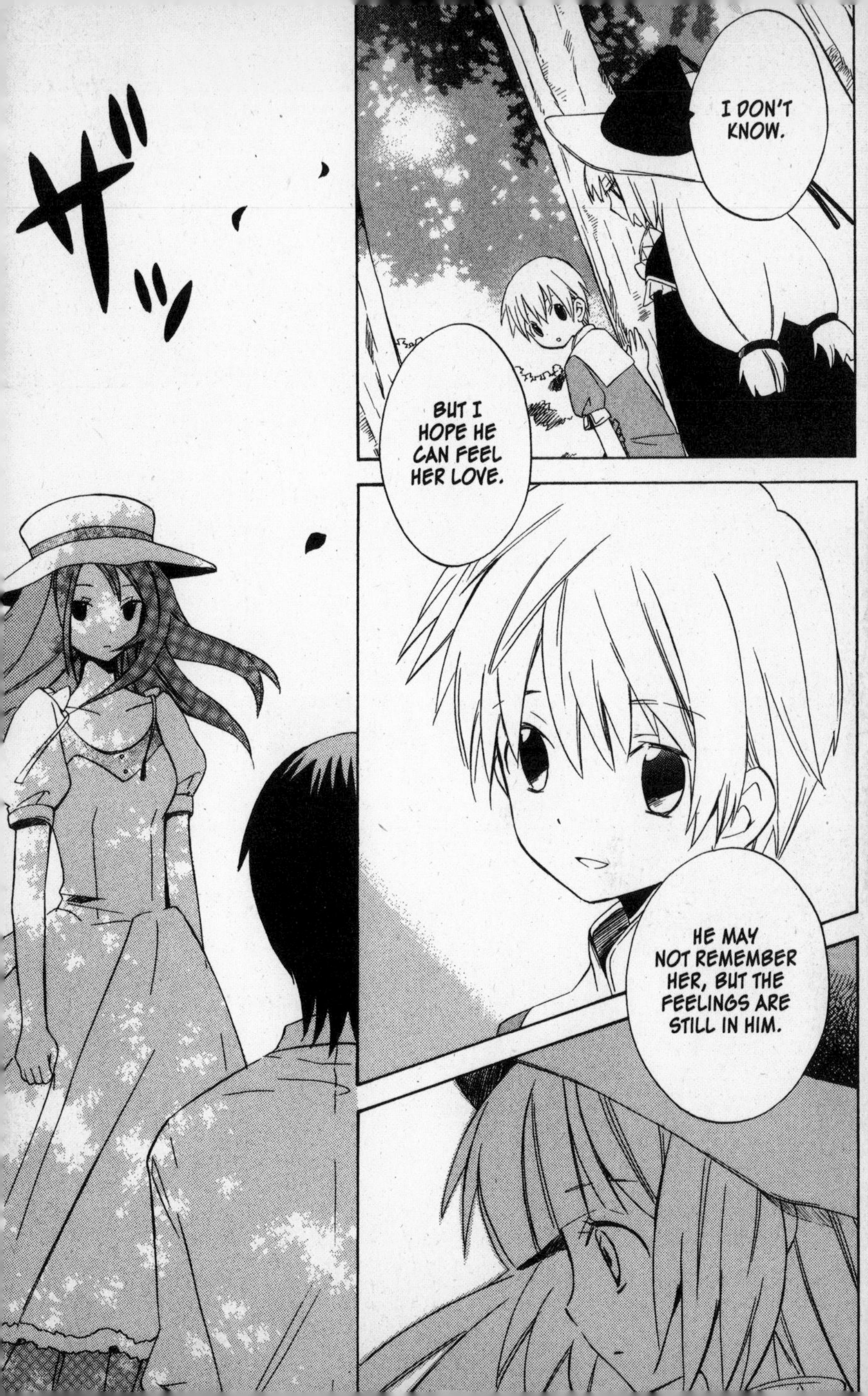
I DON'T KNOW.
BUT I HOPE HE CAN FEEL HER LOVE.
HE MAY NOT REMEMBER HER, BUT THE FEELINGS ARE STILL IN HIM.
ザッ

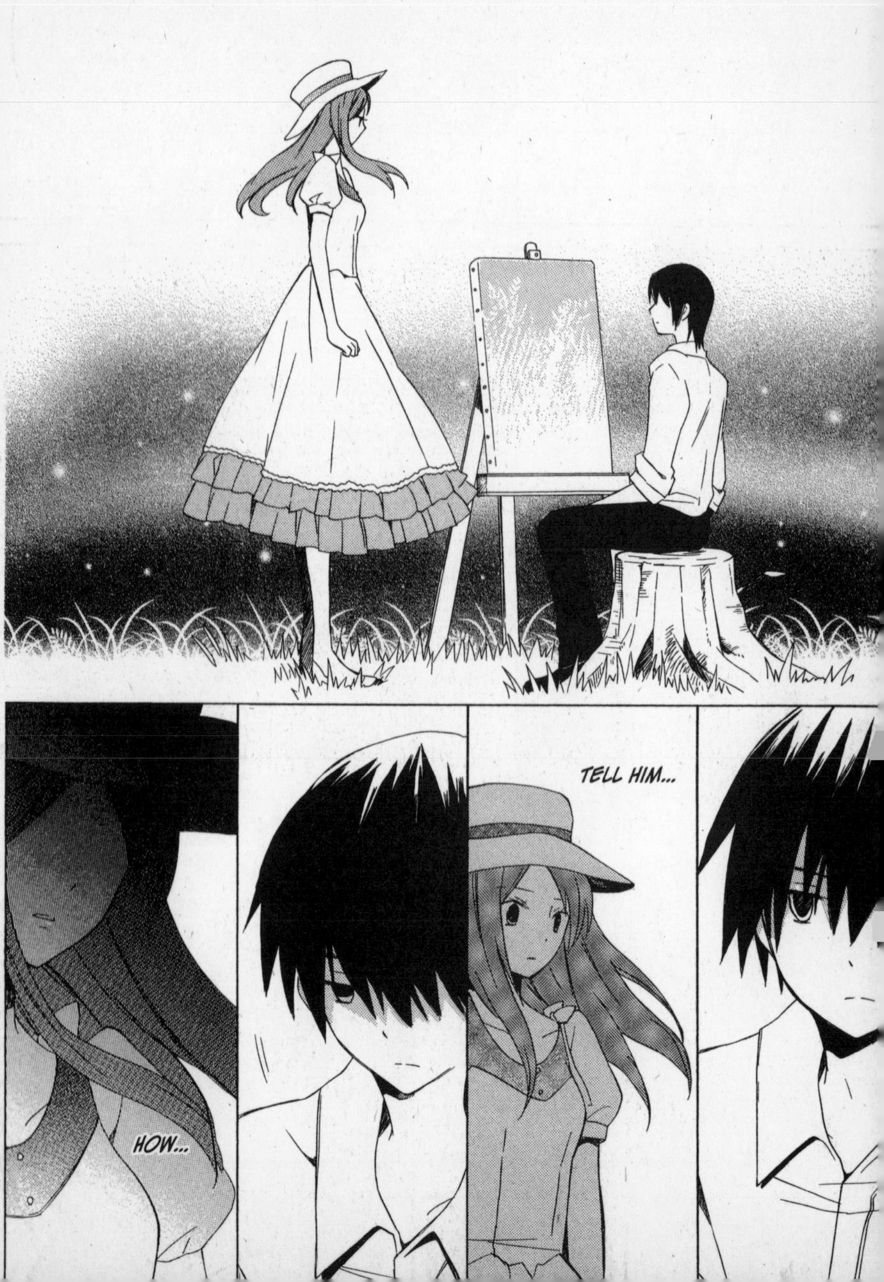
TELL HIM...
HOW...

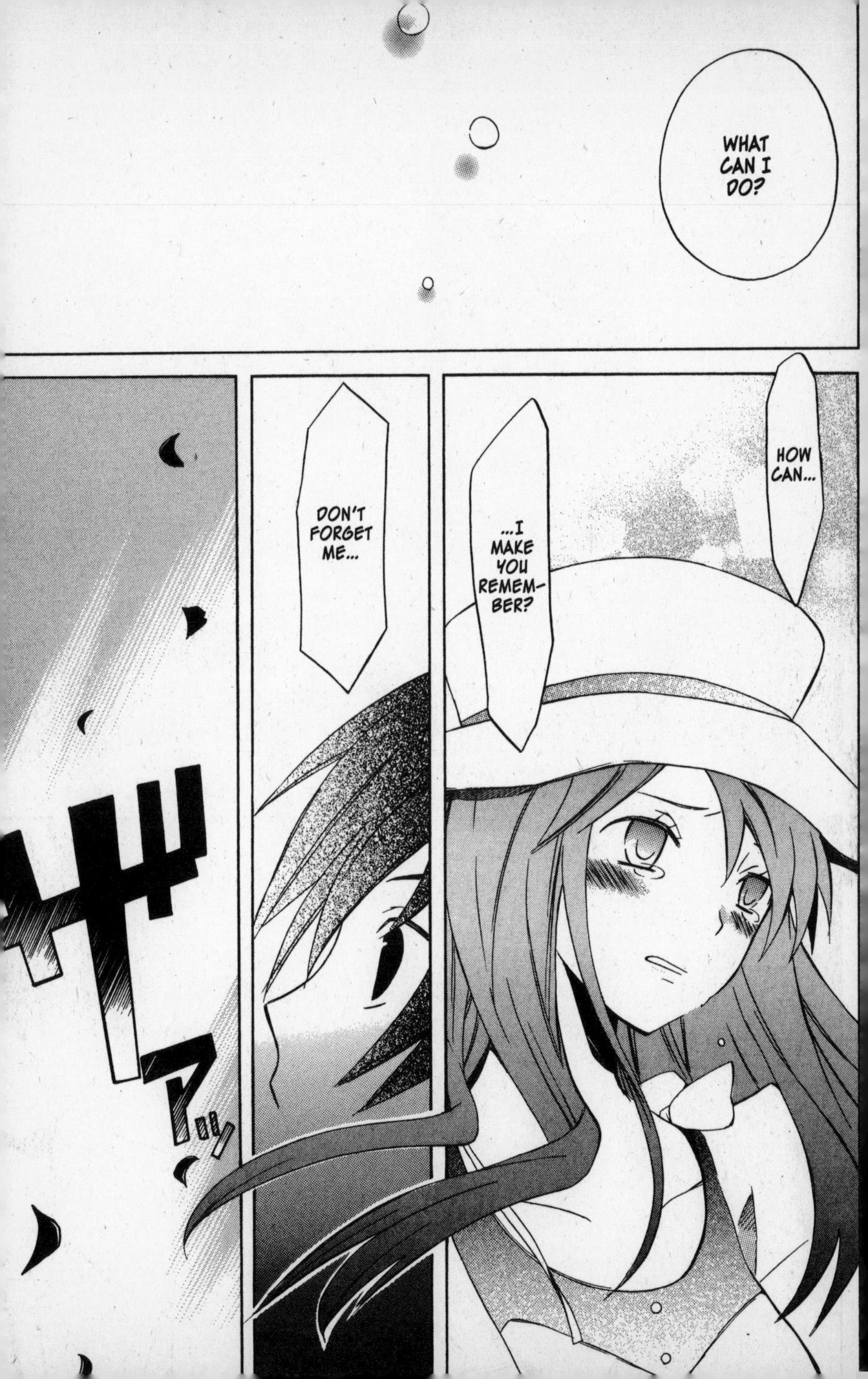
WHAT CAN I DO?
HOW CAN...
...I MAKE YOU REMEMBER?
DON'T FORGET ME...
ザァアッ

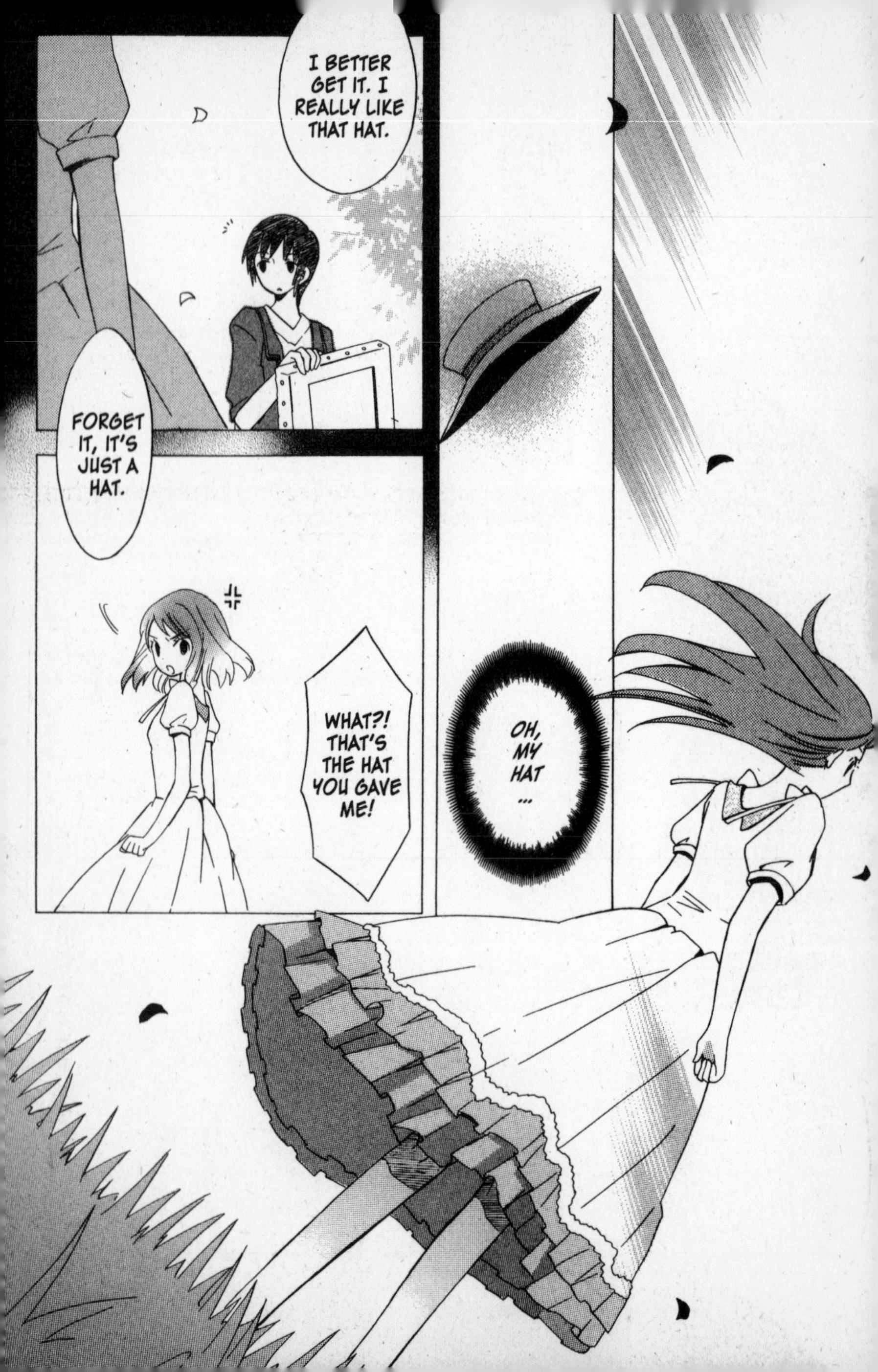
OH, MY HAT ...
I BETTER GET IT. I REALLY LIKE THAT HAT.
FORGET IT, IT'S JUST A HAT.
WHAT?! THAT'S THE HAT YOU GAVE ME!

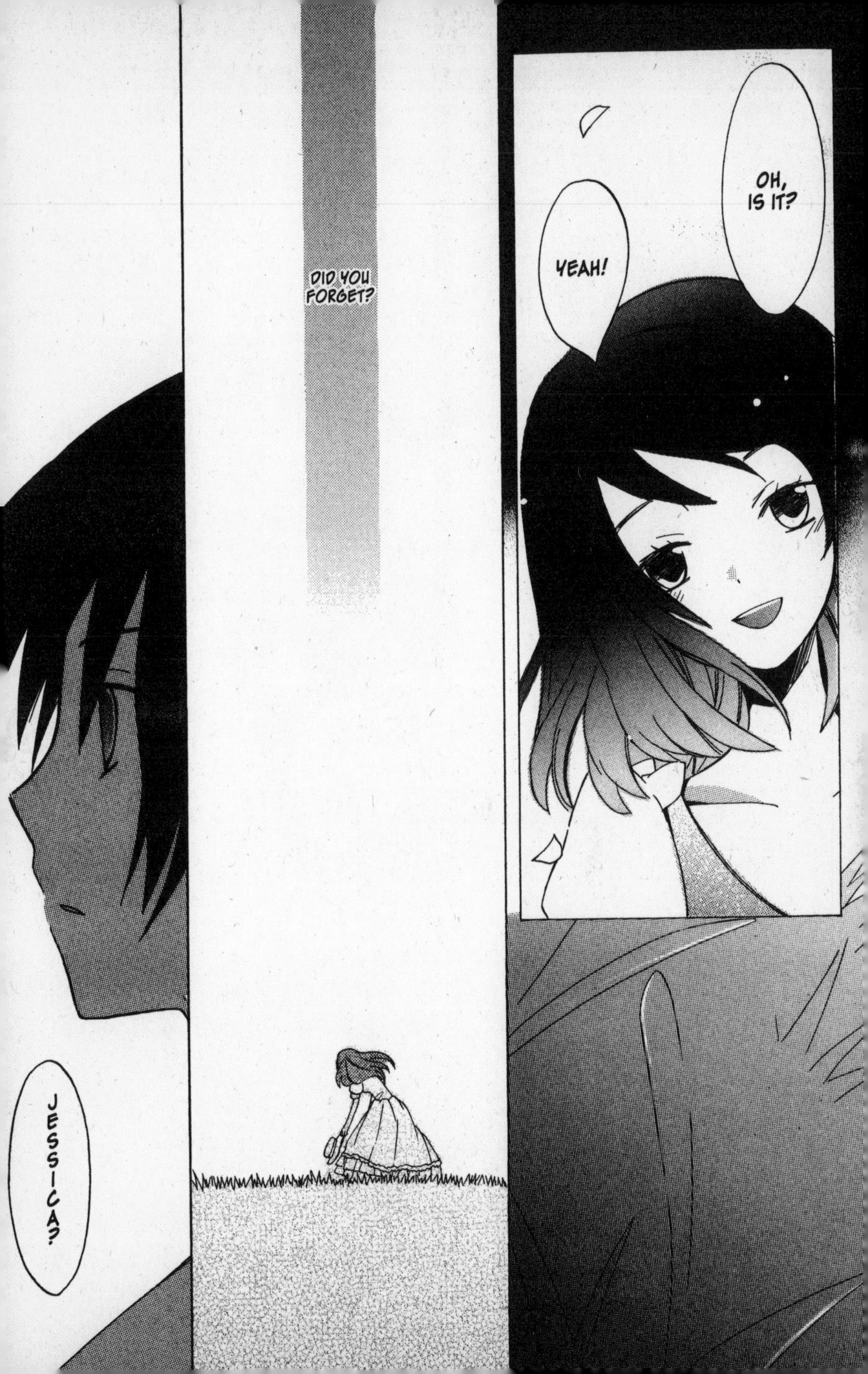
OH, IS IT?
YEAH!
DID YOU FORGET?
JESSICA?

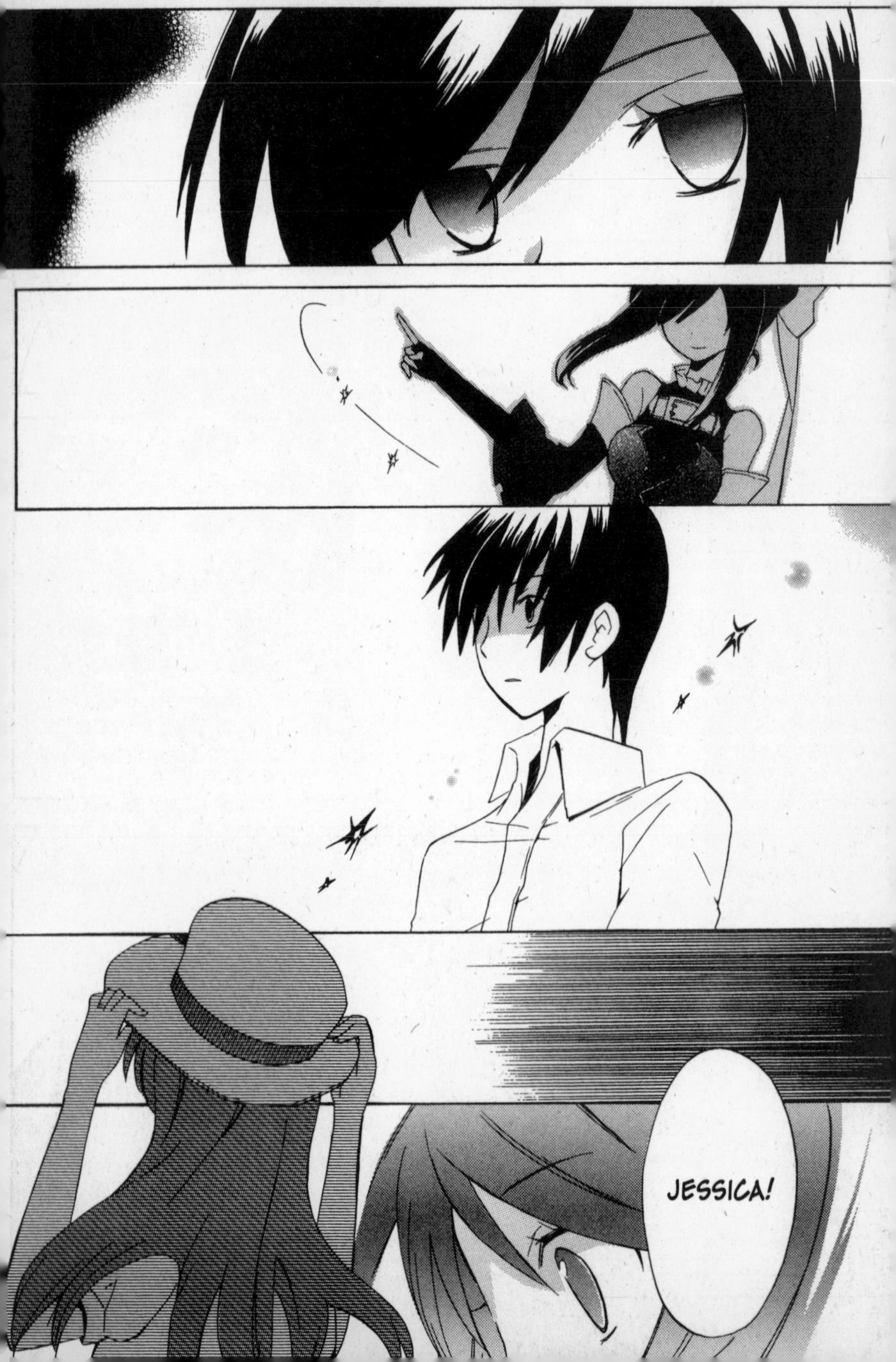
JESSICA!

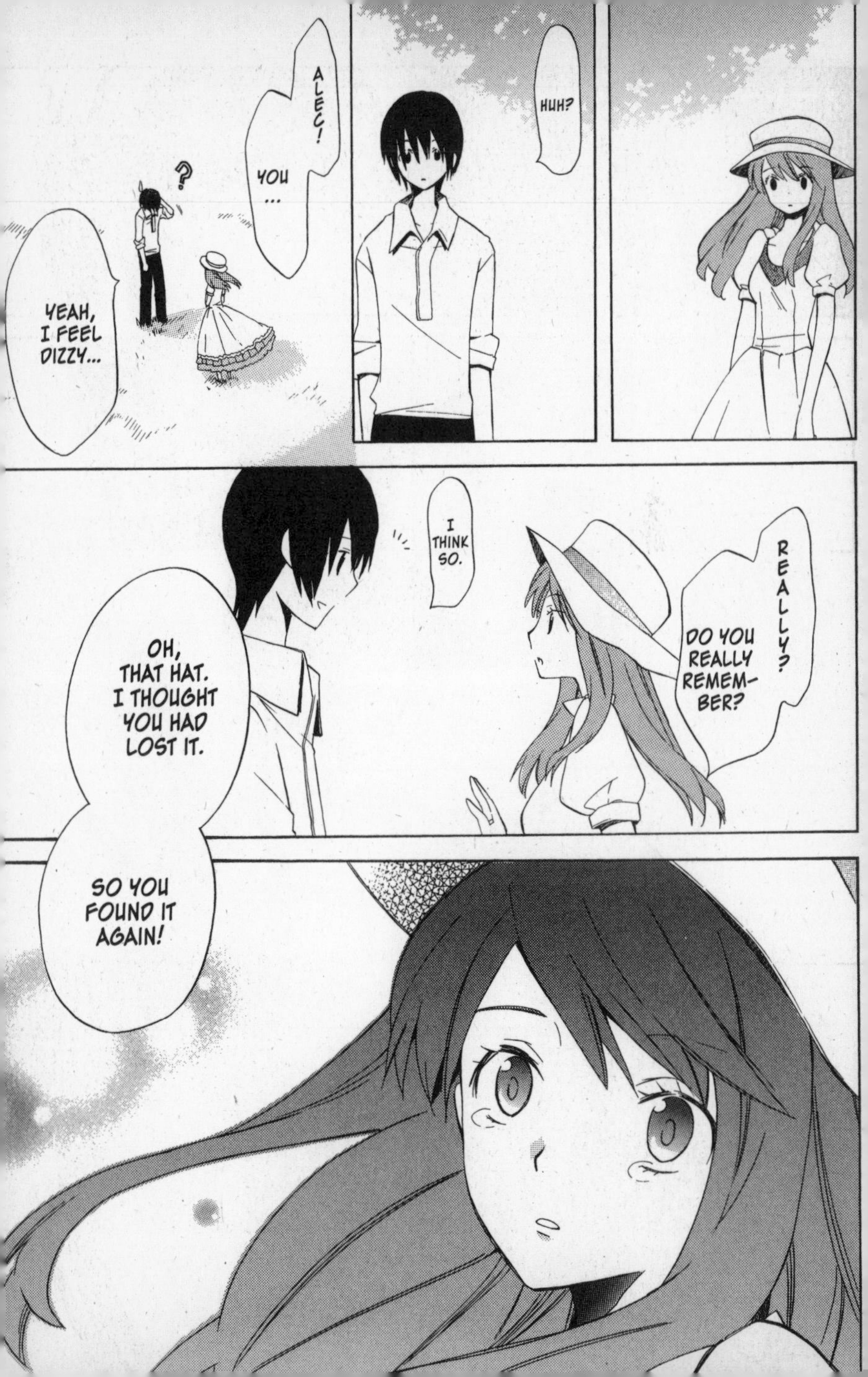
HUH?
ALEC!
YOU ...
YEAH, I FEEL DIZZY...
REALLY?
DO YOU REALLY REMEM-BER?
I THINK SO.
OH, THAT HAT. I THOUGHT YOU HAD LOST IT.
SO YOU FOUND IT AGAIN!

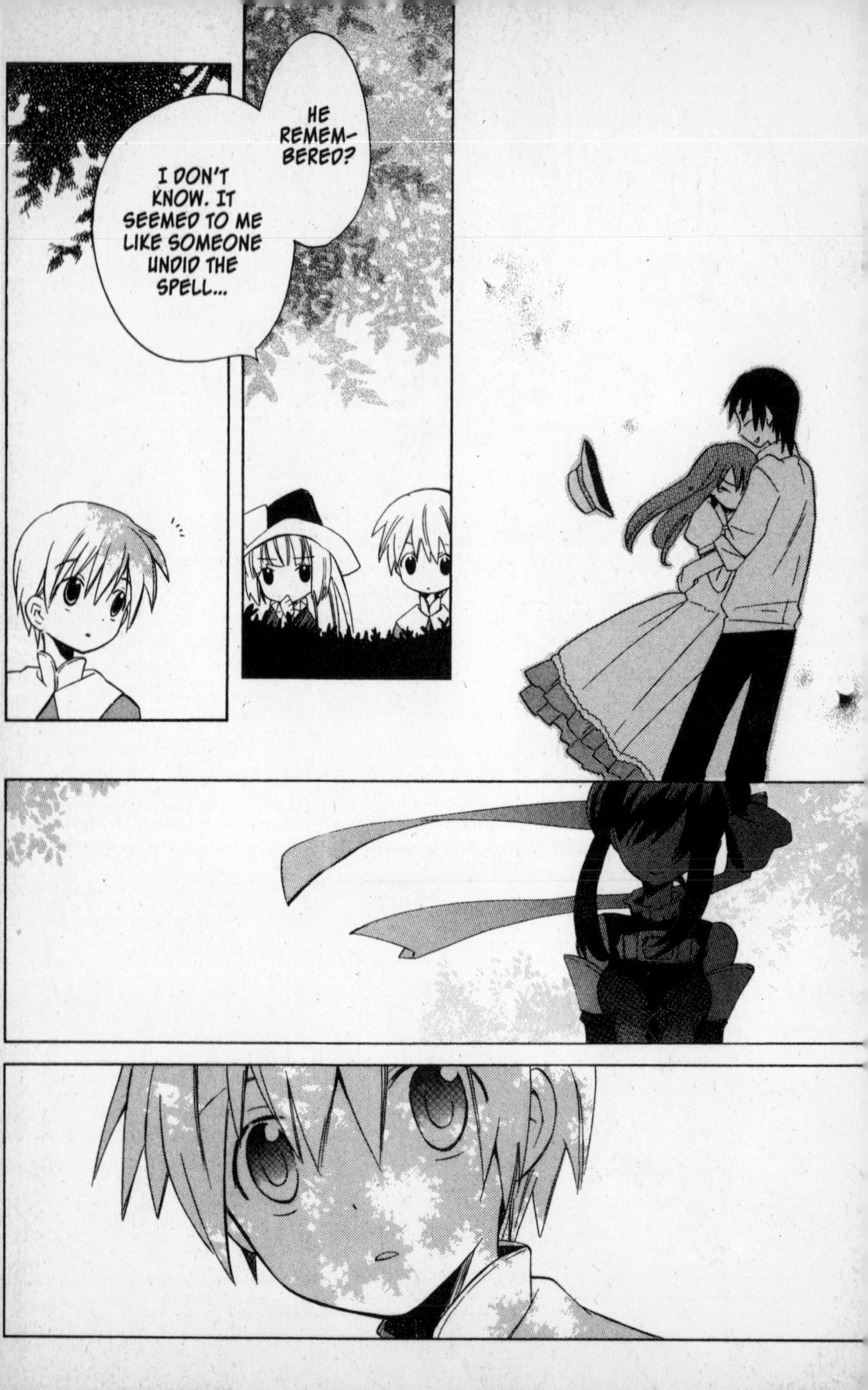
HE REMEMBERED?
I DON'T KNOW. IT SEEMED TO ME LIKE SOMEONE UNDID THE SPELL...

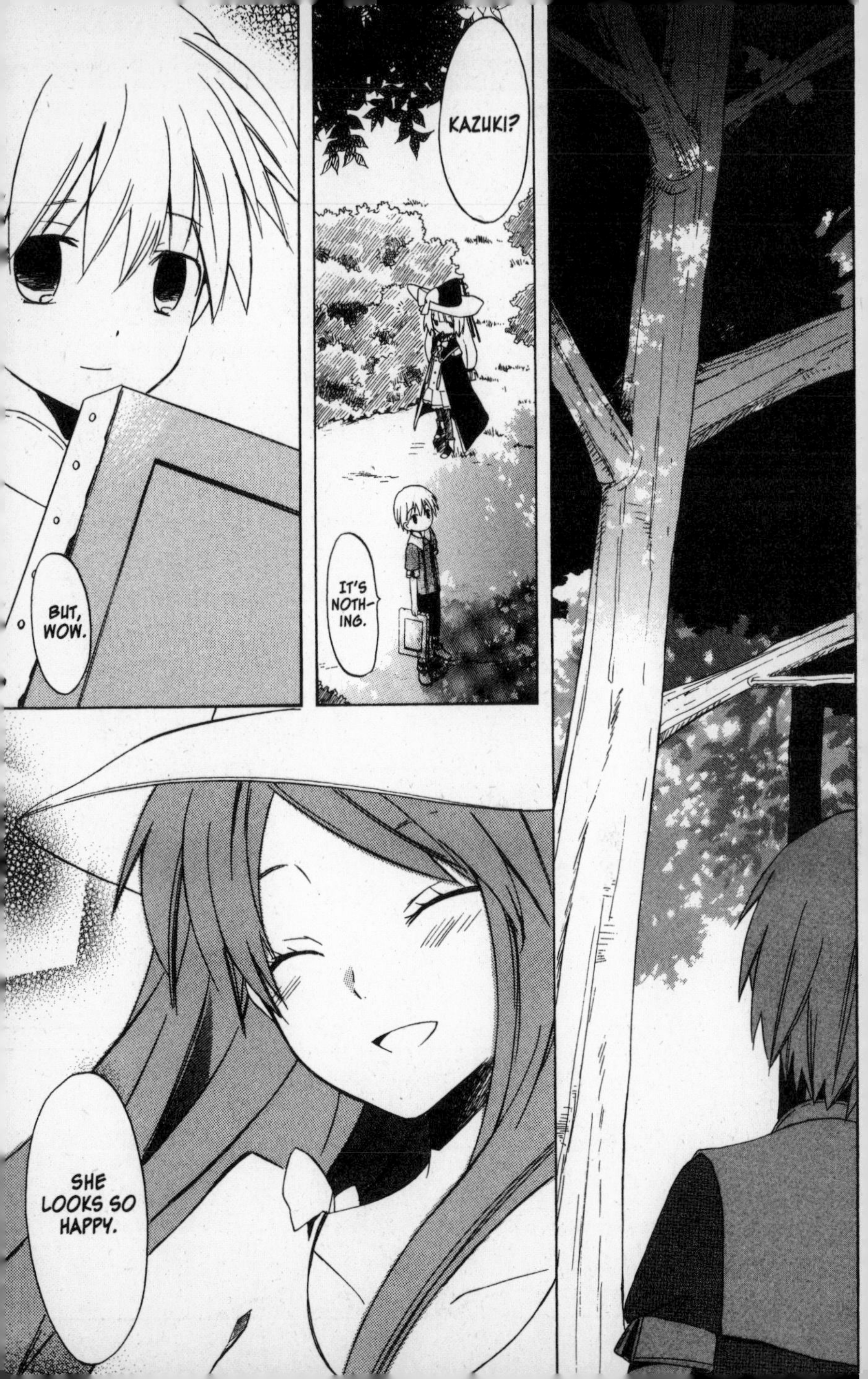
KAZUKI?
IT'S NOTHING.
BUT, WOW.
SHE LOOKS SO HAPPY.

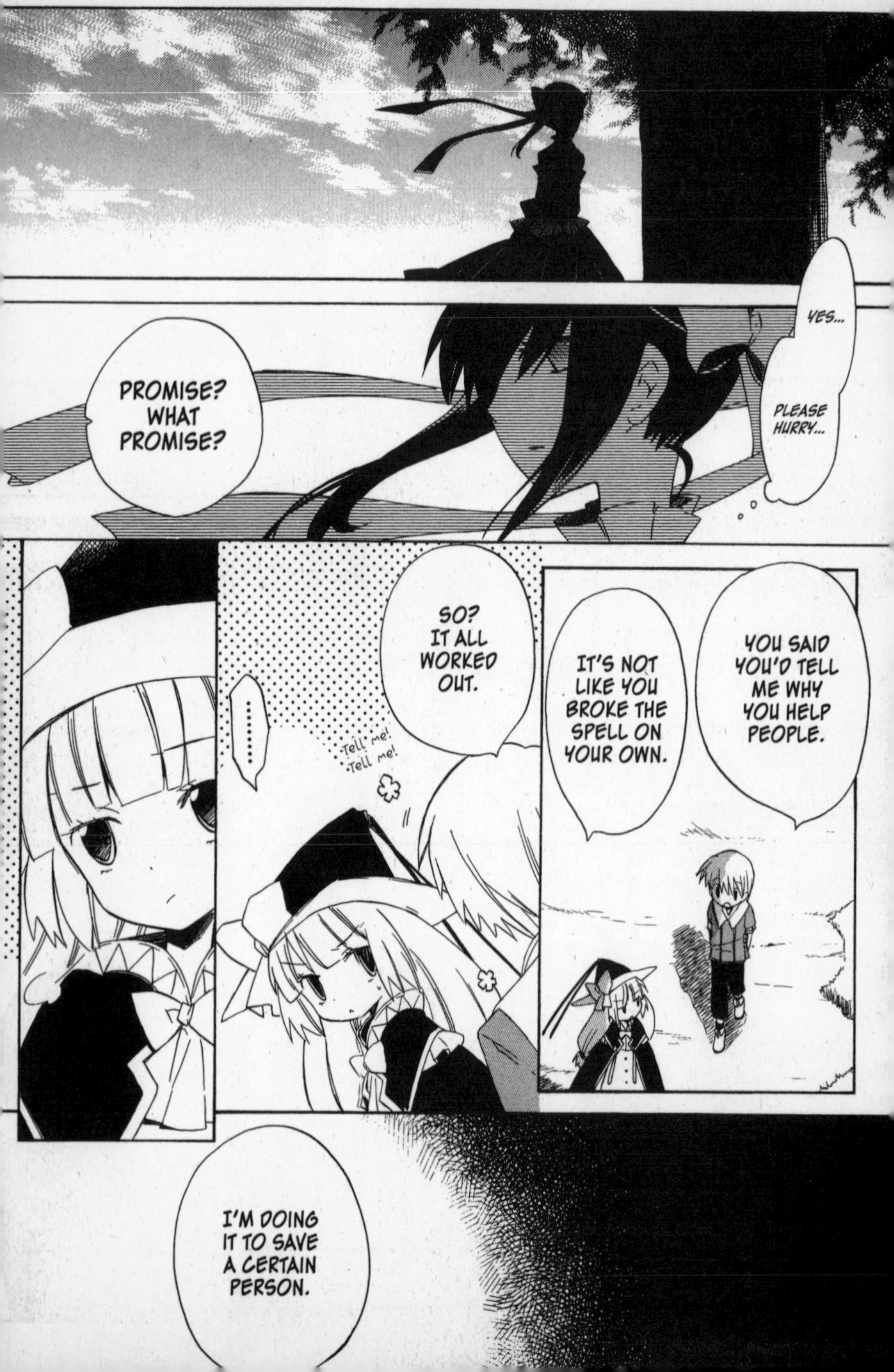
YES...
PLEASE HURRY...
PROMISE? WHAT PROMISE?
YOU SAID YOU'D TELL ME WHY YOU HELP PEOPLE.
IT'S NOT LIKE YOU BROKE THE SPELL ON YOUR OWN.
SO? IT ALL WORKED OUT.
Tell me! Tell me!
......
I'M DOING IT TO SAVE A CERTAIN PERSON.

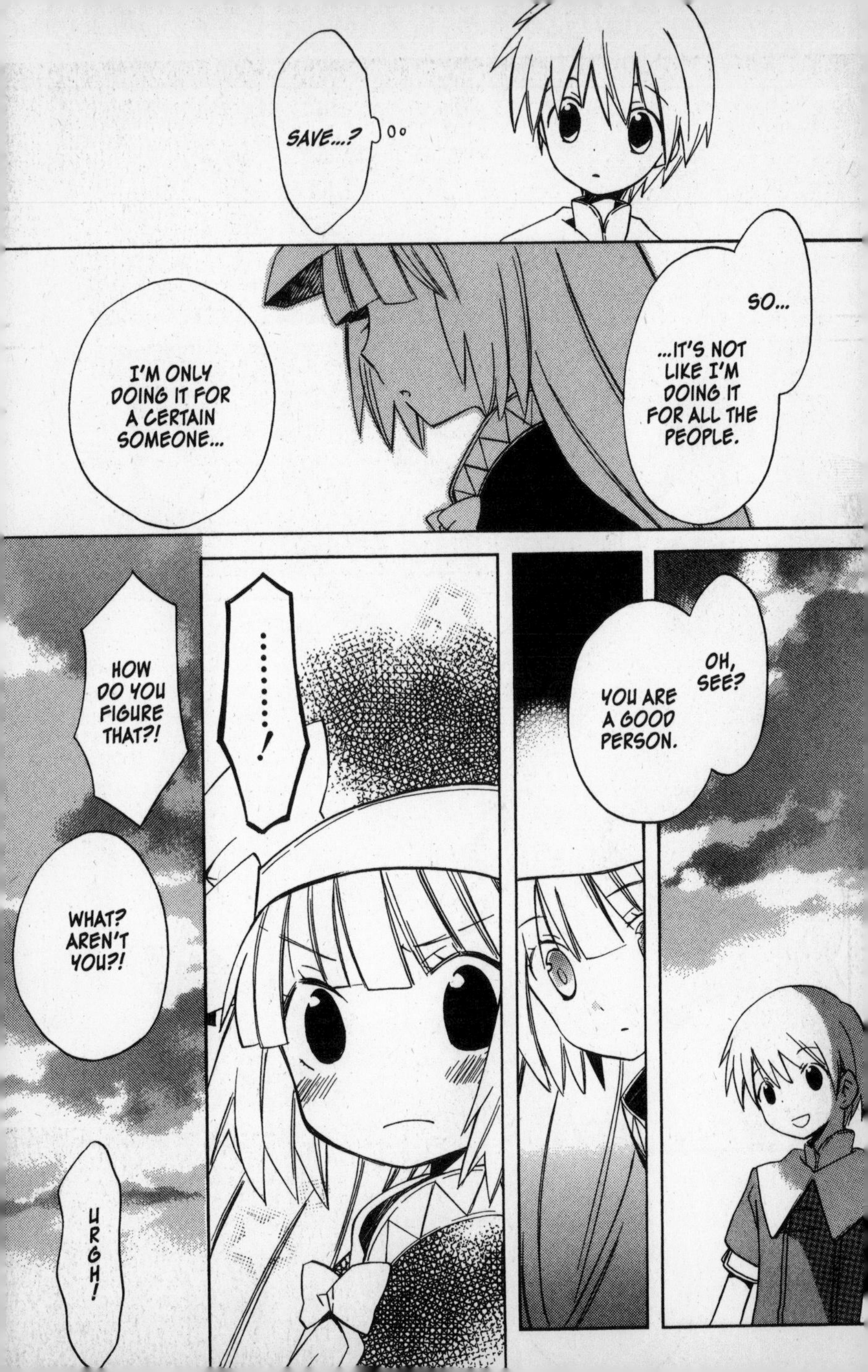
SAVE...?
SO...
...IT'S NOT LIKE I'M DOING IT FOR ALL THE PEOPLE.
I'M ONLY DOING IT FOR A CERTAIN SOMEONE...
OH, SEE?
YOU ARE A GOOD PERSON.
......!
HOW DO YOU FIGURE THAT?!
WHAT? AREN'T YOU?!
URGH!

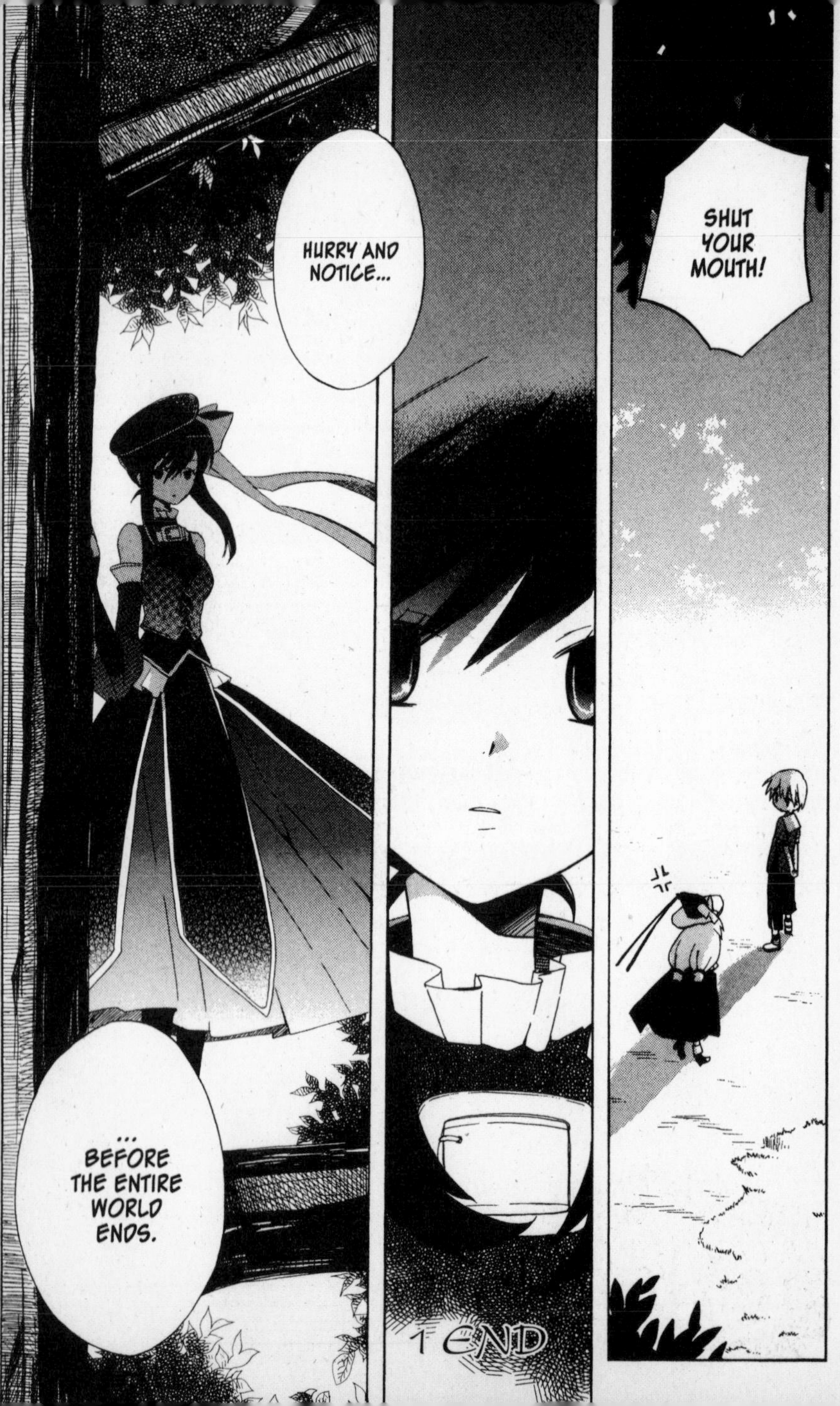
SHUT YOUR MOUTH!
HURRY AND NOTICE...
... BEFORE THE ENTIRE WORLD ENDS.
1 END

the Witch of Artemis

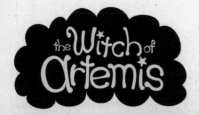

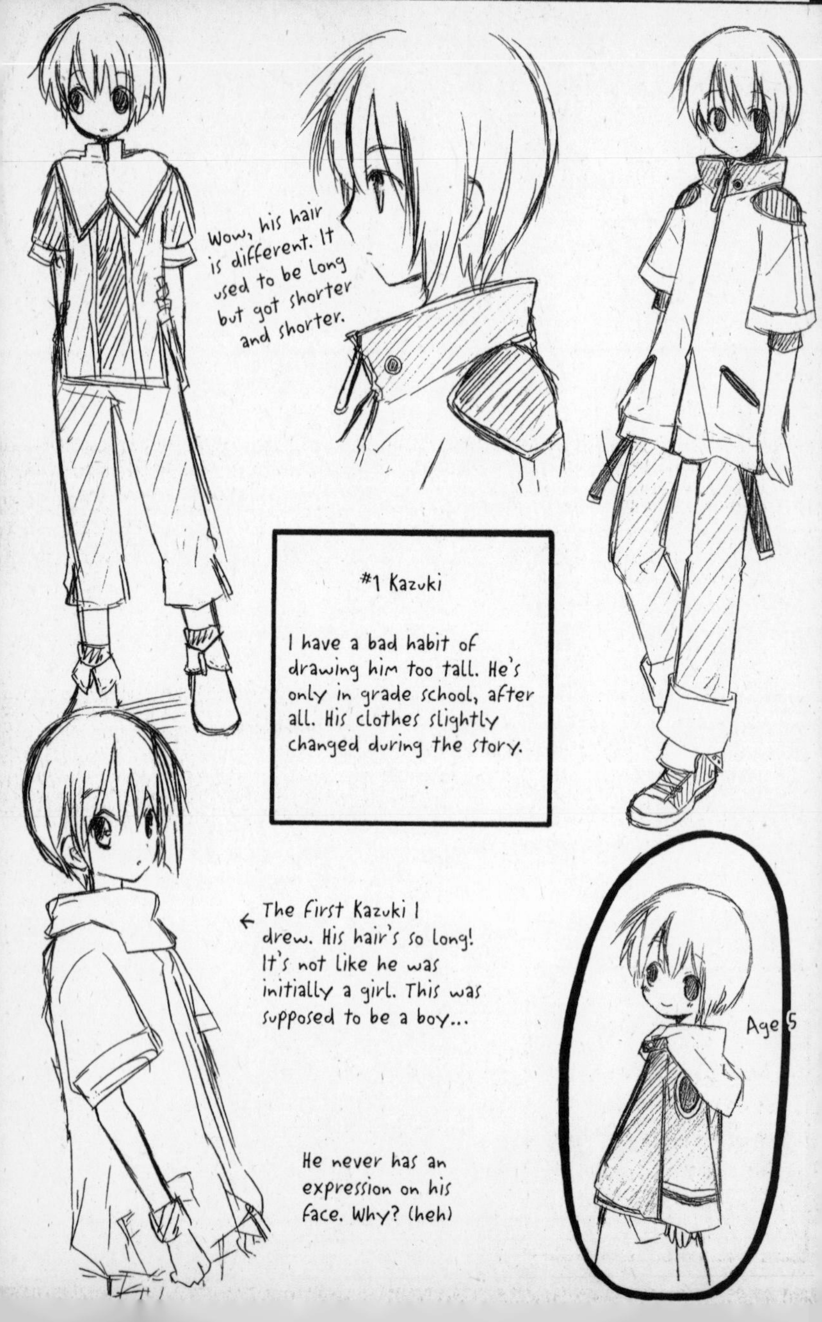
Wow, his hair is different. It used to be long but got shorter and shorter.
#1 Kazuki
I have a bad habit of drawing him too tall. He's only in grade school, after all. His clothes slightly changed during the story.
← The first Kazuki I drew. His hair's so long! It's not like he was initially a girl. This was supposed to be a boy...
Age 5
He never has an expression on his face. Why? (heh)

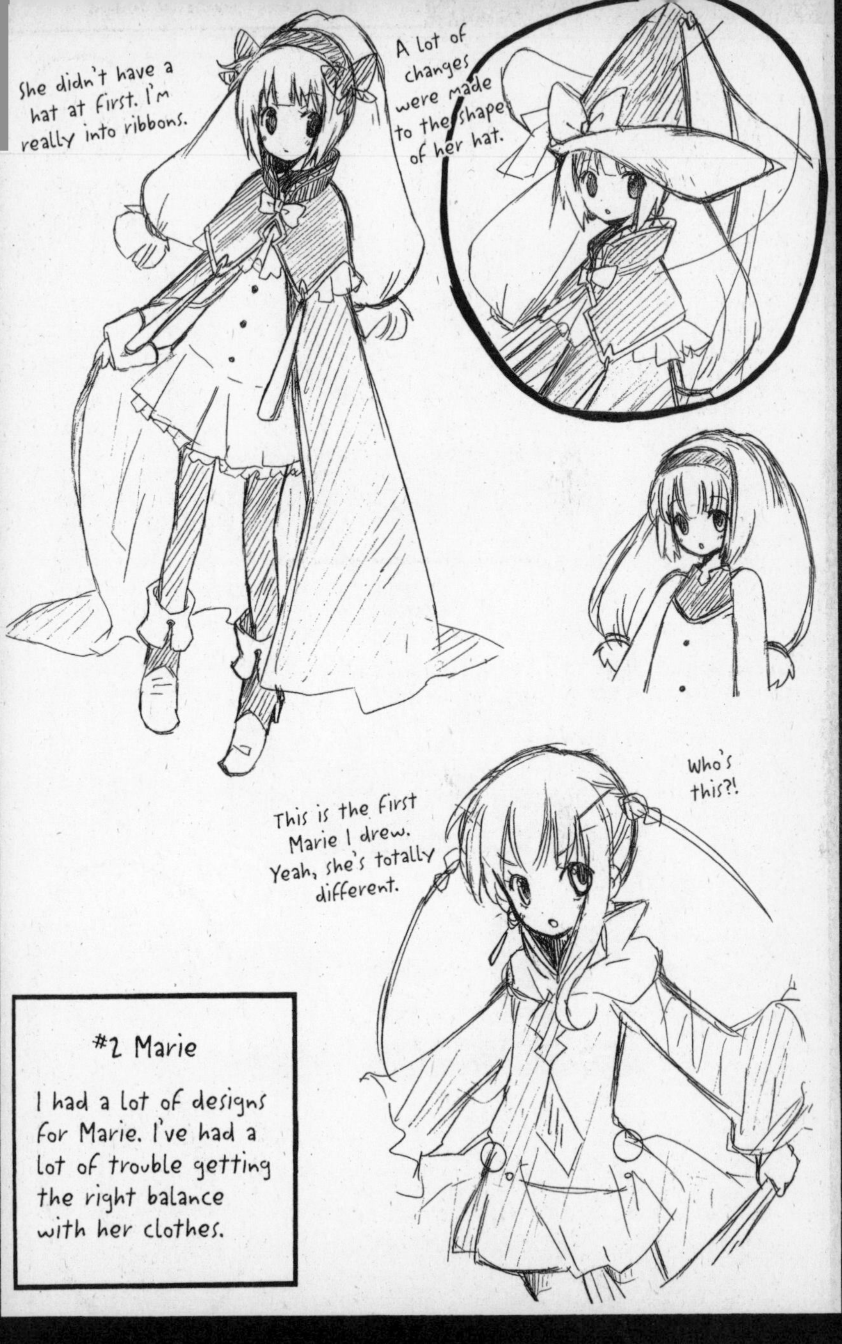
She didn't have a hat at first. I'm really into ribbons.
A lot of changes were made to the shape of her hat.
Who's this?!
This is the first Marie I drew. Yeah, she's totally different.

#2 Marie

I had a lot of designs for Marie. I've had a lot of trouble getting the right balance with her clothes.

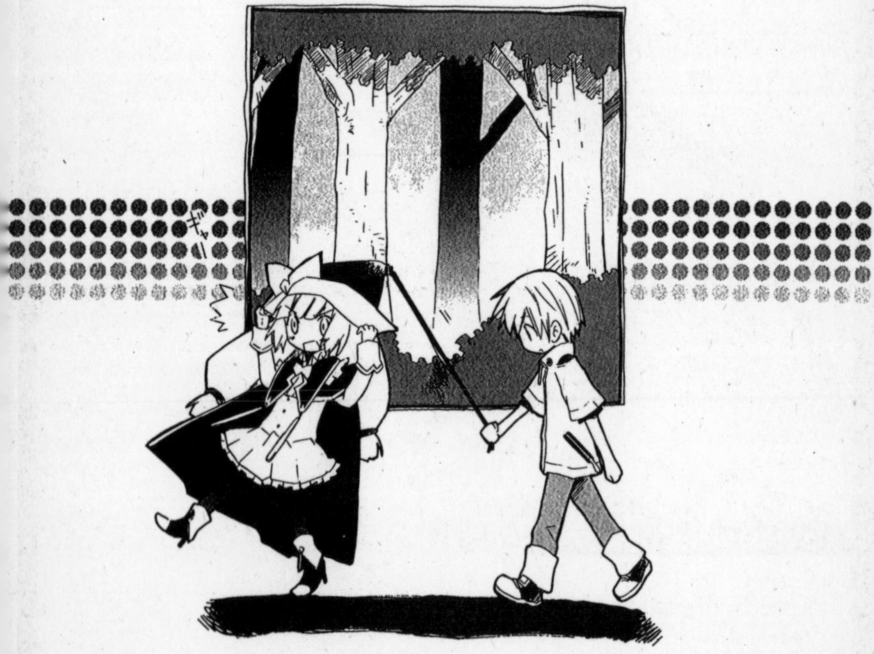
ギャー

Since it's the first volume...

Character Introductions.

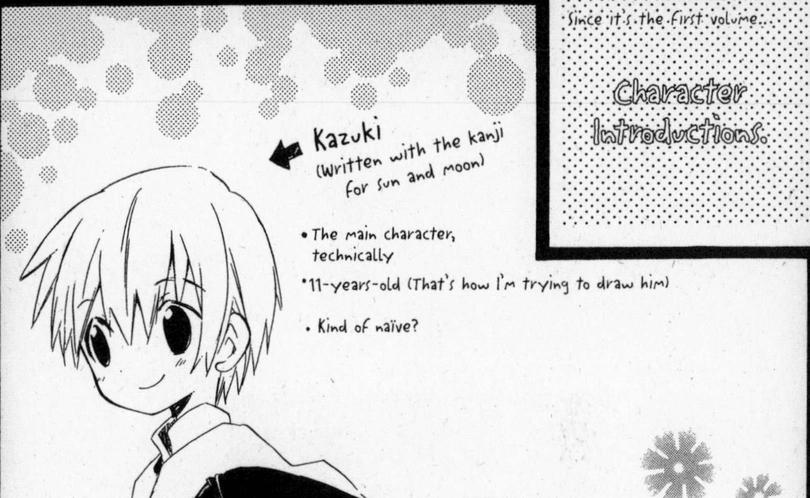
Kazuki
(Written with the kanji for sun and moon)
• The main character, technically
• 11-years-old (That's how I'm trying to draw him)
• Kind of naïve?
Marie
(I wanted something easy to remember)
• She's supposed to look Kazuki's age
• For an amazing witch, she sure can be dumb
• I have her talk like an old lady, though it seems to keep changing
Sorry for the crappy introductions!

This is my first longer serialization, and I've been struggling, learning and enjoying myself every month. My art is still evolving so I apologize for the ugly portions. Oh, this is actually the first time I've created something so "super" fantasy. I'm dedicating myself for the first time! The plot can get a bit clumsy at times, but I hope you can enjoy it even a little bit. The story continues in the next volume so I hope to see you there! -Yui Hara

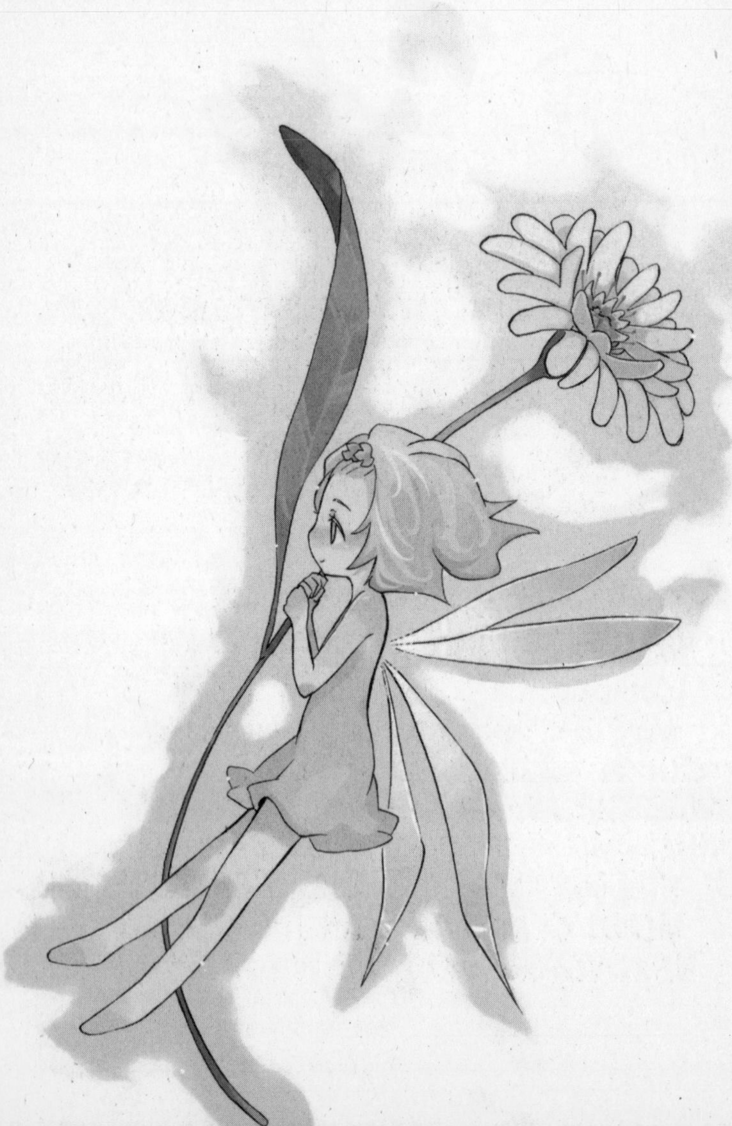

IN THE NEXT VOLUME OF...

the Witch of Artemis

AS KAZUKI ADJUSTS TO LIFE ON ARTEMIS, HE MEETS NEW FRIENDS AND FACES NEW CHALLENGES. THIS GIVES RISE TO NEW MYSTERIES AS WELL, AND HE BEGINS A QUEST TO UNRAVEL THOSE ANSWERS! WHO WAS THE MYSTERIOUS WOMAN WHO CURSED HIM, AND WHAT WAS HER PURPOSE IN HAVING HIM BROUGHT TO ARTEMIS? THINGS ARE MORE COMPLEX THAN THEY SEEM IN THE NEXT VOLUME OF THE WITCH OF ARTEMIS!

the Witch of Artemis

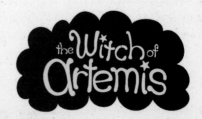

Editor's Notes
Cindy Suzuki

It was yet another busy month here in the TOKYOPOP editorial department! There are many reasons why this month has been a bit crazier than the previous months. One reason being that we have a lot of big titles coming up! We've been plugging away trying to make these titles very special just for you.

Another reason why we're so busy is that it's intern rotation time. Meaning, our lovely interns Sarah and Noora have concluded their internship. Most editorial internships last for about three months, sometimes longer depending on whether the university is on a quarter or semester system. Anyhow, as we said sayonara to Sarah and Noora, we said konnichiwa to our new interns Tim and Joey. It's fantastic that we always get brilliant editorial interns, but training and re-training constantly keeps us on our toes.

Interested in the life of a TOKYOPOP editorial intern? Well, you can find out more by subscribing to our newsletter at www.TOKYOPOP.com or LIKING us on Facebook. Our interns write tons of neat articles that show off their incredible knowledge and love of manga, anime and Japanese culture. It's really inspiring to work with such a talented bunch. So, thanks all interns, current and past. We love ya <3

See you again next month!

Cindy Suzuki, Editor

For exclusive updates, be sure to find us here:

www.TOKYOPOP.com
www.Facebook.com/TOKYOPOP
www.Twitter.com/TOKYOPOP

A **TOKYOPOP** Manga
E-mail: info@TOKYOPOP.com
Come visit us online at www.TOKYOPOP.com

WHEN YOU CAN OWN ANY SERIES
FOR UNDER 30 BUCKS,
ONLY ONE QUESTION REMAINS UNANSWERED...

WHICH ONE DO I CHOOSE?!

THIS ONE?

OR... BOTH?

WALTER
Addictus Animemus

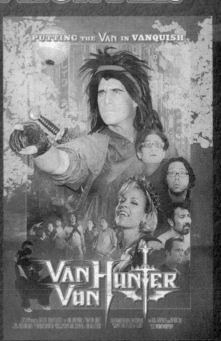

STOP!

This is the back of the book.
You wouldn't want to spoil a great ending!

This book is printed "manga-style," in the authentic Japanese right-to-left format. Since none of the artwork has been flipped or altered, readers get to experience the story just as the creator intended. You've been asking for it, so TOKYOPOP® delivered: authentic, hot-off-the-press, and far more fun!

1
2
3
4
5
6
7
8
9
10

DIRECTIONS

If this is your first time reading manga-style, here's a quick guide to help you understand how it works.

It's easy... just start in the top right panel and follow the numbers. Have fun, and look for more 100% authentic manga from TOKYOPOP®!

THE MANGA REVOLUTION · LEADING THE MANGA REVOLUTION · LEADING

漫画革命